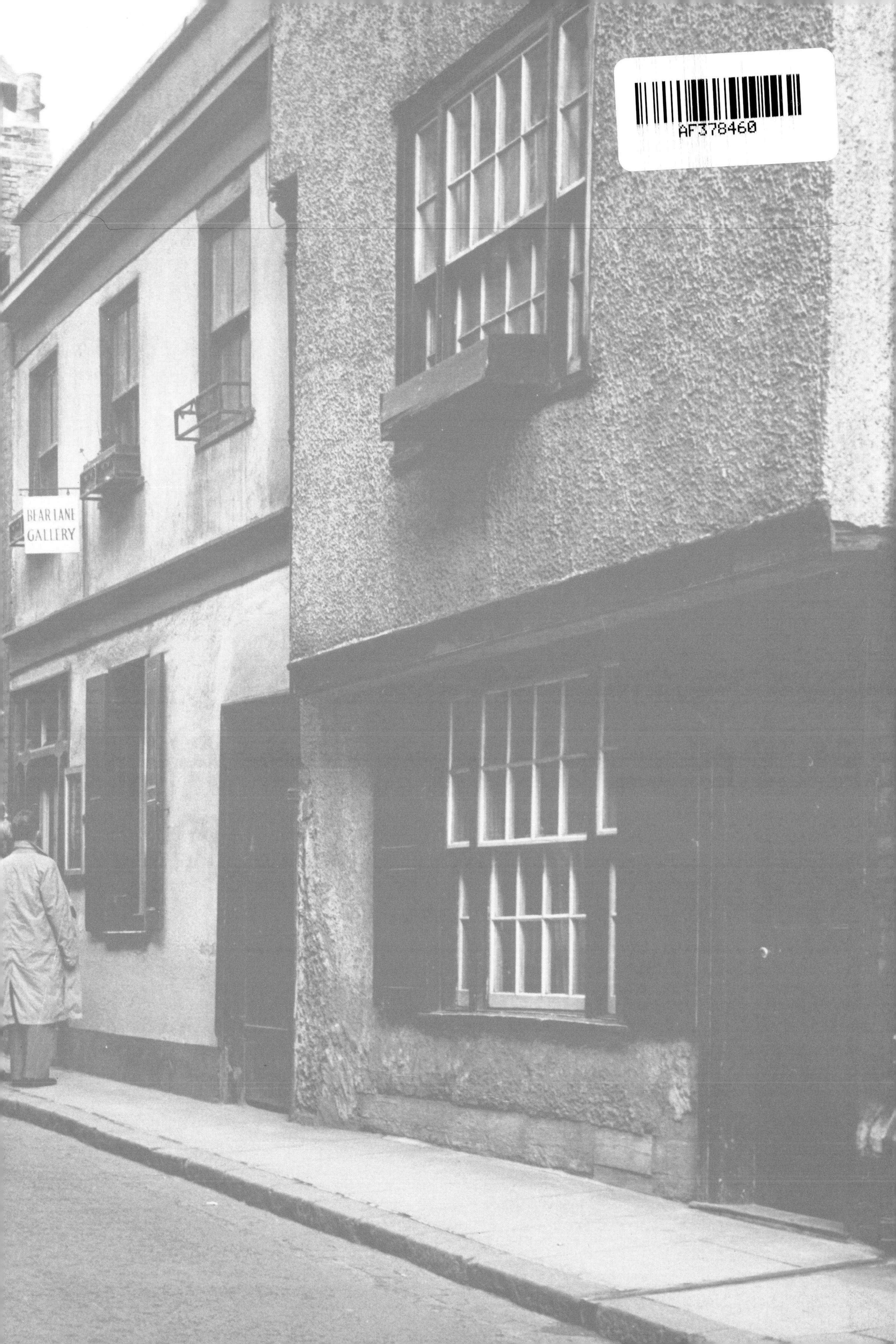
BEAR LANE
GALLERY

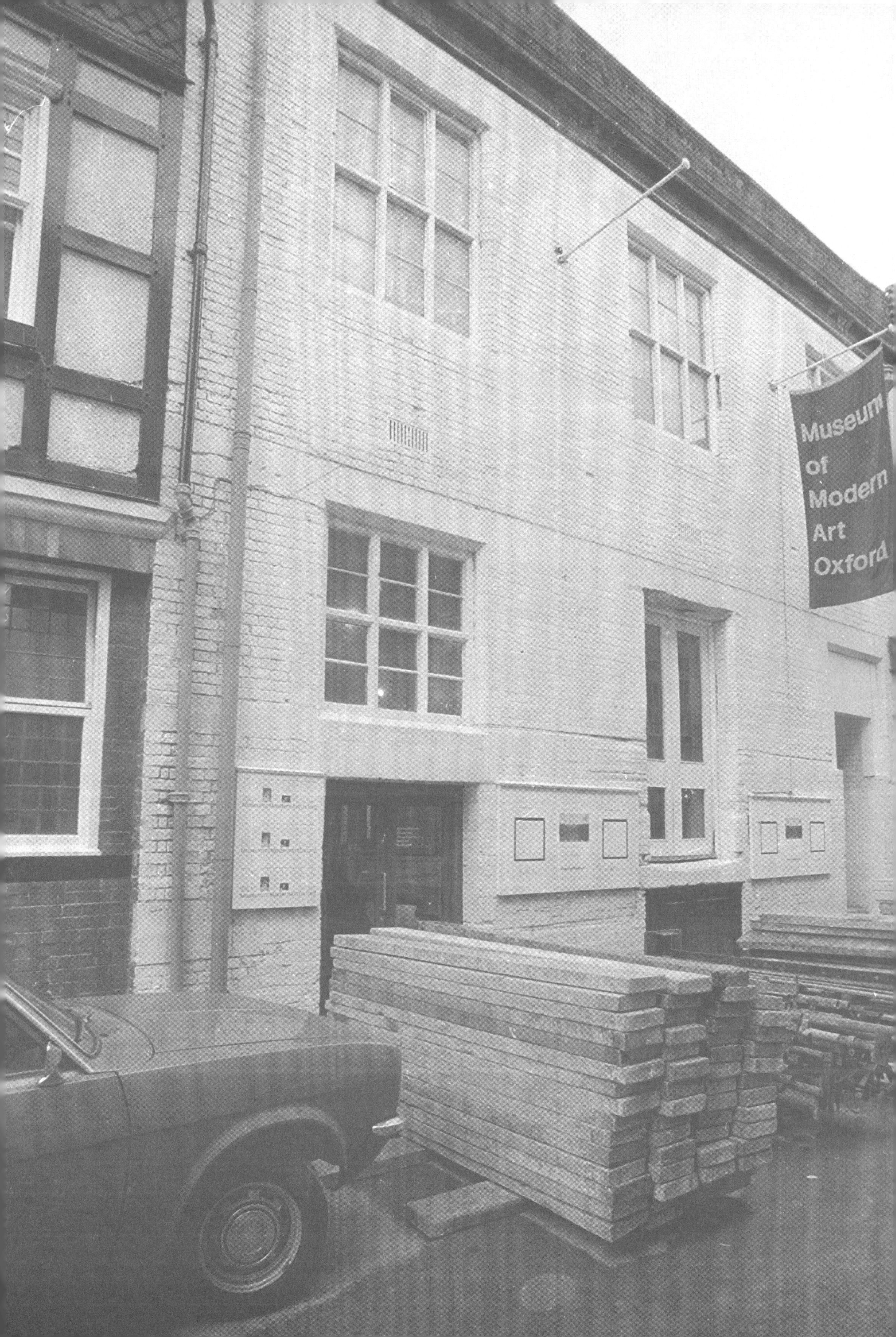

Museum
of
Modern
Art
Oxford

Sponsor's Foreword

Founded in Turin in 1895, and now in its fourth generation
as a family run business, Lavazza is the symbol of Italian
coffee around the world. In recent decades, the company
has developed a vibrant and unique brand founded on
creativity and innovation, forged through a striking range
of advertising campaigns, which take contemporary art
and fashion as its inspiration.

In particular, Lavazza has become known for its collaborations
with internationally acclaimed photographers. Commencing
with Helmut Newton in 1993 and including celebrated artists
such as David LaChapelle, Annie Leibovitz, Ellen von Unwerth
and Albert Watson to name just a few, our annual calendar
draws together our passion for culture and coffee in a much-
coveted photographic project. Lavazza represents Italian style
around the world, with a strong commitment to 'image' through
our promotion of photography and art. The Lavazza Calendar
has been an extraordinary international advertising campaign
to communicate the quality and style of Lavazza coffee and
our belief in creativity, style, the power of images and ideas.

Lavazza's latest evolution takes the brand into the world of
modern and contemporary art. Partnerships have been forged
with world-renowned institutions such as the Guggenheim
in New York and the Venice Biennale. Our association
with Modern Art Oxford extends this relationship with
internationally acclaimed contemporary art, and we are
delighted to be supporting the gallery's 50th anniversary
during this landmark year.

David Rogers
Managing Director, Lavazza Coffee UK

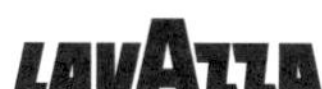

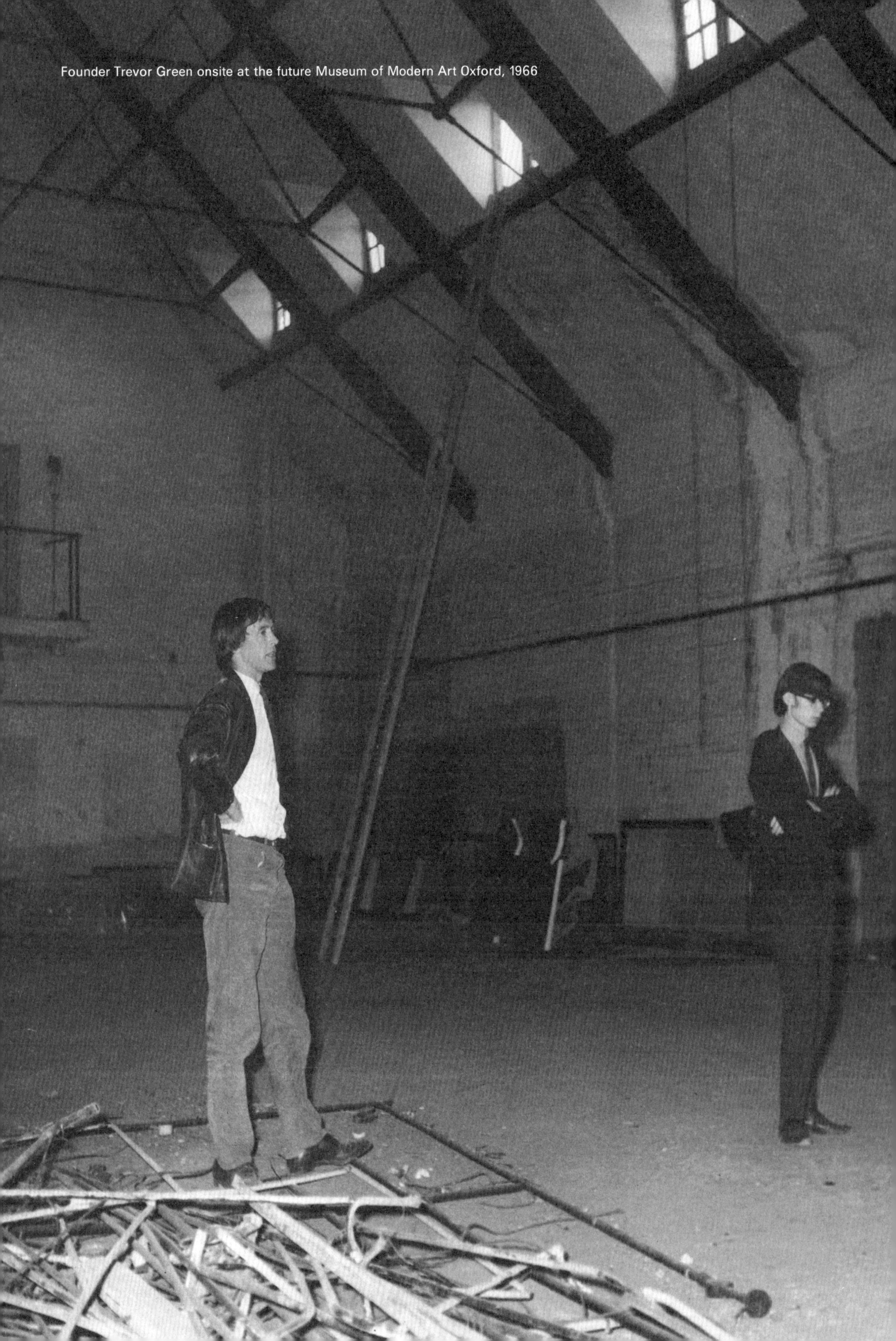

Founder Trevor Green onsite at the future Museum of Modern Art Oxford, 1966

Foreword

In 1966, a group of artists and architects led by Trevor Green
was given a temporary lease on a former Victorian brewery
in the centre of Oxford which was then being used as a furniture
warehouse. The building was in poor condition and a number
of makeshift interventions and remodelling of the spaces were
undertaken in the early years to make the building fit for public
use as a venue for temporary exhibitions. Although the founders
intended for the so-called 'Museum of Modern Art Oxford'
to develop a permanent collection of modern and contemporary
art – inspired by the New York institution – this never materialised
due to a lack of finance, space and resources. However, over
the decades, a series of pioneering directors – Peter Ibsen
(1970–73), Nicholas Serota (1973–76), David Elliott (1976–96),
Kerry Brougher (1996–2000), Andrew Nairne (2000–08) and
Michael Stanley (2009–12) – and their talented teams, built
a formidable reputation for the gallery as one of the most
innovative and influential contemporary art spaces in Europe.

Fifty years later in 2016, we are celebrating the extraordinary
history of what is now called 'Modern Art Oxford' with a
highly innovative year-long exhibition called KALEIDOSCOPE.
The exhibition restages moments in the history of the gallery
through the return of works of art from the rich programmatic
history of Modern Art Oxford. These works, which have returned
to Oxford from important institutions and private collections
across the world, are shown as part of an evolving set of thematic
displays that reference some of the key developments in the
ideas and forms of contemporary visual practice over the past
half century. They are presented in dialogue with recent and
newly commissioned work by a new generation of internationally
acclaimed and emerging artists. The exhibition is designed
to remain open at all times, even during installation periods,
enabling audiences to see the institution at work with
artworks and artists, and in order to provide some insight
into the construction of exhibitions and the creation of visual
culture. Furthermore, works come and go, and some return
again to be re-sited with other works in order to show the
shifting nature of works of art and the importance of context.
All in all, the year-long programme – which also includes

performances, talks, events, digital projects, archival displays
and a major 50th anniversary gala event – aims to offer new
insight on a dynamic history that celebrates the way in which
artists transform our perception of our world.

During the preparation of the anniversary programme, we
learned that one of the gallery's defining characteristics throughout
its history has been the consistently generous and open-ended
nature of its invitations to artists – something touched upon by
many of those whose reflections are collected in the 'Memories'
section of the book. We felt, therefore, that an artist-focused
approach made the most sense for an anniversary catalogue
and each of the artists in this year's programme was invited
to create an 'artist's page', the content of which was up to them
to decide. These pages are accompanied by a selection of the
archival material relating to the artists' previous exhibitions at
the gallery and, for those artists who are new to Oxford, images
of work in progress. Just as the exhibition this year enables
viewers to catch a glimpse of the ways in which the institution
works, so too do the numerous letters and images generated
during the making of our programme.

We offer our heartfelt thanks to the many individuals, organisations
and funders who have made KALEIDOSCOPE possible, which
are too extensive to list in the limited space here. However,
I would like to take this opportunity to most sincerely thank
all of the contributors to this publication, the exhibiting artists
and their estates, their commercial representatives and lenders,
for their participation and support in presenting this landmark
show. I would like to to thank the Modern Art Oxford trustees
and team, especially the programming and technical teams,
for the realisation of this ambitious and complex project which
challenged us logistically and in terms of planning and resources.
We are indebted to Arts Council England and Oxford City Council
as well as our corporate and individual benefactors and friends,
Lavazza UK, which has generously sponsored our 50th anniversary
gala event. Last, but by no means least, I would like to thank
our audiences for their generosity and openness in responding
so enthusiastically to our continual quest for experimentation.

Paul Hobson, Director of Modern Art Oxford

50 Inspirational Years

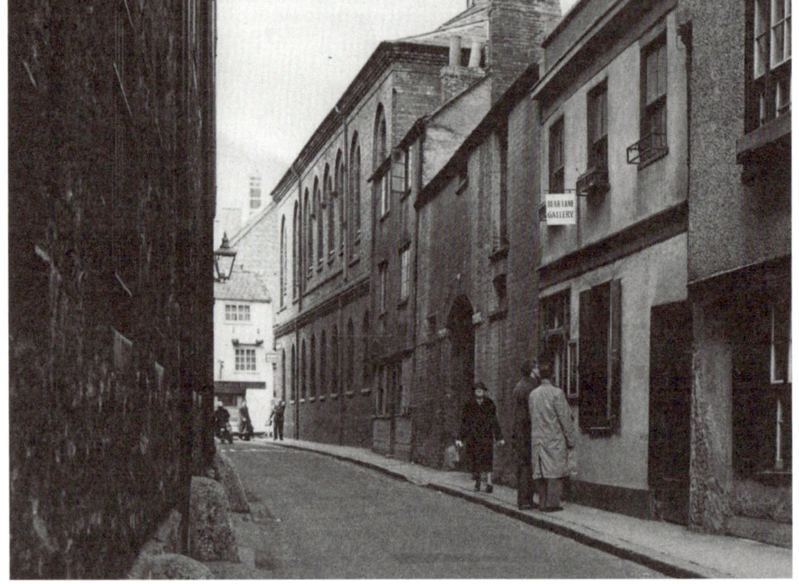

1966

First Collection

*Aspects:
American Painting 1960–65*

New Sculpture: 1966

New Generation: 1966

*Space Place: Constructed
Space Participation*

1967

Edition Art

German Expressionist Prints

Young Oxfam Exhibition

Archigram: *Beyond Architecture:
An Extension of Pop Culture
and Technology*

*Early 20th-Century
Painting and Sculpture*

Arts Council Exhibition: Painting

Contemporary Italian Art

Ventures

Anthony Benjamin:
Paintings, Prints and Sculpture

Sixteen Polish Artists

CUBA!

Light/Sound Workshop

1968

Transatlantic Graphics

*29: Recent work by
29 Post-graduates from
Chelsea School of Art*

Derek Southall:
Recent Paintings

*CASSA: Centre for Advanced
Study of Science in Art*

*8 Painters from the College
of Art and Design, Birmingham*

*Modern Drawings:
British Drawings of the Last 50 years*

Patrick Heron: *48 Works 1957–68*

*What is Man?
World Photography Exhibition*

Harold Cohen: *New Paintings*

*Littlemore Associated Schools:
An Exhibition of Art Work
Made by Pupils*

*Contemporary British
Painting and Sculpture*

Painting 1964–67

Stephen Willats:
*Visual Automatics
and Visual Transmitters*

*OSA EX68:
Oxfordshire Society of Architects*

Eventstructure Research Group:
Pneu Show

Inflatable Furniture

1969

*New Editions: Editions of Prints by
British Printmakers Published in 1968*

Franco Colavecchia:
Drawings and Stage Designs

Enzo Ragazzini: *Photographer*

Design Onstage

Tim Scott: *New Sculpture*

*Unlimited Art:
Multiples, the Art of the Future?*

Terry Frost: *Recent Paintings*

*Brighton Prints: Young Printmakers
from Brighton Art College*

*Man: Films by Dr. Hans Hass for BBC,
German and Austrian TV*

*Humber City: Fifth-Year Students
from Oxford School of Architecture*

*Woman: Second World Exhibition
of Photography*

*Painting '68: An Arts Council
Survey of Painting in 1968*

*Summer Show: Contemporary
British Painting and Sculpture*

Roelof Louw: *Location*

Henri Cartier-Bresson: *Photographs*

Bob Janz, Dante Leonelli and
Michael McKinnon: *Continuum*

1970

Vasarely Graphics

One: American Contemporary Prints

CoID Design Awards

Jon Bird and David Shepherd:
Somethings

Richard Hamilton: *Graphics*

John Heartfield: *Photomontages*

*The Black Box:
An Experiment in Visual theatre*

Mary Martin and Kenneth Martin:
Constructions

Josef Albers: *25 Years of Graphic Art*

Jan Kaliciak: *CONCRETE light YEAR*

*East Midlands 2000:
Sixth-Year Project from
Oxford School of Architecture*

Platform '70

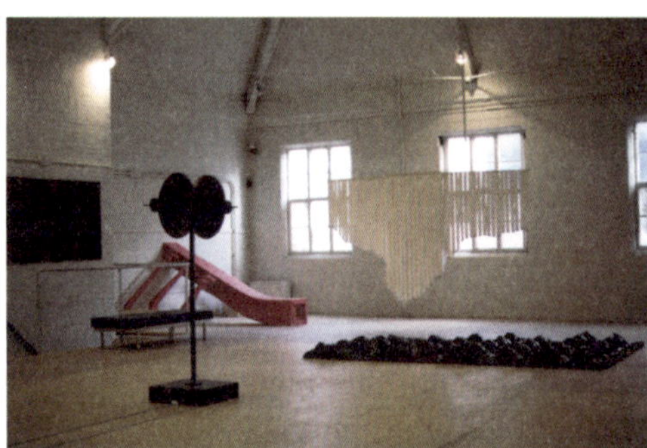

Platform '70, Museum of Modern Art Oxford, 1970

Czechoslovak Graphics 1960–70

Robert Carruthers: *Sculptures*

Basil Beattie, Bernard Cohen,
Mario Dubsky, Alan Gouk,
John Hoyland, Tess Jaray and
John Walker: *Large Paintings*

Richard Smith: *Retrospective
Exhibition of Graphics and Multiples*

Justin Knowles

Chris Jennings

1971

*Kinetics and Multiples
from Galerie Denise René*

Bart Phillips

Ad Reinhardt: *Cartoons*

PoPA at MoMA: Pioneers of Part-Art

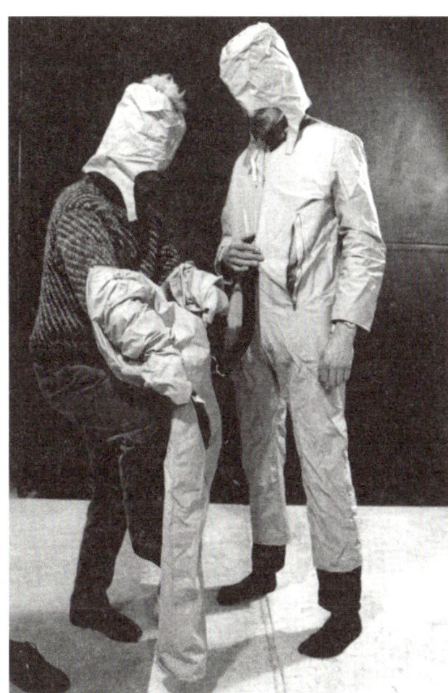

PoPA at MoMA: Pioneers of Part-Art,
Museum of Modern Art Oxford, 1971

Geoffrey Ridgen, Basil Beattie,
Alan Gouk and John McLean:
Recent Paintings

Bill Brandt

*Music in Indian Painting:
Miniatures from the V&A Museum*

Oxford Student Exhibition

Robert Frankland, Douglas Gray,
Peter Hoogenboom, George Hostler,
Tony Ingram and Alan Welsford:
Six Sculptors

*Platform '71:
2nd Annual Post-Graduate Exhibition*

Jacques Caumont:
Travel Art: Documentary exhibition

John Golding, Gerald Newman
and Colin Crumplin

Christopher Hampton: *Total Eclipse*

Brower Hatcher

*Modern Paintings from
Oxford College Collections*

Richard Long

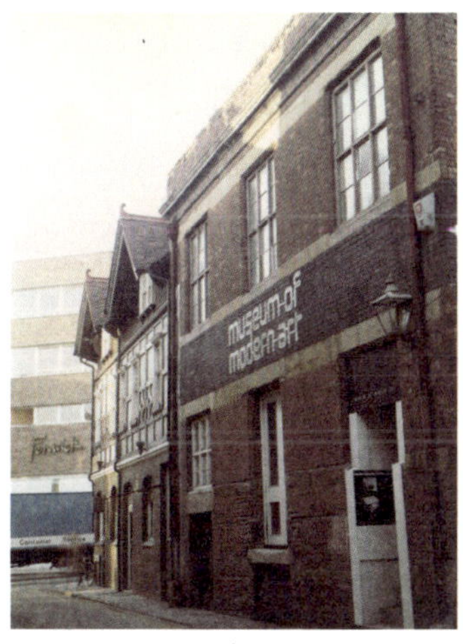

Museum of Modern Art Oxford façade, 1971

1972

John Murphy and Peter Waldron

The Casual Eye: Snapshot Photography

*Pattern In Islamic Art:
Photographs, Graphic Analyses
& Projected Colour Slides*

Concrete Poetry

Hamish Fulton:
Walking on the Road Ahead

A Selection of Works on Loan

*100 Paintings/Drawings/Graphics/
Sculptures from Oxfordshire
County Schools*

The LBW Private Collection

Richard Smith: *Paintings*

Malcolm Carder: *Island*

Modern Chairs

Gerard Hemsworth

Tim Head: *Installation*

*Platform '72:
3rd Annual Post-Graduate Exhibition*

Fourteen BIG Prints

*Cognition and Control Project:
Insight Development*

Pier 18

*Drawing: An Exhibition
Involving 42 Artists*

1973

Constantine Manos:
A Greek Portfolio: 50 Photographs

Open Field: Work by Southern Artists

Fluxshoe

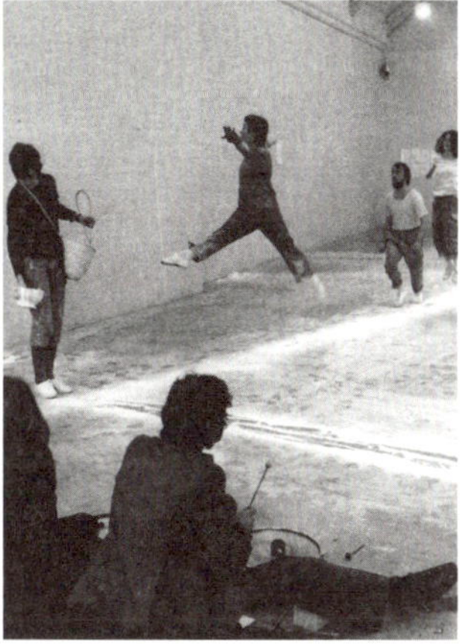

Fluxshoe, performance documentation,
Museum of Modern Art Oxford, 1973

Ian Colverson and David Masi:
*Berlin Suite: Prints, Photographs,
Process Material, Slides and Books*

John Blake: *Glass is a Rigid Liquid:
5 Glass Panes 'Permutations' Broken/
Not Borken 1971*

Francis Picabia: *Documentary Exhibition*

John Stezaker: *Objects of Reason*

Daniel Buren: *Sanction of the Museum*

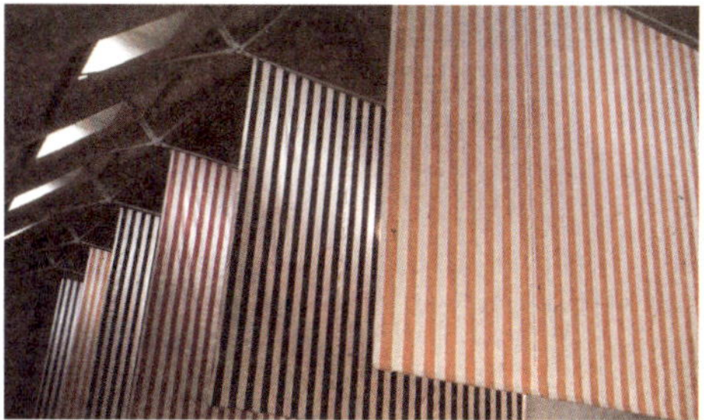

Daniel Buren, Museum of Modern Art Oxford, 1973

Ed Herring

Douglas Huebler:
Selected Works 1968–73

Sol LeWitt: *Wall Drawings*

Michael Druks: *Flexible Geography
and Location Piece*

Christian Boltanski

Jean Le Gac

*Systems: 12 Artists Using Order,
Sequence and Permutation*

*Platform '73:
4th Annual Post-Graduate Exhibition*

Staging the Romans

*Objects and Documents:
Bought by Richard Smith
for the Arts Council Collection*

Keith Critchlow: *Working Order*

Howard Rogers and Neil Davies:
Recent Kinetic Work

1974

Paul Nash: *Photography*

Joseph Beuys:
*The Secret Block for a Secret Person
in Ireland, Drawings 1948–72*

Daniel Meadows:
The Free Photographs Omnibus

Bob Law: *10 Black Paintings 1965–1970*

*Obmokhu 1921: Reconstructions
of Russian Constructivist Sculpture*

Hamish Fulton

Anthony McCall:
Performance and Screening

*Edinburgh Arts 1973/1974:
A Look Forward and Back*

Bruce Robbins:
Considerations of a Situation

Hanne Darboven

Charlier, Lohaus, Mees, Panamarenko,
Roquet and Van Snick

*Ten from Co-optic:
Real Britain*

Harvey Breverman,
Chris Orr and Tom Piper

Elliot Erwitt: *Son of Bitch*

Jasper Johns: *Drawings*

Pictures from Space

Chinese Contemporary Posters

Barry Flanagan: *Drawings 1966–74*

John Hilliard 1969–74

*Compassionate Camera:
Dustbowl Pictures*

François Morellet

David Tremlett:
Work Done in Australia and England

1975

Young British Photographers

Matisse Lithographs

Agnes Martin:
On a Clear Day

*Oxfordshire Young Artists 1975:
Secondary Schools Exhibition*

*The University of East Anglia
Art Collection*

Paul Neagu and his Generative
Art Group: *Horizontal Seed*

Christopher Watts:
Drawings Made in 1974

*The Photographs of
Eadweard Muybridge*

Bruce McLean: *Early Works 1967–71*

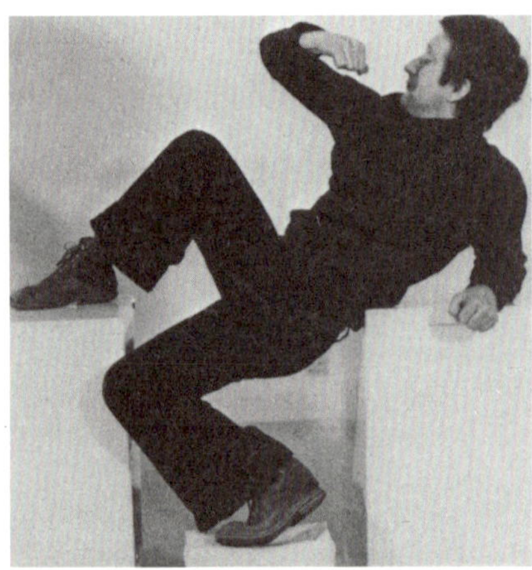

Bruce McLean, exhibition invitation, 1975

Marcel Broodthaers:
Le Privilège de l'Art

Ansel Adams

John Murphy

Carl Andre:
Poems 1958–74

*Mirrors of the Mind:
Prints and Objects*

Lesley Foxcroft

Duncan Grant:
90th Birthday Exhibition

Stephen Buckley:
Recent Drawings and Paintings

Art and Language 1966–75

Kim Lim: *Prints*

Bryan Pearce: *Paintings,
Watercolours & Drawings 1952–75*

Alan Charlton:
Paintings From a Series Begun in 1970

Philip Glass Ensemble

Jeff Clarke:
Prints and Drawings

1976

*Andre Flavin Judd LeWitt:
Sculpture, Prints and Drawings*

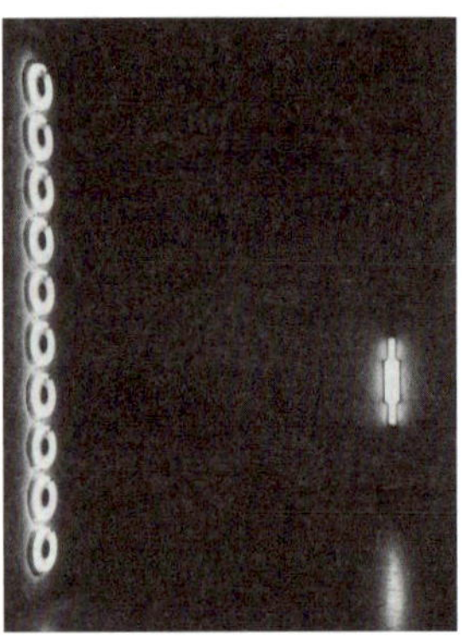

Andre Flavin Judd LeWitt, Museum
of Modern Art Oxford, 1976

Klaus Rinke: *Ex-hi-bi-tion*

Charlie Meecham:
Photographs of Oxfordshire

The Young in Art

Howard Hodgkin:
45 Paintings 1949–75

Eugene Atget:
Photographs 1857–1927

Ulrich Ruckriem

Dr. Harold E. Edgeton:
*Seeing the Unseen:
High Speed Photography*

Kevin Atherton:
Two Places, Two Performances

David Larcher: *Monkey's Birthday*

Noel Forster

Paddy Summerfield:
Beneath the Dreaming Spires

*The Complete Chris Orr: Published
and Unpublished Prints 1967–76*

Walker Evans

David Evison: *Recent Sculpture*

Alfred Wallis: P*aintings from
the Collection of Kettle's Yard*

Donald Judd: *Drawings 1956–76*

Arnulf Rainer: *Hiroshima Zyklus*

Martin Naylor:
Sculpture and Drawings 1973–76

Kurt Schwitters: *Merzbilder*

Arshile Gorky: *Paintings and Drawings*

1977

A Terrific Thing: British Art 1910–16

Andrew Pitcairn-Knowles: *Photographs*

Yvonne Rainer: *Films and Talk*

Jan Dibbets

*Art in Action:
A Workshop Demonstration by
Pupils and Students of Oxfordshire
Schools and Colleges*

Darcy Lange: *Work Studies in Schools*

Hans Hofmann: *The American Years*

Sol LeWitt: *Incomplete Open Cubes*

Jacky Lansey, Rose English
and Sally Potter: *Mounting*

Frank Stella:
Aluminium Reliefs 1976–77

Howard Hodgkin: *Complete Prints*

El Lissitzky 1890–1941

Dziga Vertov: *Films*

Ralph Gibson: *Quadrants*

Rita Donagh: *Paintings and Drawings*

Jasper Johns and Samuel Beckett:
Foirades/Fizzles

Brian French: *Recent Work*

Jo Baer: *Paintings 1962–74*

Brian Alterio: *Photographs*

Simone Forti and Peter Van Riper:
Performance and Workshop

Stan Brakhage: *Films*

*A Survey Conducted by Students
of the City University, London*

August Sander: *Photographs*

Mary Kelly: *Post-Partum Document*

Joel Fisher: *Installation*

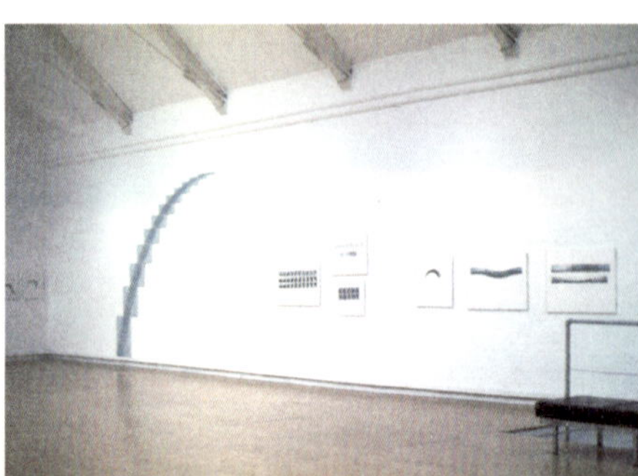

Jan Dibbets, Museum of Modern Art Oxford, 1977

1978

*The Inner Eye: Exhibition of
Work Made in Psychiatric Hospitals*

Victor Burgin: *Work 1976–78*

Lewis Hine: *Photographs*

Susan Hiller: *Fragments*

Karl Blossfeldt: *Photographs*

Peter Roehr: *Work 1962–68*

Miranda Tufnell Dance Group

Lol Coxhill and Veryan Weston: *Concert*

Stephen Willats:
Living Within Contained Conditions

Kenneth Martin: *Drawings and Prints*

John Walker: *Drawings*

Paintings from Paris

Edward Weston: *Photographs*

Frederick Evans: *Photographs*

Dan Graham: *Installations/Photographs/
Videotapes/Performances/Architectural
Models/Publications/Films*

Alan Johnston: *From the Mountain
to the Plain & Other Drawings*

*The Falling Leaf:
Aerial Dropped Propaganda 1914-68*

Joseph Kosuth: *Text/Context*

Bill Brandt: *Photographs
of Air-Raid Shelters 1940*

Paul Strand:
The Hebridean Photographs

Hans Haacke: *Works 1970-78*

Jean-Luc Godard: *Films*

Peer Gynt Project:
A Secondary School Project

1979

Alexander Rodchenko 1891-1956

Hans Namuth: *Photographs*

Jackson Pollock: *Drawing into Painting*

Rosemary Butcher Dance Company:
Performance

John Piper: *Fifty Years of Work*

Helen Muspratt: *Photographs*

Wells Coates:
Architect and Designer 1895–1958

*Open Attitudes:
New Painting and Sculpture*

Aaron Siskind: *Photographs*

A World Without War

A Clearer Picture

The Art of the Invisible

Kandinsky: The Munich Years 1900–14

Roy Grayson: *Contiguities*

Rick Florsheim: *Photographs*

Richard Long

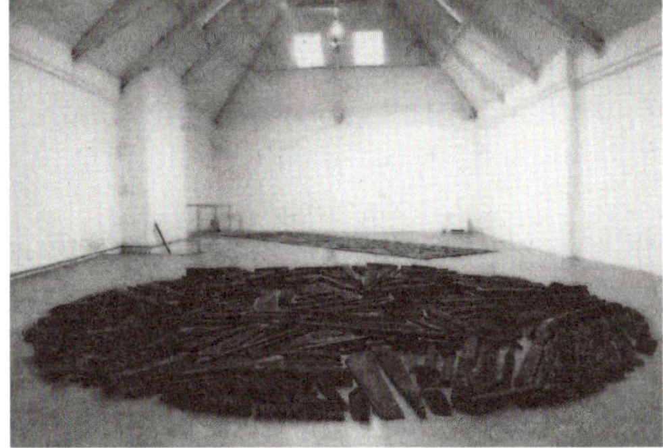

Richard Long, Museum of Modern Art Oxford, 1979

1980

Typography in Britain 1919–1980

Tubular Steel Furniture: The Survivors

Terry Pope, Tony Longson and
John Law: *Non-Standard Constructions*

Plans for the Eighties

Alan Green: *Paintings 1969–80*

Merryle Johnson: *Circus*

*Dekor: Patterning and Decoration
in Recent American Art*

Roger Hilton: *The Last Paintings*

Giulio Paolini: *Et Quid Amabo
Nisi Quod Aenigma Est?*

Sjoerd Buisman: *The Living Landscape*

Modern British Photography 1919–1939

*Imagined Journeys: An Exhibition
of Work by Oxfordshire School Pupils
from the Education Programme
at the Museum of Modern Art*

Jennifer Durrant: *Recent Paintings*

Jan Groth:
Tapestries and Thematic Drawings

José Clemente Orozco:
*A Major Exhibition of Murals,
Paintings and Graphics*

1981

The Red Mother (Røde Mor) Collective:
Posters

Peter Lanyon:
Drawings and Graphic Work

Leon Kossoff:
Paintings From a Decade 1970–80

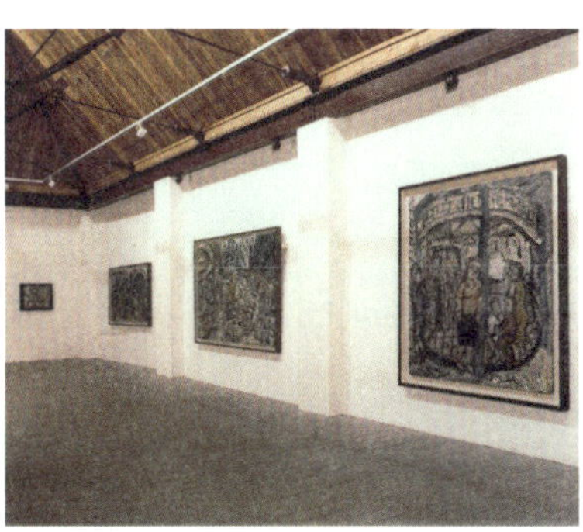

Leon Kossoff, Museum of Modern Art Oxford,
1981

R.W. Fassbinder: *Films*

Bernard Meninsky

*Six from Oxford, Seven from Leiden:
An Exchange Exhibition of Artists
from Twin Towns*

Ron Haselden: *Seaham Harbour*

Bill Brandt: *Photographs*

Gillian Ayres: *Paintings*

Orson Welles: *Films*

*Beaverbrook's England 1940–1965:
Cartoons by Cummings, Low,
Strube and Vicky*

Winsor McCay: *Little Nemo in
Slumberland and Other Cartoons*

Posy Simmonds: *Drawings for
Mrs Weber's Diary and True Romance*

Glen Baxter: *Paintings, Watercolours
and Drawings 1970–81*

1982

John Goto, Franta Provaznik and
Paddy Summerfield: *The Third Meaning*

Lubetkin and Tecton:
Architecture and Social Commitment

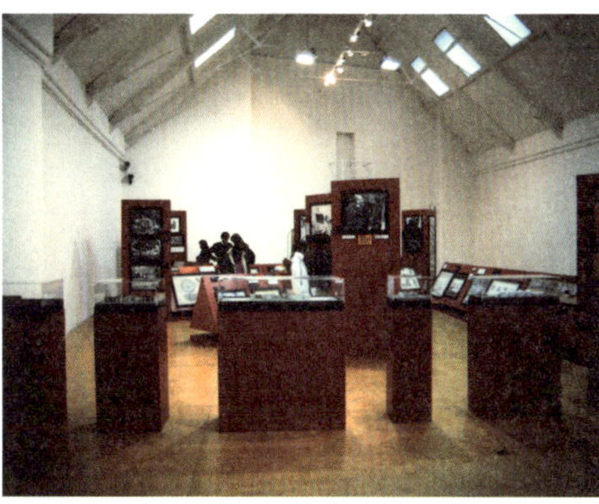

Lubetkin and Tecton, Museum of Modern Art Oxford,
1982

Ian McKeever:
Islands and Night Flak Series

Francis Davison: *Collages*

*Supercolor UK: Ten Professional
Photographers Using Polaroid*

Vladimir Mayakovsky:
Twenty Years of Work

Early Soviet Photographers

Peter Kinley: *Paintings 1956-1982*

*Screen Idols: Indian Film Posters
from the 1950s to the Present*

*India: Myth and Reality, Part One:
Gods of the Byways*

The Indian Calendar

Elizabeth Simpson:
People of Rajasthan

*India: Myth and Reality, Part Two:
Aspects of Modern Indian Art*

*The Other India:
Seven Contemporary Photographers*

Peter Phillips:
retroVISION: Paintings 1960–1982

Ex Libris Japan

Sixth Form Paintings and Prints

Jože Plečnik:
Architecture and the City 1872 1957

Jewel Stern: *Project Skyline*

The Subject of Painting

Jan Svoboda

Ernest George Trobridge 1884-1942

1983

Stephen Farthing and Glenn Sujo:
Twice-Told Tales

Rotha as Film Socialist

Bruce Gilbert, Graham Lewis and
Russell Mills: *MU/ZE/UM: Traces*

Leonid Pasternak 1862-1945

Brian Eno: *Mistaken Memories
of Mediaeval Manhattan*

Painter as Photographer

Raymond Manson:
*Coloured Sculptures, Bronzes
and Drawings 1952–1982*

*Impressions and Imprints: Prints
and Drawings by Members of
Oxford Printmakers' Co-operative*

*Focus on Drawings:
Recent Work by Ruskin Students*

*AIA: The Story of the Artists'
International Association 1933-1953*

Peter Kennard: *Despatches
from an Unofficial War Artist*

Oxfordshire Visual Artists Week

Bill Woodrow:
Beaver, Bomb and Fossil

*New Blood on Paper:
Drawings by Five Young Artists*

Jean Arp: *Papiers Déchirés
and Related Works 1929-1943*

Graham Crowley: *Home Comforts*

Dada and After (Concert)

Joaquim Gomis:
Homage to Miro for his 90th Birthday

Tolly Cobbold:
Eastern Arts Fourth National Exhibition

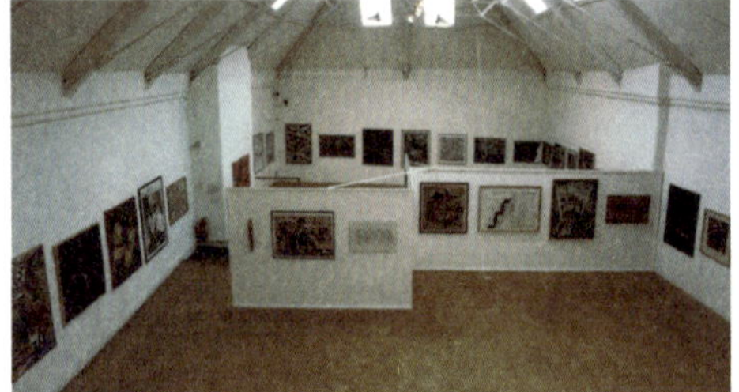
Tolly Cobbold, Museum of Modern Art Oxford, 1983

Paul Klee:
His Life and Work 1879-1940

Julio González:
1876-1942 Drawings

Stephen McKenna: *Paintings*

John Ruskin

Humphrey Spender:
The Thirties and After

*Blood and Laughter: Caricatures
from the Revolution of 1905*

*Master Pieces:
Furniture from Paintings*

Leonard McComb

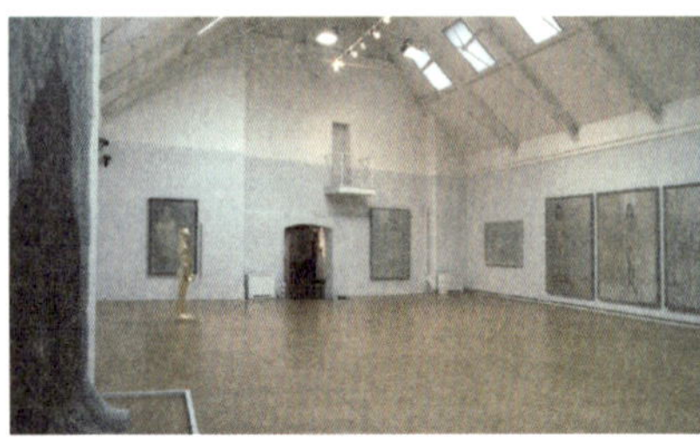
Leonard McComb, Museum of Modern Art
Oxford, 1983

1984

Observers of Man

Thirty-Five Artists Printmaking

New French Painting

Robert Medley: *Paintings 1928-1984*

Robert Mapplethorpe 1970-1983

Markéta Luskacová: *Oxford Schools
Sculpture Project: A Documentation*

Louise Shenstone: *Working Lines*

Oxfordshire Visual Artists Week

*Tradition and Renewal: Contemporary
Art in the German Democratic Republic*

Ron McCormick, Keith Arnatt and
John Davies: *The Prosaic Landscape*

Henri Cartier-Bresson:
Paintings and Drawings 1927-1984

*Smagic: Original illustrations
from Children's Books*

Constructivism in Poland 1923-1936

Pierre Bonnard: *Drawings*

Peter Hagerty: *36 Views and the State*

*Dreams-Visions-Metaphors:
Photographs of Manuel Álvarez Bravo*

Jirí Kolár: *Diary 1968*

Matta: The Logic of Hallucination

Jörg Immendorff:
Café Deutschland and Related Works

*Lee Miller and Roland Penrose
in Sussex: Recent Collages*

Peter Greenham:
Paintings and Drawings

Duane Michaels: *Photographs,
Sequences, Texts 1958-1984*

*Art into Production: Soviet Ceramics,
Textiles and Fashion 1917-1985*

1985

Thérèse Oulton: *Recent Paintings*

Roger Hilton: *The Early Years*

Judy Goldhill:
*A British Portrait: Photographs
of the Anglo-Jewish Community*

David Mach:
Towards a Landscape

Birgit Skiöld: *Memorial Exhibition*

The Late De Chirico 1940-76

Stephen Buckley: *Many Angles*

*Colour Photographs from
the Farm Security Administration*

John Hubbard:
*The Breath of Nature:
Work from 1981-1985*

*Tierra y Libertad: Photographs
of Mexico 1900-1935 from
the Casasola Archive*

Edward Wright:
Graphic Work and Painting

Stephen Cox: *We Must Always
Turn South – Sculpture 1977-1985*

Hiroshima: Paintings by Survivors

Arnulf Rainer: *Hiroshima Zyklus*

Graham Ashton:
The Tools of the Trade

Photography in the Anglo-Boer War

History Painting: Komar and Melamid

The Architecture of Adolf Loos

Markéta Luskacová: *Pilgrims*

Otto Wagner:
Designs for Architecture

Black Sun: The Eyes of Four

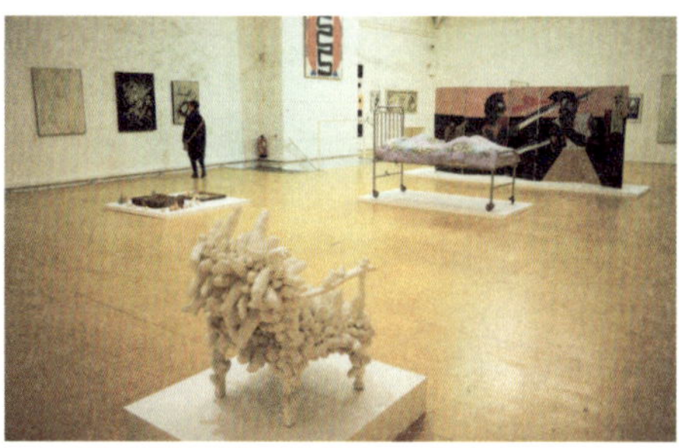
Reconstructions: Avant-Garde Art in Japan
1945–65, Museum of Modern Art Oxford, 1985

*Reconstructions:
Avant-Garde Art in Japan 1945–65*

Dada in Japan 1920–1970

1986

*Sixteen Studios: Work by Artists
Living In and Around Oxford*

Photographs of Miro, Picasso and Dali

*Dobles Figuras:
Contemporary Spanish Painting*

Gerald Incandela and Christopher Hobbs:
*The Making of Derek Jarman's
Caravaggio*

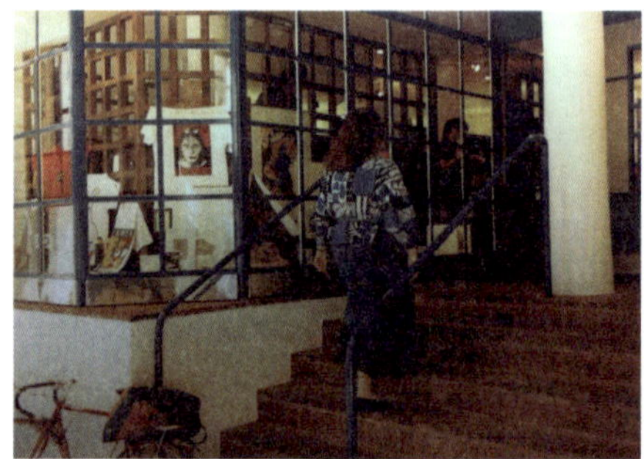
Entrance to Museum of Modern Art Oxford, 1986

1987

*Current Affairs: British Painting
and Sculpture in the 1980s*

Satyajit Ray:
Rabindranath Tagore

Sunil Janah:
Images of Bengal

*Rabindranath Tagore:
A Celebration of His Life and Work*

Vera Lehndorff and Holger Trülzsch:
Trans-Figurations

The Boyle Family: *Beyond Image*

Arthur Tress: *Talisman*

Reflections of Technology

Soviet Posters of Silent Cinema

Chinese Picture Stories

Stephen Farthing: *Mute Accomplices*

Balla: The Futurist

Naum Gabo:
*The Constructive Idea: Sculpture,
Drawings, Paintings, Monoprints*

*Another Russia:
Unofficial Contemporary
Photography from the Soviet Union*

1988

K.G. Subramanyan: *Fairy Tales
of Oxford and Other Paintings*

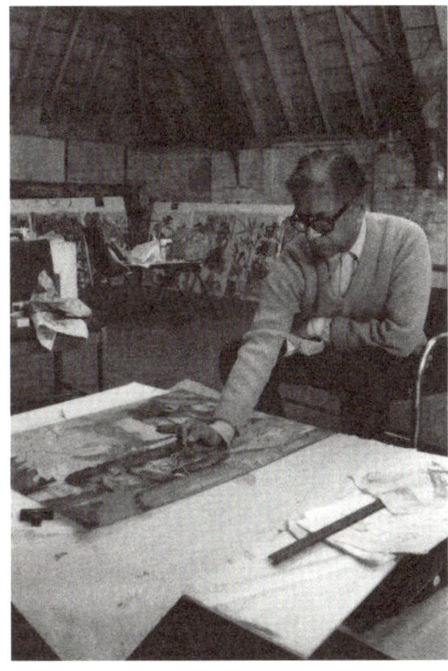

K.G. Subramanyan at work in temporary studio,
Museum of Modern Art Oxford, 1988

Giacomo Manzù:
Themes and Variations

*Short Stories:
Prints and Drawings by John Hewitt*

*Prints and Drawings
of the Weimar Republic*

Boris Birger: *Paintings*

The Drawings of Roy Lichtenstein

Richard Hamilton: *Installations*

Time: Oxford Photography Exhibition

Eisenstein at Ninety

*Art at the Edge:
Contemporary Art from Poland*

Steve Farrer: *Against the Steady Stare*

*The Fallen: Work by Artists Who Lost
Their Lives in the First World War*

Shirazeh Houshiary

1989

Neil Libbert: *Photographs*

Sue Coe: *Police State*

*Performances:
Testament of Youth: Dance Events*

Richard Wilson: *High-Tec*

*Makonde: Wooden Sculpture
from East Africa*

Brian Catling:
An Installation and Five Performances

Mexico: Mythical Objects

Posada: Messenger of Mortality

Phillip Guston: *Works on Paper*

John Buckley:
What's Up Doc?

*Lies, Lies, Lies:
Oxford Photography Open
Submission Exhibition*

100 Years of Russian Art

Links: New Work by Bonn Artists

Andy Walton: *Drawings*

*Wols: Photography,
Watercolours and Graphics*

Helen Chadwick: *Viral Landscapes*

Denise Evans: *Preservations*

Yayoi Kusama: *Soul Burning Flashes*

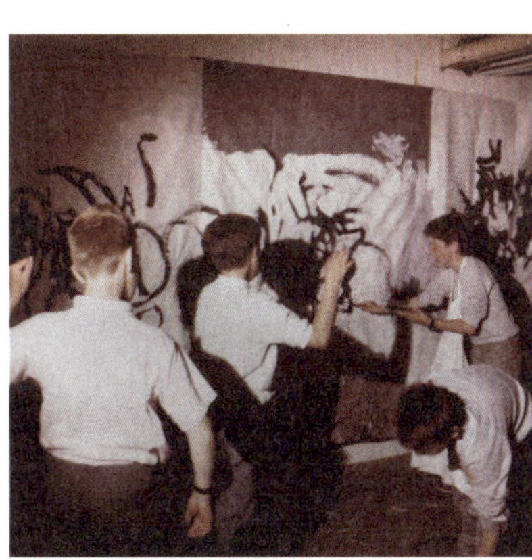

Young people use movement and shadow to
transpose Indian dance into paint, Museum
of Modern Art Oxford, 1989

1990

Northlands: New Art from Scandinavia

Ken Campbell:
A Few Ways Through the Window

Edvard Munch and Photography

*Movers and Shakers:
Dance for the 1990s*

Yannis Kourakis:
Banana Paintings

Devětsil: *Czech Avant-Garde Art,
Architecture and Design of the
1920s and 30s*

Martin Parr:
The Cost of Living

*Boundaries:
Oxford Photographic Open Submission*

Art Creating Society

Art from South Africa

*Signs of the Times
Part 1: A Decade of Video,
Films and Slide-tape Installation
in Britain 1980-1990*

John Trigg: *Inside the Whale,
Sculpture and Painting*

*Signs of the Times
Part 2: A Decade of Video,
Films and Slide-tape Installation
in Britain 1980-1990*

Derain: The Late Work

1991

*Real Time/Real Space:
New Dance Dimension*

Arturo di Stefano

Andrew Logan: *An Artistic Adventure*

*Small World:
Oxford Photography Lecture Series*

Eitan Lee Al:
*Quoted Images: Reconstructed Images
of Political and Personal History*

Jac Leirner

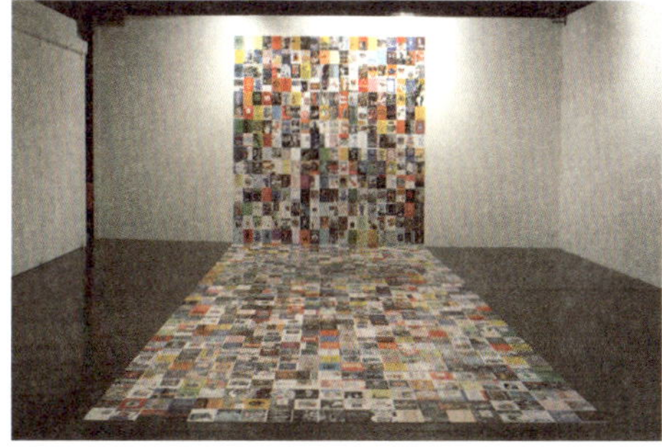

Jac Leirner, Museum of Modern Art Oxford, 1991

David Smith:
Medals for Dishonour 1937–1940

Ana Maria Pacheco

Panayiotis Kalorkoti:
Homage to Goya and Soldier

*The Dragon in the Treasure House:
Behind the Myths of Tibet*

John Muafangejo: *I Was Lonelyness*

John Latham: *Art After Physics*

Ken Kiff: *Graphics*

1992

*Life After Chernobyl:
A Hard Rain (Yuri Ivanov)*

*Engineers of the Human Soul: Soviet
Social Realist Painting 1930s–1960s*

Ernst Barlach:
Woodcuts, Lithographs and Sculpture

*Writers Under Stalin and other
Collage Portraits by Vladmir Sulyagin*

*Oxford Arts Society: A Century
of Art in Oxford 1891-1991*

Brian Cohen: *Photographs*

Arnold Newman: *Five Decades*

Robert Doisneau: A Retrospective

*The Critical Decade: Black British
Photography in the Eighties*

Helen Escobedo

Brave New Worlds:
Michael McDonough: *Prints;*
Stuart Turner: *Sculpture*

Photography in Russia 1840–1940

Marley Stone:
'Horse Series' and 'Dog Face'

*East Timor 1974-1992:
Years of Silence, Images of Resistance*

Bill Jacklin:
Urban Portraits, New York 1986–1992

A World of Difference:
Images of Oxfam across the World

A Cleaner Picture

Shanti Panchal: *Paintings*

1993

Sol LeWitt: *Drawings 1958–1992*

Sol LeWitt: *Structures 1962–1993*

Signs and Emblems:
Marcel Broodthaers:
Complete Prints and Editions

Signs and Emblems: Asafo:
The Flags of the Fante Regiments

Signs and Emblems: Bracha
Lichtenberg Ettinger: *Matrix-Borderlines*

Signs and Emblems:
Anthony Freestone: *Paintings*

Posters and Pots of
the Cultural Revolution

New Art from China, Part 1:
Silent Energy

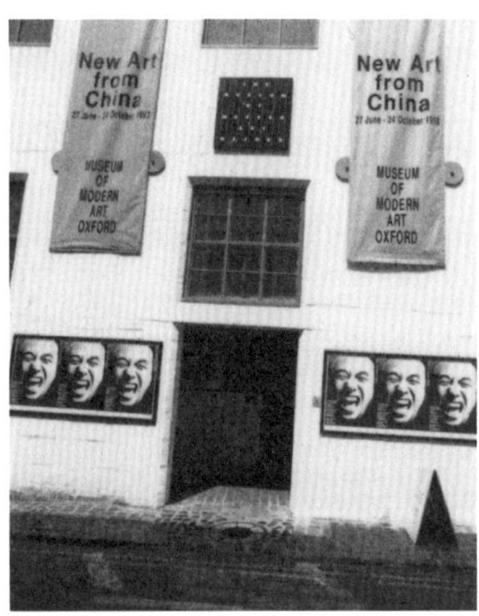

Museum of Modern Art Oxford façade during
New Art from China, 1993

Stuart Franklin:
A Tale of Two Cities: Photographs
of Mexico City and Beijing

New Art from China, Part 2:
China Avant-Garde

Paul Kilsby: *Inflections*

Gary Hill: *In Light of the Other*

1994

Drawing into Clay

The Raw and the Cooked:
New Work in Clay in Britain

Blue Peter

The Reading Room

Positive Lives: Responses to HIV

Mrinalini Mukherjee: *Sculpture*

Kalighat:
Indian Popular Painting 1800–1930

Contemporary Art Society:
Recent Purchases

Stuart Dawson: *Paintings*

Josef Albers: *A Retrospective*

Peter Joseph:
Paintings and Works on Paper

Print et L'Estampe:
Oxford-Montreal Printmaking Exchange

Strange Territory

Art from Argentina

1995

Susan Trangmar: *Interval*

Donald Judd: *Posters*

Donald Judd: *Sculpture,*
Furniture, Prints, Architecture

John Comino-James:
Nearly Every Tuesday: Photographs
at Thame Market 1989–1994

Adam Lowe:
Littoral Deposits and Other Works

Marina Abramović:
Objects Performance Video Sound

Jacqueline Poncelet:
The Decorative Smile

Willy Ronis: *Photographs 1926–1995*

Judah Catalan: *Works on Paper*

Louise Bourgeois: *Sculpture, Prints*

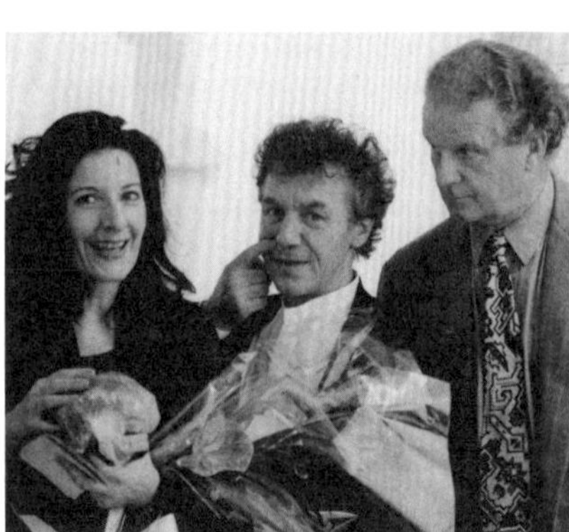

Marina Abramović, private view, Museum of
Modern Art Oxford, 1995

1996

Perm, Open City:
Recent Photographs from the Urals

Heri Dono: *Blooming in Arms*

Sergio Camargo: *Sculpture 1960–1990*

Jenny Greep: *Motorway Paintings*

The Director's Eye:
Drawings and Photographs
by European Filmmakers

Terry Smith: *Page-Specific Works*

Carl Andre

Bartholomew Dudley: *Short Stories*

Scream and Scream Again:
Film in Art

About Vision:
New British Painting in the 1990s

1997

Ally Stott

In Visible Light: Photography
and Classification in Art,
Science and The Everyday

The ART of Driving

In Place (Out of Time):
Contemporary Art in Australia

Yoko Ono:
Have you seen the horizon lately?

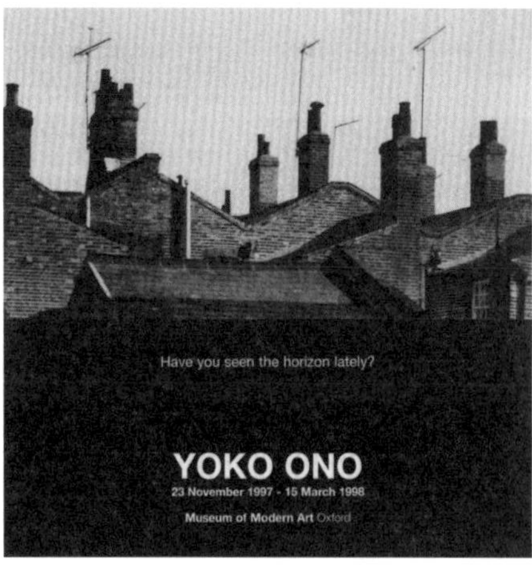

Yoko Ono, exhibition invitation, 1997

1998

Mona Hatoum

John Murphy and Julião Sarmento:
A Conversation Piece

Gary Stevens: *And*

Mitja Tusek

Gustav Metzger

1999

James Casebere:
New Photographs

Sarah Morris

Anna Gaskell

Notorious: Alfred Hitchcock
and Contemporary Art

Michelangelo Pistoletto:
Shifting Perspective (I Am the Other)

2000

Audible Light

Weegee

Enclosed and Enchanted

Matt Mullican: *More Details*
from an Imaginary Universe

2001

Katarzyna Kozyra

Alison Turnbull

Mark Lewis

Open City:
Street Photographs Since 1950

*Experiment/Experiencia:
Art in Brazil 1958–2000*

Ed Ruscha: *Paintings,
Drawings and Books 1961–2001*

2002

Matthew Cooper Lewis

Laura Quarmby

Trauma

*How To Be Modern:
Arne Jacobsen in the 21st Century*

Concrete Garden

Tracey Emin: *This is Another Place*

2003

David Goldblatt: *Fifty-one Years*

Jake and Dinos Chapman:
The Rape of Creativity

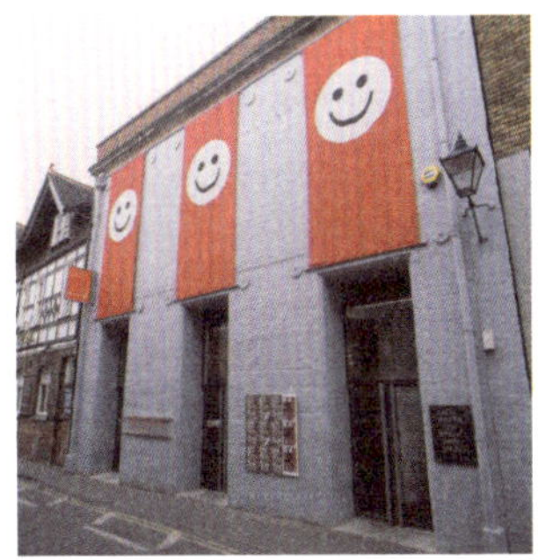

Jake and Dinos Chapman,
Modern Art Oxford, 2003

Monica Bonvicini: *Anxiety Attack*

Jim Lambie: *Male Stripper*

Candice Breitz: *Re-Animations*

*Veil: Veiling, Representation
and Contemporary Art*

2004

The Oxford Show

Phil Collins, Jeremy Deller
and Jasmila Zbanic: *Recall*

Mike Nelson: *Triple Bluff Canyon*

Yael Bartana, Emily Jacir and
Lee Miller: *Wherever I Am*

*Real World:
The Dissolving Space of Experience*

Jannis Kounellis

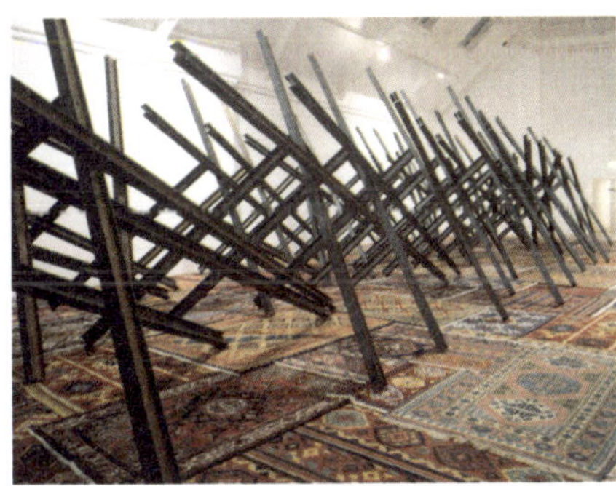

Jannis Kounellis, Modern Art Oxford, 2004

2005

Fiona Tan

Arrivals > Poland:
Pawel Althamer and Artur Zmijewski

Oxford 2015: Dreams Plans Visions

Cecily Brown: *Paintings*

Arrivals > Slovenia: Miha Knific

Imagine

Angela Bulloch

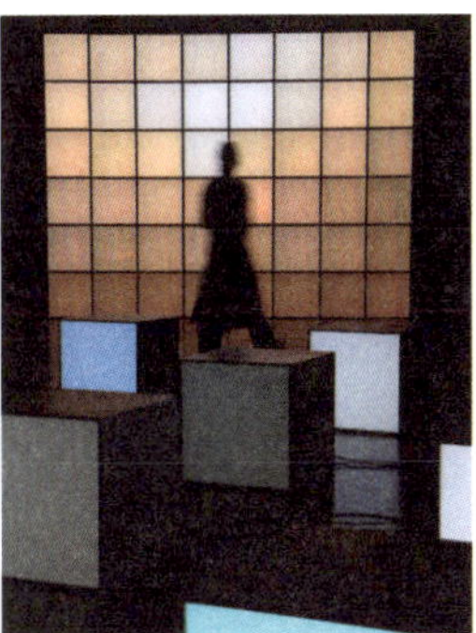

Angela Bulloch, Modern Art
Oxford, 2005

Arrivals > Lithuania:
Zilvinas Landzbergas

2006

Arrivals > Latvia: Alnis Stakle

Filmperformance

Ulrich Ruckriem:
The Shadows of The Stones

Local Stories

Out of Beirut

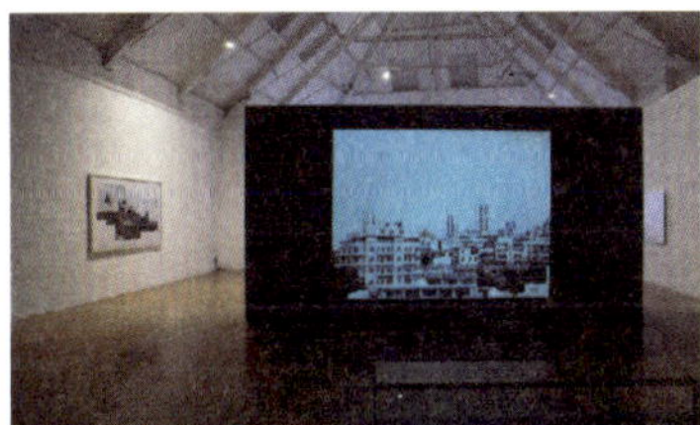

Out of Beirut, Modern Art Oxford, 2006

Kerry James Marshall: *Along the Way*

Arrivals > Cyprus:
Christodoulos Panayiotou

Arrivals > Slovakia:
Ilona Nemeth, The Wall

Daniel Buren: *Intervention II*

Arrivals > Estonia:
Kristina Norman: *The Pribalts*

2007

Arrivals > Hungary: Beáta Veszely

Callum Innes: *From Memory*

Arrivals > Malta:
Raphael Vella: *Reading Cabinets*

Seth Price, Kelley Walker
and Continuous Project

Stella Vine: *Paintings*

Encounters: Moshekwa Langa

Trisha Donnelly

Encounters: Imran Qureshi

2008

The Oxford Open

Helen Ganly: *Journey into Light*

Encounters: Lina Saneh

Box Ladder

Obsessions

Encounters: Katie Paterson

Ansel Adams: *Photographs*

Mircea Cantor:
The Need for Uncertainty

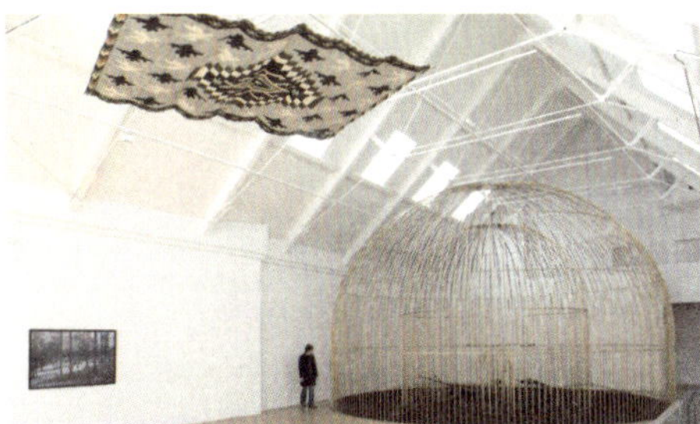

Mircea Cantor, Modern Art Oxford, 2008

Gary Hume: *Door Paintings*

Encounters: Victor Alimpiev

*Oxfordshire Schools Art Exhibition:
MY...*

Janet Cardiff and George Bures Miller:
The House of Books Has No Windows

2009

Regina José Galindo:
The Body of Others

Encounters: Raphaël Zarka

Transmission Interrupted

Silke Otto-Knapp:
Present Time Exercise

Polaroids: Mapplethorpe

Karla Black

Encounters: Cova Macias

Pawel Althamer: *Common Task*

Miroslaw Balka: *Topography*

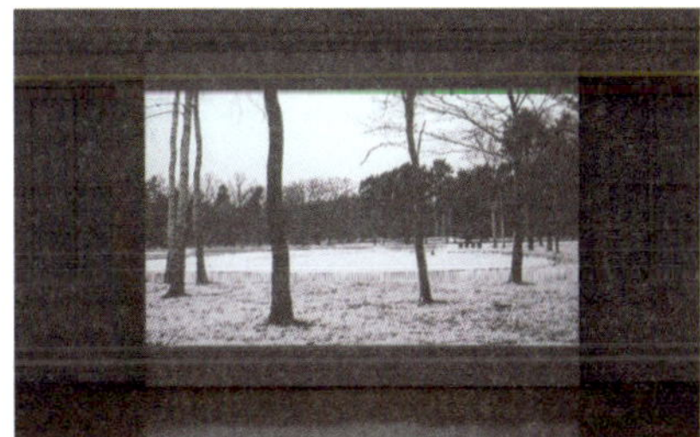

Miroslaw Balka, Modern Art Oxford, 2009

Susan Philipsz: *You Are Not Alone*
(offsite at the Radcliffe Observatory)

2010

Maria Pask: *Déjà vu*

Johanna Billing:
I'm Lost Without Your Rhythm

Howard Hodgkin: *Time and Place*

Simon and Tom Bloor: *Hit and Miss*

Manfred Pernice: *Baldt1*

David Austen: *End of Love*

Thomas Houseago: *What Went Down*

2011

Michael Sailstorfer: *Clouds*

Roman Ondak: *Time Capsule*

Haegue Yang: *Teacher of Dance*

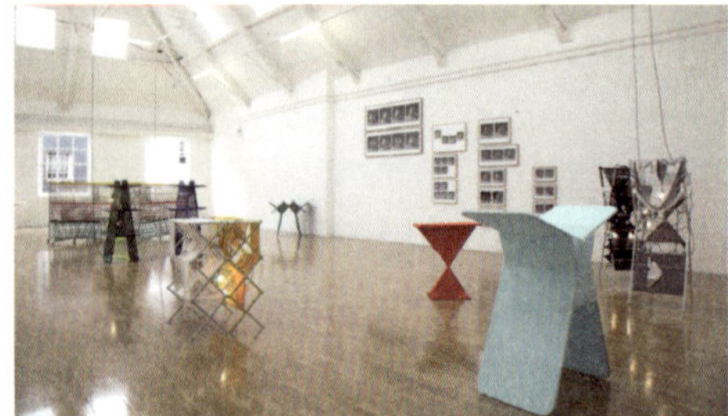

Haegue Yang, Modern Art Oxford, 2011

Dead Star Light (3 Project)

Abraham Cruzvillegas:
*Autoconstrucción: The Optimistic
Failure of a Simultaneous Promise*

brook & black:
Residency and Open Studio

James Capper:
Ripper Teeth in Action

Graham Sutherland:
An Unfinished World

2012

Tamarin Norwood: *Keeping Time*

Stephen Cornford and Ben Gwilliam:
Audiograft

Jordan Baseman: *Green Lady*
(offsite at The Story Museum)

Shezad Dawood: *Piercing Brightness*

Simon Murison-Bowie: *Artweeks*

Lost in Time and Space

Mistaken Identities: Oxford Pride 2012

Jenny Saville

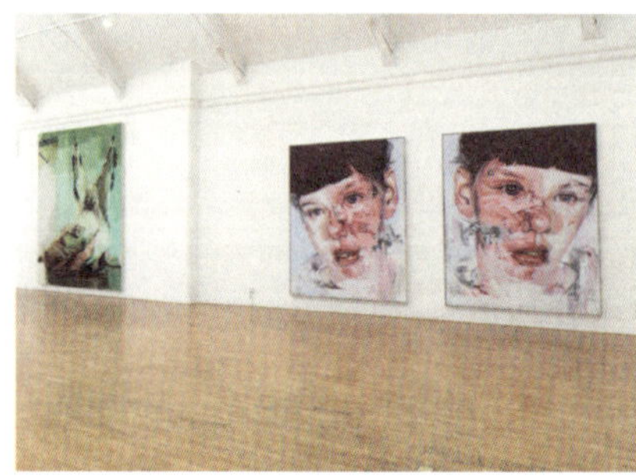

Jenny Saville, Modern Art Oxford, 2012

John Gerrard: *Exercise (Djibouti) 2012*
(offsite at The Old Power Station)

Urbonas Studio:
Residency & Open Studio

Jean-Luc Moulène

Platform

Julian Wild: *Making the Connection*

André Cadere:
Documenting Cadere: 1972–1978

Amalia Pica

2013

Hans Josephsohn

Simon Starling: *Black Drop*
(offsite at The Radcliffe Observatory)

Rolf Julius: *Audiograft*

Zsuzsanna Nyúl:
Residency and Open Studio

Stephen Willats:
*Conscious Unconscious:
In and Out the Reality Check*

Archigram Beyond Architecture REMIX

Haris Epaminonda: *Chapters*

Simon Starling: *Black Drop*

Stephanie Douet: *Real/Non Real*

David Raymond Conroy:
PPE, or It is Spring and I am Blind

Friedrich Kunath:
Raymond Moody's Blues

Tim Head: *Displacement*

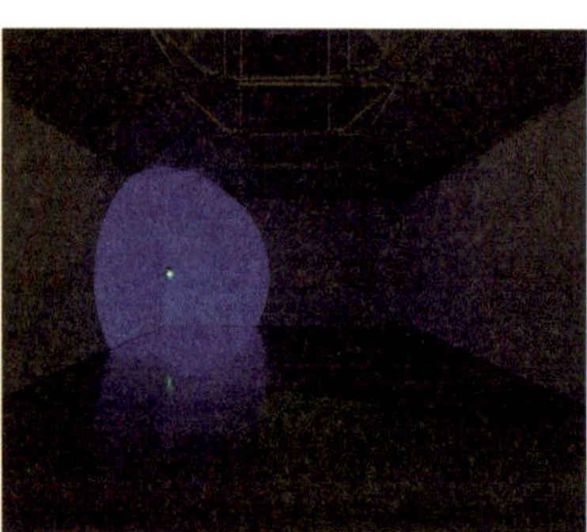

Tim Head, Modern Art Oxford, 2013

Platform 2013

Eva Kotatkova:
A Storyteller's Inadequacy

*Notice! Modern Art Oxford in Print
1966–2013*

After / Hours / Drop / Box

2014

Roelof Louw

Hannah Rickards: *To enable me
to fix my attention on any one of these
symbols I was to imagine that I was
looking at the colours as I might see
them on a moving picture screen*

Sean Lynch:
*A blow-by-blow account
of stone carving in Oxford*

Test Run

Patricia Lennox Boyd: *Metrics*

Barbara Kruger

Stuart Brisley: *State of Denmark*

*Straight to Camera:
Performance for Film*

*Love is Enough:
William Morris & Andy Warhol*

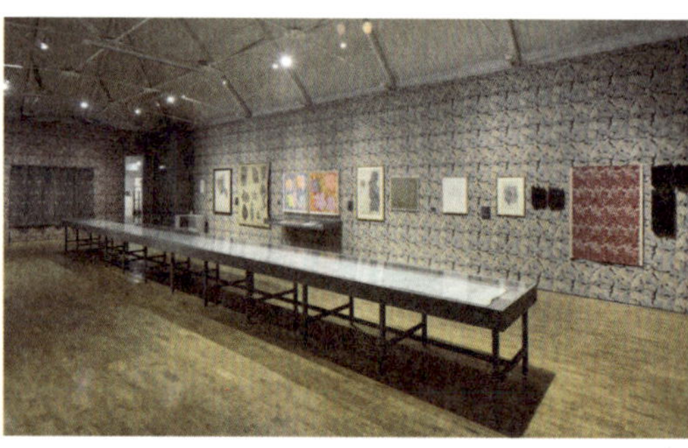

Love is Enough, Modern Art Oxford, 2014

Christian Boltanski:
*Inventory of Objects Belonging
to a Young Man of Oxford*

2015

The Film Studio

Debora Delmar Corp:
Upward Mobility

Test Run: Performance in Public

Lynn Hershman Leeson:
Origins of the Species (Part 2)

Platform

Josh Kline: *Freedom*

Kiki Kogelnik: *Fly Me to the Moon*

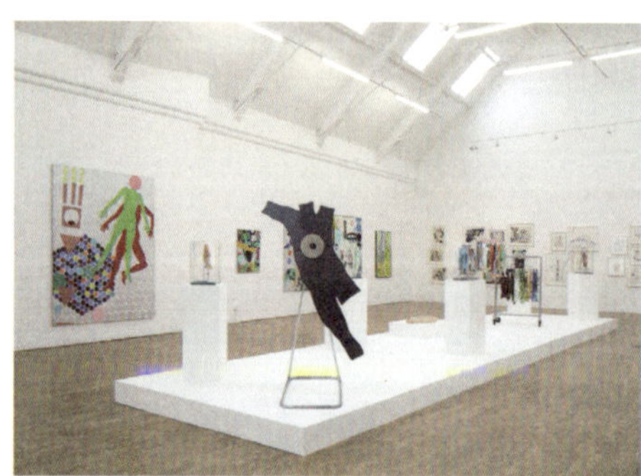

Kiki Kogelnik, Modern Art Oxford, 2015

Anne Hardy: *FIELD*

2016

*KALEIDOSCOPE:
The Indivisible Present*

*KALEIDOSCOPE:
A Moment of Grace*

*KALEIDOSCOPE:
Mystics and Rationalists*

*KALEIDOSCOPE:
It's Me to the World*

*KALEIDOSCOPE:
The Vanished Reality*

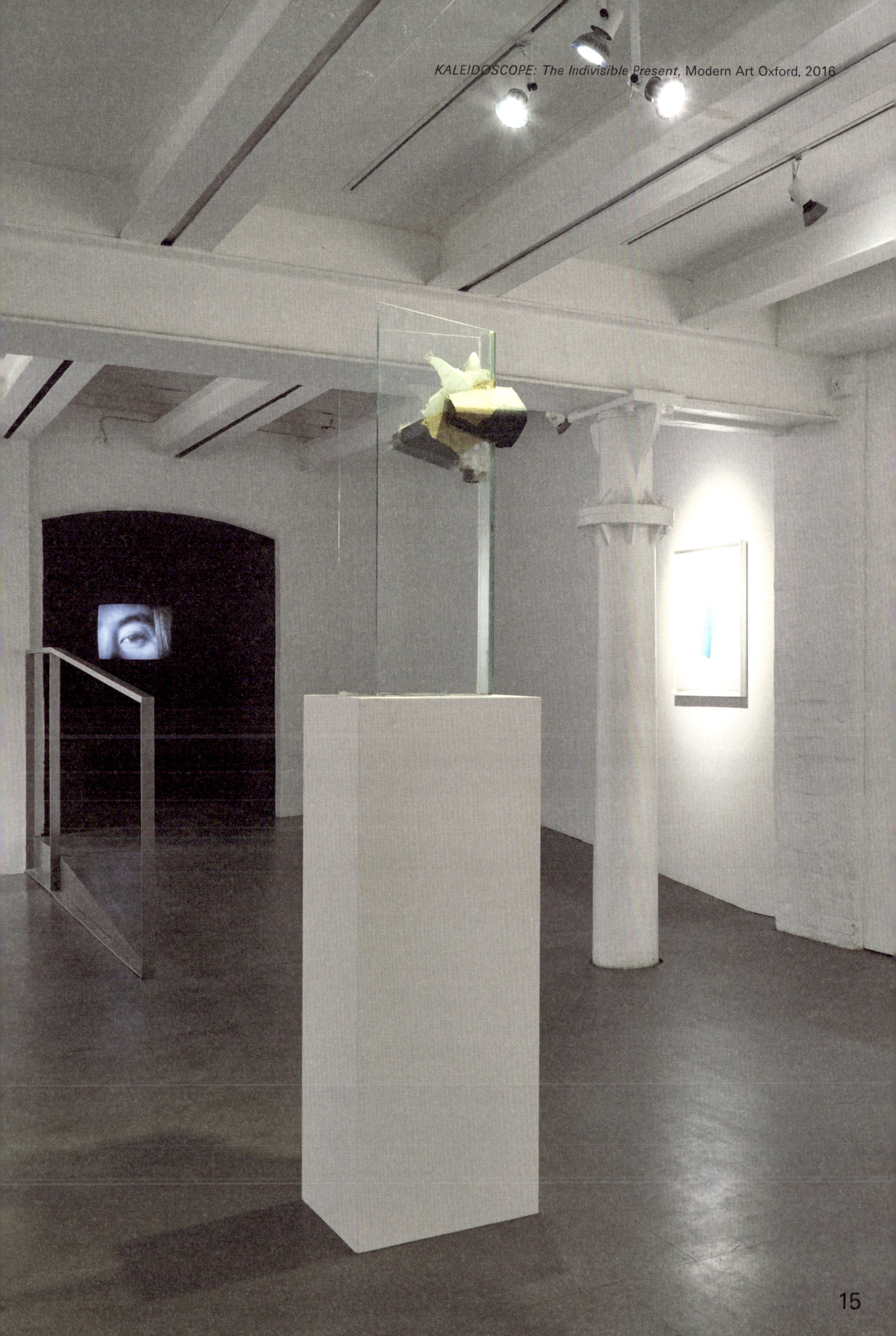

KALEIDOSCOPE: The Indivisible Present, Modern Art Oxford, 2016

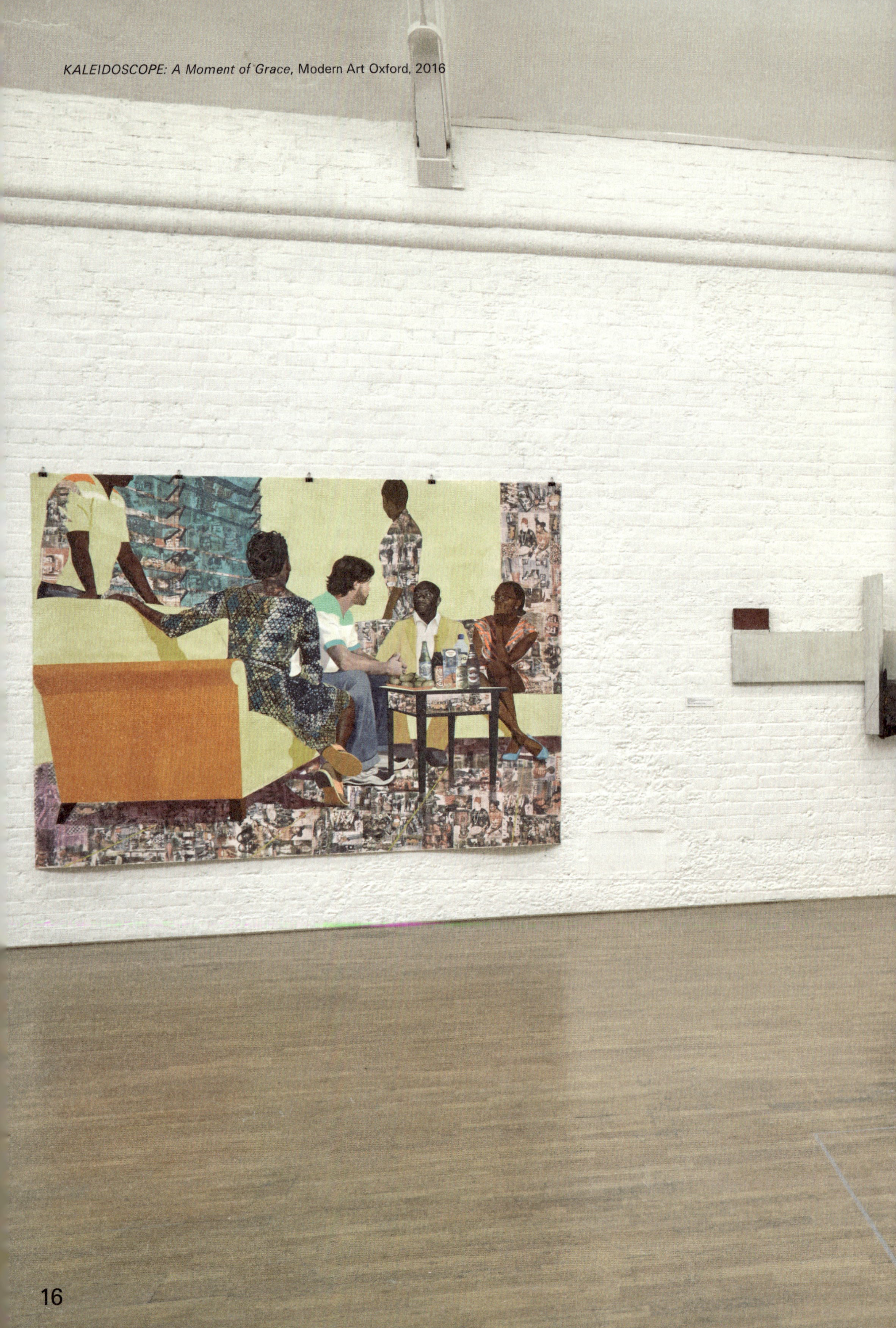

KALEIDOSCOPE: A Moment of Grace, Modern Art Oxford, 2016

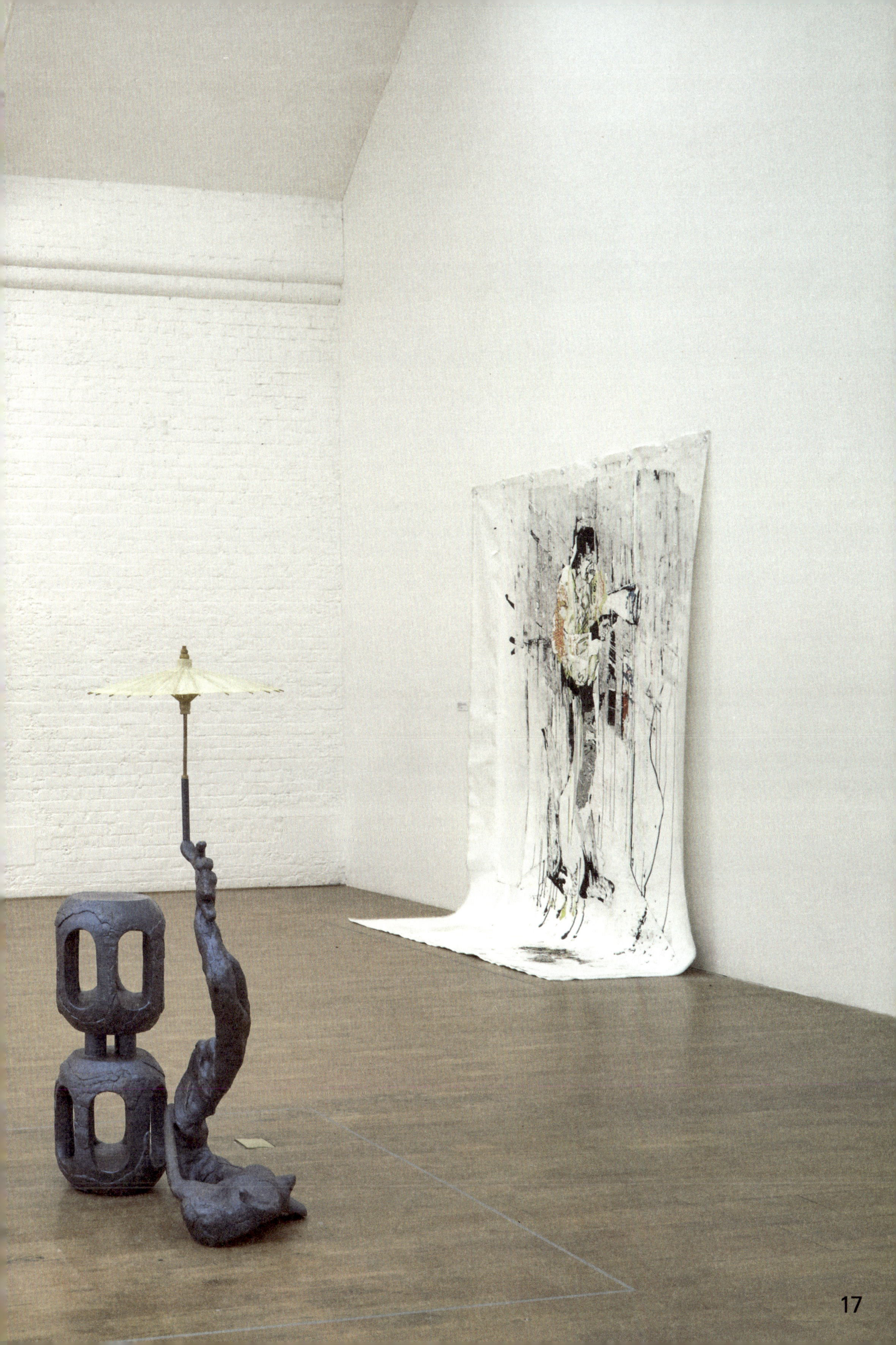

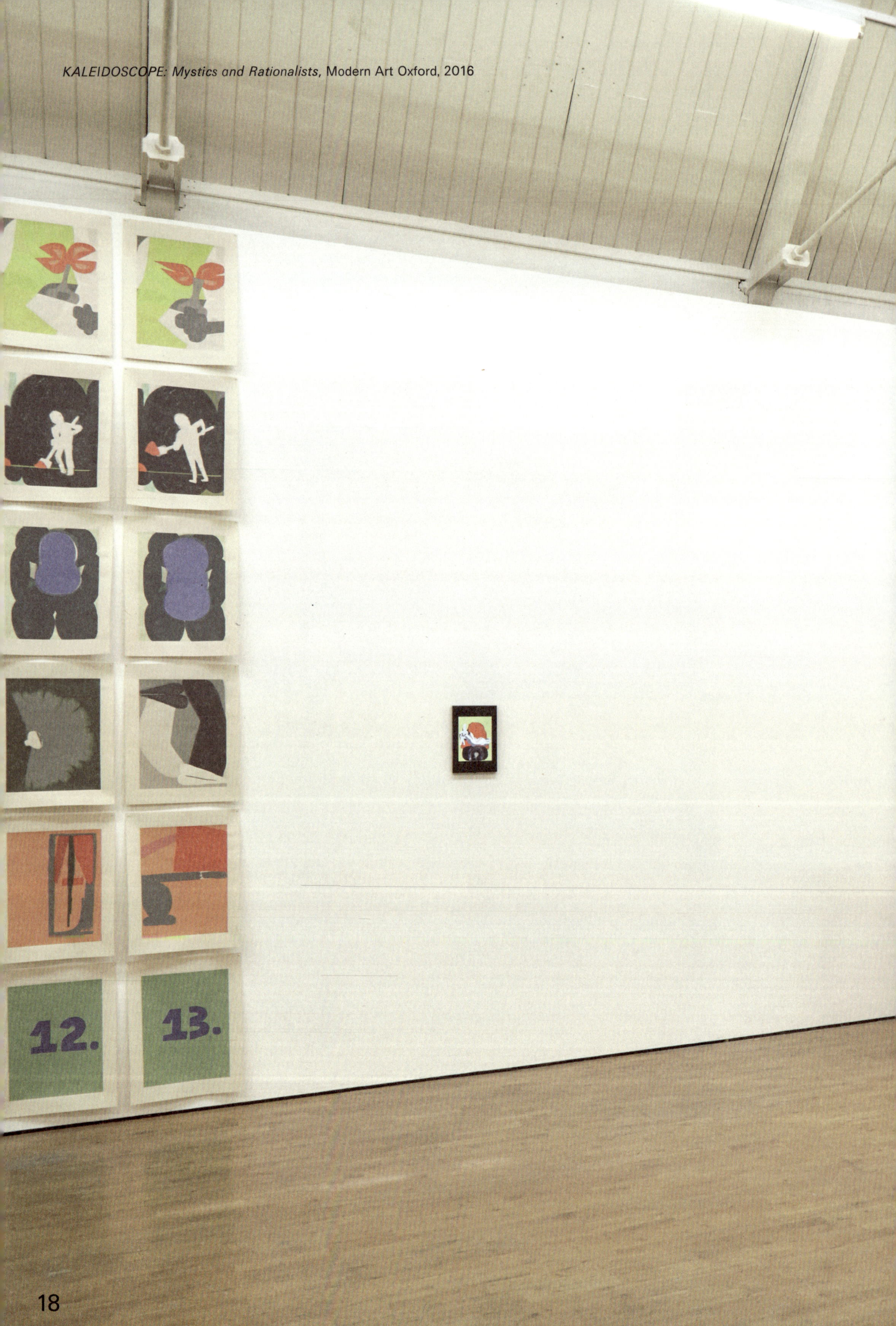

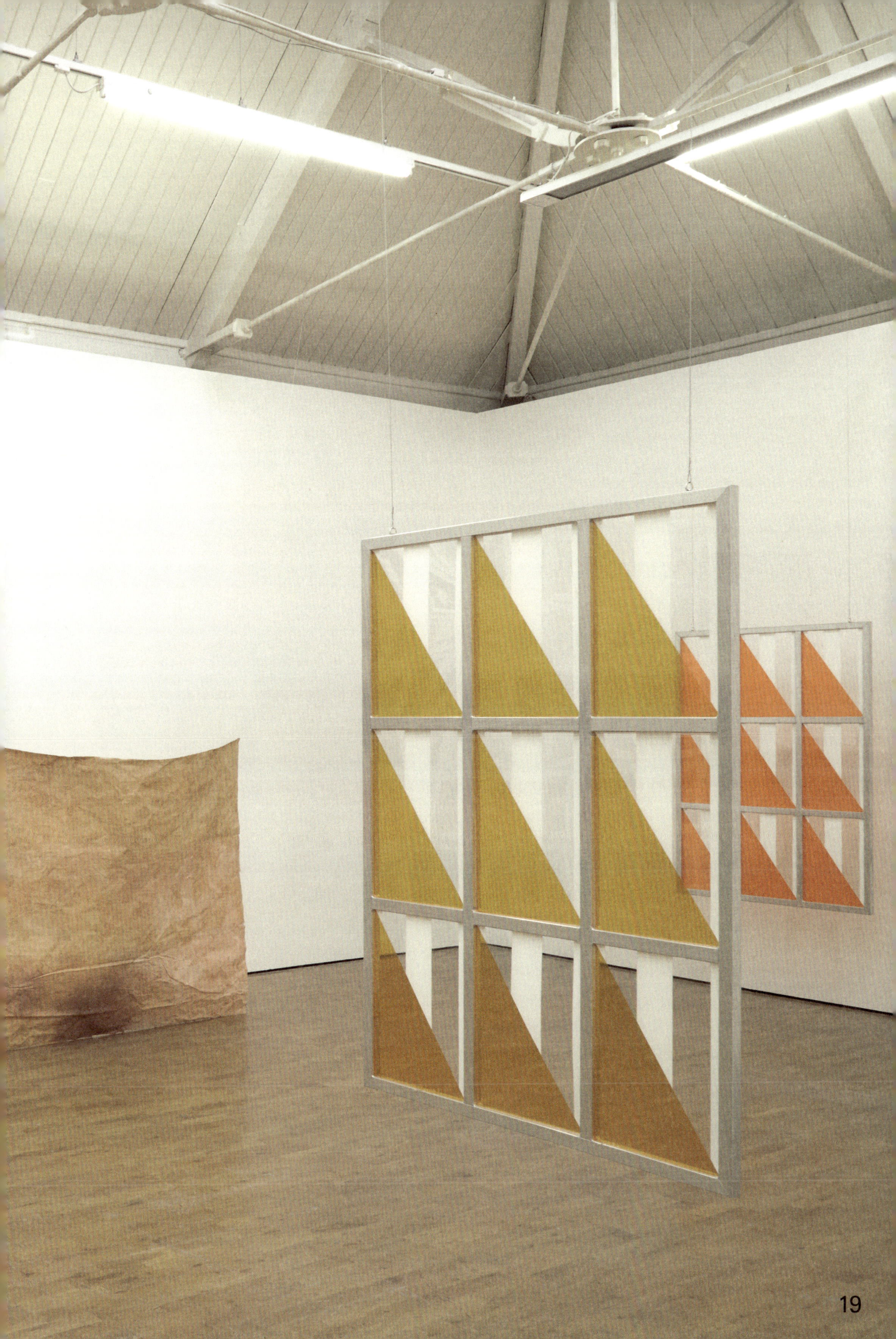

Memories

Being a child of the 1940s from a small market town, I had not grown up in an art-orientated environment nor received any art education. As a result I had only a vague notion of the subject, which was not really something of relevance to me. This all changed in 1984 when, because of my passion for photography, I visited the Duane Michals exhibition at the Museum of Modern Art Oxford. What a revelation. Suddenly this obscure subject called 'Art' became interesting and important to me, which it has been ever since. I have visited numerous exhibitions at the Museum of Modern Art Oxford / Modern Art Oxford as well as many other venues over the subsequent 39 years, but I always regard Modern Art Oxford as the most important. I am forever grateful to the gallery and its approachable, helpful staff for 'switching on the light' and revealing to me this fascinating, exciting, stimulating world called art.

**Stu Allsopp, Friend
of Modern Art Oxford**

I began visiting Oxford in the 1990s as someone with no connection to the University for which the city is famous. Instead I was a regular at what was then known as the Museum of Modern Art and in particular its bookshop, where I attempted to sell books to the man who ran it, a Scotsman named Alistair. At the time the shop carried the best selection of art books in town, as well as an idiosyncratic selection of experimental fiction and film theory, anything that interested Ali, an aspiring novelist who gave me his work to read. At lunchtime I would wander through the gallery and take in the shows: Donald Judd, Carl Andre, Yoko Ono, some of the greatest names in international contemporary art. Somehow the city and the gallery became mixed up in my mind. Both were built on a human scale: both were containers of a multitude of ideas. Perhaps I could live here? Modern Art Oxford was the portal through which my family and I arrived in the city; how many others have travelled the same route we will never know. What is certain is that Modern Art Oxford has remained somewhere to encounter art and new ways of thinking, to be challenged, stimulated and entertained.

James Attlee, writer

I joined the Museum of Modern Art on the 25 October 2000, however, my first encounter with the Museum was in September 1975 during my two postgraduate years at the Slade School of Fine Art. As I recall, we were brought to attend a talk during an exhibition in the Upper Gallery entitled *Art and Language 1966–75*.

My position as part of the Modern Art Oxford team (for 16 years) allowed me to view several shows that varied in their nature as well as approaches to materials and visual visions, which I perceived as a source of research and an inspiration to my work as a painter. Such shows also assisted in exposing my eyes and mind to highly variable sources of visual adventures which ignited my hunger for further knowledge.

Much of my inspiration is drawn from my exposure to new approaches in other forms of arts, such as, cinema, photography, architecture, video art, theatre and contemporary dance-performance, finding captivation in the correlation between performance and drawing. I feel that these sources enhanced my expertise and practice to a novel and deeper level, also setting ground to my research and practice here as well as abroad, especially in places such as Tangier, Paris and Barcelona.

I have always been fascinated by the way curators transform space and light for each show, from painting to installation, as was displayed in the Mike Nelson show in 2004 when the Upper Gallery was filled with sand, or that of Jim Lambie's 2003 show and Jannis Kounellis's 2004 show.

According to Brian O'Doherty in *The Ideology of the Gallery Space*, '... From the 20s to the 70s, the gallery has a history as distinct as that of the art shown in it.'

The space became the new God.

The Upper Gallery is a 'text' open to all possibilities,

it looks like a 'ship' waiting for light and whispers to sail to new visual horizons...

It is Magic....

I sometimes wonder if the spirits of those who worked here since the late 19th century are wandering around us full of wonder.

Long live the Line,
Long live the Shadow,
Long live the Light.

**Mohamed Omer Bishara,
Visitor Assistant and painter/
collagist/printmaker**

Modern Art Oxford exhibited us directly post-graduation, and later commissioned us over several years to work beyond the gallery with community and educational groups. More recently *Plot 16*, our two-year residency in Rose Hill, enabled us to re-site the architectural drawing of Modern Art Oxford into a scaled up sculpture on an allotment, grow hops to reflect Modern Art Oxford's former use as a brewery, make beer and open up new routes and means of exchange between different communities across Oxford and beyond. Modern Art Oxford is a powerhouse with staff and audiences that encourage artists to take risks for which we are enormously grateful. It mediates the local with the international and claims the precious edge of what defines contemporary culture.

brook & black, artists

The Museum of Modern Art Oxford offered me the opportunity to engage with and build on a highly regarded, socially relevant platform. It was a museum known for the creation of meaningful exhibitions that had a kind of unusual artistic integrity and energy, and it was clearly an institution willing to experiment and take risks. The Museum of Modern Art Oxford punched way beyond its weight class, with international reverberations. The institution had the kind of expansive thinking and openness that I was looking for. There, one could bring a variety of art forms together; not just painting and sculpture, but photography, performance, film, video, and installation art. Oxford was also an arena in which we could do surveys of the then under-appreciated, socially engaged work of Yoko Ono and Gustav Metzger or retrospectives as diverse as Weegee and Ed Ruscha; and we could bring together an array of artists working in diverse media who were influenced by the garden or even by Alfred Hitchcock. Hopefully we made the Museum of Modern Art Oxford even more 'notorious'.

Kerry Brougher, Director, 1996–2000

I have been working as a Visitor
Service Assistant for 28 years,
since Roy Lichtenstein's *Drawings*
and Richard Hamilton's *Installations*
in 1988.

I enjoy being around the exhibitions
and talking to visitors; their reactions
can be so varied. The other day a visitor
told me how much she enjoyed visiting
the gallery with her young daughter
and how welcoming we were; that's
very satisfying to know.

I think that Modern Art Oxford can be
a showcase of reflection and debate
about the society we live in, bringing
rigorous thought and dimensions
about life, human pain, pleasure and
joy through what we continue to show
and present.

**Andrew Charlwood,
Visitor Assistant**

Modern Art Oxford was still the
Museum of Modern Art Oxford in
2002 when I first arrived as Senior
Curator. With then director Andrew
Nairne, I had the pleasure of building
on the institution's pioneering history
that dates back to the 1960s. It
has always been a vital platform for
contemporary art for Britain, serving
not only the remarkable university
town but also the landscape of art
making and ideas across the country.
Among my many great memories of
Modern Art Oxford are the exhibition
of Mona Hatoum in the late 1990s,
and in the early 2000s the remarkable
project of Mike Nelson, who turned
the entire building into a sculpture
studio worthy of Rodin, or better still,
Cecil B. de Mille. Inviting Daniel Buren
back to the gallery some 40 years
after his radical intervention in the
1970s was a special moment for
the gallery and its many publics.
Long may they continue to thrive.

**Suzanne Cotter, Senior Curator
and Deputy Director, 2002–2009**

As an artist you are always looking
to work with institutions and people
that help you to do what you want
to do! Modern Art Oxford is such
an institution.

Jeremy Deller, artist

Becoming Director of the Museum
of Modern Art Oxford in 1976 enabled
me to think about the social, political
and aesthetic contexts within which
modern and contemporary art was
being made and to reflect this in
continuing programmes of exhibitions,
publications and events.

From the outset I, with my colleagues,
began to challenge the predominantly
white, male consensus of the
British art world first by showing
more exhibitions by women artists
(Mary Kelly, Susan Hiller, Jo Baer,
Gillian Ayres, Sally Potter, Yayoi
Kusama, Louise Bourgeois...) and
then by stepping outside the western
stockade to research and show art
from the USSR, Mexico, India, Japan,
Mozambique, Tanzania, South Africa,
Brazil, Argentina, Indonesia and China.

This was not as an 'exotic' footnote
to any 'main' programme. Museum
of Modern Art Oxford was one of the
first museums anywhere to create an
open, equal platform for showing some
of the best artists from Britain, Europe
and the US alongside many 'others'
from elsewhere.

David Elliott, Director, 1976–1996

It's fantastic to have such a
sophisticated art gallery/museum
in a thriving university town full
of young excited people.

Tracey Emin, artist

To me, Modern Art Oxford has been
a playground. It is a place that allowed
me to fully explore my ideas and push
my abilities, which is an experience
I am most grateful for. Although
it is its 50th anniversary this year,
Modern Art Oxford always maintains
a fresh and youthful mindset. Having
had the chance to dig through the
gallery's archives and meet many
of its wonderful staff as a part of my
volunteering experience, I strongly felt
the institution's drive to challenge and
strive towards creating something new.

**Sarka Fenclova, Modern Art
Oxford intern and University
of Oxford student**

I came to Modern Art Oxford in
late 2011, funded by a scholarship
to write a doctorate on the gallery's
half century of programming.
To spend four and a half years
in the archives, poring over
paper records of long-gone events,
was a curious and fascinating
experience. Modern Art Oxford
is unusual in having continuously
occupied a single historic building
for its entire period of existence.
Exhibitions even from the late 1960s
seem almost uncannily contemporary
when seen in photographs set within
the familiar brick-walled 19th century
spaces, spaces that are instantly
recognisable, largely unchanged,
and yet subject to profound
reinvention. For me, as I suspect
for many who have worked in or
wandered the gallery over the past
five decades, 30 Pembroke Street
is haunted by the many ghosts
of its exhibitionary incarnations.

Dr. Hilary Floe, curatorial researcher

I grew up in Wheatley, ten miles
outside Oxford. I was your typical
arty teenager, and the Museum of
Modern Art Oxford was a beacon of
intellectual and romantic possibility.
At first, it was less the exhibitions
and more the museum bookshop
and cafe I was drawn to. I liked their
bean salads. I would go on awkward
dates there with similarly arty girls
from school. In the pre-internet 1990s,
the bookshop was truly a mine of
information about art and culture.
I'd scour the art magazines, buy
postcards of artworks and I vividly
recall saving money for their copy of
Stewart Home's *What Is Situationism?*
at a precocious age when I had no
clue what Situationism was but knew
it sounded cool. Later, as a student at
the nearby Ruskin School of Fine Art,
I gravitated towards the exhibitions.
Here I first saw work by Chris Ofili,
Marina Abramović, Carl Andre, and
Yoko Ono. On graduation, I was thrilled
to have the opportunity to show in
the cafe a short video I'd made.

I'm proud that this small museum
in my home town has such an
internationally important history.
But I'm also forever indebted
to Modern Art Oxford for those
teenage years spent in its bookshop
and cafe.

**Dan Fox, Co-editor
of *frieze* magazine**

As a student in the early 1970s,
I put on jazz events in the basement
of the museum, and inadvertently saw
the shows of Sol LeWitt wall drawings,
Hamish Fulton photos and others
organised by Peter Ibsen over which
we philistines argued furiously –
'could this be art?'

Sandy Nairne, Chris Aggs and I went
to Richard Demarco's Edinburgh Arts
summer schools, which transformed
my appreciation of contemporary art
and consequently we were among
the very few Oxford students who
had heard of Joseph Beuys when
Nick Serota arrived in 1974, and
so I was privileged to work on
the installation of *The Secret Block*
exhibition of Beuys drawings and
to meet Joseph and Caroline Tisdall.

A couple of years later in 1976 I
came back to the museum as Assistant
Director at the age of 24, almost
entirely unqualified, except that
I had spent some time in the small
contemporary art world (such as
it then was) in London and then in
Germany, and had seen Germano
Celant's *Arte/Ambiente* show in
Venice, which expanded my view
of art and became very influential
in my art-historical formation.

David Elliott had become the director
following Nick, and we were able to
present exhibitions of Rita Donagh,
Jo Baer, Mary Kelly, Susan Hiller,
a performance by Sally Potter,
Rose English and Jacky Lansley,
film programmes, and projects
with Darcy Lange, Dan Graham,
Steve Willats, Victor Burgin, Joseph
Kosuth, and historical shows which
informed the social and political
work of these contemporary artists.
My last exhibition before I moved
to work at the Whitechapel was
a beautiful show by Alan Johnston.
Howard Hodgkin was then resident
artist at BNC Oxford, and had the
first artist's studio I had seen.

Some years later when I worked at
the Fruitmarket gallery in Edinburgh,
we took David's show of postwar
Japanese art and organised exhibitions
of Komar and Melamid and then
of Richard Hamilton installations.

For many years Oxford has played
a crucial part in bringing a modern
and cosmopolitan 20th century culture
to a largely philistine and traditional
society. Long may it continue.

**Mark Francis, Assistant Director,
1976–1978**

Having lived in Oxford for 50 years
I remember the beginning of the
Museum of Modern Art Oxford
with Trevor and Eileen Green.

As an exhibitor, tutor and friend I
have been closely involved as the
years unfolded, and always approached
the gallery with a sense of anticipation
and excitement. You never knew what
you would find within. Awareness of
the risks taken by the gallery and its
different directors, whose personal
choices were inevitably reflected,
continues to this day.

One of the most powerful experiences
has been walking around in these huge
spaces and seeing how they have been
utterly transformed by light, sound and
substance. An ash wall which collapsed
in on itself, live peacocks in vast gilded
cages, a mirror crashing to the ground
in a thousand splinters, and seas of
sand undulating across the floor of
the Upper Gallery. Modern Art Oxford
has enriched my life.

**Helen Ganly, Friend of Modern
Art Oxford**

Modern Art Oxford's ambitious,
meticulously researched and ever-
prescient programming has played
a fundamental role in shaping the
discussion around contemporary
art in Britain and beyond. It has
introduced the public to a wide
range of artists of whom they
had never heard, but having seen
them, will never forget. For Modern
Art Oxford to steadfastly exhibit
the intellectual avant-garde in
our age of vacuous celebrity and
arts austerity takes a good deal
of courage for which it should
be supported and applauded.

Will Gompertz, broadcaster

Living in Oxford 35 years ago,
Modern Art Oxford was my introduction
to Modern Art. I often found it
challenging – and still do – but
the white spaces and their changing
content always intrigued me, I went
on to spend a lot of time in the Musée
d'Art Moderne de la Ville de Paris and
the Arnolfini, Bristol.

Barbara Grodecka Lewis, visitor

The luminous presence of Modern
Art Oxford has been a constant source
of inspiration for the Ruskin School
of Art. Rooted in the present day,
but with our the eyes focused on
the future, we have been brothers
in arms in the historical city of
Oxford. For Ruskin's lively community
of students and staff, Modern Art
Oxford is a touchstone for advanced
studio practice and groundbreaking
exhibitions, a place to gather new ideas
and a platform for rigorous thinking.
Modern Art Oxford's bold commitment
to experimentation and innovation
will continue to be an inspiration for
future generations of young artists.

**Professor Hanneke Grootenboer,
Head of the Ruskin School of Art,
University of Oxford**

It was at Modern Art Oxford (or the
Museum of Modern Art Oxford as
it then was) that I first saw an exhibition
by a living artist. It was a show of
Bill Woodrow's work: a washing
machine which had been cut and
twisted into an electric guitar, an
umbrella transformed into a crow,
a telephone hanging from a car
bonnet... In some small way it changed
my life. I've been visiting the museum
regularly ever since. Not just for the
exhibitions – from David Mach and
Yoko Ono to Jenny Saville and Graham
Sutherland – but often just to sit in
the cafe. Like many people in Oxford
I think of Modern Art Oxford as one
of our most important public spaces,
for experiencing art, yes, but also
for meeting, for talking, for just being
still. It's like Port Meadow or Shotover
or the Thames Path. Quietly we think
it belongs to us. It's part of the fabric
of Oxford and it's hard to imagine
the city without it.

Mark Haddon, author

In 2010, I was seconded to Modern Art Oxford, working mainly on the archive. I had two key motivations:

It was modern; being used to historical art, I wanted a change.

It was exhibition driven and I perceived this as the challenge of an ever-changing identity.

What I learnt was that Modern Art Oxford's archive is its institutional memory. When the temporary exhibition has long gone, the joy of discovering handwritten letters between artists and past directors remains. The wonderful poster archive presents, at points, a history of British graphic design. The archive tells the organisation's story in multiple creative ways; curatorial, educational, communicative. My understanding of how creativity manifests itself in many ways to contribute to the success of an organisation is something I found in boxes in the archive of Modern Art Oxford and it has influenced me ever since.

Gill Hart, Head of Education, The National Gallery (at time of secondment: Museums Fellow, Clore Leadership Programme)

Arts Council England has supported Modern Art Oxford since its founding in 1966. The 50th anniversary reflects a proud history of presenting work by leading contemporary artists, supported by visionary leadership that has helped to build and shape the institution to one of international cultural significance. The Arts Council continues to support Modern Art Oxford as we believe these traditions are still alive and thriving.

Darren Henley, Chief Executive of Arts Council England

I still remember the vivid impact that the Upper Gallery space had upon me as a visiting student in 1974 when I first walked up the steps into it.

Bob Law's mystic *Black Paintings* were a shock (were they all really black?).

Then, Nick Serota's exhibition programming at the Museum of Modern Art Oxford spurred my interest in contemporary work and my education increased exponentially when I was fortunate to start work under David Elliott's tutelege in 1978. As for so many other visitors to the Museum of Modern Art Oxford during his brilliant directorship, I found the gallery a place of inspiration, somewhere one might discover unknown viewpoints, social, political, conceptual, that challenged one's own experience, and broadened it hugely.

The Museum of Modern Art Oxford under David was a place where one also learnt to take risks. For me, smuggling sensitive artwork from behind the Iron Curtain taught me that life only expands if you learn to handle risk.

John Hoole, Deputy Director, 1978–1982

Peter's total commitment to artists and their work enabled him to develop the Museum of Modern Art Oxford into one of the most exciting provincial galleries in England, putting on an extraordinary variety and number of exhibitions. He led the way with his *Drawing* show, which was one of the first of its kind and which encouraged further purely drawing exhibitions. The success of the *Drawing* show opened the door to him showing more international artists. As an artist himself, he studied Fine Art at Chelsea, he encouraged young talent and was proud of his *Platform* shows which gave postgraduate students the chance to show their work.

His three exciting, busy years at the museum gave him the opportunity to develop his ideas and gave him the freedom to experiment. Our house was full of artists coming and going, staying for a night or week – even the shed was used on one occasion. Lack of funds led to some creative solutions: I travelled to Paris with my nine-month old son to fetch an exhibition; Peter often designed the posters while I typed the invitations to the private views. The night before a private view, Peter would stay up all night installing the show, finally sweeping the stairs before coming home for breakfast. He did a remarkable job against overwhelming, mainly monetary obstacles.

Antoinette Ibsen, widow of Peter Ibsen, Director, 1970–1973

For 50 years, Modern Art Oxford had championed the very best of international talent. Constantly innovating, the gallery has worked with both world-renowned as well as emerging artists. We have played an important role in developing new approaches to exhibition making and artistic practices. In this landmark year, we can be hugely proud of our track record, the audiences we have reached and the lives we have changed. We continue to show the very best of contemporary art and our ambition is undimmed by the challenging environment in which most galleries now operate. I am confident that those who established the gallery would be delighted to see how we continue to deliver their vision – working closely with artists to make critically engaged visual culture relevant for our times.

David Isaac, Chairman of the Trustees, 2007–2016

I had the privilege of being taken to what was a furniture warehouse belonging to Oxford City Council by Trevor Green, a local architect. Trevor took myself and my late husband Brian, to see the building and no way could I have seen this as an art gallery, but Trevor did and now look at it 50 years later!

Over the years I have been to most of the exhibitions, met all the directors and have been lucky enough to meet most of the artists. As a volunteer I have worked in the archives, sorting posters and other museum material, organised overseas trips for volunteers to Berlin, Barcelona, Rome, St Petersburg, Amsterdam, Paris and other places. My late husband carried out the legal work for the museum over many years until his death in 2007. We also had a Volunteers Committee and many Friends, who promoted the gallery to the public.

I feel very honoured to be a Modern Art Oxford patron and also now with my son.

Vera Jefferson, Modern Art Oxford patron

Modern Art Oxford allows us to express art as a whole. The large variety of conceptual pieces allows us to work our subconscious and develop our own subjective view. We are free here, able to deal with what we feel.

Leah Jones, visitor

For me, as an Oxford student it's an important place to see contemporary art in Oxford. I'm looking forward to seeing more. Thank you!

Armin Kekil, visitor

Modern Art Oxford is an extraordinary place. Its rich history, exemplary curatorial programme, intellectually generative location, and rigorous regard for the centrality of art and cultural production make it a singularly important institution.

Barbara Kruger, artist

As Deputy Director between 1982 and 1986 I worked with David Elliott and his indefatigable secretary Carol Brown on about 25 exhibitions a year in the museum's various spaces, with only a five-day turnaround between each set of exhibitions. The scant financial resources at our disposal did not prevent us from presenting a very international programme. I curated exhibitions of the American photographer-philosopher Duane Michals, the Scottish sculptor David Mach and the English abstract painter Stephen Buckley, among others, and gave a platform to the video installations of musician Brian Eno, the dazzling dancer and choreographer Michael Clark, the Bow Gamelan Ensemble and the reformed post-punk band Wire. It was a heady mix and an exciting time for presenting contemporary art when there were few such dedicated venues in the country. We worked to the point of exhaustion, but with the thrill of knowing anything was possible.

Marco Livingstone, Deputy Director, 1982–1986

I was fortunate enough to work alongside Modern Art Oxford's education team on many projects. Most notable were *Art in Rose Hill* and *Lost in Time and Space*.

These projects cut to the heart of what it genuinely means to share, experiment with and collaborate through contemporary art.

I led activities, adventures and enquiries with young people, toddlers, their dads and carers and older participants in the early stages of Alzheimer's. Modern Art Oxford has and continues to be, a steadfast beacon, transmitting and communicating the message inherent in cutting edge artistic expression. It broadcasts the visions of artists into every corner of its building and then, it figuratively breaks down these walls through innovative, meaningful, progressive educational programmes.

Long live Modern Art Oxford and its inclusive, open and instinctive understanding of how art should be raised to the status of life itself, without forgetting those lives as yet living without art.

Jon Lockhart, artist and teacher

One of the real pleasures of Modern Art Oxford is the way in which the building surprises you. A walk past the gallery's unprepossessing façade on Pembroke Street suggests a modest space. However, those who venture upstairs are rewarded by the soaring heights of the Upper Gallery, which has played host to so many epic installations throughout the gallery's 50 year history. The rest of the building is equally captivating in its idiosyncrasy. As a curator, the rhythm of these spaces are a joy to work with, offering both vast tracts of space suitable for monumental works of art as well as small nooks and crannies to host more intimate encounters.

The institution has never been afraid to take risks, which has led to some quite incredible experimental exhibitions and events. Blessed with a rich history, enthusiastic staff and dedicated visitors, the gallery is sure to continue to surprise and delight audiences throughout the next 50 years.

Ciara Moloney, Curator of Exhibitions and Projects

I worked with many exceptional people at Modern Art Oxford and through offsite collaborations – in schools, hospitals, a prison, museums, youth clubs, artists' studios and community settings... and on an allotment! Education / learning / engagement / participation – whatever you call it, it's the area of a gallery's activity that often reaches the widest audience, and through providing intriguing and meaningful encounters has the greatest impact on people's way of thinking about and interacting with art.

Sarah Mossop, Head of Education, 2002–2012

I think the history of Modern Art Oxford is a story of artists and curators with the ambition to reimagine what art can be and what it can do. Their talent and vision has given audiences 50 years of extraordinary experiences in the galleries and beyond, through exhibitions, projects and publications.

During my time as Director we loved the tradition of inviting artists to respond to the unique spaces, with their differing scales, brick walls and metal pillars recalling the former brewery. Artists such as Jannis Kounellis, Jim Lambie, Tracey Emin, Mike Nelson and Janet Cardiff/ George Bures Miller transformed the galleries. They and many other artists who I had the privilege to work with at Modern Art Oxford have hugely enriched my life. When I look back I remember incredible art, a great staff team who made it all happen, and passionate audiences.

Andrew Nairne, Director, 2000–2008

I remember my first encounters with contemporary art in Pembroke Street as moments of discovery and surprise. As a first-year student of History and Economics I knew little about avant-garde art, but here was a place that put new ideas and images directly in front of you. It was exciting, if sometimes unnerving or even bewildering. Later, as a student volunteer and then as a staff member working alongside Nick Serota in the mid-70s, I began to learn much more about new art and how to offer people the chance to appreciate it.

At the centre of that endeavour was a direct encounter with artists and their work – offered as a conversation or exchange. And that spirit has remained at the heart of the work of Modern Art Oxford through subsequent years.

Sandy Nairne, Assistant Director, 1974–1976

I have a longstanding connection with Modern Art Oxford. Its history of courageously supporting and showing work by international artists and exposing its community and audience to relevant, overlooked and sometimes challenging practices has served a significant contribution beyond its local community. Artists like Monica Bonvicini and Haegue Yang have had their major solo institutional exhibitions here in Oxford. Its consistent keen eye, over the years, on influential and key figures in art-making is invaluable.

Valeria Napoleone, collector and Modern Art Oxford patron

The Museum of Modern Art Oxford was reaching the end of its first decade when I came to Oxford, but it had already established a unique local and national reputation. Nationally, it had carved out a niche as a leading innovator in contemporary art venues under Nick Serota, and David Elliott was building on that early period with groundbreaking shows featuring cutting edge global figures such as Marina Abramović, Sol LeWitt and Gustav Metzger. Locally, the Museum of Modern Art Oxford cafe was the 'go to' place for young people and families and an early pioneer of the cafe culture. I was a member of the Management Board for nearly a decade and was particularly involved with the expansion of the education programme under Andrew Nairne's leadership. That programme has been of immense value to the young people of Oxford, particularly in the more deprived neighbourhoods such as Rose Hill. As we move boldly into life beyond 50, Modern Art Oxford is an indispensable jewel in Oxford's world class cultural portfolio.

Councillor Bob Price, Leader of Oxford City Council

I had a five-minute gap between meetings on my first day working at Modern Art Oxford. An old cardboard box had grabbed my curiosity, so I flipped open the lid. 'Education Archive' was scrawled on the box front. The documents inside were energising. Charismatic proclamations jumped off the 50-year-old pages. The faded typing by the first director explained: 'the new museum is a place for everyone, a creative, dynamic, exciting, different sort of place.' Ingenious. Since opening that box in summer 2015, I've found that ethos of enthusiastic ambition within easy reach at Modern Art Oxford. It feels infused through the building. Every day I enjoy hearing people's interesting experiences of the art gallery. Modern Art Oxford is a civic space for art that will reward anyone's curiosity. It is abundant with creativity, fuelled by dedication, powered by art and generous-spirited people.

Emma Ridgway, Head of Programme

My first encounter with Modern Art Oxford was in 1996. I came to the gallery when I was 18 and studying Art on Foundation at Trowbridge College.

I had just emerged from rural secondary school education and was realising for the first time that art is a world in which any question can be asked and any answer is valid. A simultaneously terrifying and liberating experience.

I came to see the Donald Judd exhibition and remember thinking I knew I liked what I was seeing, I wasn't sure why and that was a feeling I should trust and follow wherever it might take me.

My interest since that moment throughout my career and in returning to Modern Art Oxford as Head of Programme has been to attempt to make more circumstances in which many others might have their own equivalent experience.

In researching ideas for the 50th anniversary programme I came across the expression 'delicate monumentality' which was used to describe one of the earliest exhibitions. This totally sums up Modern Art Oxford's influence and impact on art and society more broadly – gradually and incrementally changing lives and building a vast knowledge of the contemporary visual world over many generations.

Sally Shaw, Head of Programme, 2013–2016

Nestled in the nooks and crannies of Oxford and within the walls of a mightily-built brewery, Modern Art Oxford is a bastion of contemporaneity mere minutes away from the Ashmolean, the oldest museum in the world. I absolutely loved visiting this jewel of a museum when we first started a conversation about working with the institution on an exhibition that would also link the old and the new: Jeremy Deller's show that paired two legends from two different times and places, namely Andy Warhol and William Morris. Everything about this pairing was perfect, both in terms of site and story, as we were able to intermingle the 19th-, 20th-, and 21st-centuries together in a full-tilt and fully-covered environment of design, historicity and modernity that itself was a contemporary art installation. The show was cool, the space was cooler and the team even cooler still!

Eric Shiner, Director, Andy Warhol Museum

What a fine example of what a small gallery can do! It brings stimulation and inspiration. Well done.

Ronnie Sonneborn, visitor

For me Modern Art Oxford is more than just a building, it is an 'idea'– an idea about contemporary life that many different audiences can engage with in many different situations.*

Michael Stanley, Director, 2009–2012

In a city of such privilege, the Young Women's Music Project struggles to find space and opportunities to develop. Over the past three years we have been able to host some incredible events at Modern Art Oxford, which have opened the eyes of the young people we work with, who are some of the most vulnerable young people in the county. They usually don't feel that they are able to access such spaces and feel comfortable in them without judgement. I feel the support we have had from Modern Art Oxford has been incredibly valuable to the future of these young people and our music project.

Zahra Tehrani, Director, Young Women's Music Project

To have the opportunity to experience contemporary art of an international standard is not the rarity it once was. But 50 years ago it took a particular determination and commitment to create a platform for experimental art. In Oxford, a city where the presence of the University presides over so much cultural activity, setting up something that dealt exclusively with what artists had to say in the present day was a breakthrough that challenged the establishment and has gone on challenging it ever since. Modern Art Oxford is now one of a few independent public galleries in England that has weathered the storms of financial stringency, philistinism, elitism and conservatism to remain at the forefront of experimentation for a generation. Without a doubt there is plenty more to look forward to.

David Thorp, Interim Director, 2012–2013

Modern Art Oxford's internationalism and its ability to shine a light on politics and history are probably unsurpassed by any other public space over the last 50 years.

Richard Wentworth, artist

A place to witness true modern expression in its purest form.

Anthony White, visitor

*interview with *Oxford Mail*, 20 January 2010

Marina Abramović

KALEIDOSCOPE: It's Me to the World
20 August – 16 October 2016

Marina Abramović: *Objects Performance Video Sound*
9 April – 2 July 1995

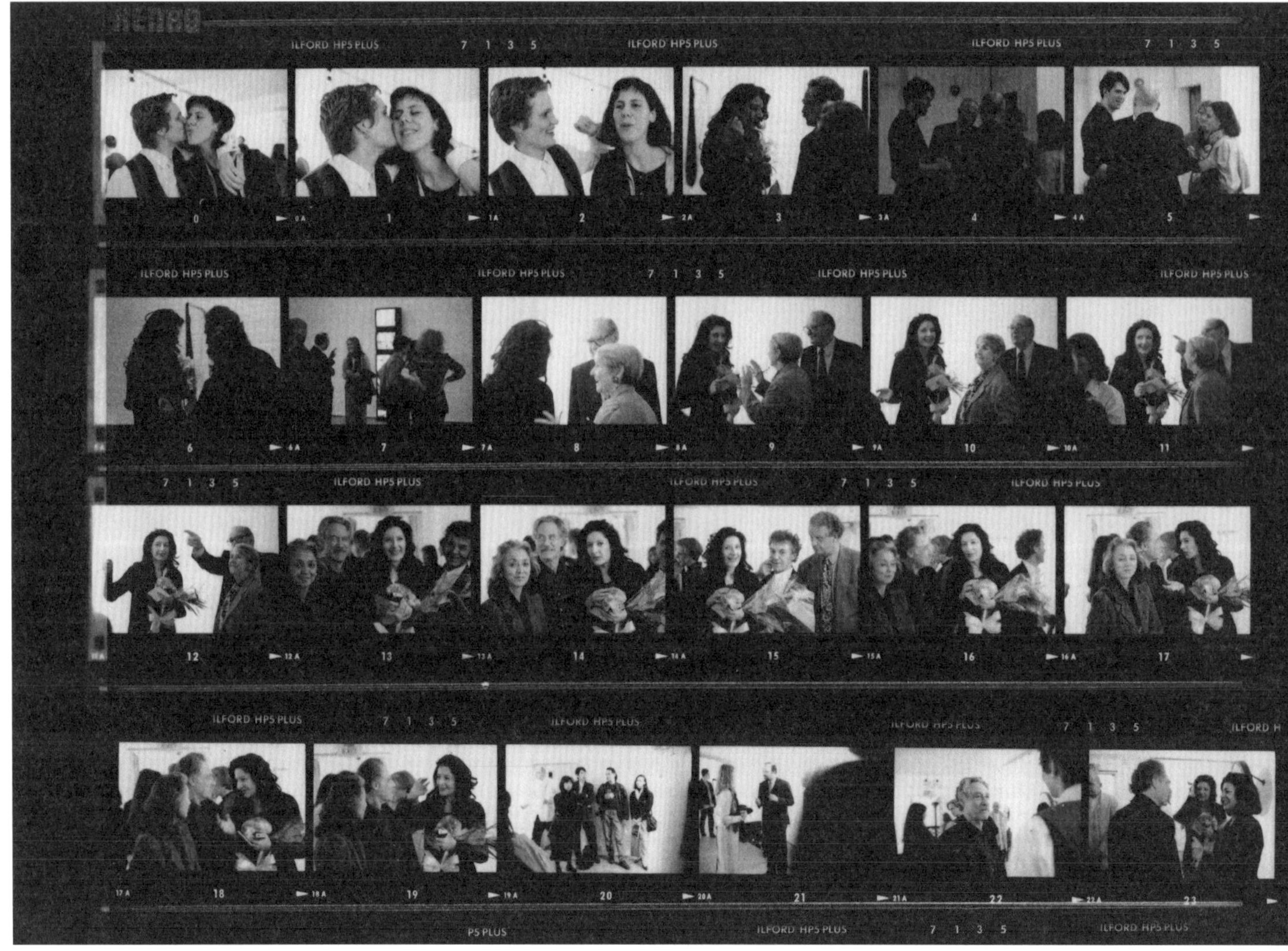

Exhibition preview, 1995

Exhibition poster, 1995

MARINA ABRAMOVIĆ

objects performance video sound
objects performance video sound
objects performance video sound
objects performance video sound
objects performance video sound
objects performance video sound
objects performance video sound
objects performance video sound
objects performance video sound
objects performance video sound
objects performance video sound
objects performance video sound
objects performance video sound
objects performance video sound
objects performance video sound
objects performance video sound
objects performance video sound
objects performance video sound

Museum of Modern Art Oxford 9 April - 2July 1995

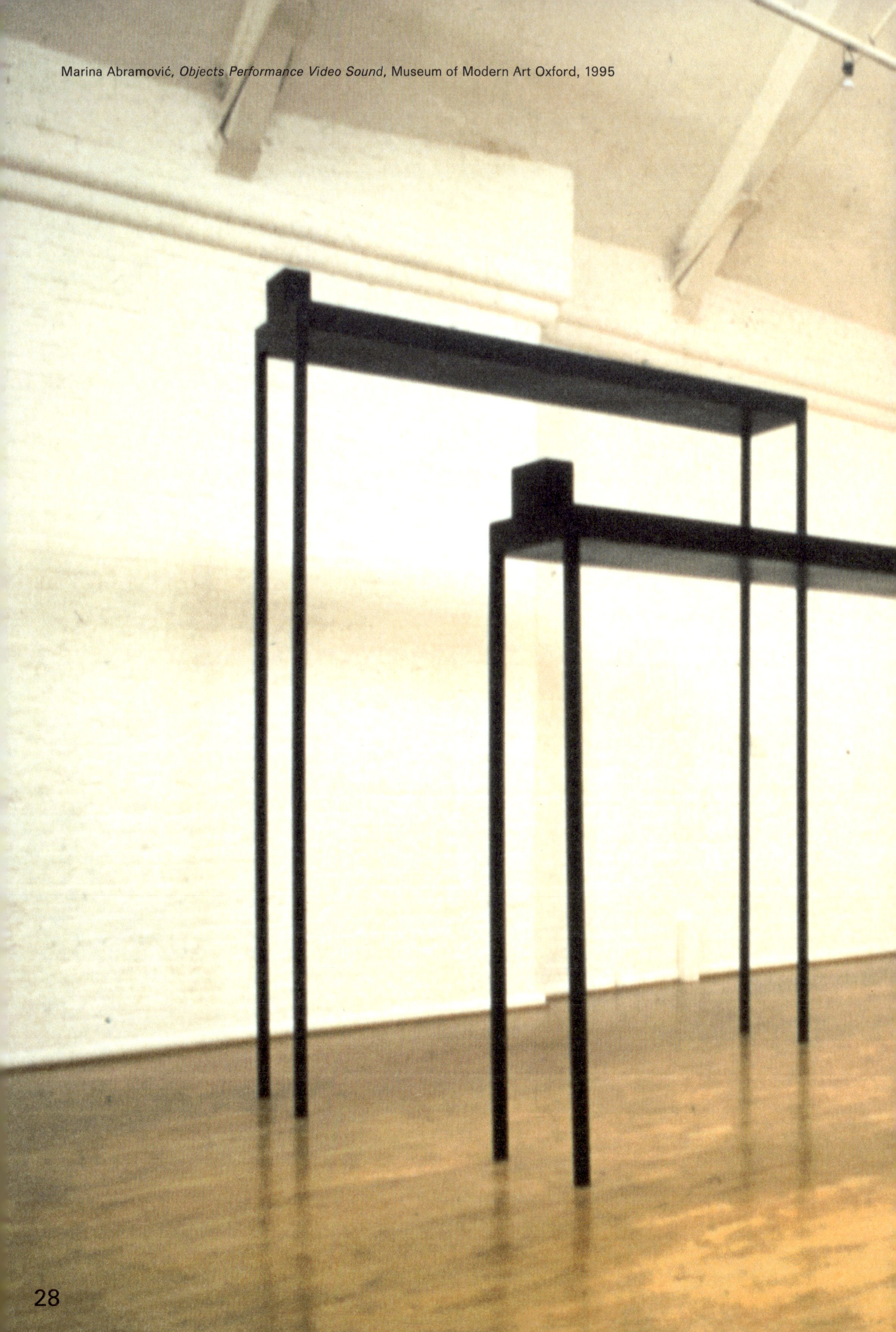

Marina Abramović, *Objects Performance Video Sound*, Museum of Modern Art Oxford, 1995

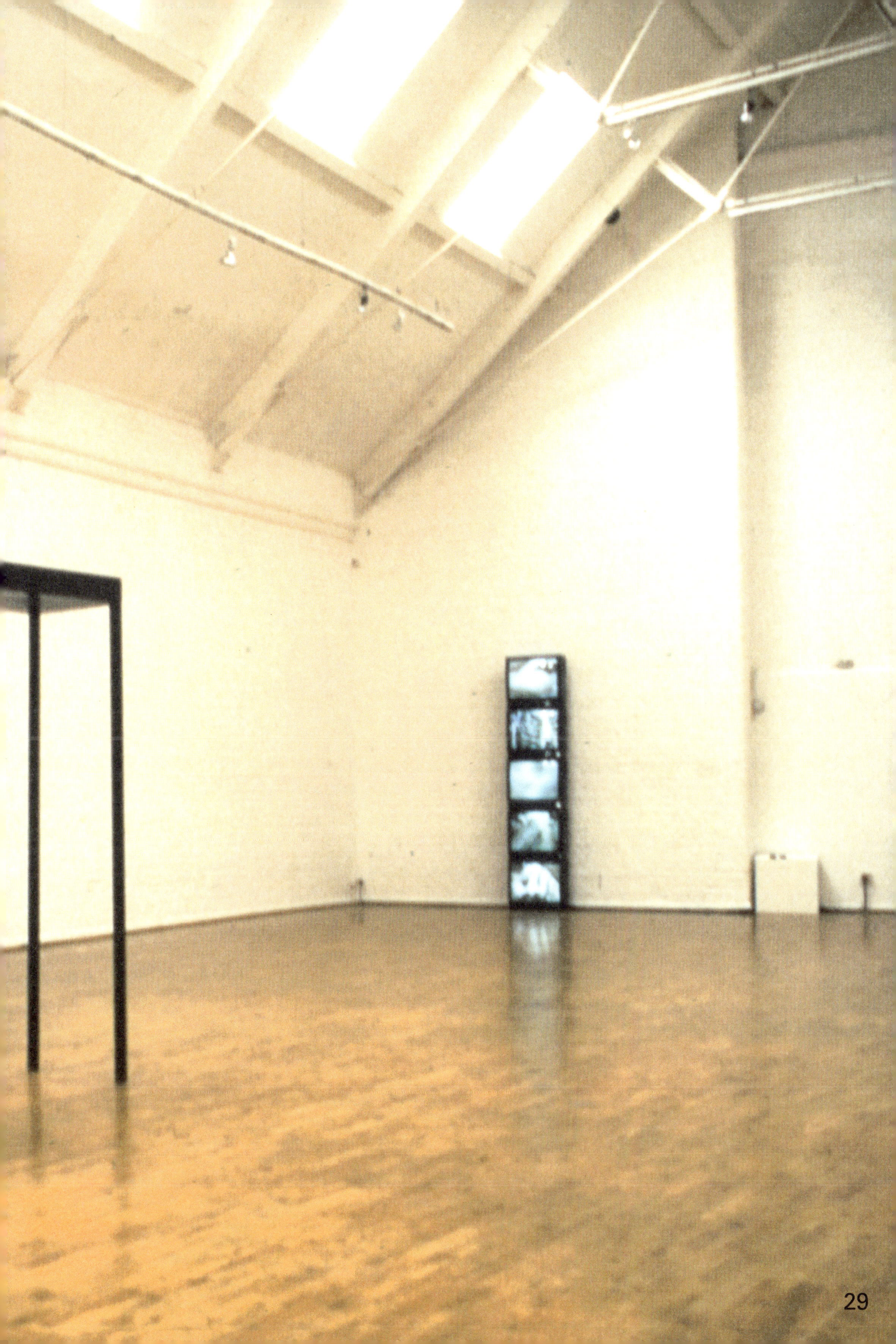

Mohammed Qasim Ashfaq

KALEIDOSCOPE: It's Me to the World
20 August – 16 October 2016

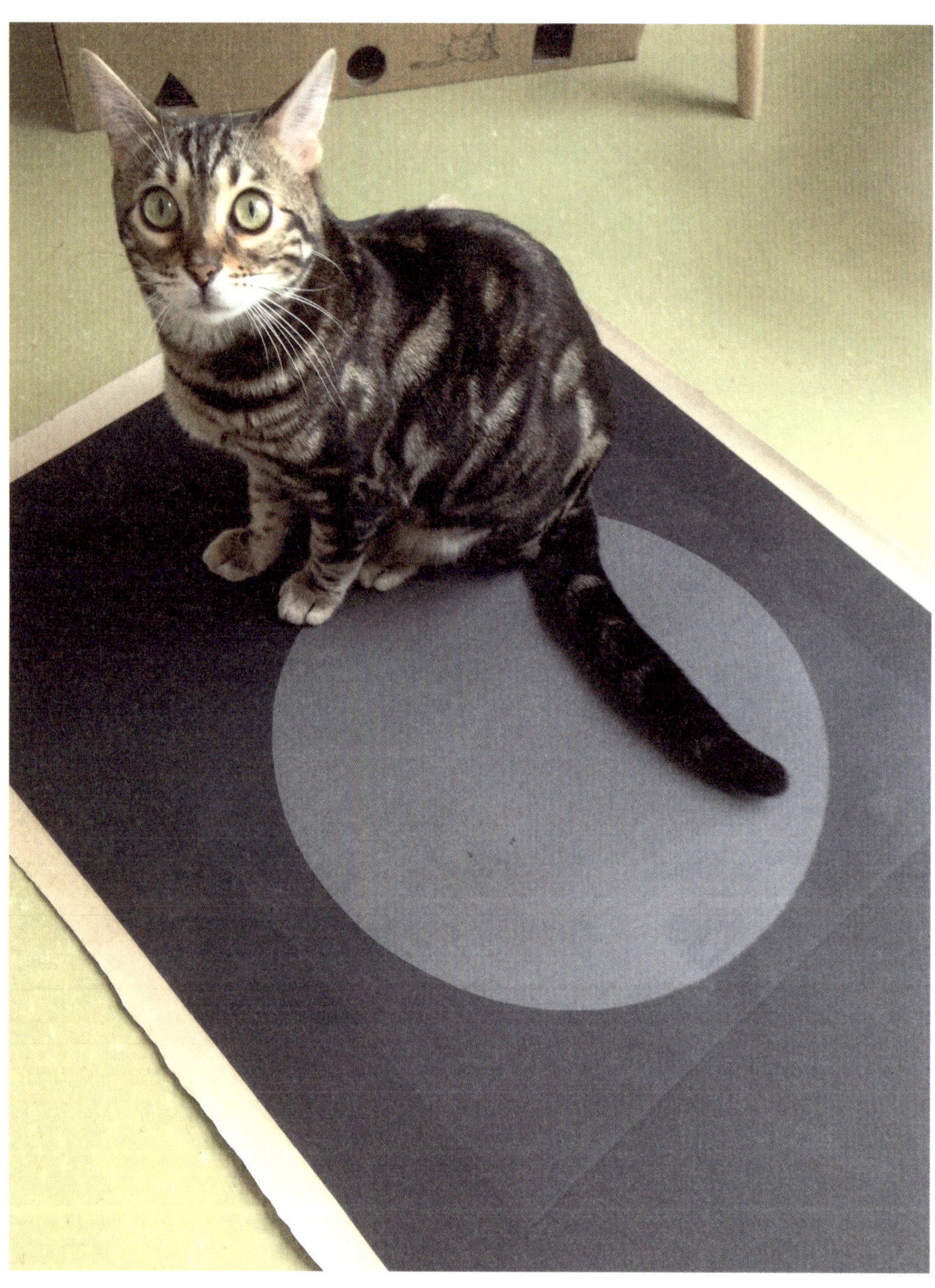

SHIFT, copperplate etching on vein arches noir with Kiki the Cat, 2016

BLACK HOLE IV, 2014

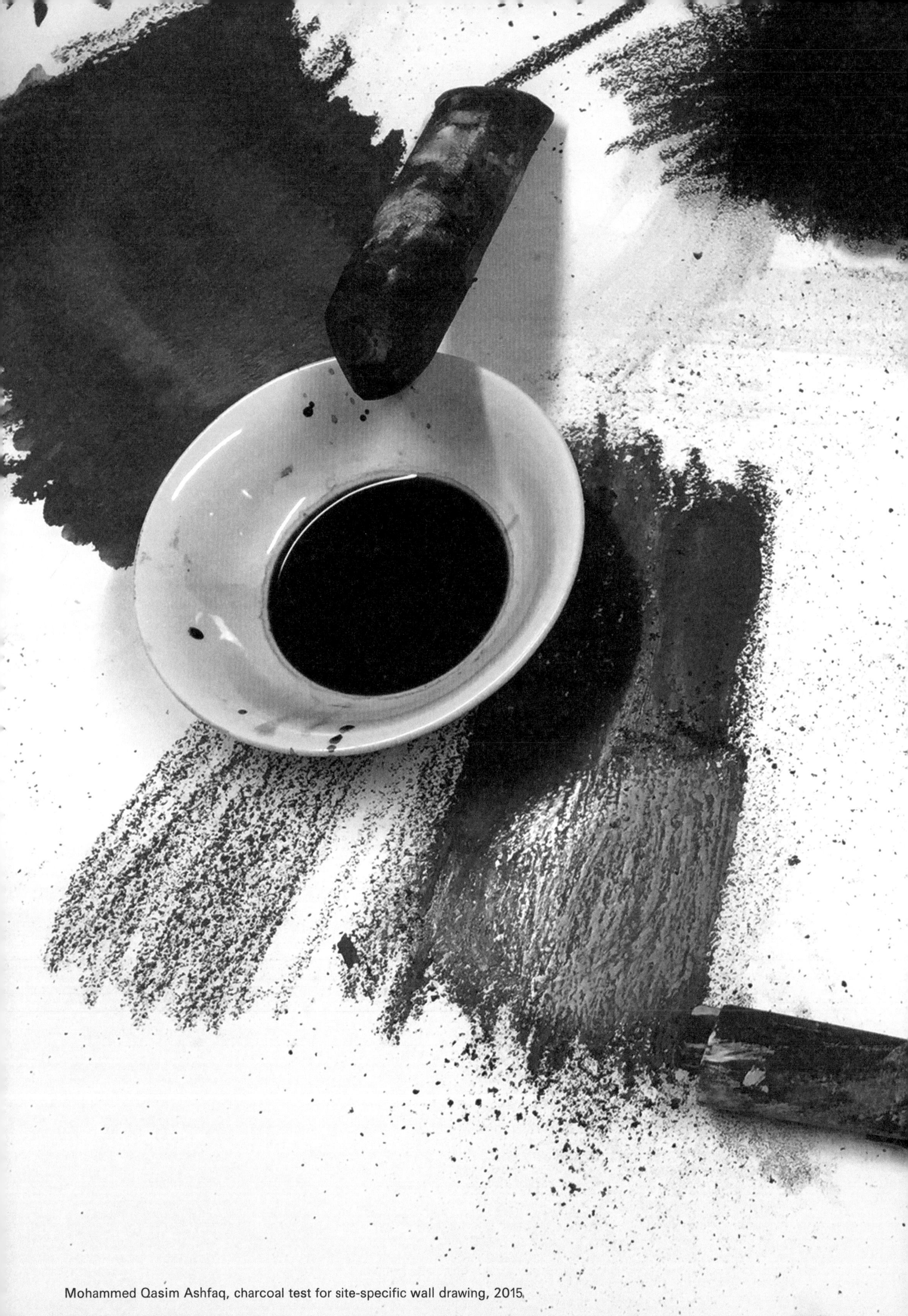

Mohammed Qasim Ashfaq, charcoal test for site-specific wall drawing, 2015.

Kevin Beasley

KALEIDOSCOPE: A Moment of Grace
16 April – 22 May 2016

A selection of thoughts that refer to notes on presence
and an arrangement of objects

…yet – from then on I realized what is essential, and
has been lacking from my train of thought, is an experience
that subsists within sentiment. Not in theory but rather
in physiological terms, the way one's body instinctually
winces upon hearing a sound as unpleasant as a squealing
megaphone. I do not wish to digress from where this
has begun, so this should be considered an anecdote
to a much larger issue. How does one stick to the wall?
Or slump into the corner? I have felt that what is most
important in a room are the objects situated within it,
because they reflect a human being. A system that can
be overtly mechanized, efficient, and fiscally driven;
or it obtains the qualities of compassion, touch, sensibility.
These are all human. Mass is a constant but I like to consider
what the ephemerality that is produced from that mass
is capable of - or to clarify, how do I reconcile the reveal
of consequences of being present in a room? Perception
and preconceived notions derived from conditioned ways
of seeing and experiencing places withers when activity
in a space is reduced to a focus on the moment at hand.
This is not completely totalitarian, but all arrows previously
painted on those banal substrates point in one direction.
At least I hope they do. Road signs do this, they actually
point in every direction, but in some way they point in
the direction you need them to, when you want them to,
where you want to go. You have to know why you are
there to begin with in order to trust the signs in front
of you. It is about being present, is it not? To gather
your belief in a collective unconscious with your knowledge,
with your desire for something inaccessible, maybe with
your pessimism, with your physical awareness/agility,
your hands, your lower back, your entire body and all
of its orifices to recognize what is in front of you. Your
most refined version of yourself acutely positioned to
experience something. This is the most revealing moment…

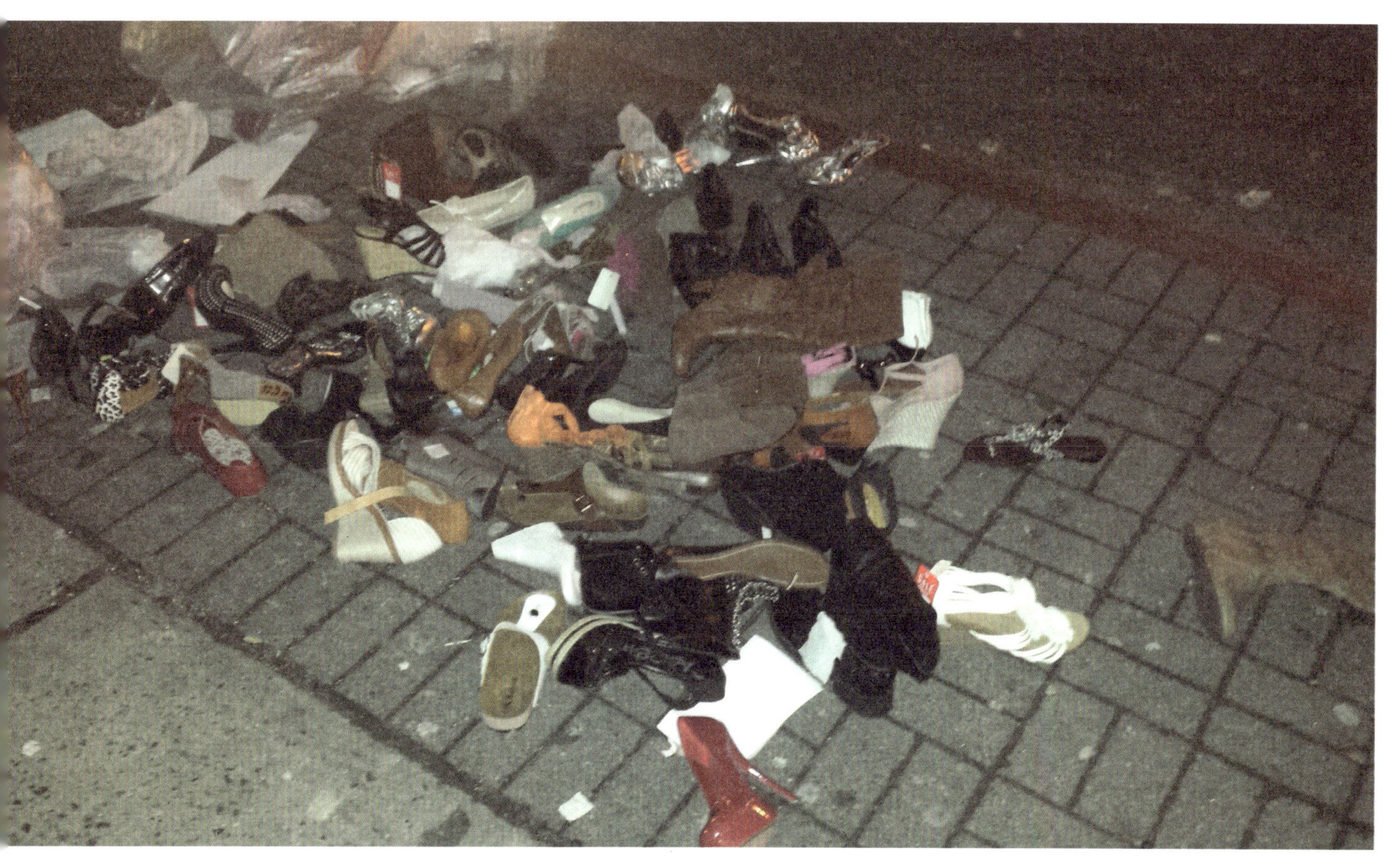

Shoes found outside the artist's studio, 2015

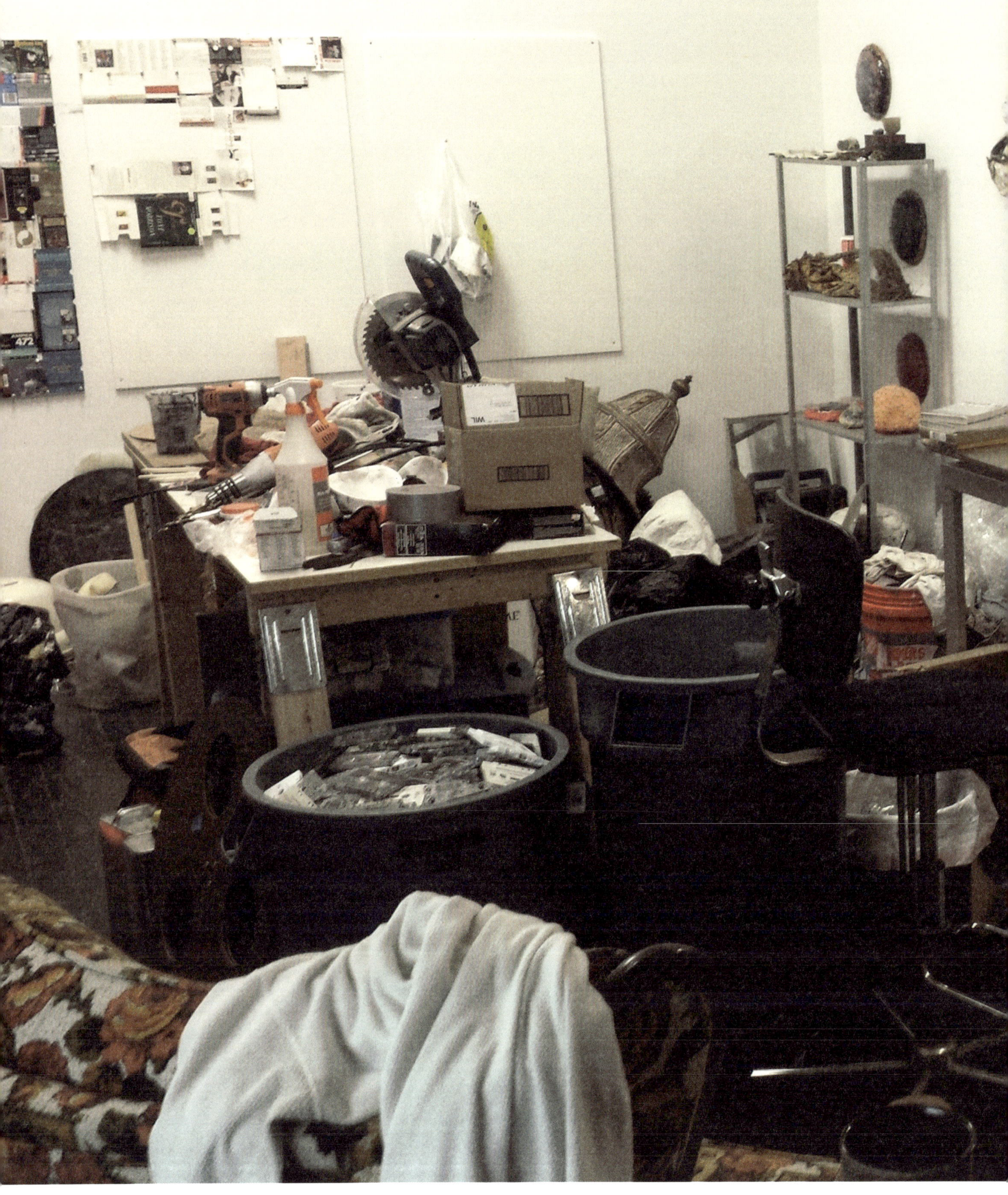

Artist's studio during the production of *...for this moment, this moment is yours...*, 2013

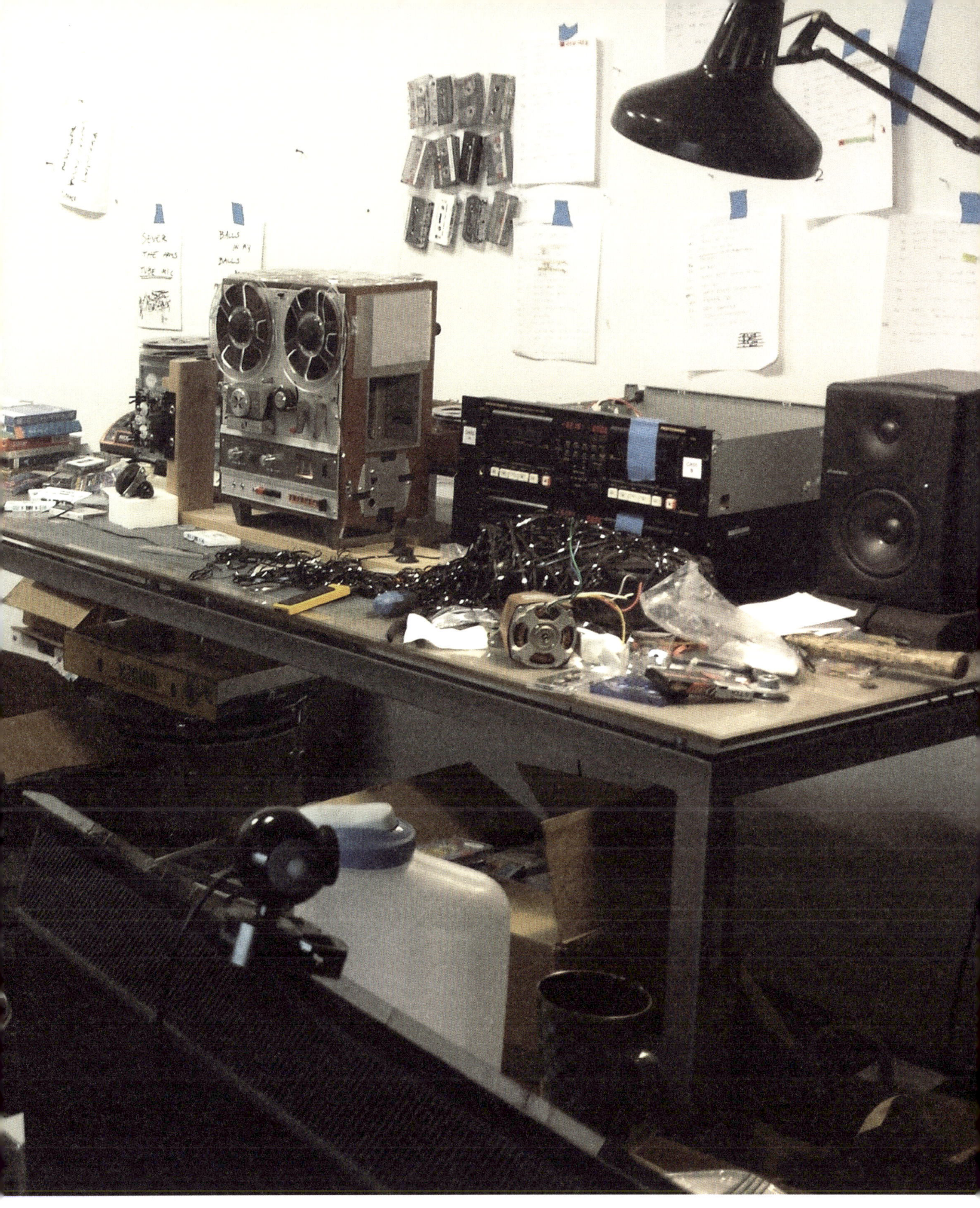

Joseph Beuys

KALEIDOSCOPE Live: lecture by Sean Rainbird
1 December 2016

Joseph Beuys: *The Secret Block for a Secret Person in Ireland, Drawings 1948–72*
7 April – 12 May 1974

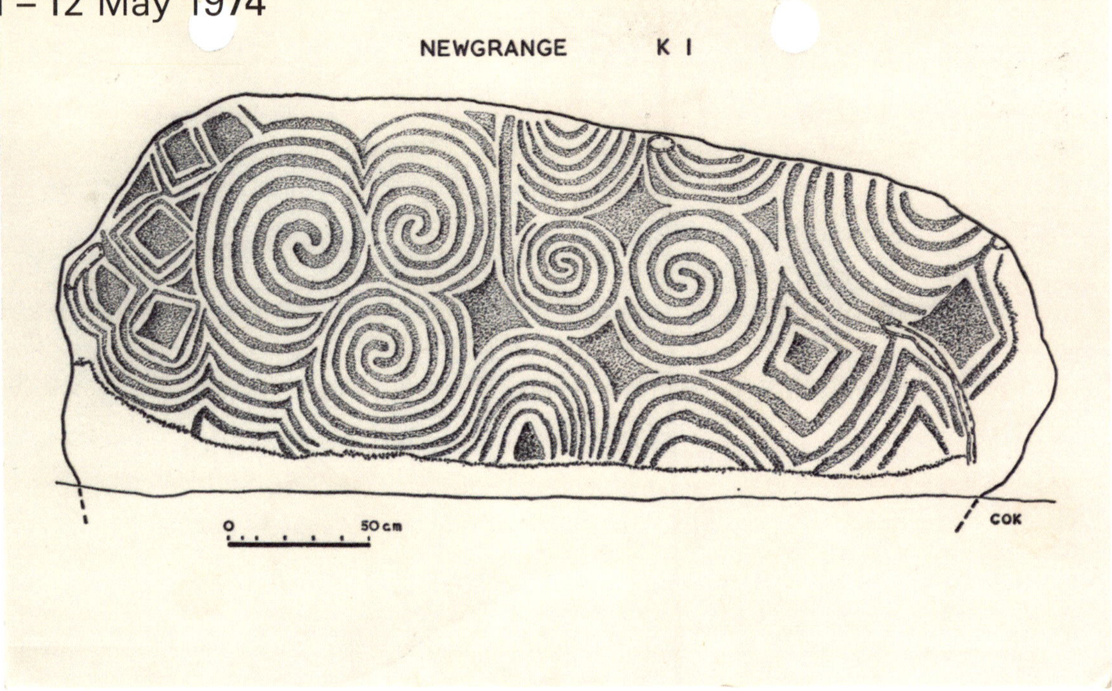

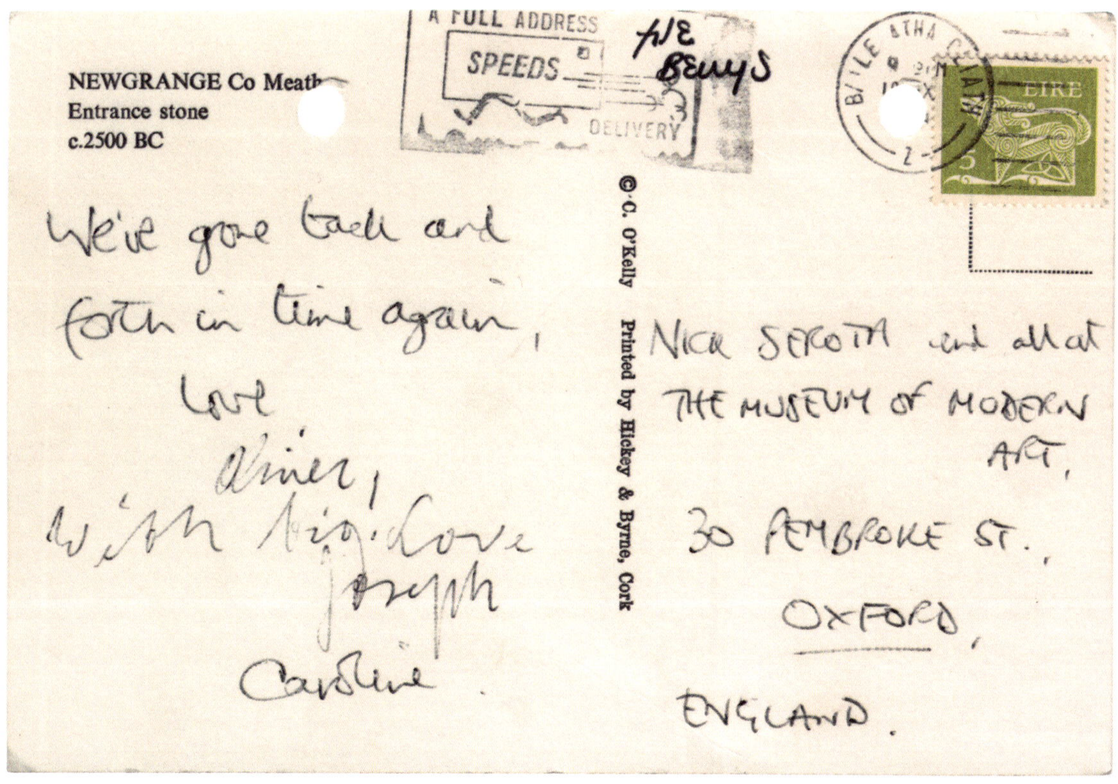

Postcard from Joseph Beuys to Nick Serota, Modern Art Oxford, undated

Artist's lecture, Museum of Modern Art Oxford, 1974

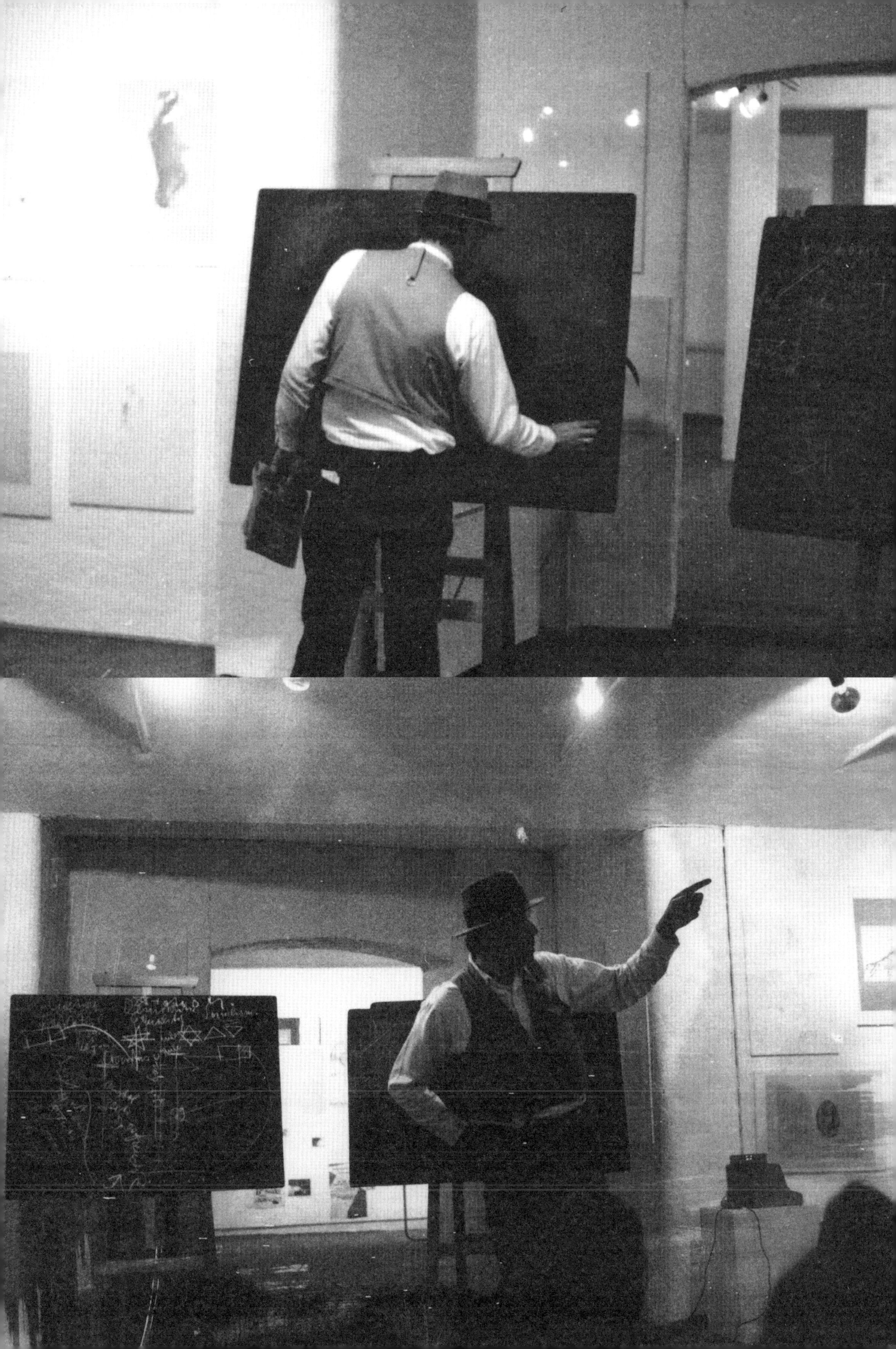

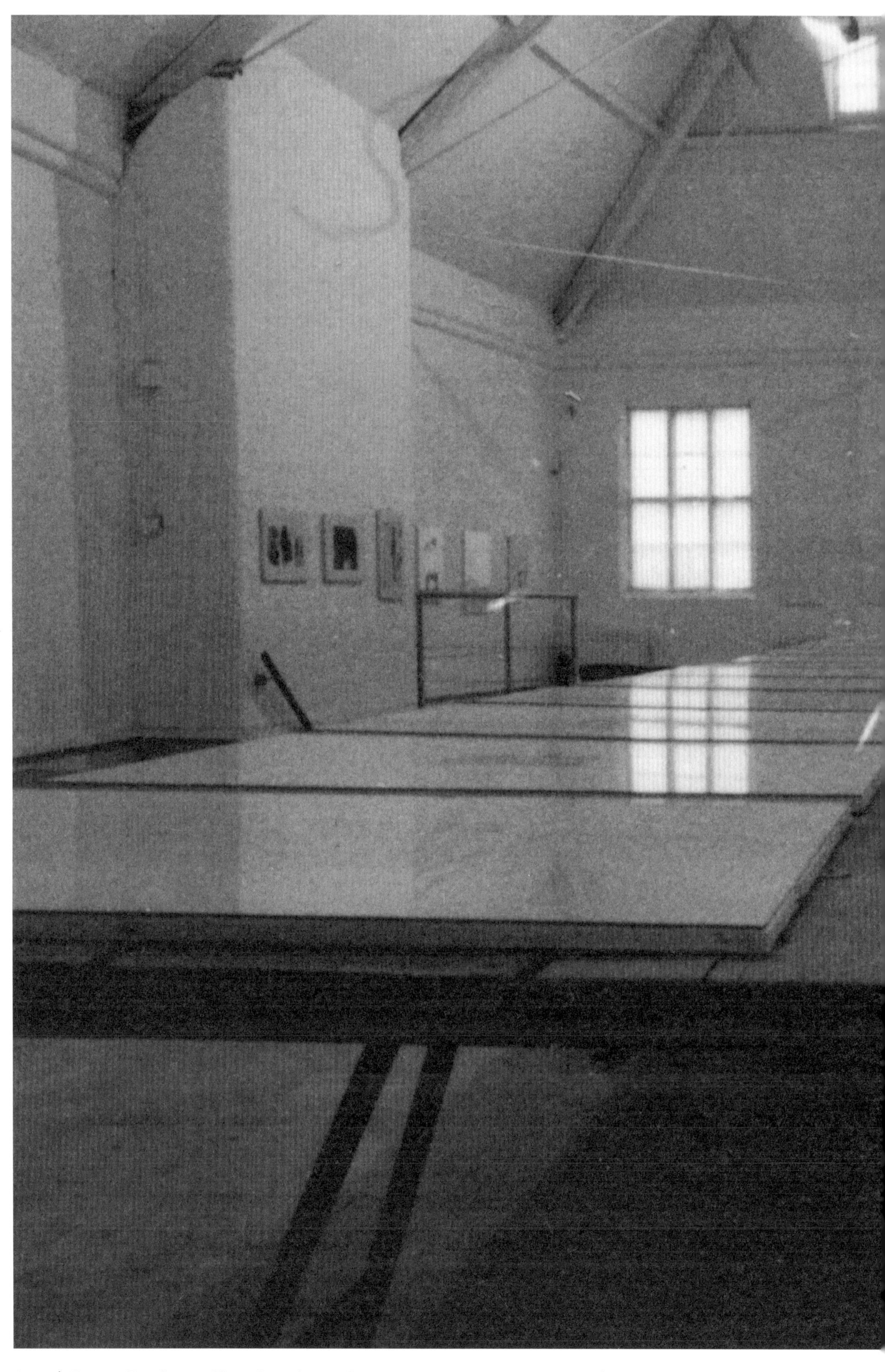

Joseph Beuys, *The Secret Block for a Secret Person in Ireland*, Museum of Modern Art Oxford, 1974

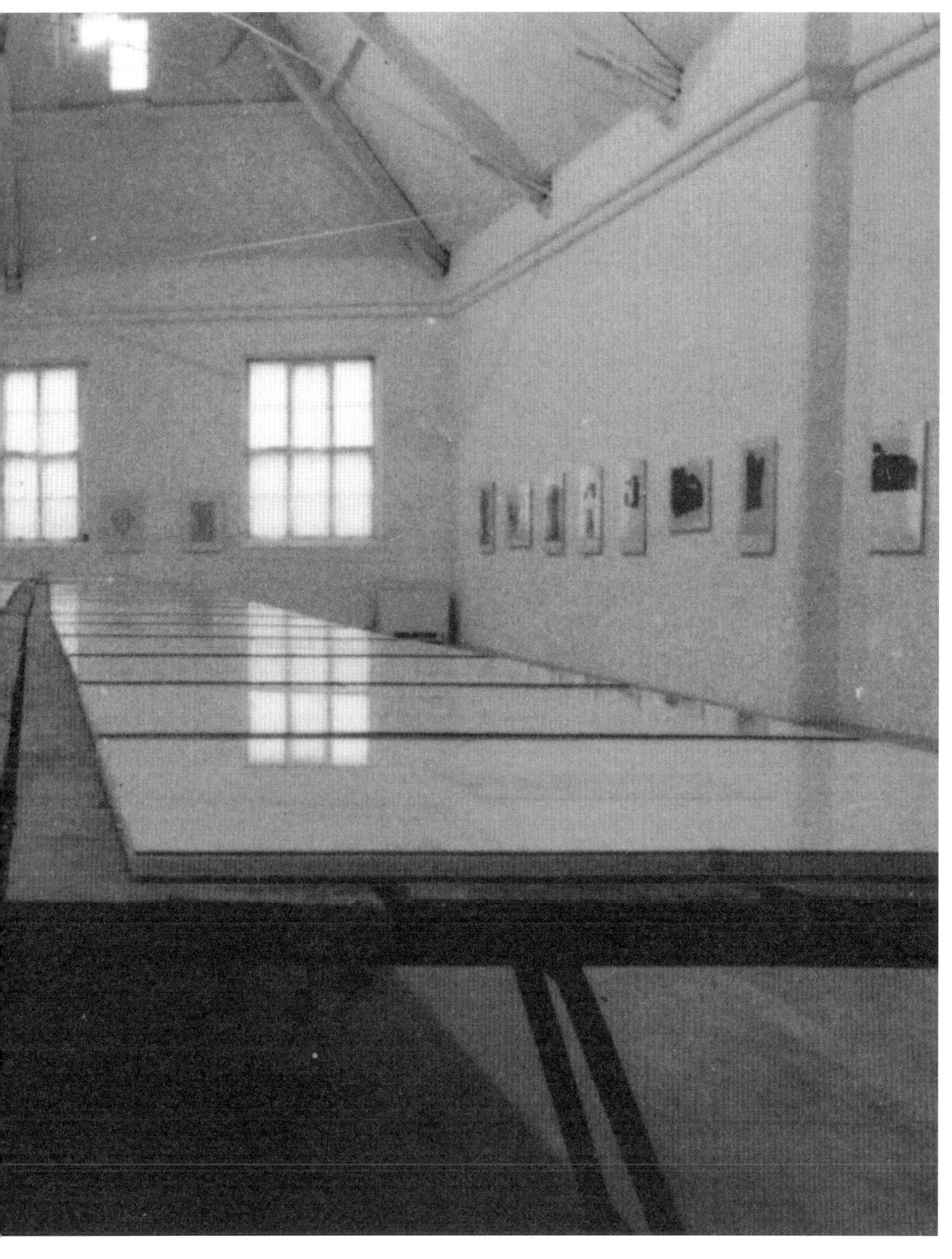

Karla Black

KALEIDOSCOPE: Mystics and Rationalists
11 June – 31 July 2016

Karla Black
30 September – 29 November 2009

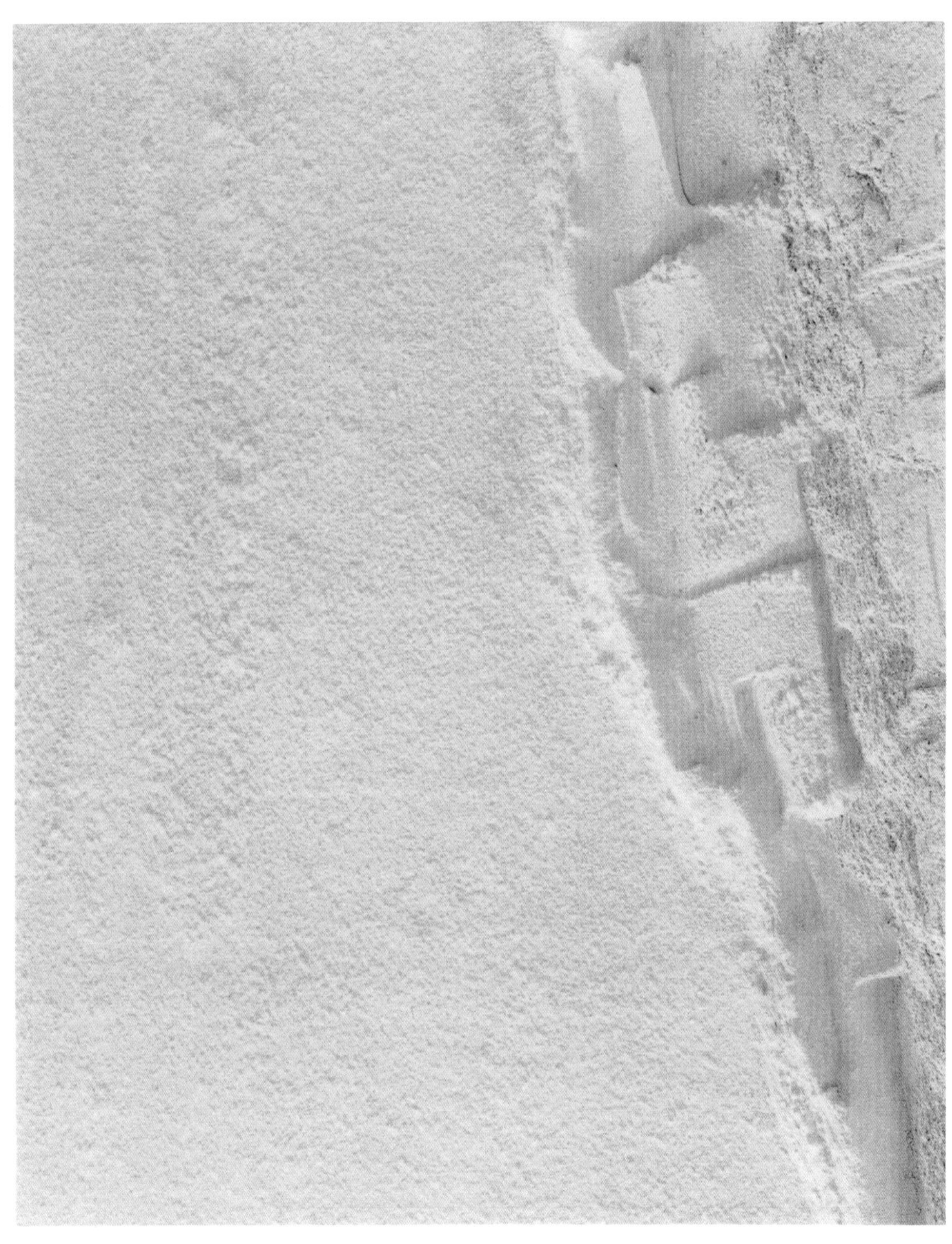

Exhibition invitation (front), 2009

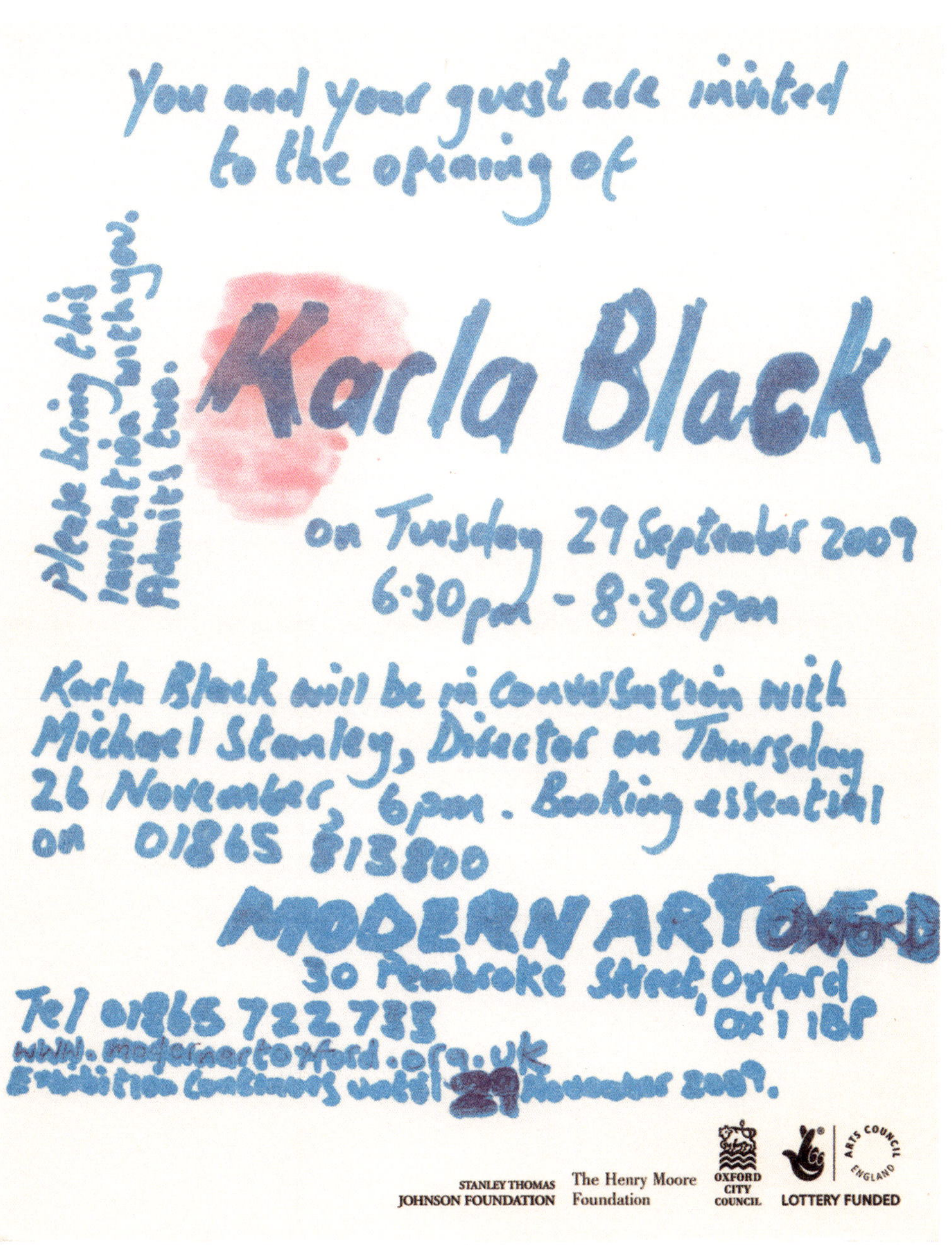

Exhibition invitation (back), 2009

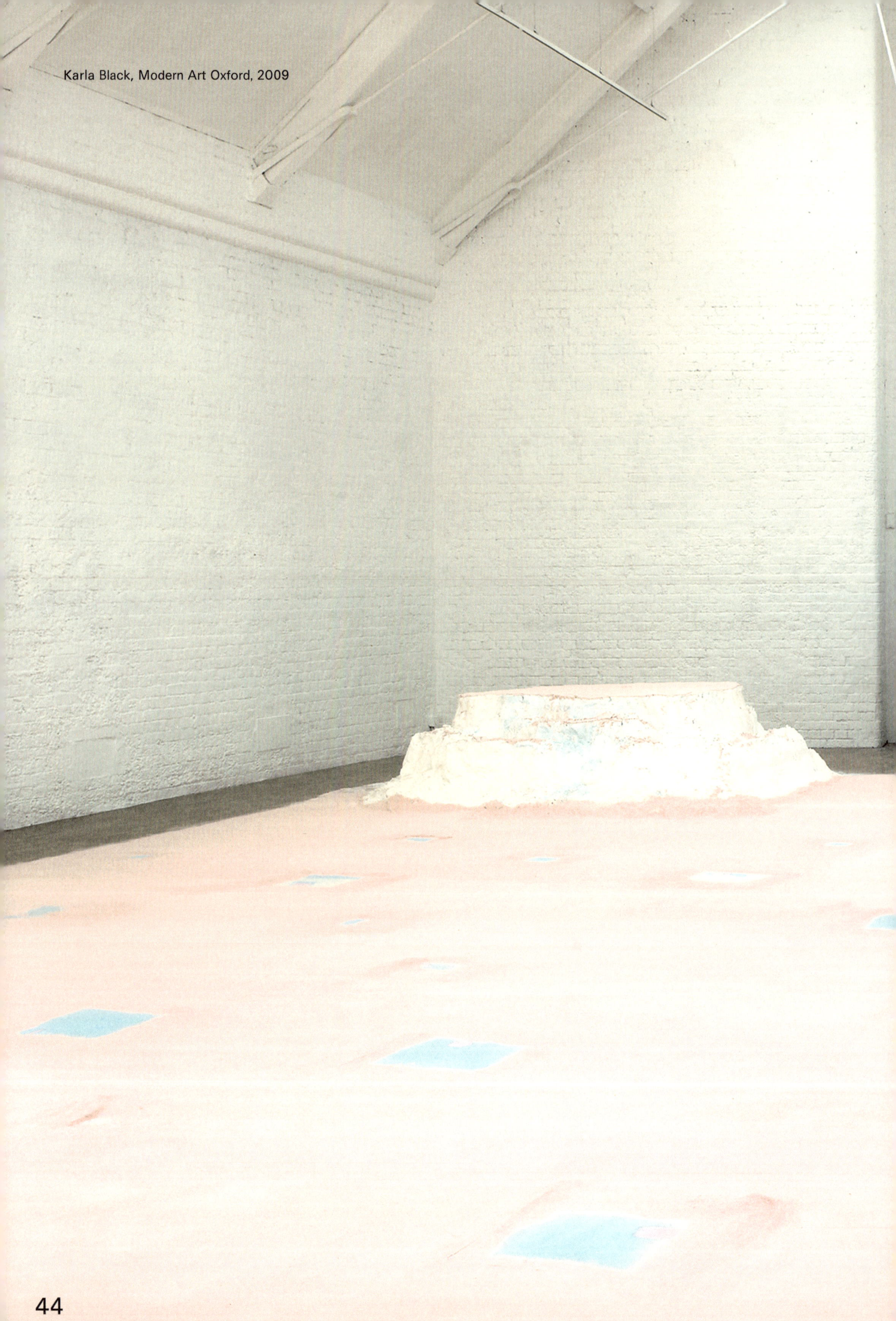

44

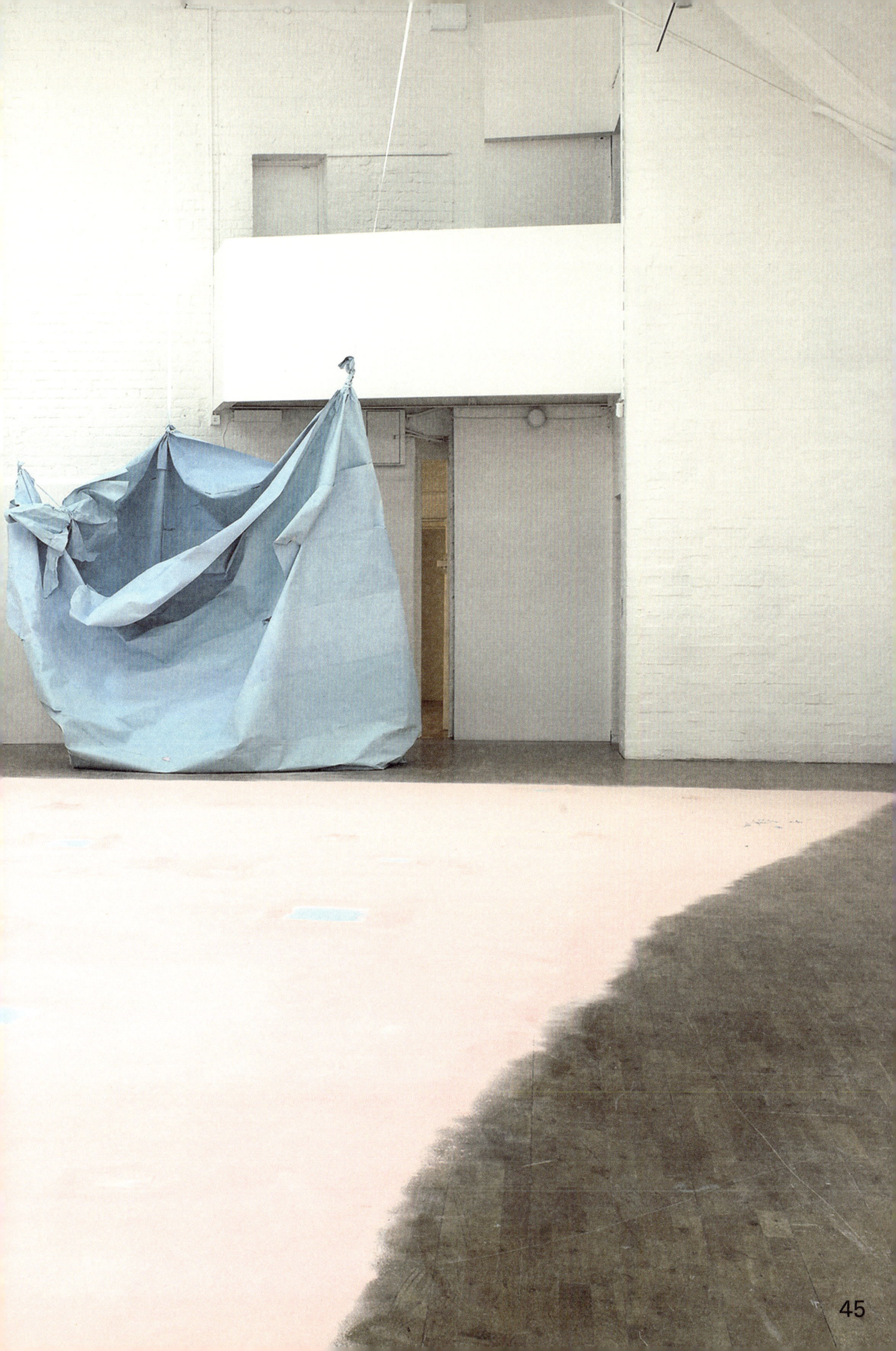

Marcel Broodthaers

KALEIDOSCOPE: The Vanished Reality
12 November – 31 December 2016

Signs and Emblems
Marcel Broodthaers: *Complete Prints and Editions*
4 April – 20 June 1993

Marcel Broodthaers: *Le Privilège de l'Art*
26 April – 1 June 1975

Museum of Modern Art Oxford

LE PRIVILÈGE DE L'ART

an exhibition by

Marcel Broodthaers

April 26 June 1 1975, Tuesday Saturday 10-5, Friday 10-7.30, Sunday 2-5, Monday closed
Private view Saturday 26 April 6-8 p.m.

Exhibition invitation, 1975

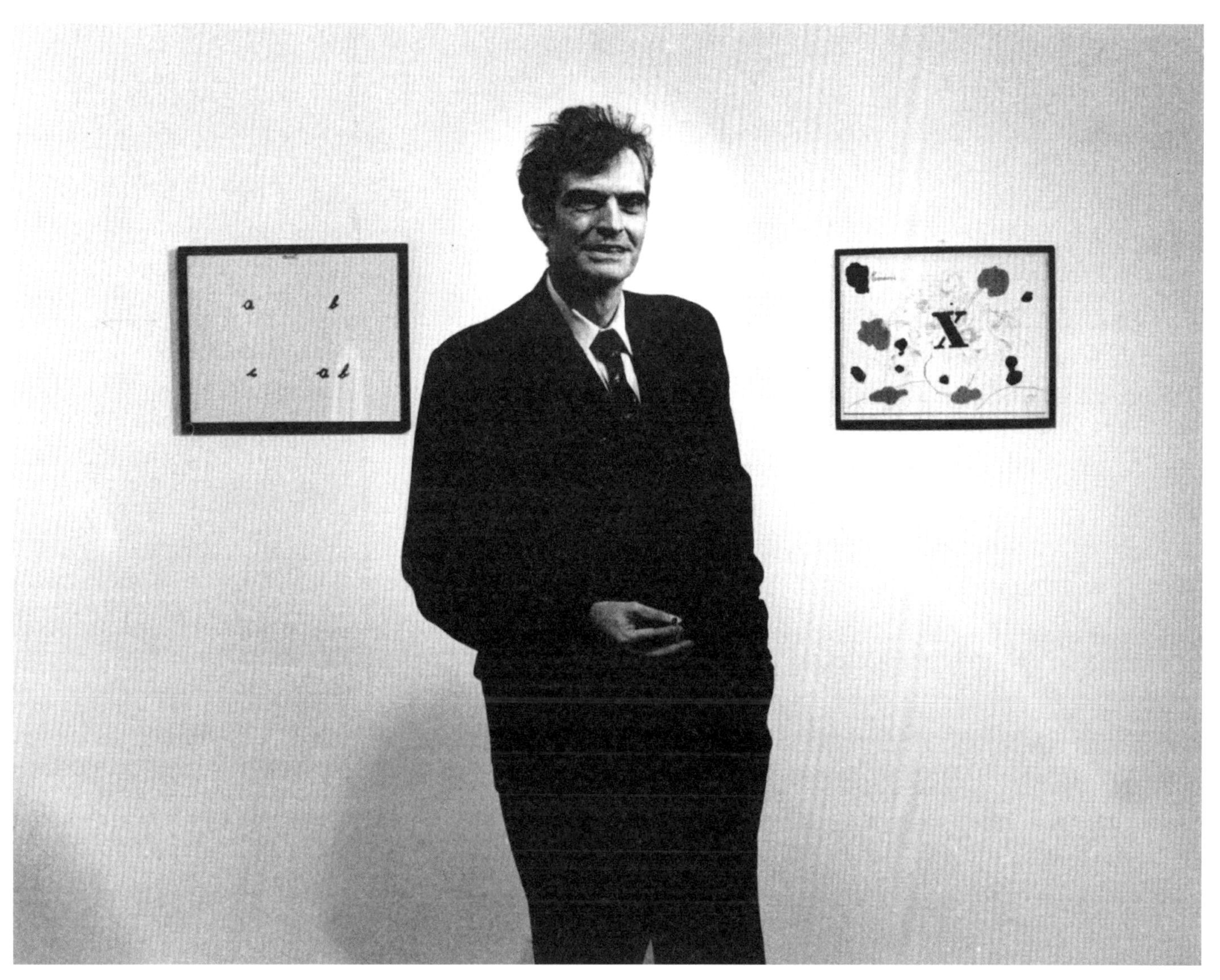

Portrait of the artist, Museum of Modern Art Oxford, 1975

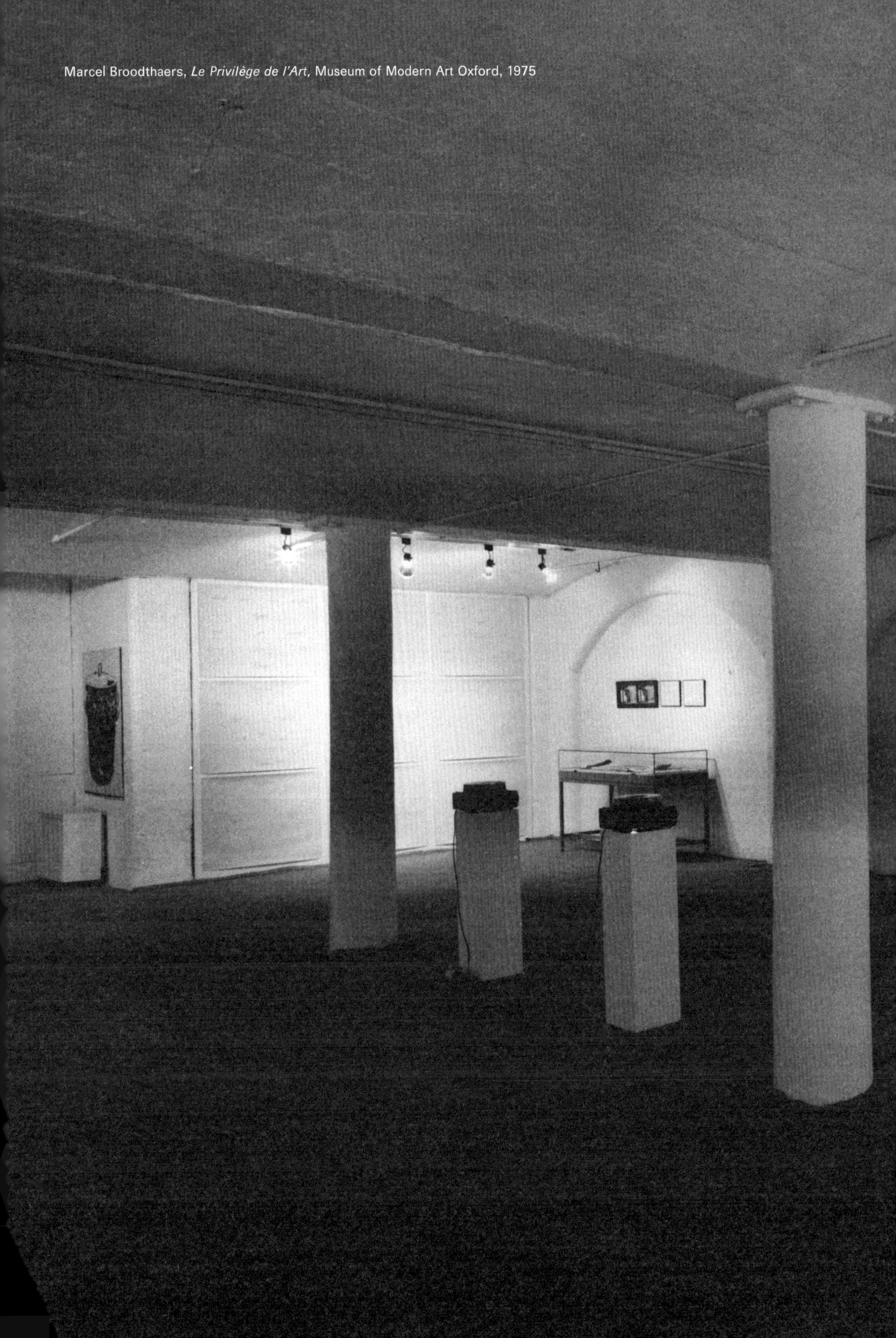

Marcel Broodthaers, *Le Privilège de l'Art,* Museum of Modern Art Oxford, 1975

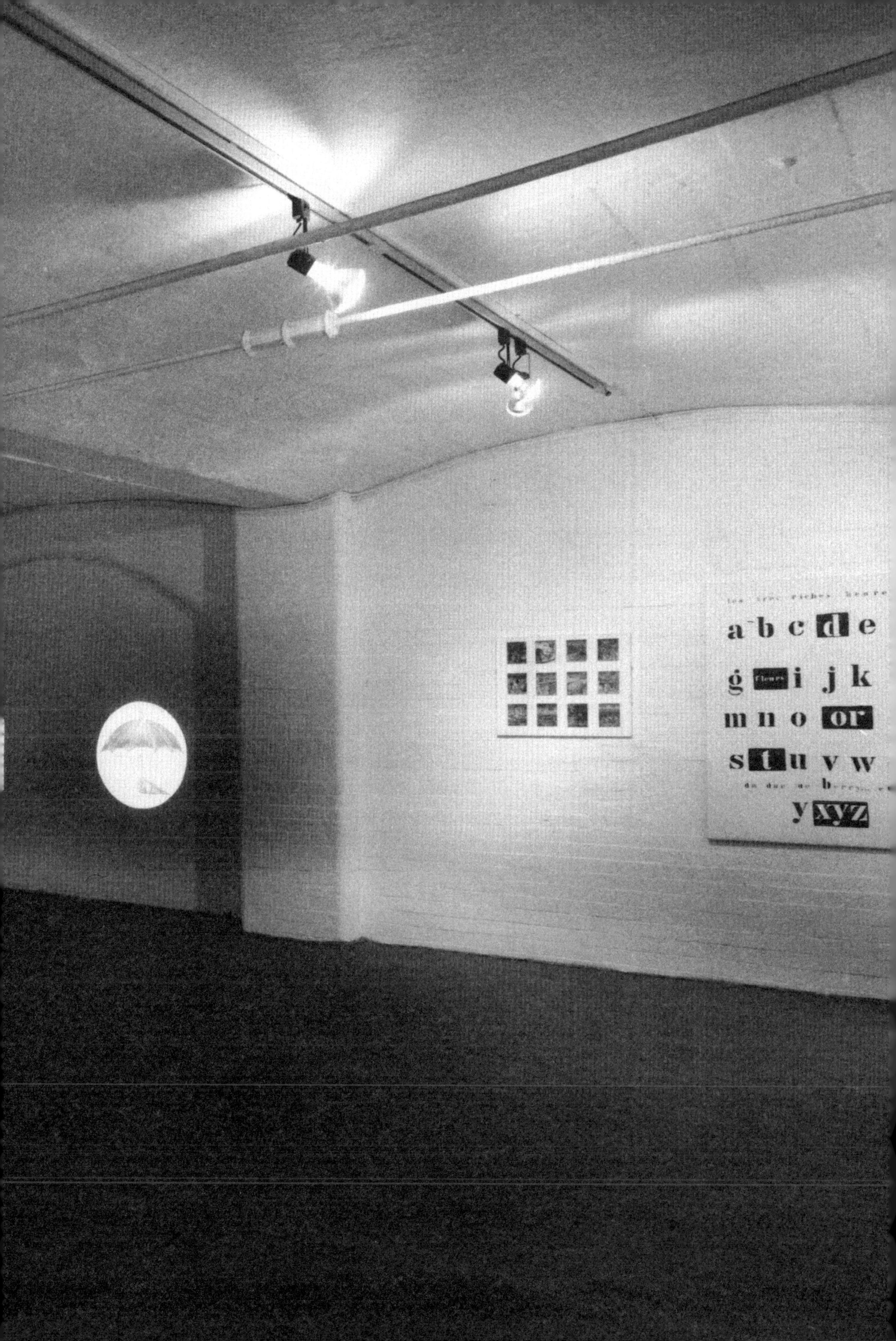

Daniel Buren

KALEIDOSCOPE: Mystics and Rationalists
11 June – 31 July 2016

Daniel Buren: *Intervention II*
4 November 2006 – 28 January 2007

Daniel Buren: *Sanction of the Museum*
31 March – 15 April 1973

Exhibition invitation, 1973

Sketch for *Sanction of the Museum*, Museum of Modern Art Oxford, 1973

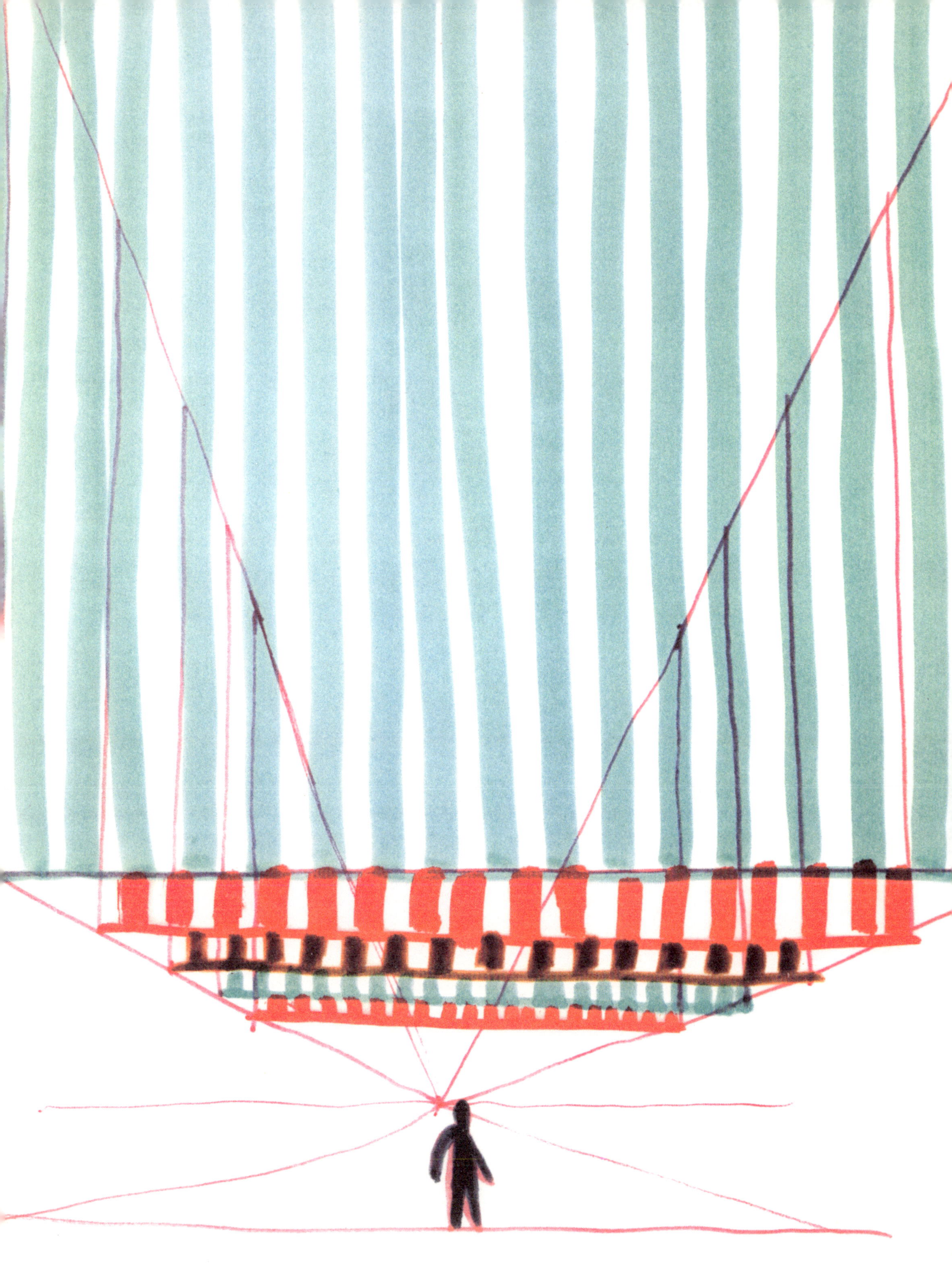

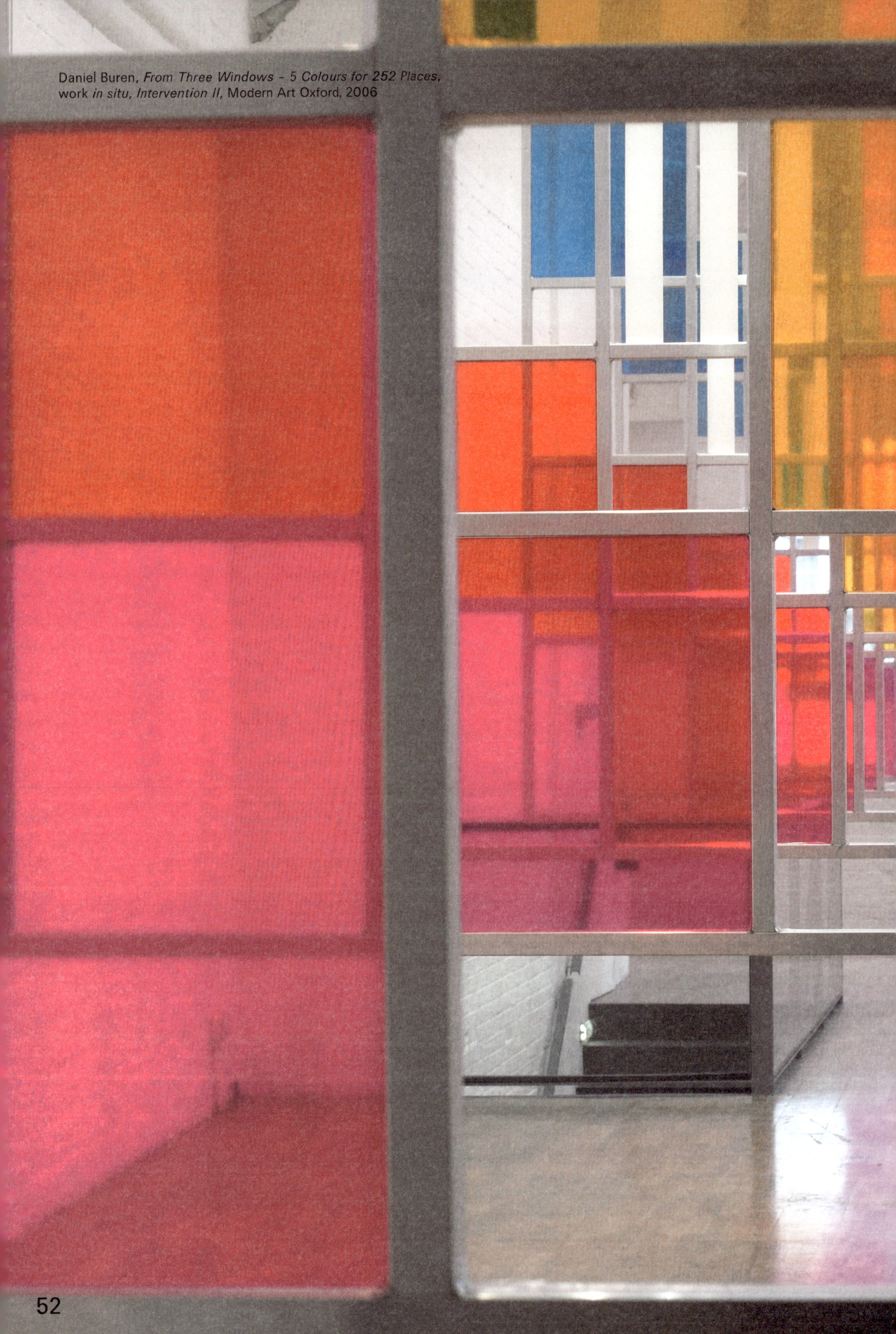

Daniel Buren, *From Three Windows - 5 Colours for 252 Places,* work *in situ, Intervention II,* Modern Art Oxford, 2006

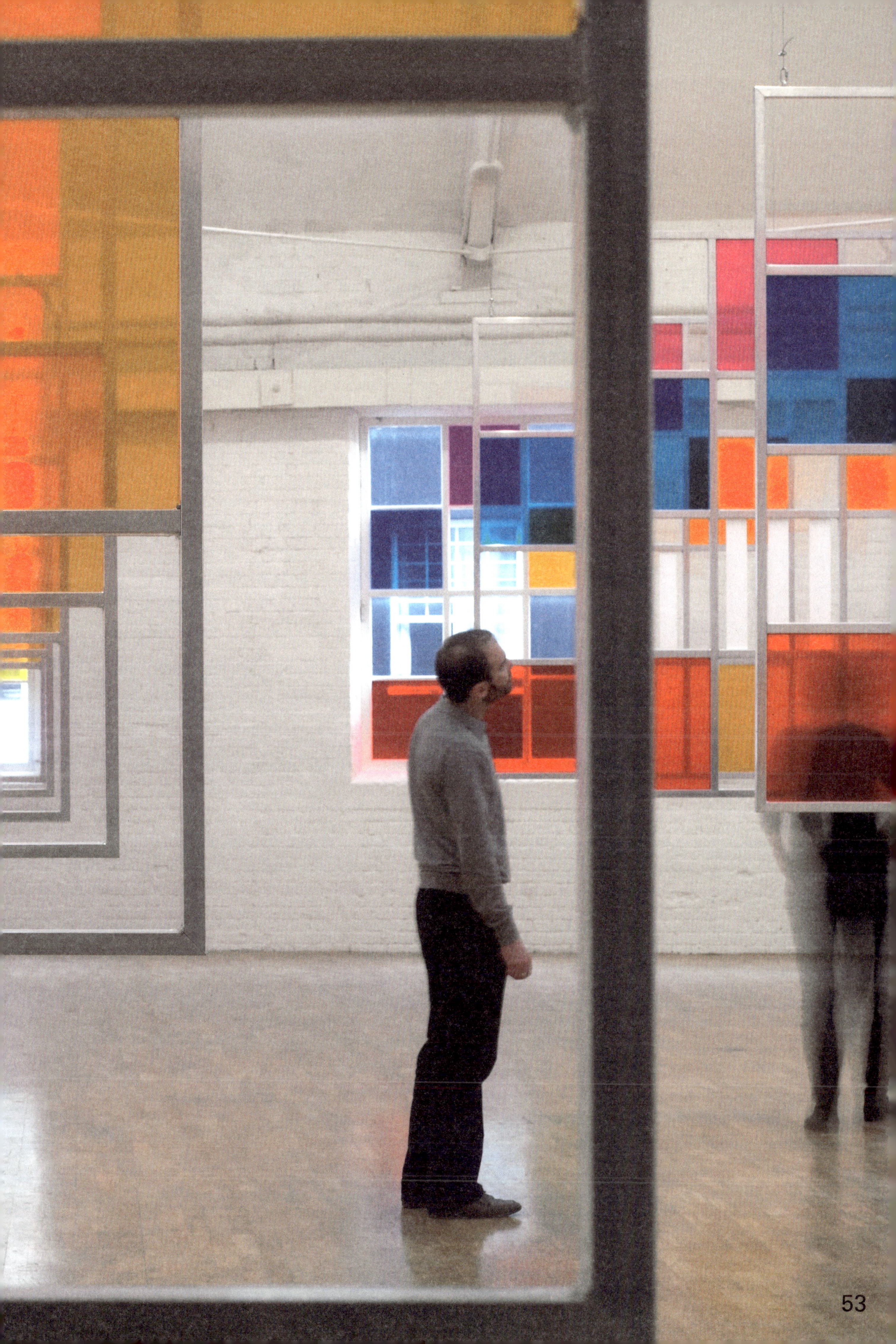

Helen Chadwick

KALEIDOSCOPE: It's Me to the World
20 August – 16 October 2016

Helen Chadwick: *Viral Landscapes*
5 November 1989 – 7 January 1990

'Meat Abstract' by Helen Chadwick
Portfolio Gallery, Edinburgh, 1989

Letter from Helen Chadwick to Chrissie Iles and David Elliott, 1989

to settle down + feed ourself till gaga
+ let digestion hold sway.
Look after my cells safely till after Xmas.
I will pop up after Chicago to
take some photos + look in greater
concentration at the shows.
Have a good Holiday Christsir — take
that sun + yield to the infinity
nets,
thankyou both for having faith to
put on the show after seeing the tiny
fractal proofs + wishing to go the
distance.
in fond greetings
yours,
Helen

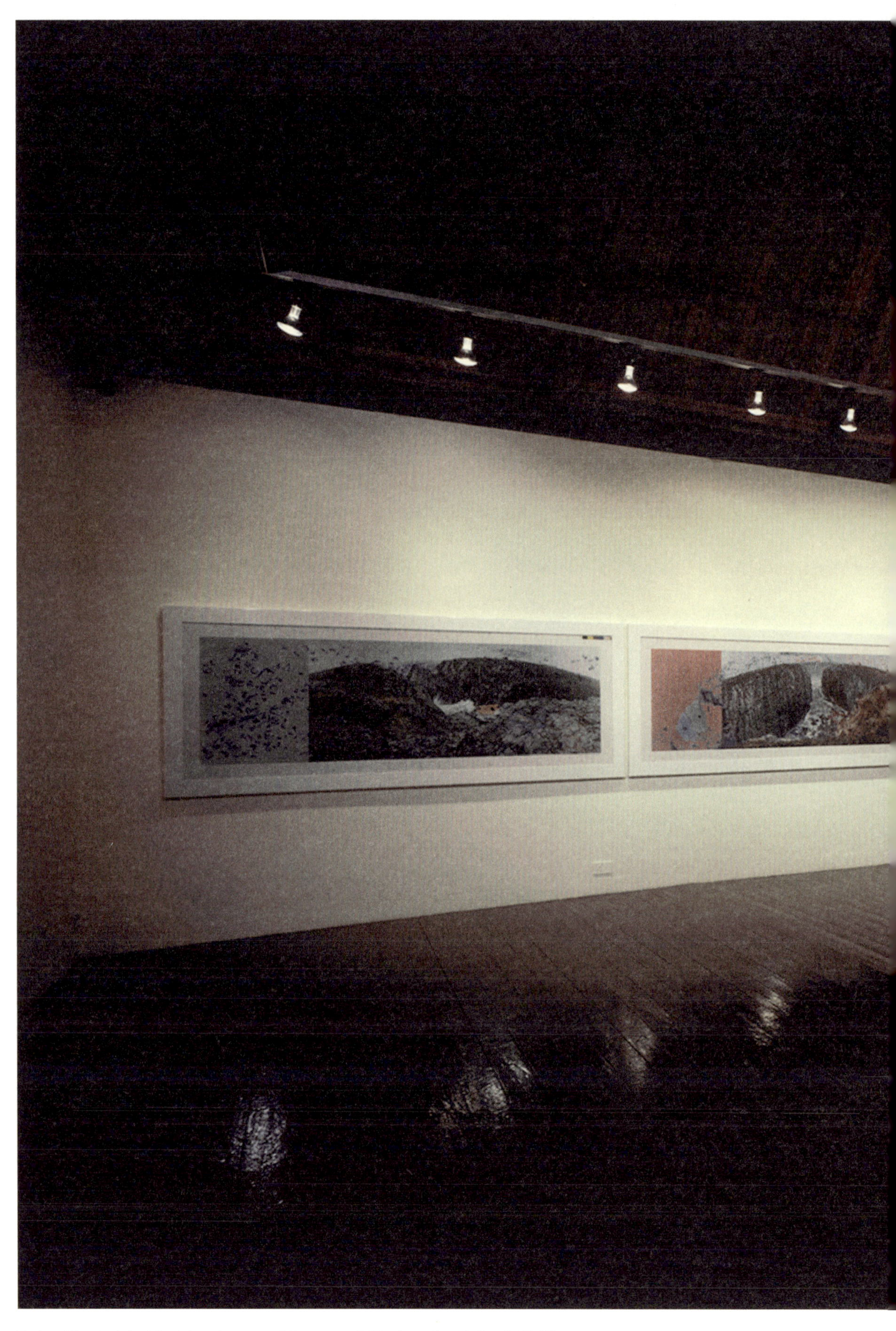

Helen Chadwick, *Viral Landscapes*, Museum of Modern Art Oxford, 1989

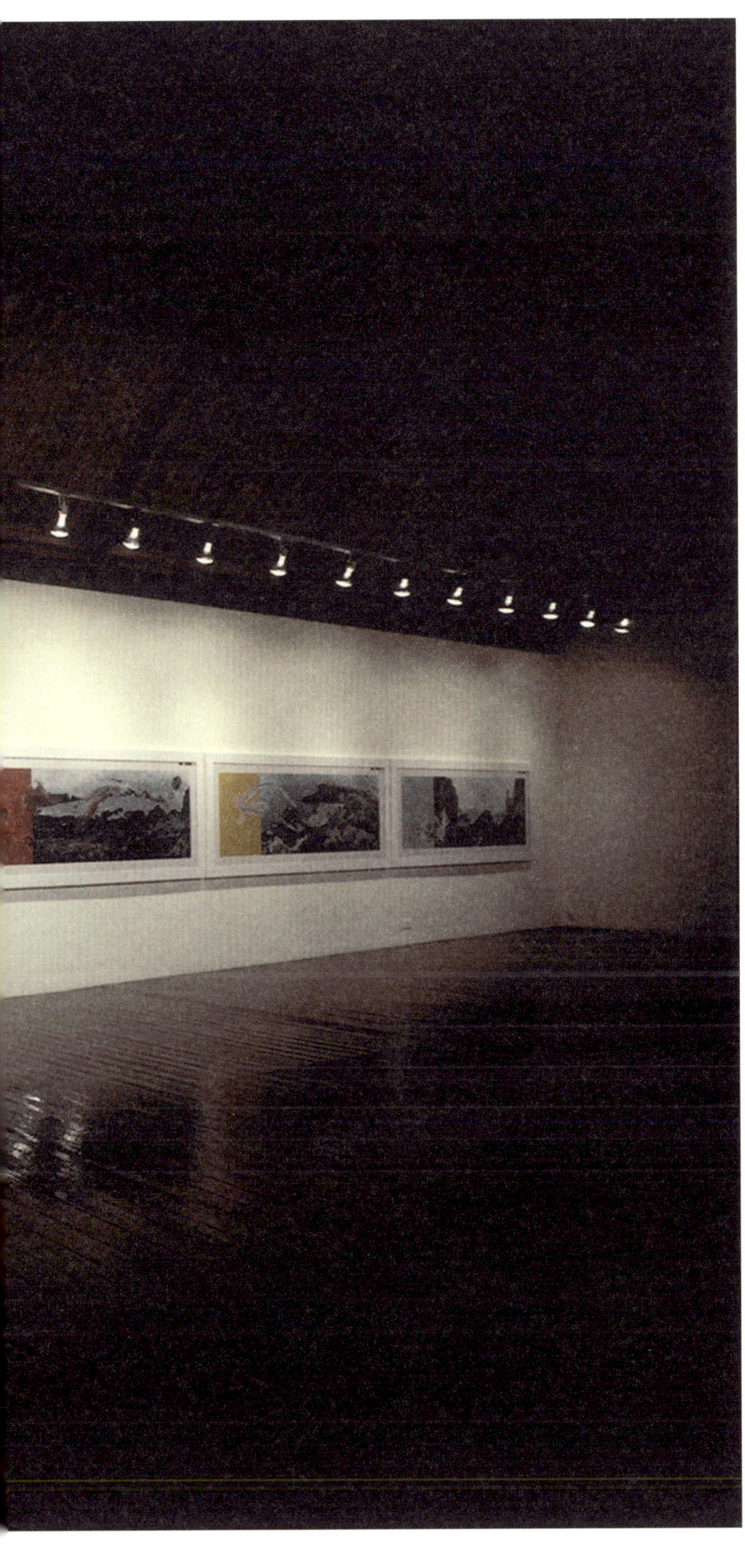

Njideka Akunyili Crosby

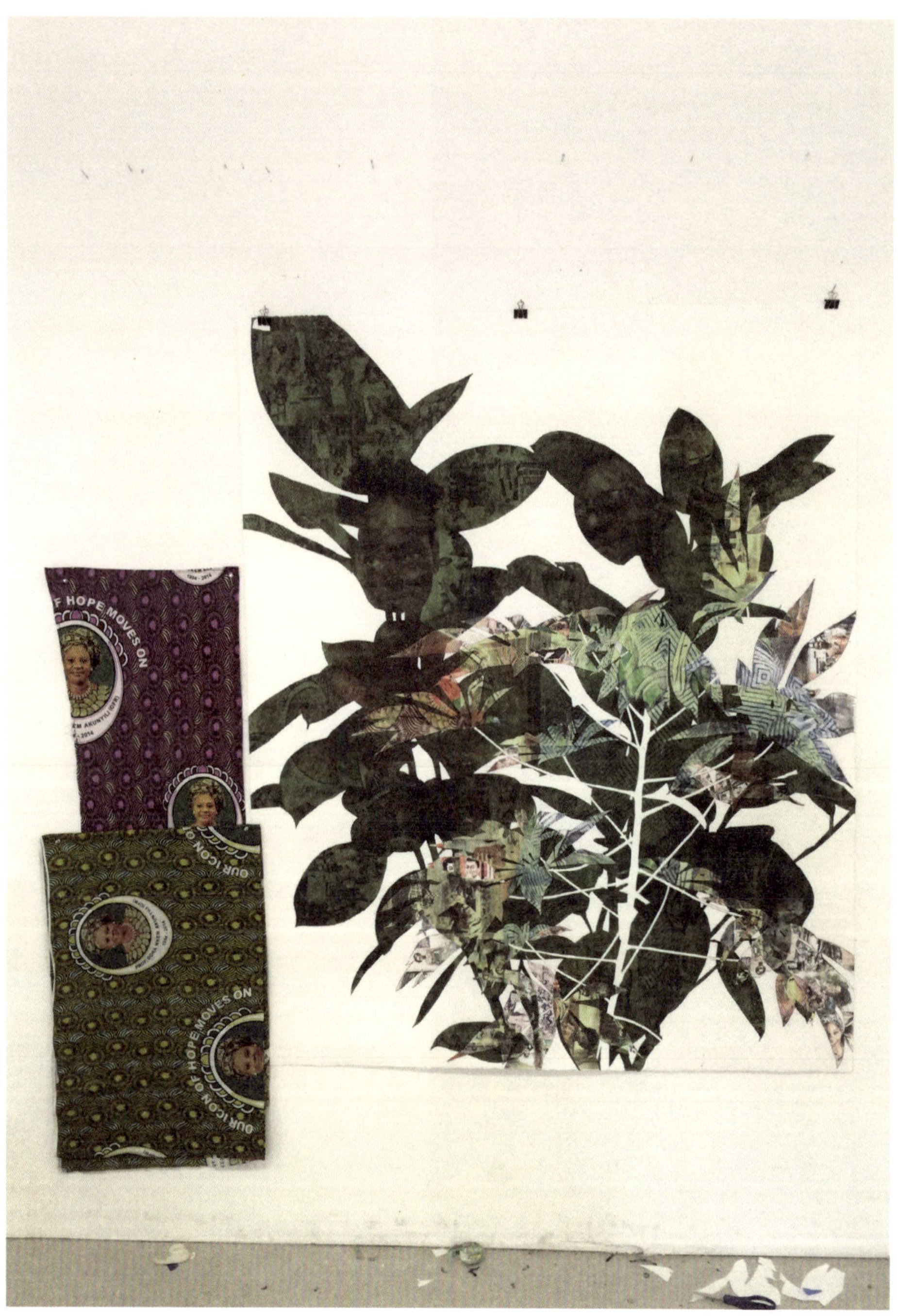

Cassava Garden (in progress), 2015

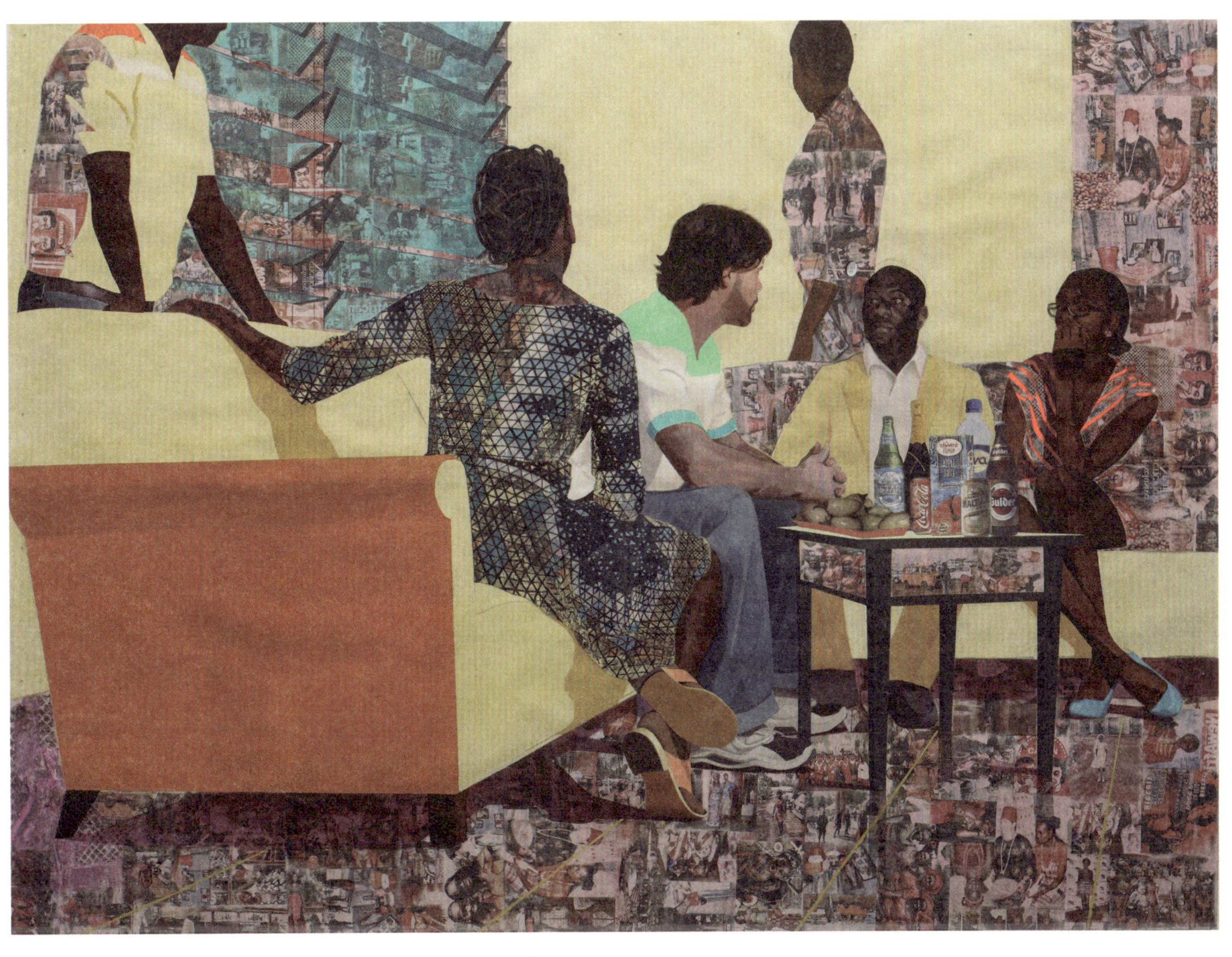

Something Split and New, 2013

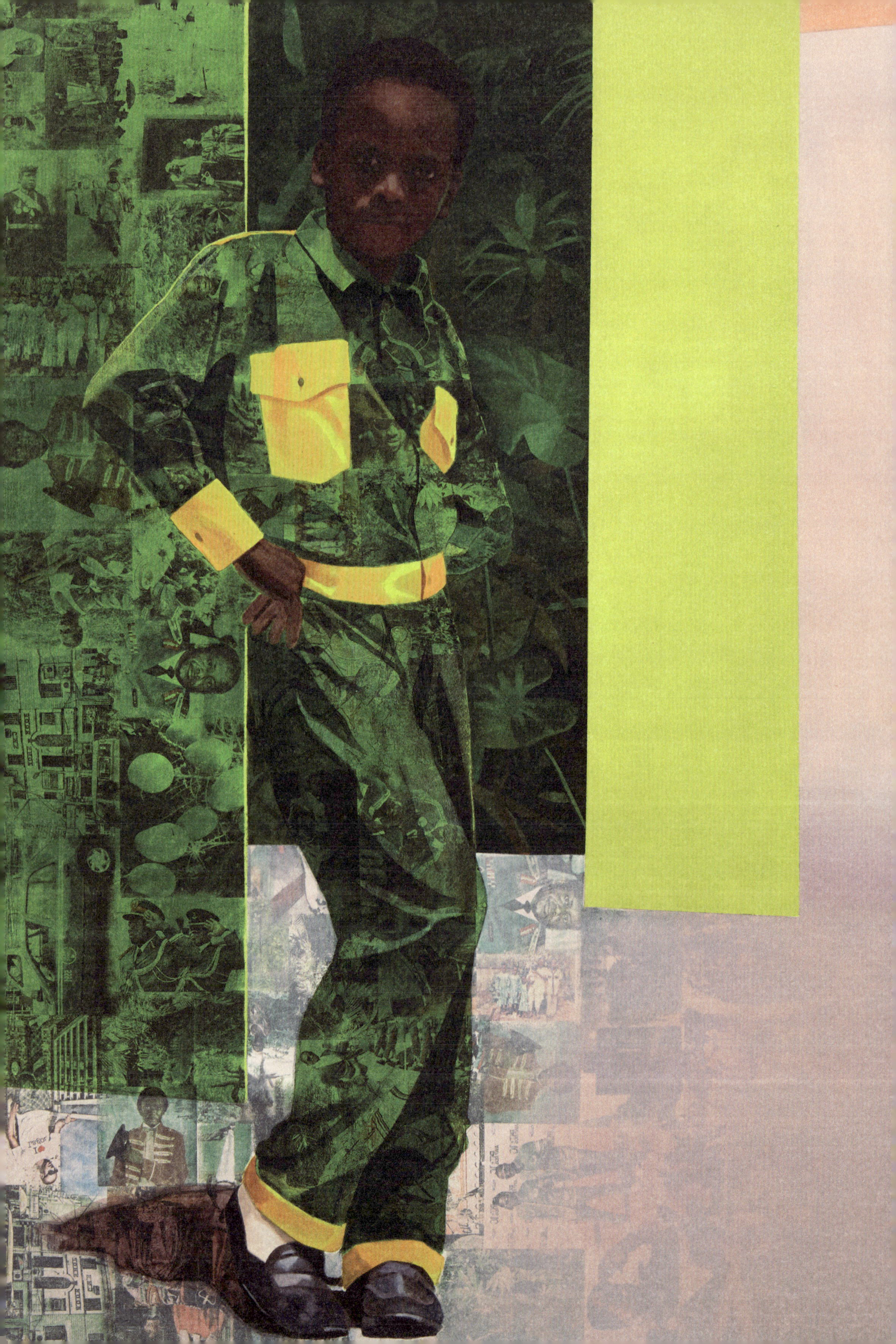

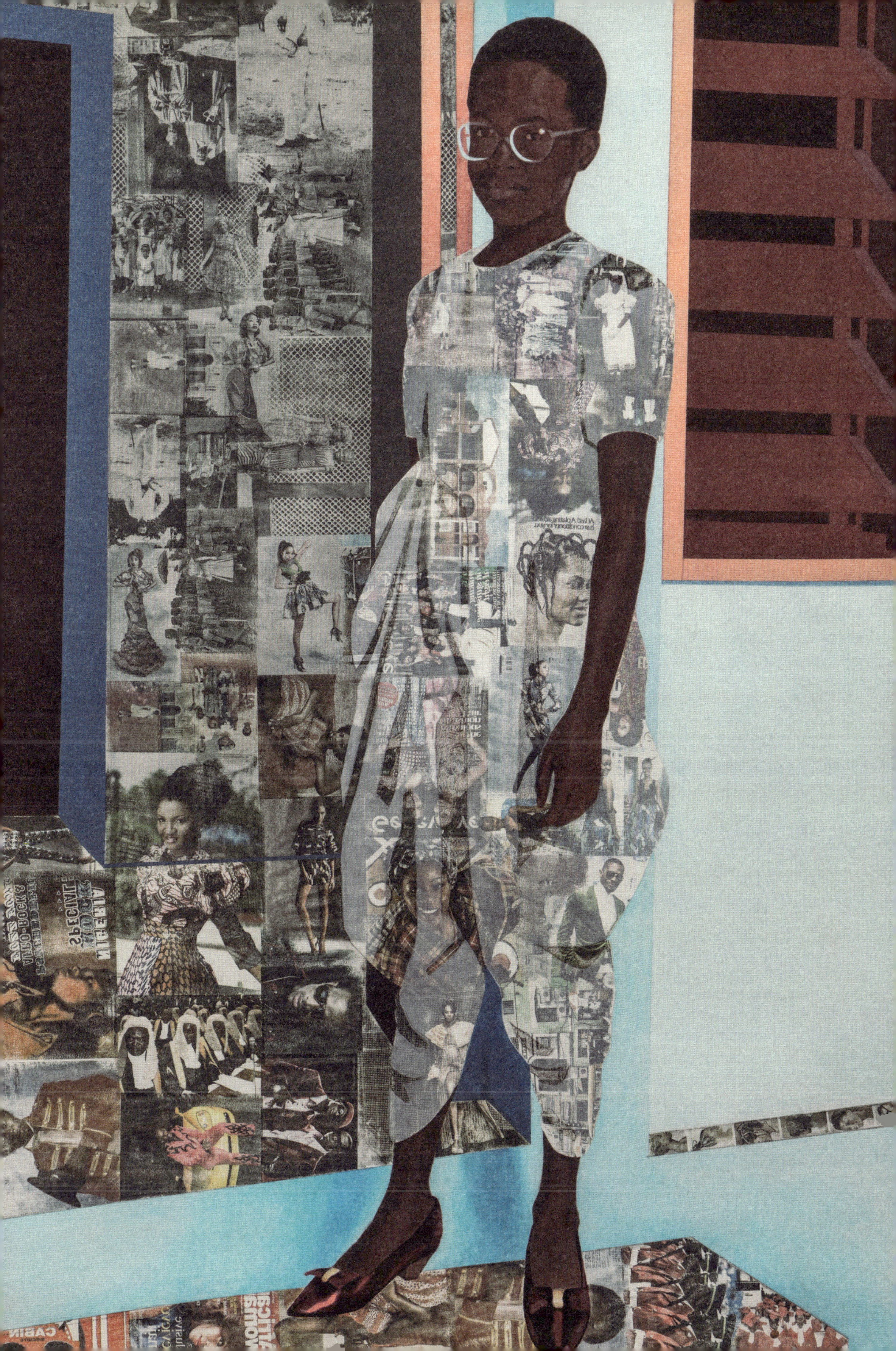

Dorothy Cross

KALEIDOSCOPE: Mystics and Rationalists
11 June – 31 July 2016

KALEIDOSCOPE: It's Me to the World
20 August – 16 October 2016

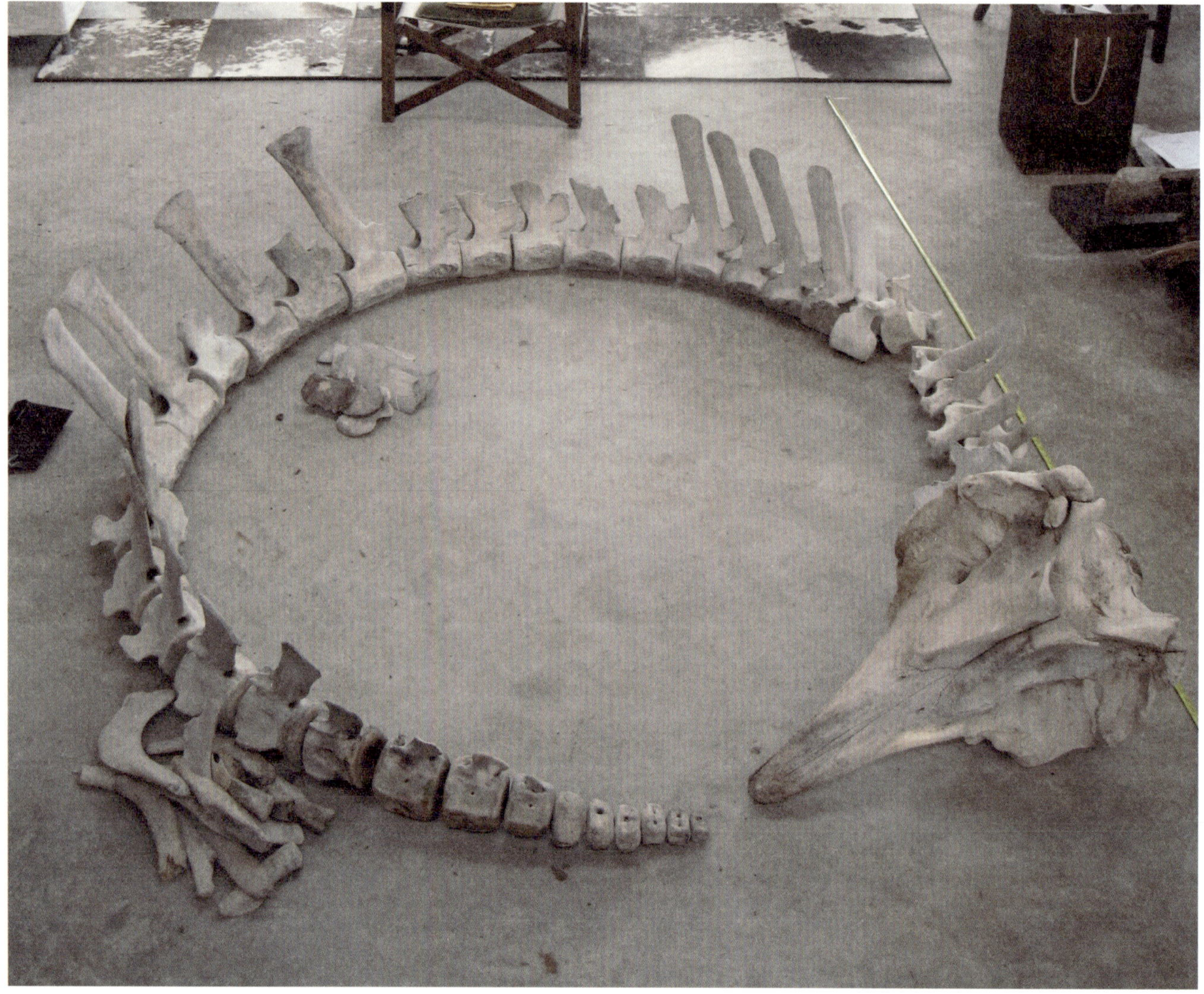

Studio with Cuvier's whale bones, 2016

Studio with Basking Shark Currach, 2016

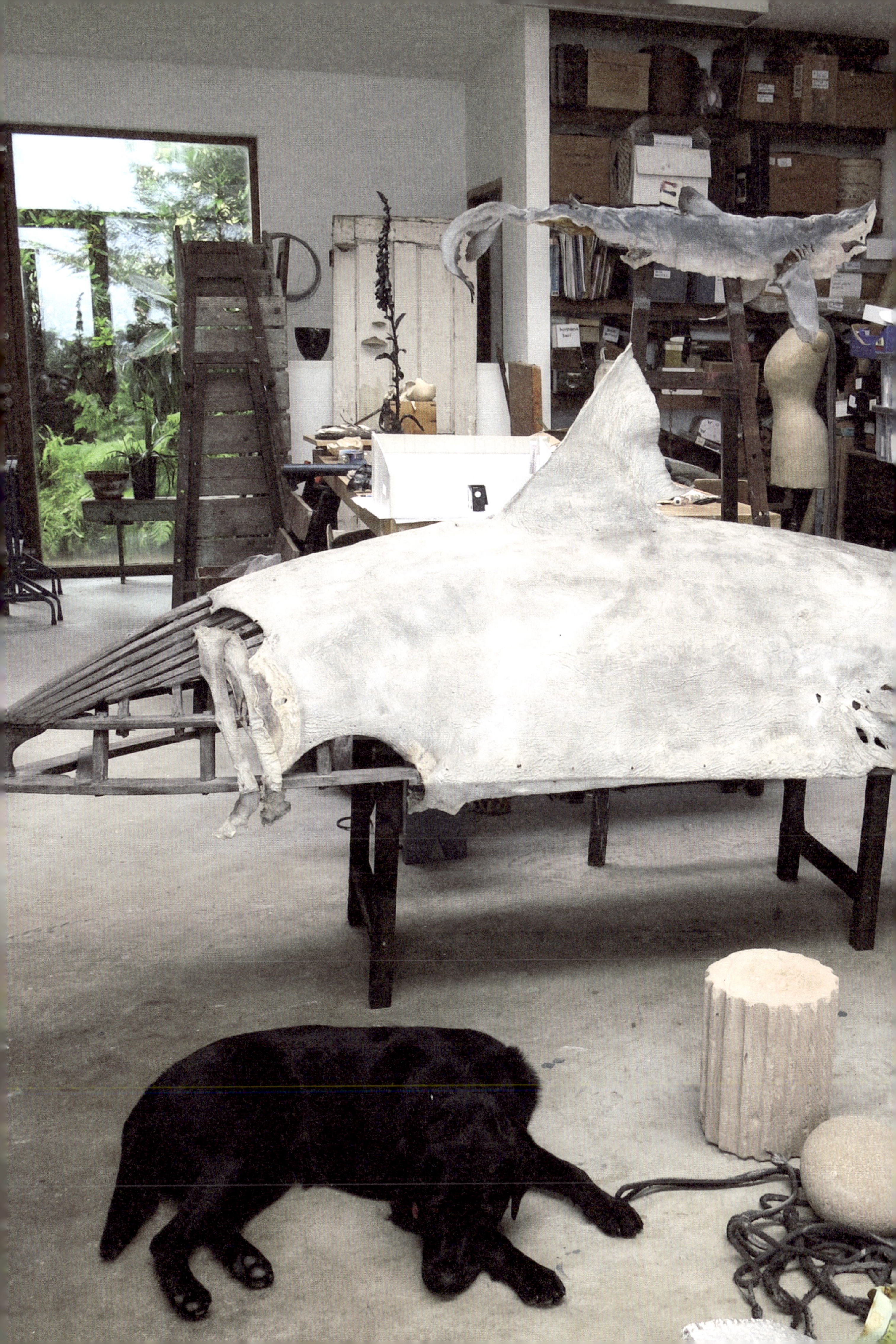

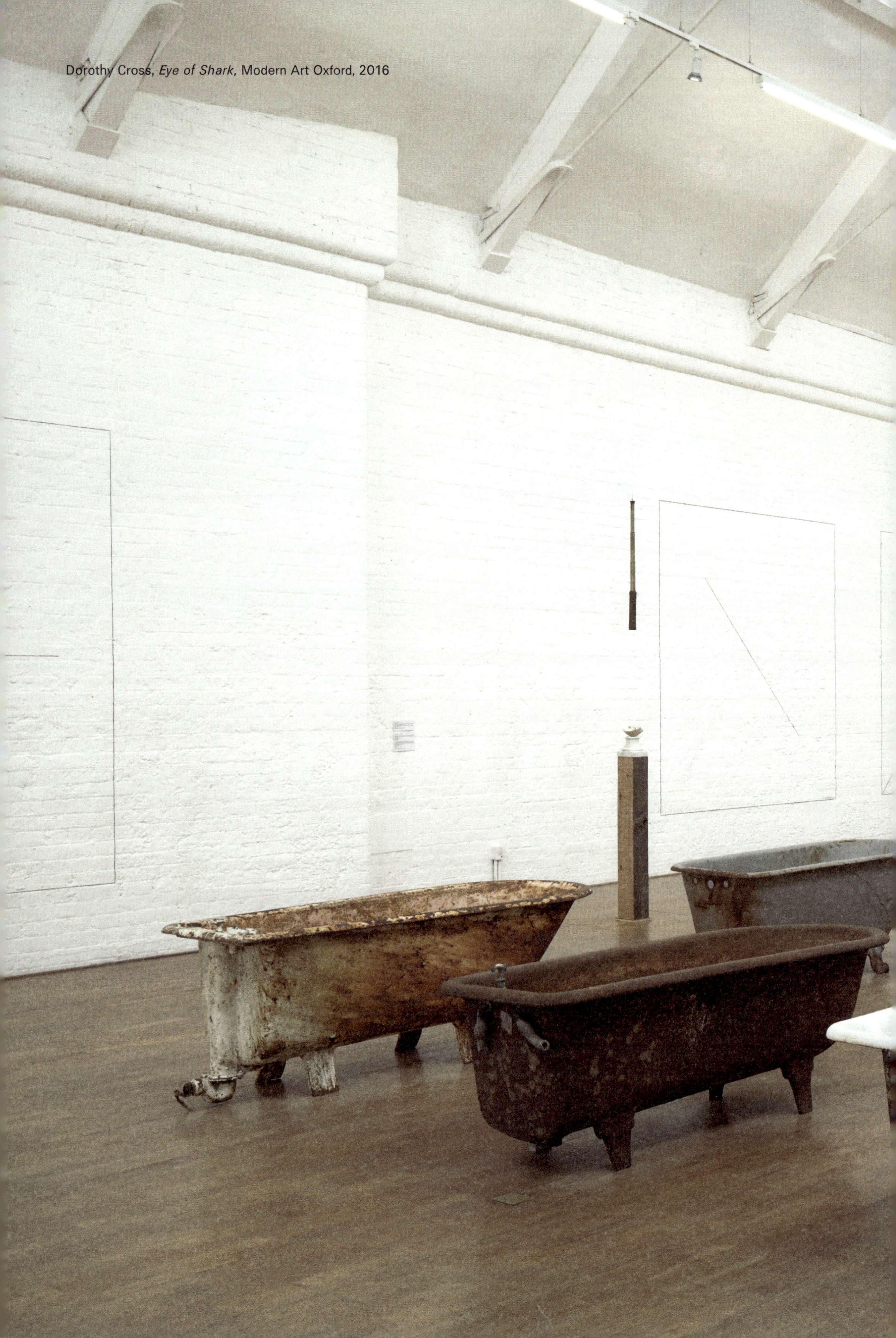

Dorothy Cross, *Eye of Shark*, Modern Art Oxford, 2016

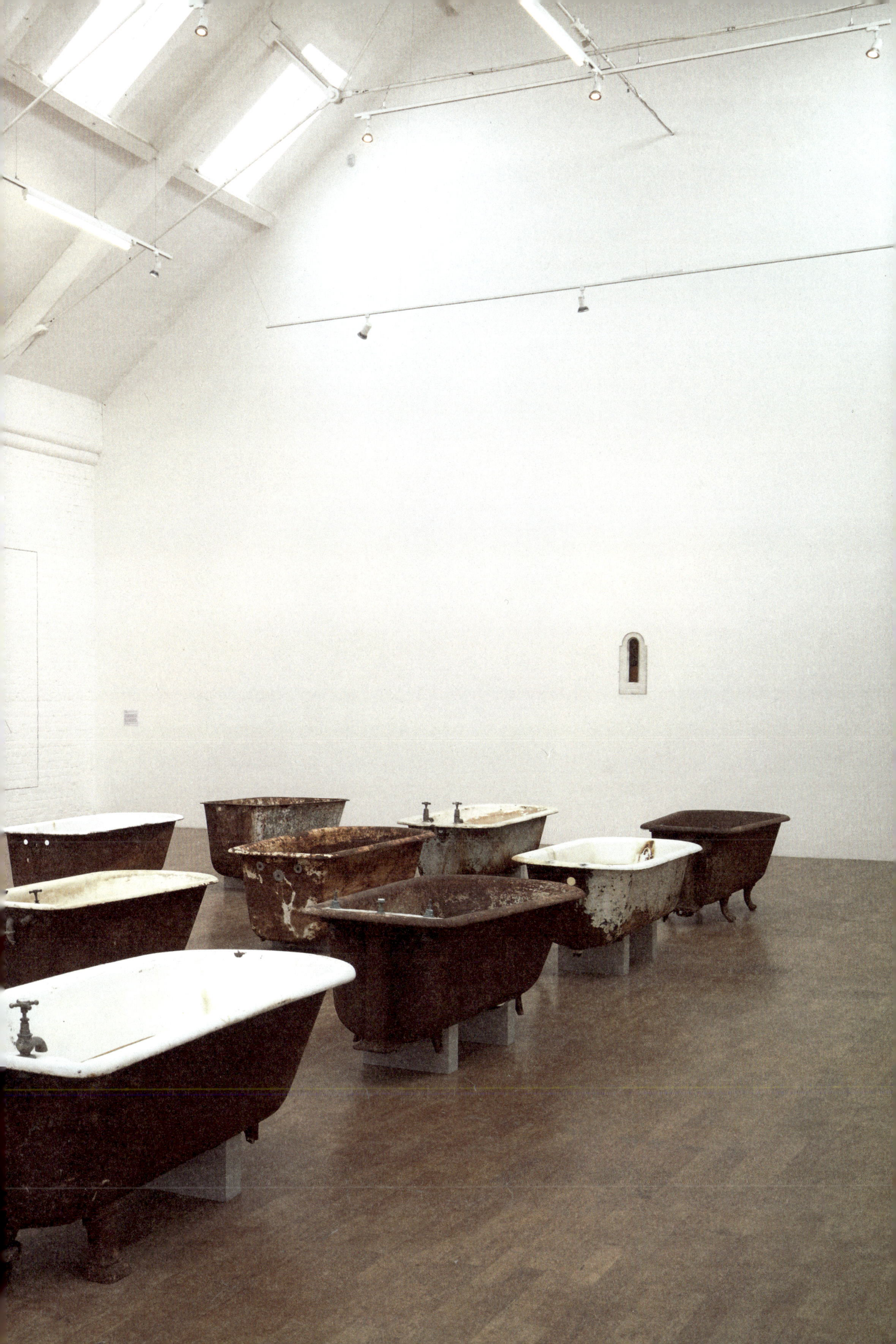

Dog Kennel Hill Project

KALEIDOSCOPE: The Indivisible Present
6 February – 20 March 2016

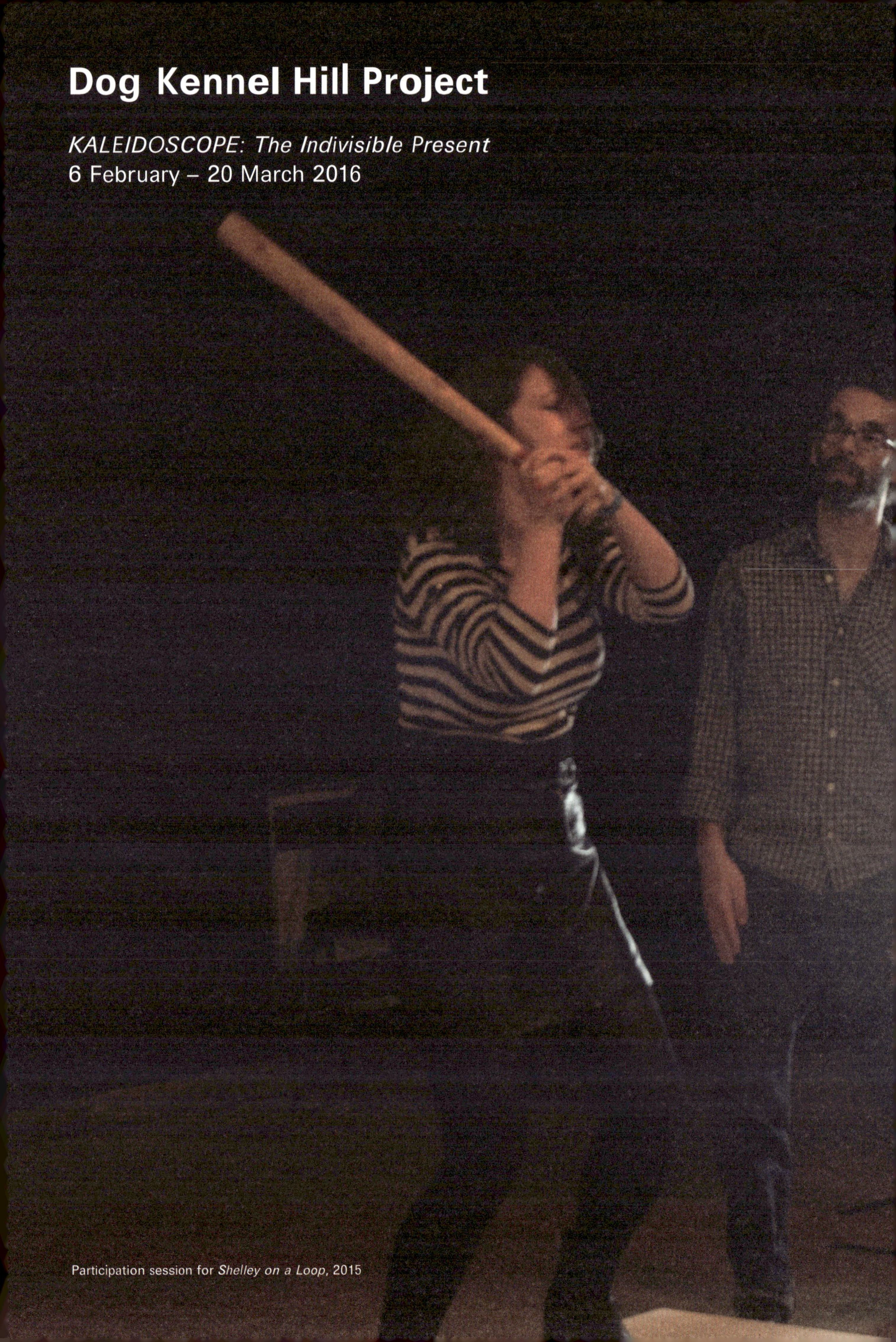

Participation session for *Shelley on a Loop*, 2015

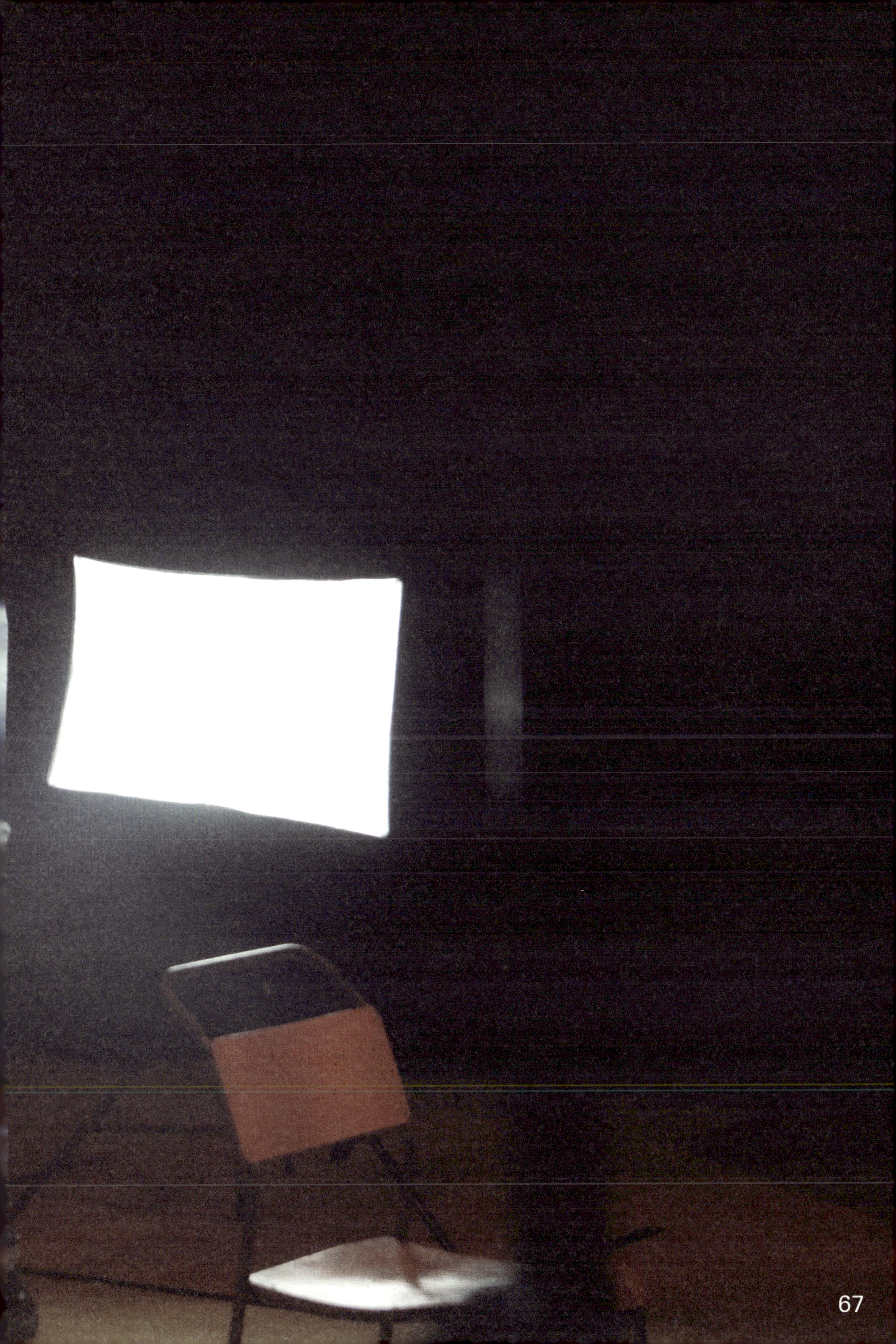

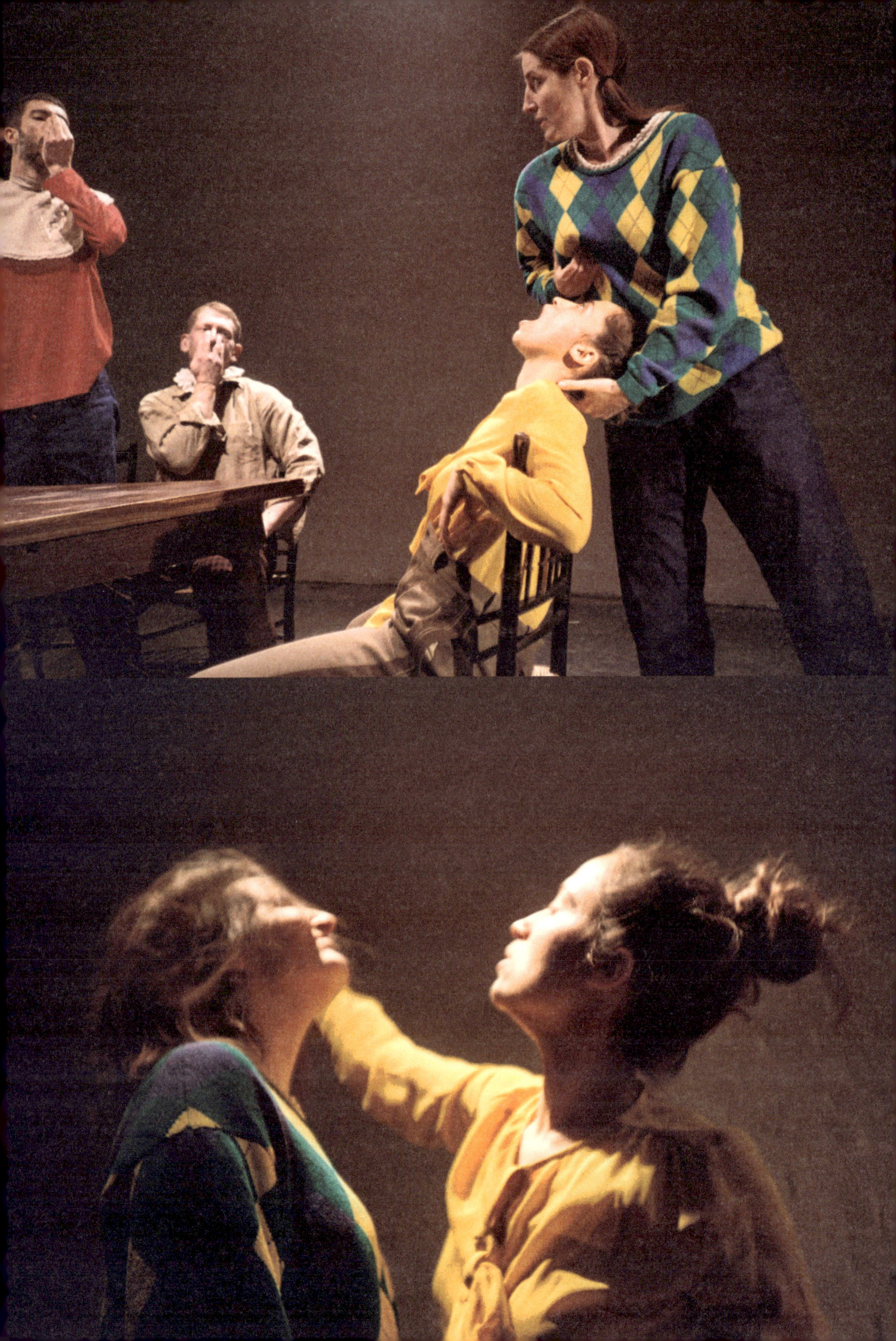

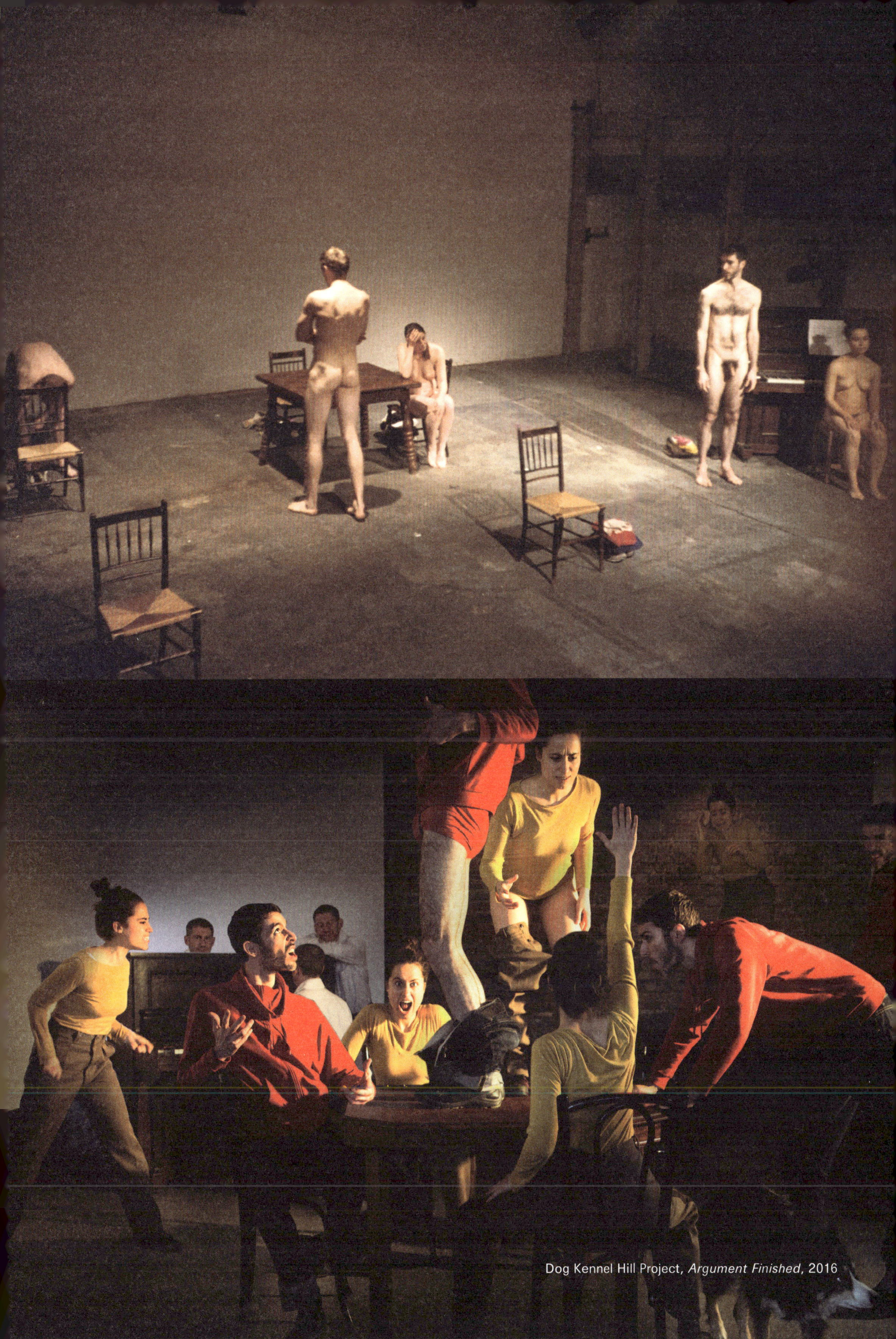

Dog Kennel Hill Project, *Argument Finished*, 2016

Ibrahim El-Salahi

KALEIDOSCOPE: Mystics and Rationalists
11 June – 31 July 2016

The Oxford Show
21 February – 21 March 2004

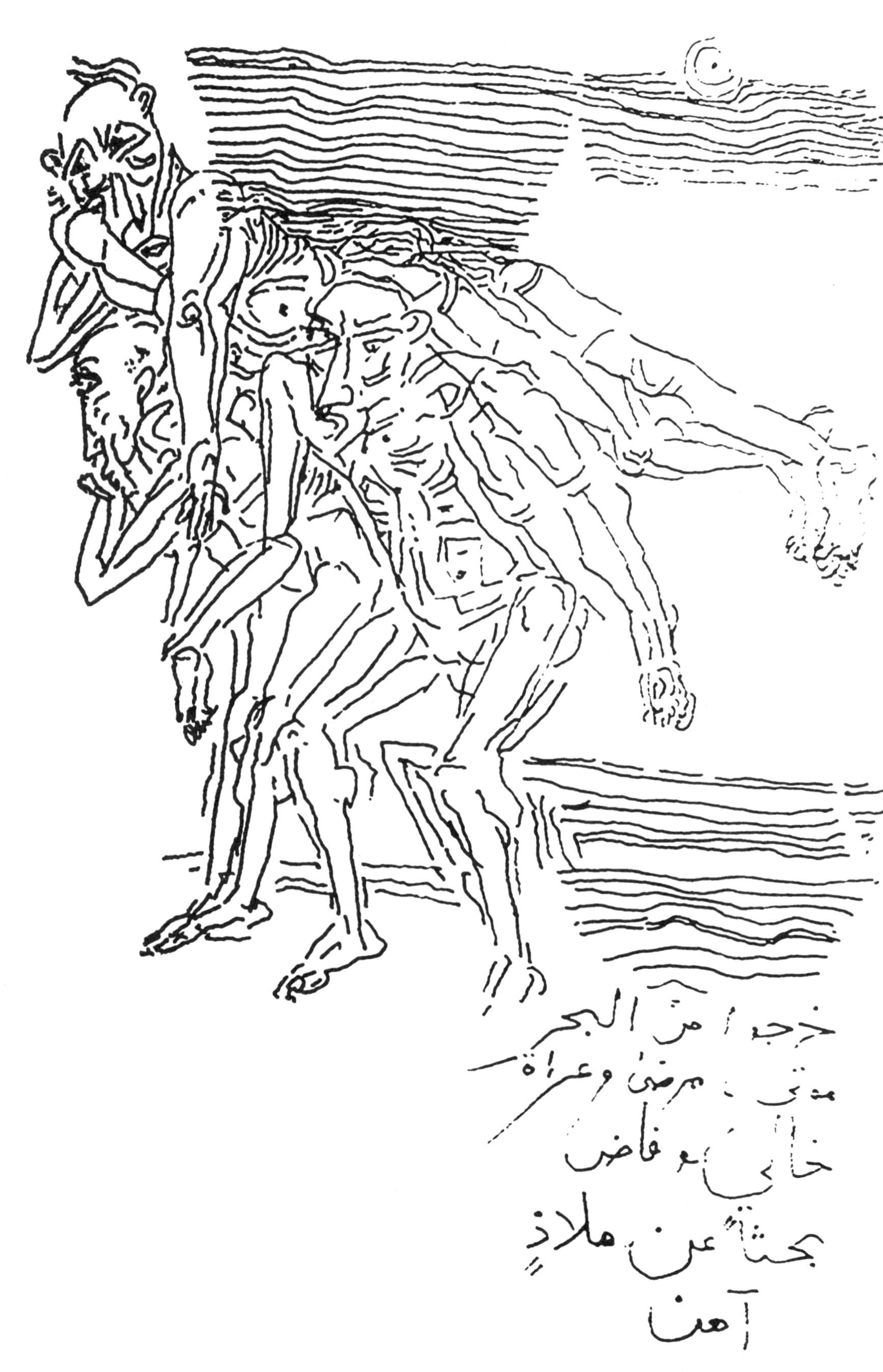

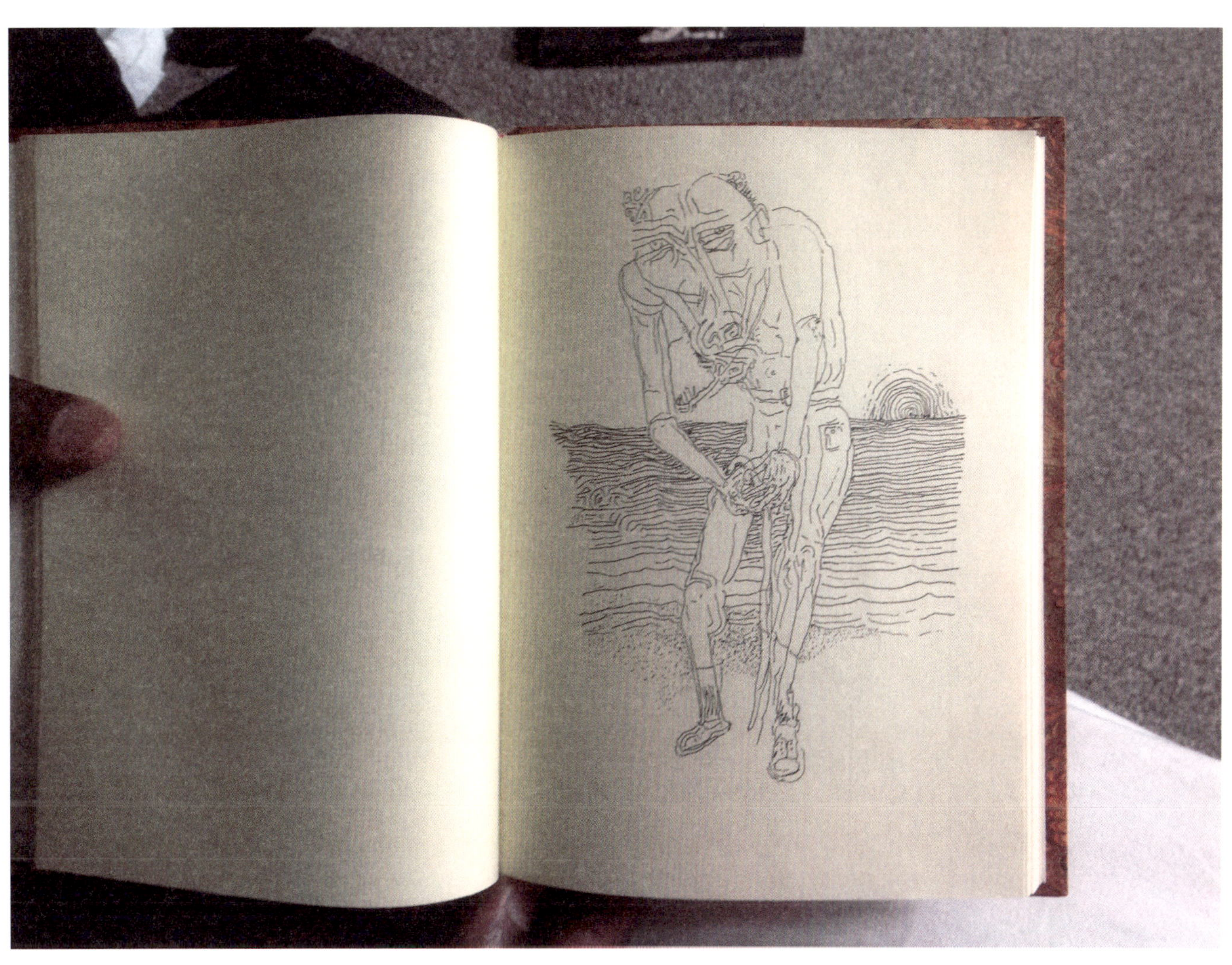

Drawings from the artist's sketchbook, 2016

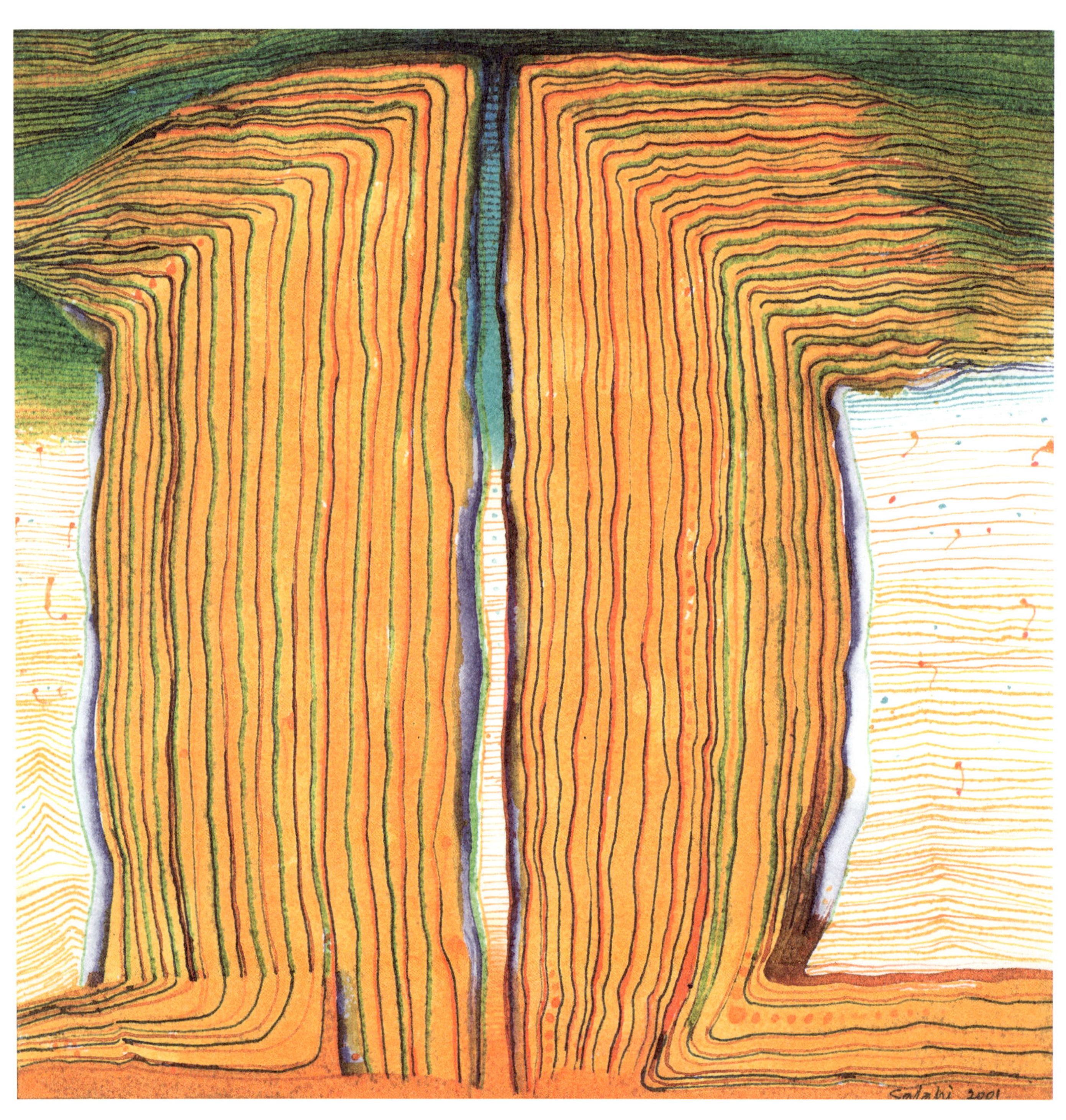

Ibrahim El-Salahi, *Untitled XII*, 2001

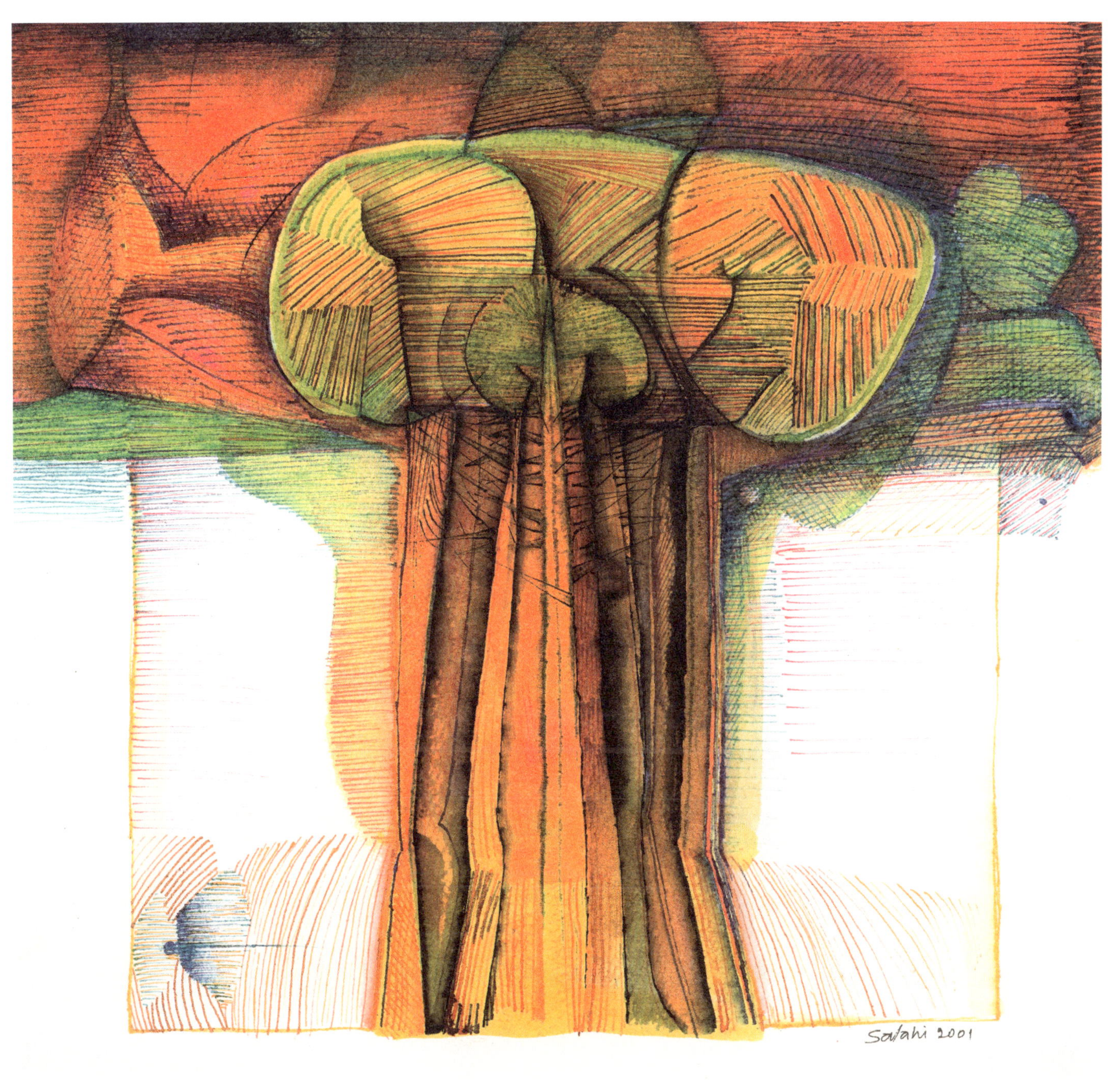

Ibrahim El-Salahi, *The Tree*, 2001

Douglas Gordon

KALEIDOSCOPE: The Indivisible Present
6 February – 20 March 2016

Notorious: Alfred Hitchcock and Contemporary Art
11 July – 3 October 1999

Height proposal:
Top of screen at 4·28 m
level with top of exhibition
wall. ∴ 1·28 m off floor.
Could go higher.

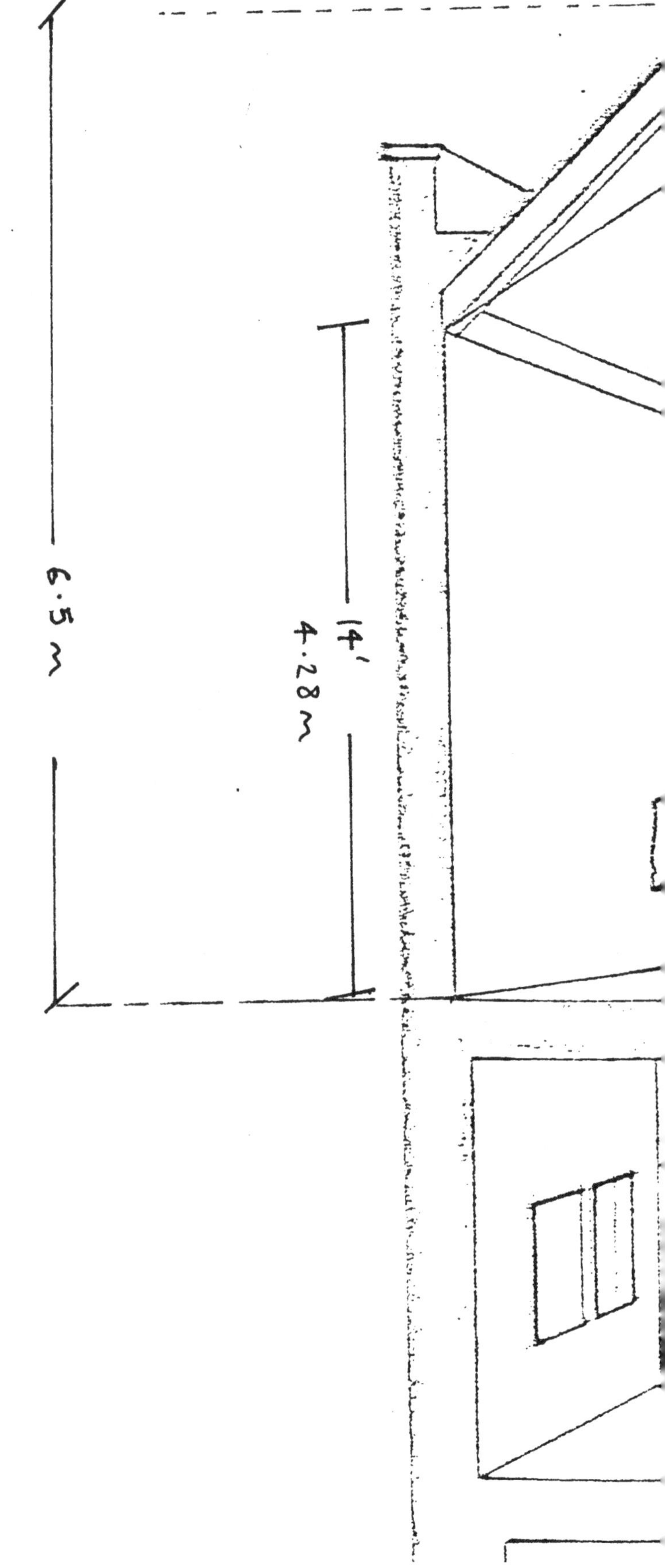

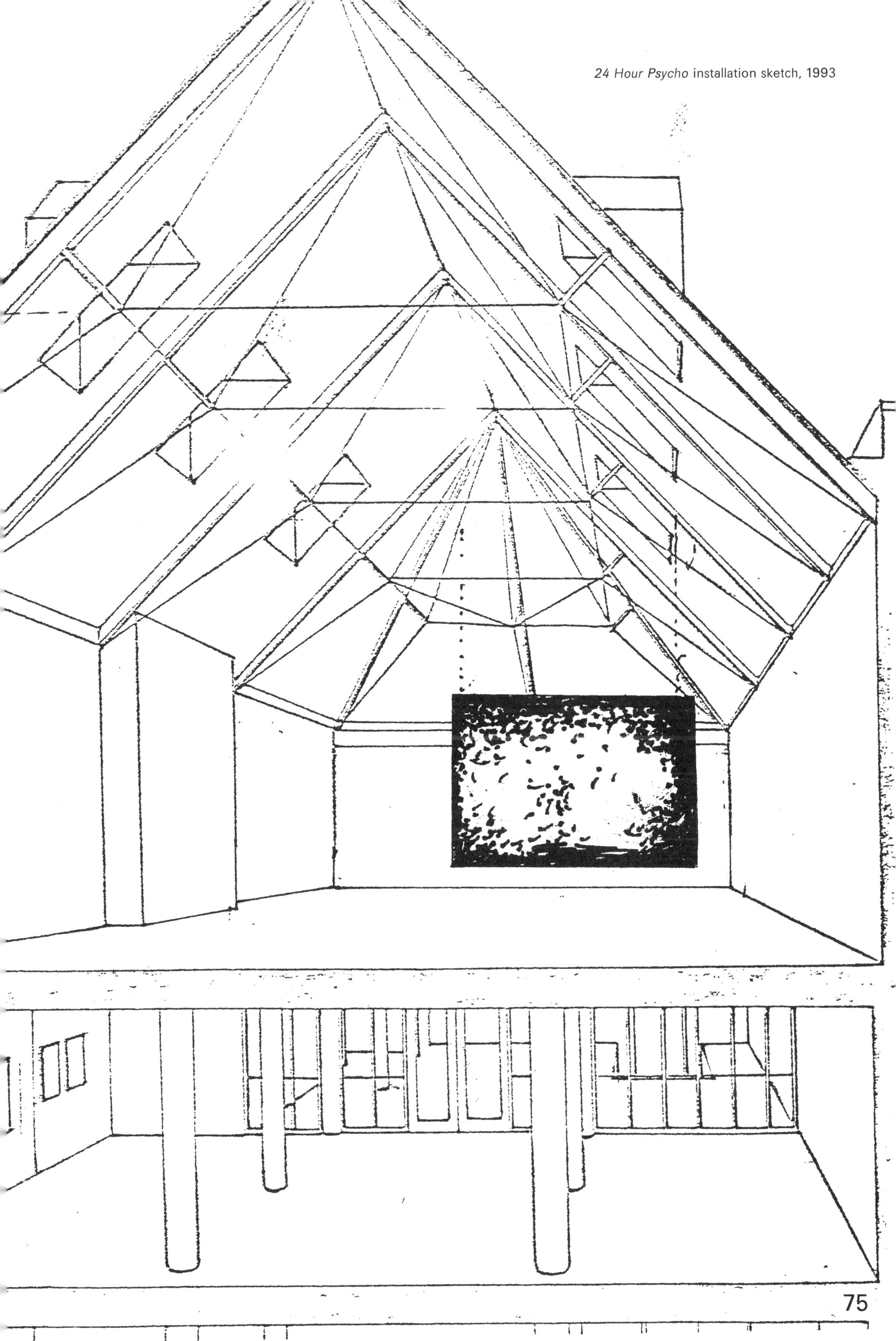

24 Hour Psycho installation sketch, 1993

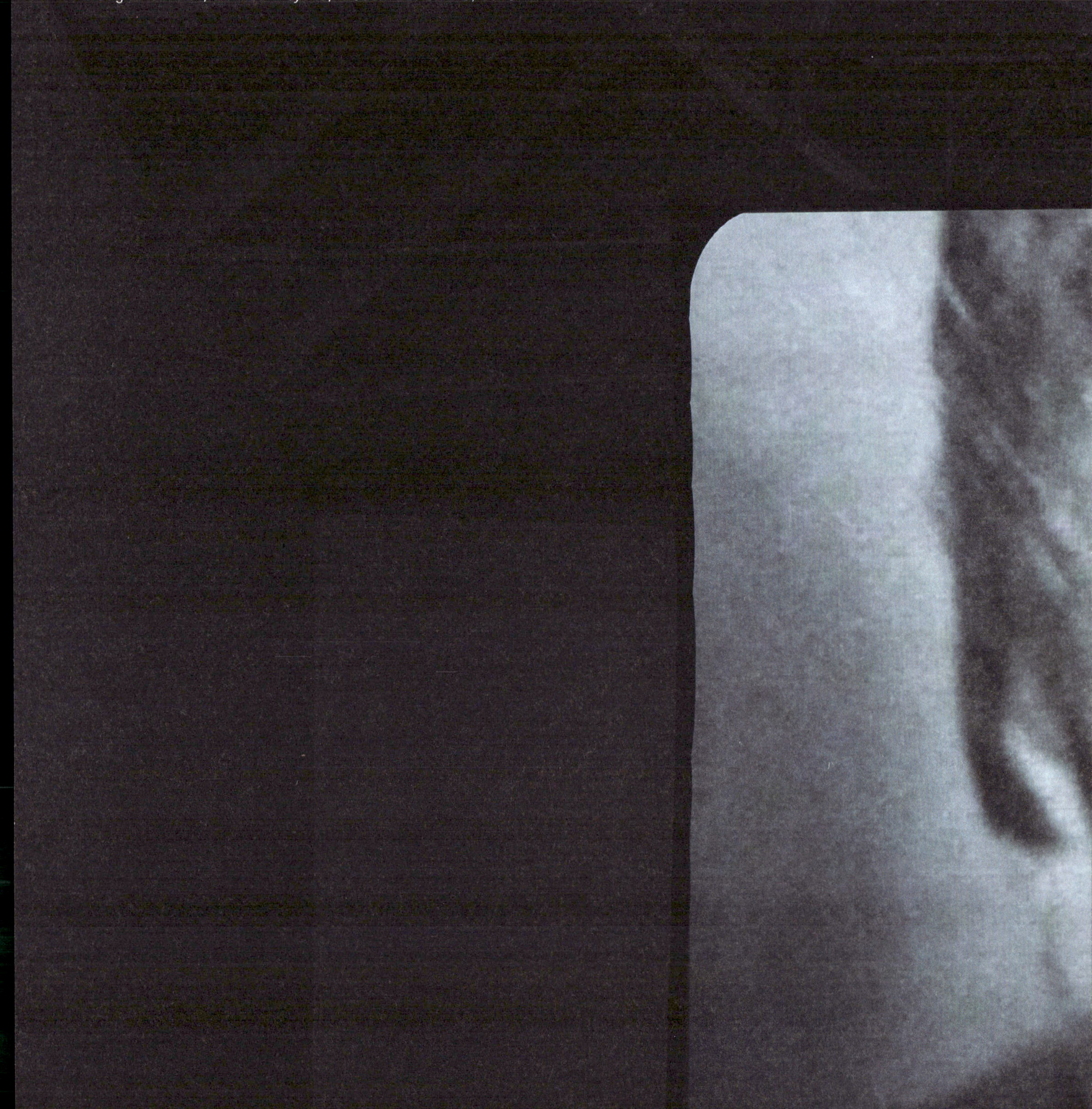

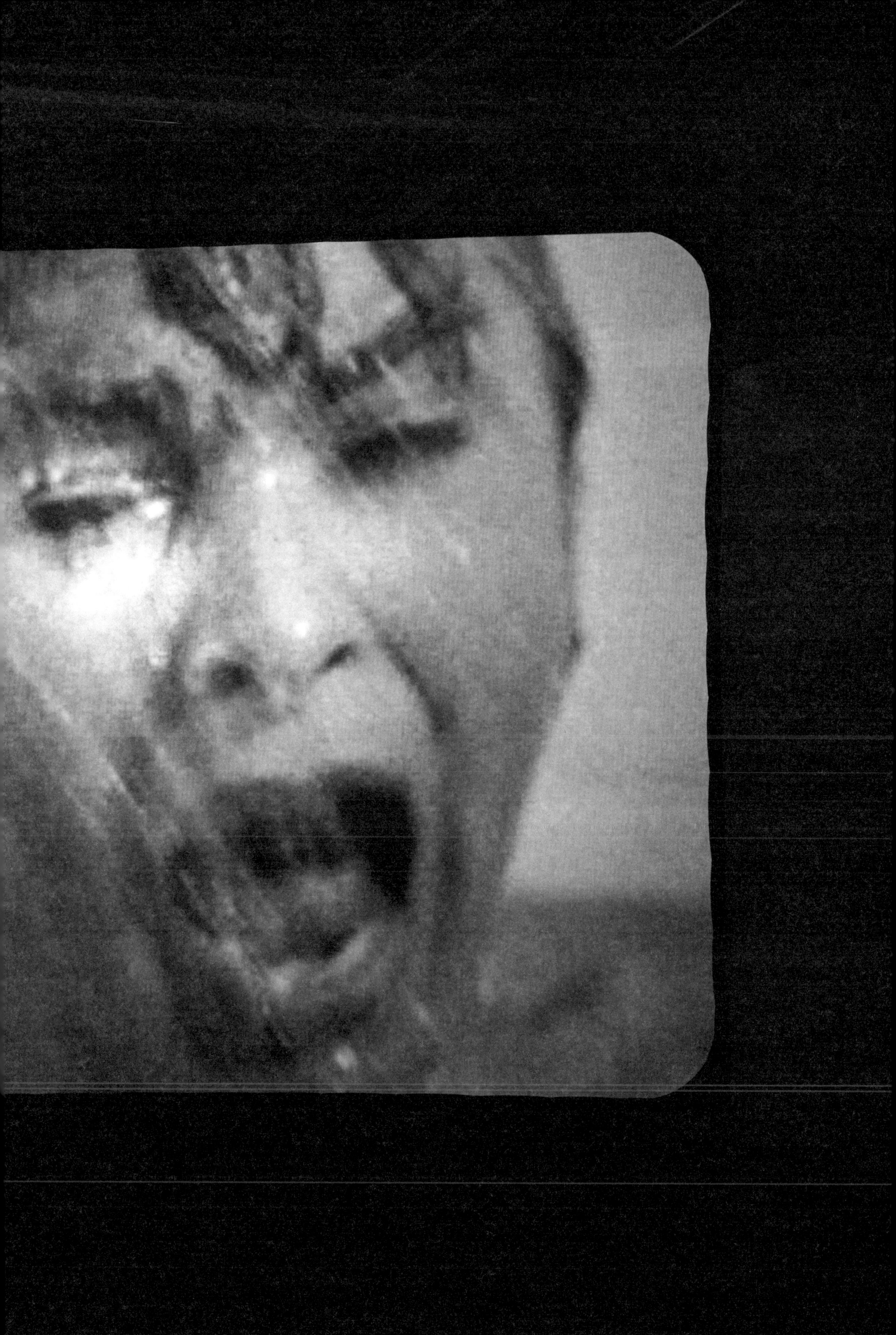

Dan Graham

KALEIDOSCOPE: Mystics and Rationalists
11 June – 31 July 2016

Dan Graham: *Installations/Photographs/Videotapes/Performances/
Architectural Models/Publications/Films*
3 September – 1 October 1978

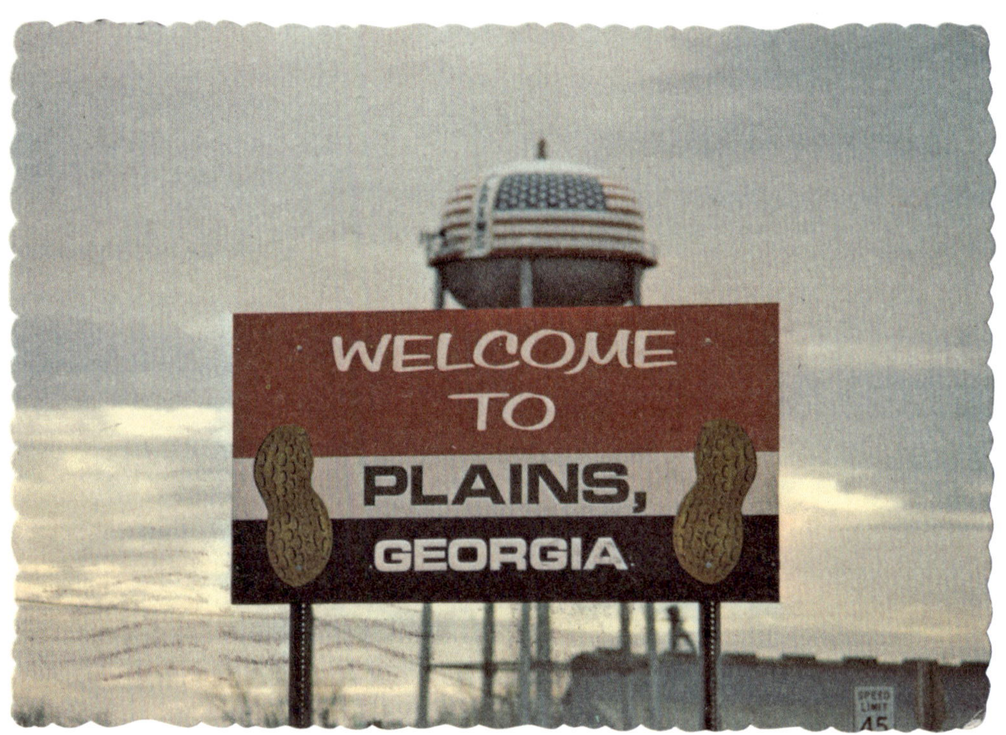

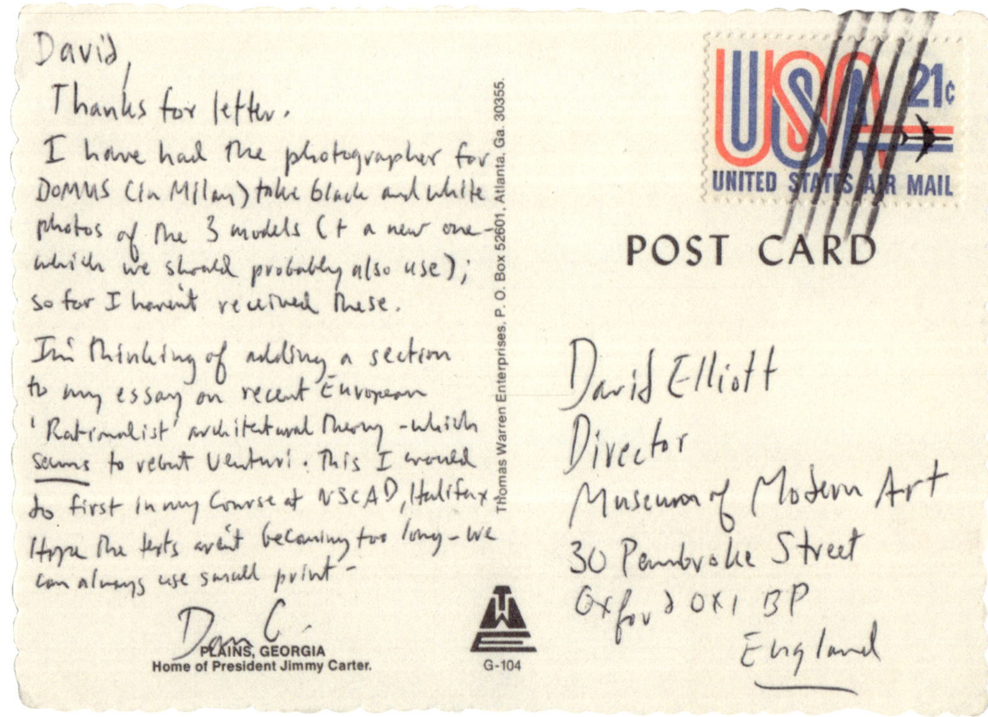

Postcard from Dan Graham to David Elliott, 1979

Past Future Split Attention   1972

video-taped performance:

transcript of performance February, 1972, London, England:

....

....

<u>Premise</u>:

Two people who know each other are in the same sapce. While one person pre-
dicts continuously the other person's future behavior, the other person

recounts (by memory) the other's past behavior.

<u>Notes</u>:
Both are in the present, so knowledge of the past is needed to continuously
deduce future behavior (in terms of causal relation). For one to see the
other in termsof the present (attention) there is a mirror reflection or
closed figure-eight feedback/feedahead loop of past/future. Both person's
behavior reciprocally reflects/depends upon the other's, so that each one's
information of his moves is seen in part as a reflection of the effect that
their own just-past behavior has had in reversed tense as perceived from
the other's view ofhimself. For instance, the expectation of the person pred
icting the other one's behavior may be thwarted if theother person deliberat
ely alters the course of his future behavior and establishes an alternate or
negating series of actions. However, unconsciously (conscious to an outside
observer in a longer span of time) he may perform as predicted, but in a dis
placed or altered sequence of responses which reflect his reaction to the
reaction of the other to his projecting a 'past' identity upon them. Or he
may be projecting the behavior that the other person is anticipating from
him onto theother person's past, trying to affect that person's future (pred
ictions)...and so on. (As part of the thinking process in termsoftime contin
uum ofcause and effect, theobserver, in dealing with what he sees, extrapola
from the observed's past behavior projected in line to the future.) For the
performance to proceed, a simultaneous - but doubled attention - of the firs
performer's 'self' in relation to the other (object) - the other's impressions - must be maintained by each performer. This affects cause and effect
directionality, as does the discrepancy in time between words as linear proj
ections and the very different (but also linear) sequential direction of
behavior. As video-tape is a continuum (unlike film, which is discontinuous,
an analytic re-construction) with separate sound (verbal) andvisual
tracks,it is an ideal medium for presenting this sequence.

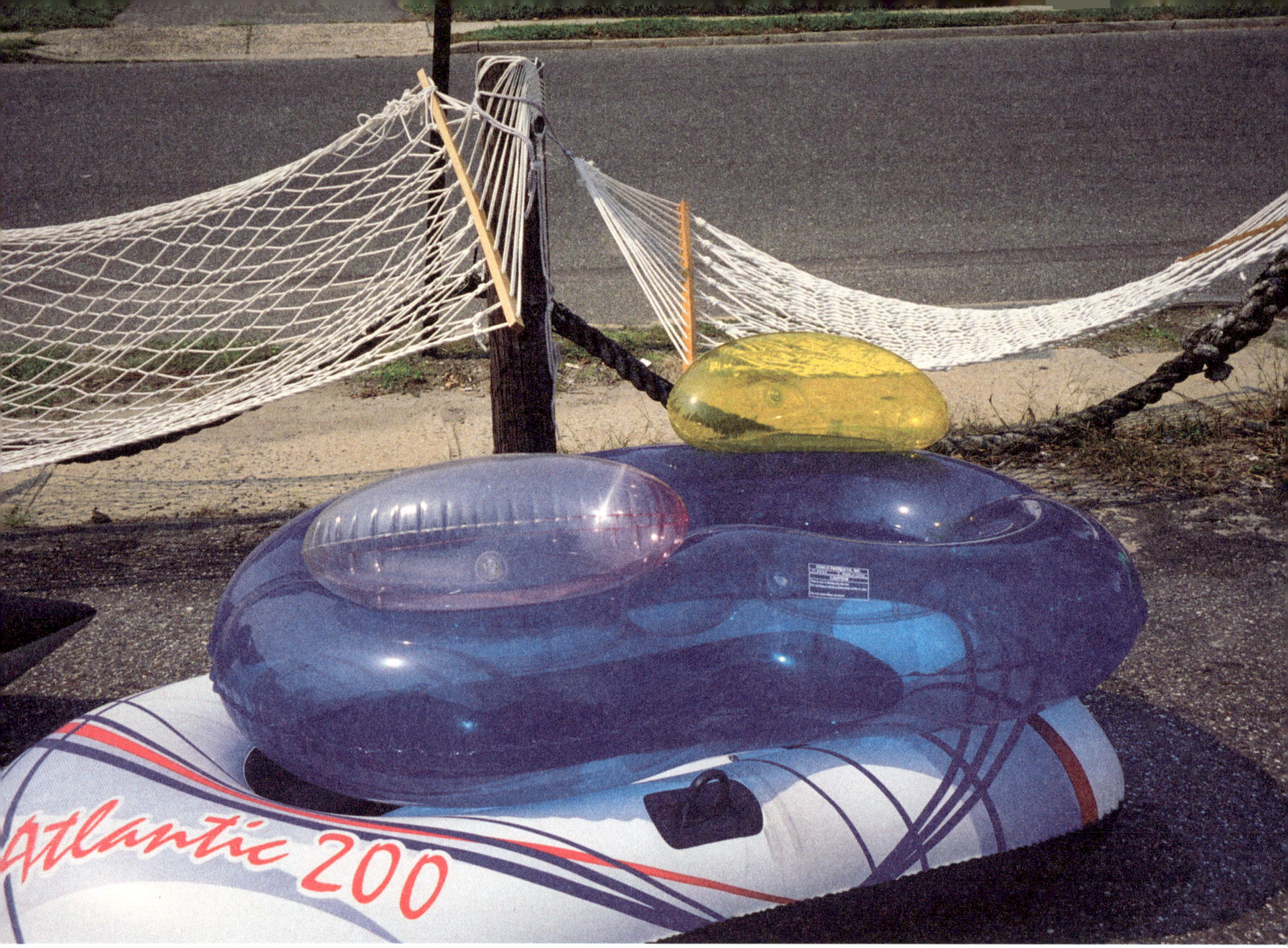

A lot of New Jersey is highway culture. This is between
Jersey City and Deal. It seems to be some kind of sea animal.
Don Judd was a Gemini. He was originally from Kansas City.
He wrote an article about the urban plan of Kansas City, which
is neoclassical. At some point he and his family moved to
New Jersey, and he became fascinated by plastics and the
materials of the new highway culture and suburban houses.
I think his work is about the conflict between American
neoclassicism and New Jersey highway culture. Plastics
were very important in the 1960s. It was a little like Milan
during those years with Joe Columbo. The oil refineries
were located in New Jersey. My father actually worked
near one of them, for a chemical company. Out of petroleum
refineries came the plastic industry.

Dan Graham, *Inflatable Beachside Floats*, Highway Store, New Jersey, 2006

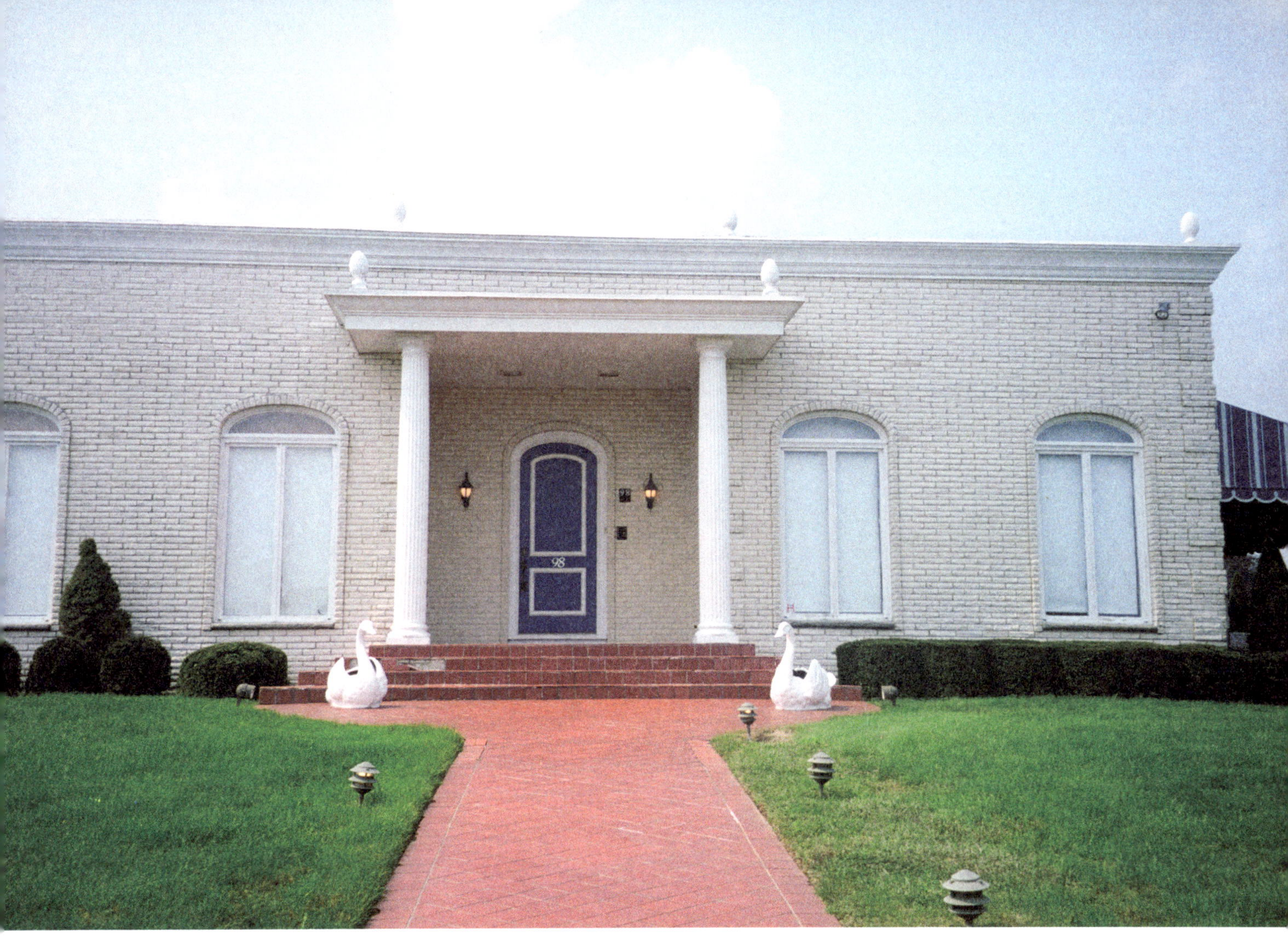

They're basically mobster houses. When we speak about
mobsters, we talk about Italian Americans. That's the same
ethnic group that Francis Ford Coppola was from, although
he is quite a nice guy. What they try to do in New Jersey in
these houses, with these swans outside of the big neoclassical
entrance to the house, is kind of like baroque ornamentation.
In his exhibition *Signs of Life*, Venturi talks a lot about this;
that people, particularly Italian Americans, like to show what
their lifestyle is like by the ornamentation on their lawns.
I guess the swan is kind of an elegant animal.

Dan Graham, *Mafia Mansion*, Deal, New Jersey, 2006

Guan Xiao

KALEIDOSCOPE: A Moment of Grace
16 April – 22 May 2016

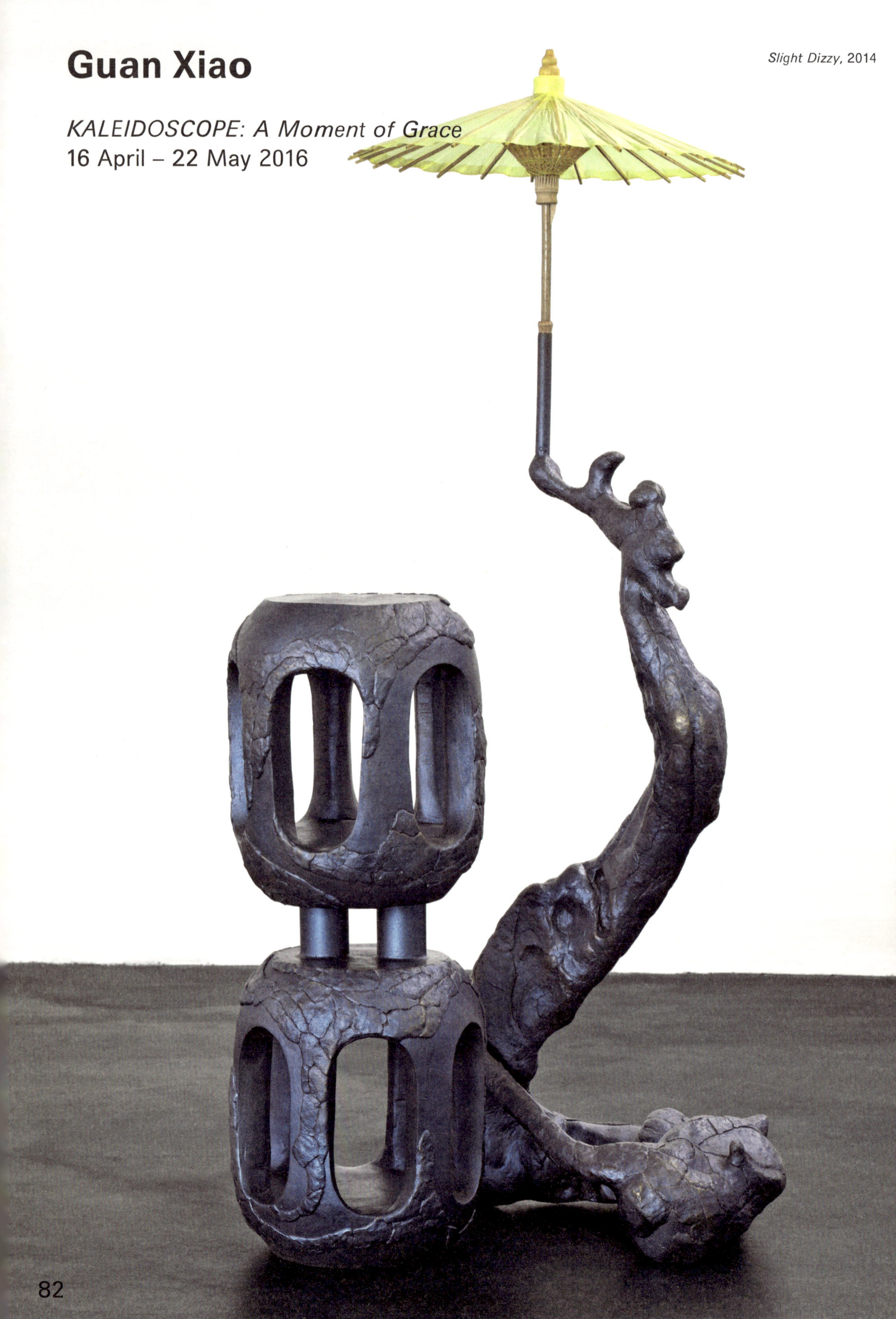

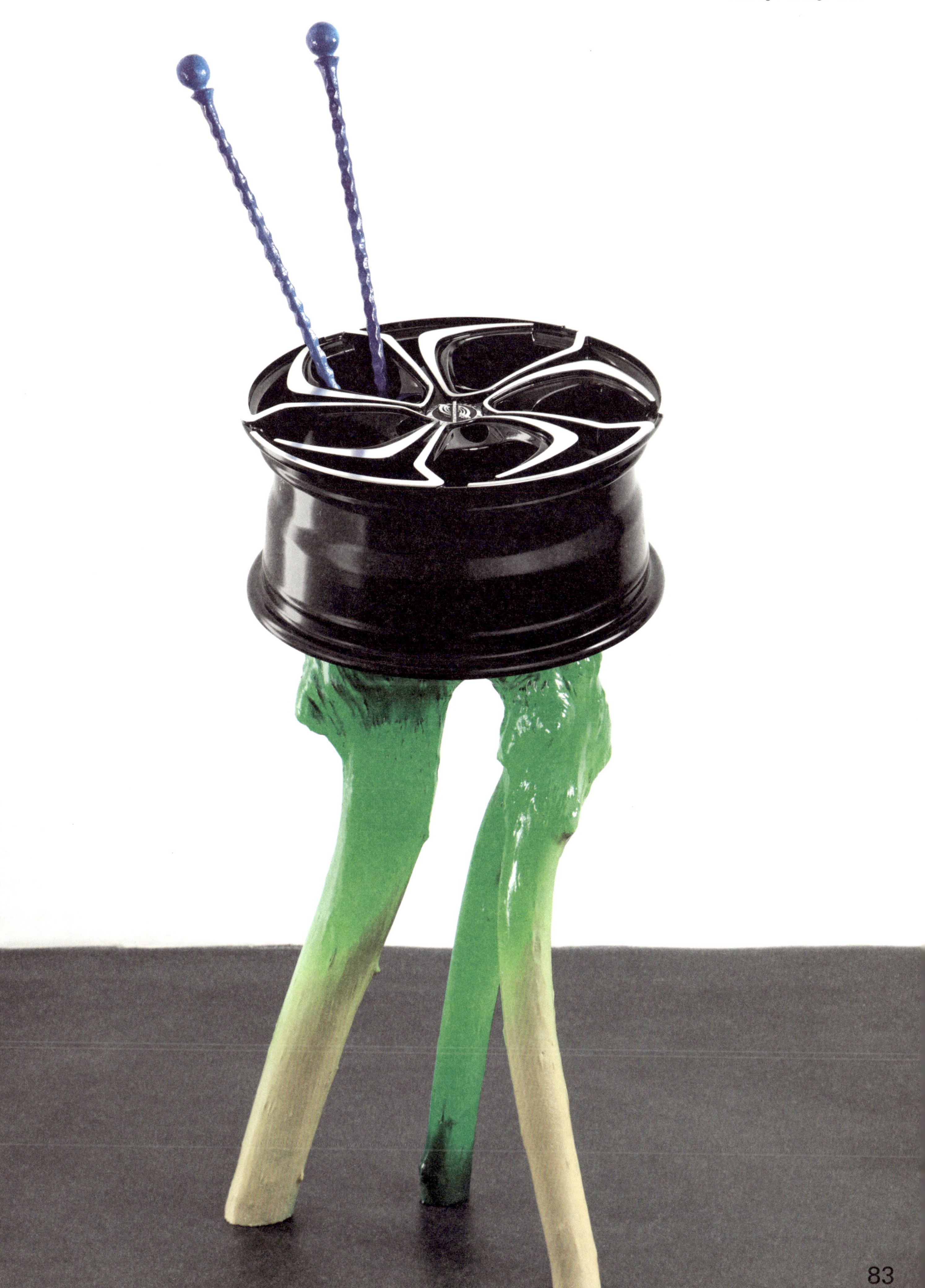

Hans Haacke

KALEIDOSCOPE: The Vanished Reality
12 November – 31 December 2016

Hans Haacke: *Works 1970-78*
19 November – 24 December 1978

I would like to start working in Oxford on Sunday, Nov. 12
in the afternoon. Unless I have difficulties in changing my
dates of departure (there was a misunderstanding, you set it
for Sunday) I shall take the night flight from Friday to Saturday and either recover from the ordeal in London or come
straight to Oxford. I shall let you know in time.

Best regards to you and David and the whole crew

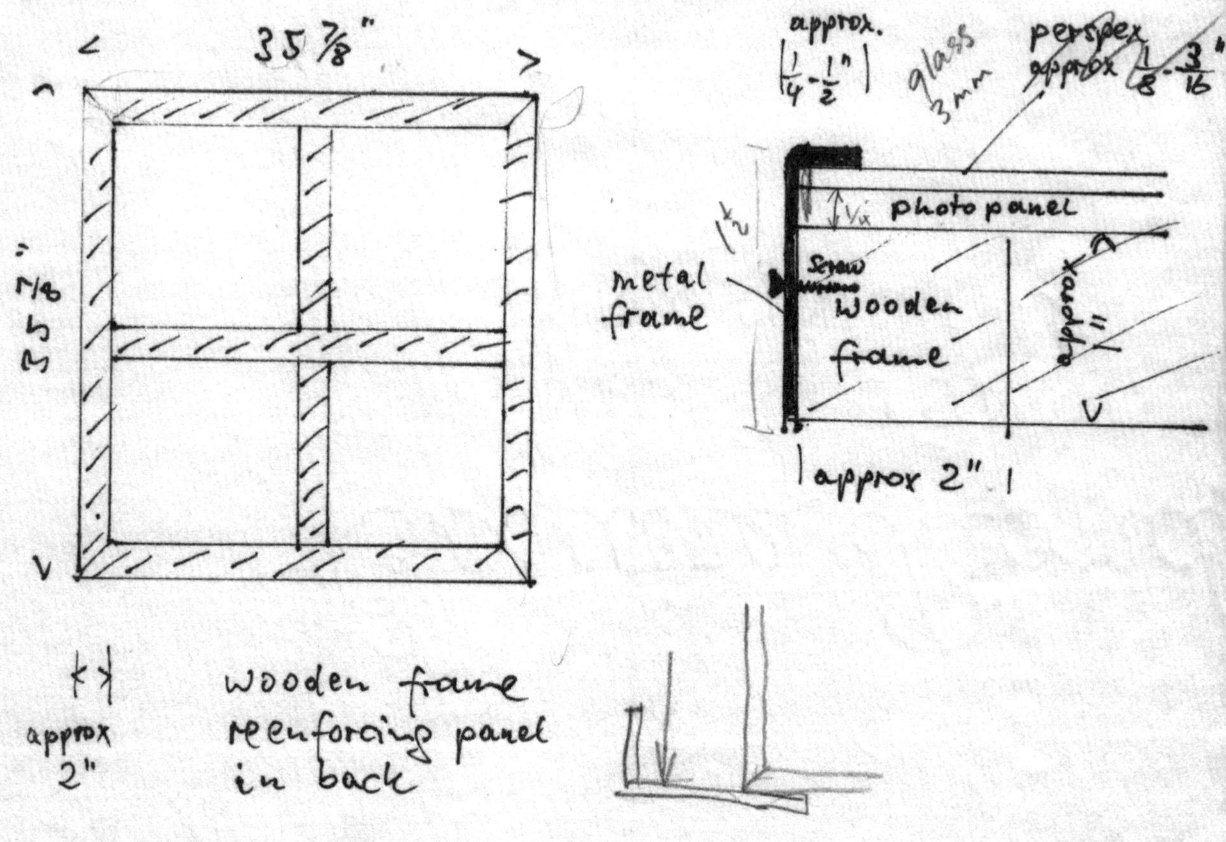

A Breed Apart exhibition drawings, 1978

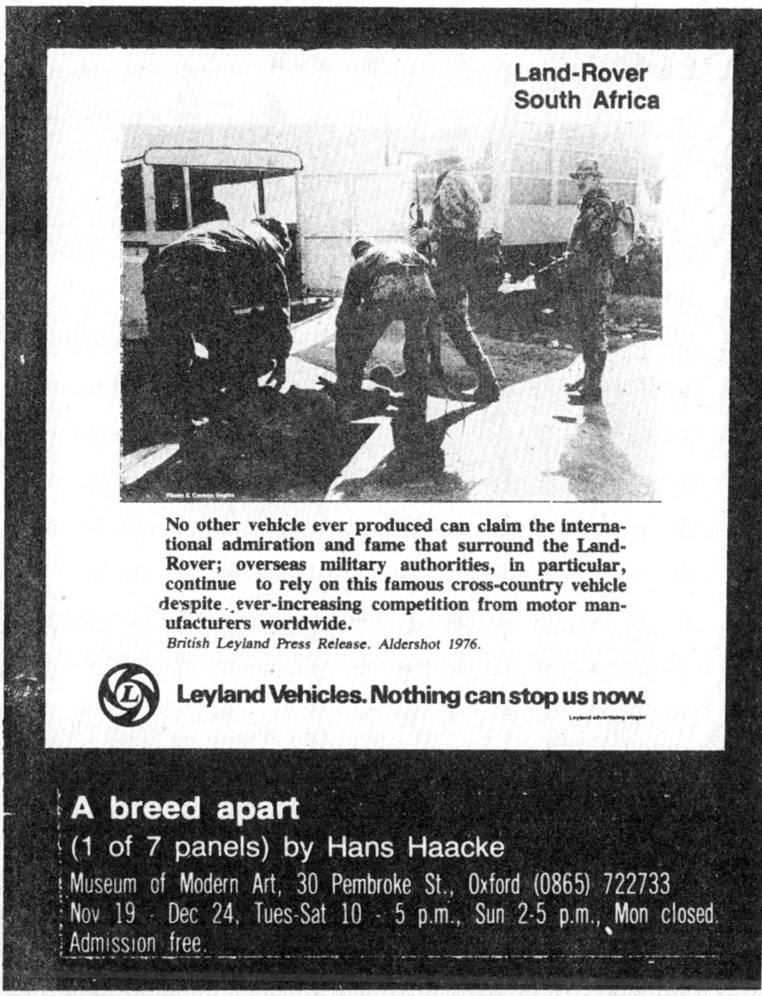

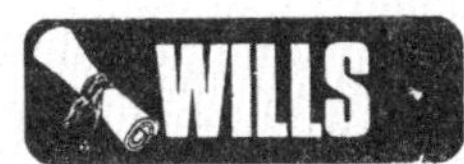

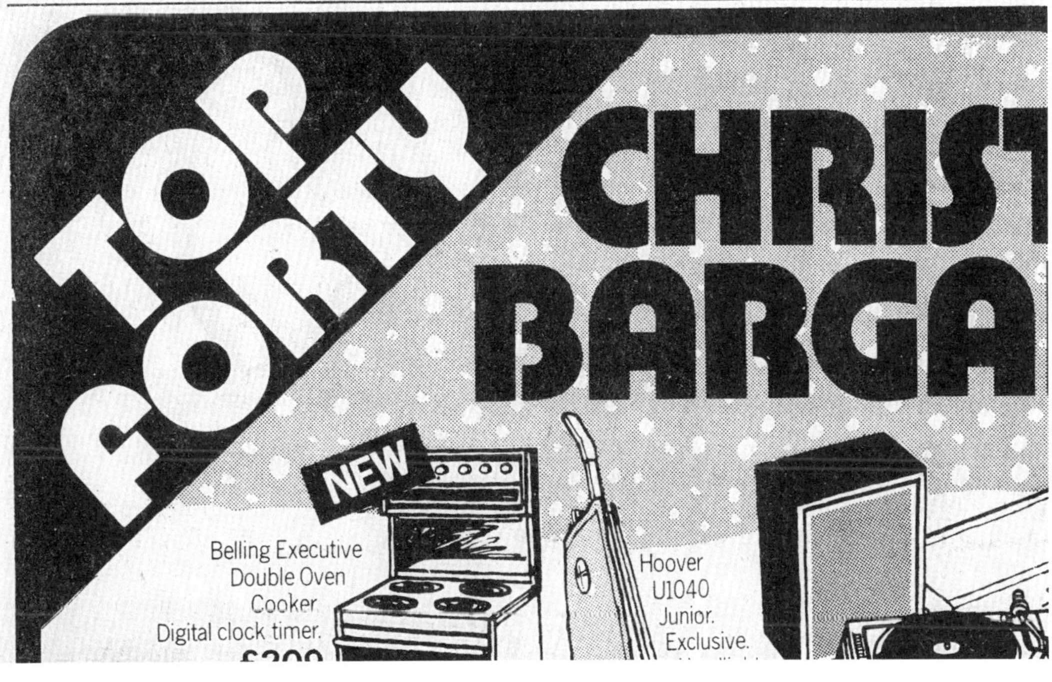

A Breed Apart newspaper advertisement, 1978

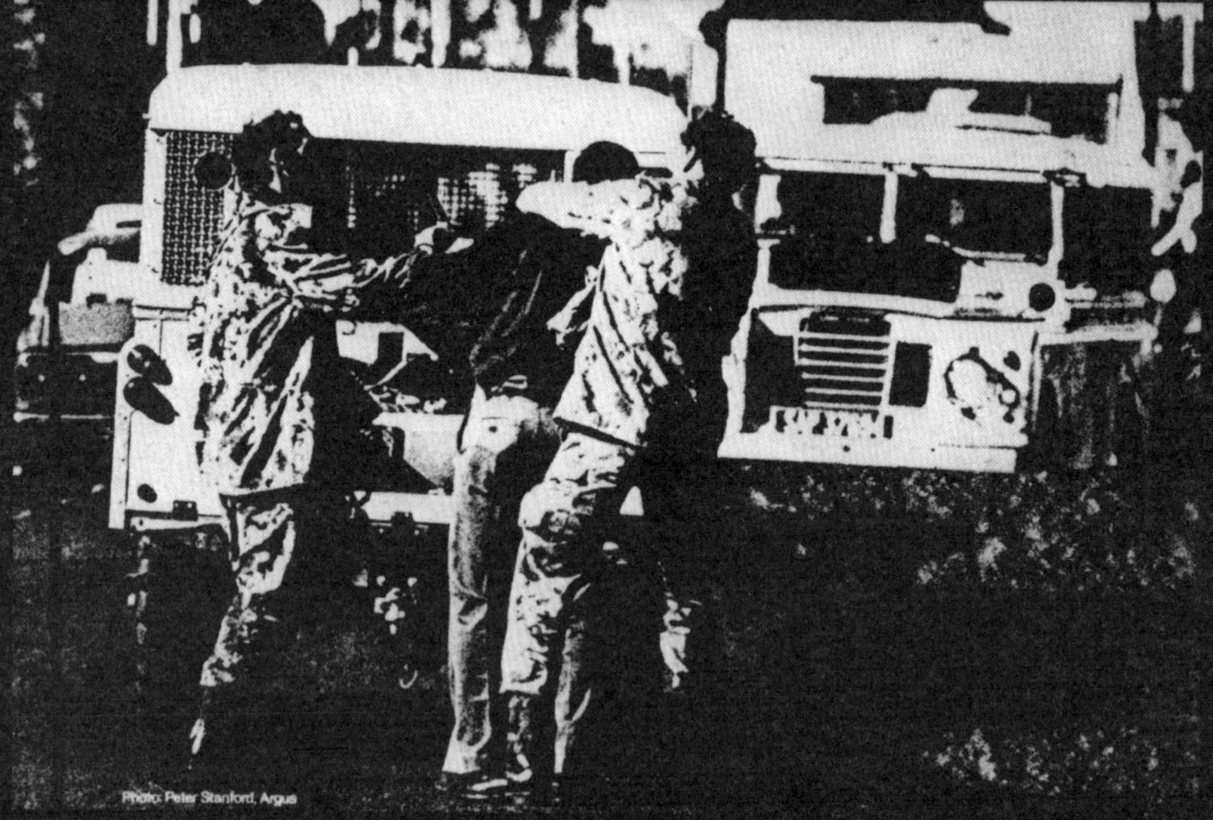

Hans Haacke, *A Breed Apart,* 2 of 7 panels, 1978

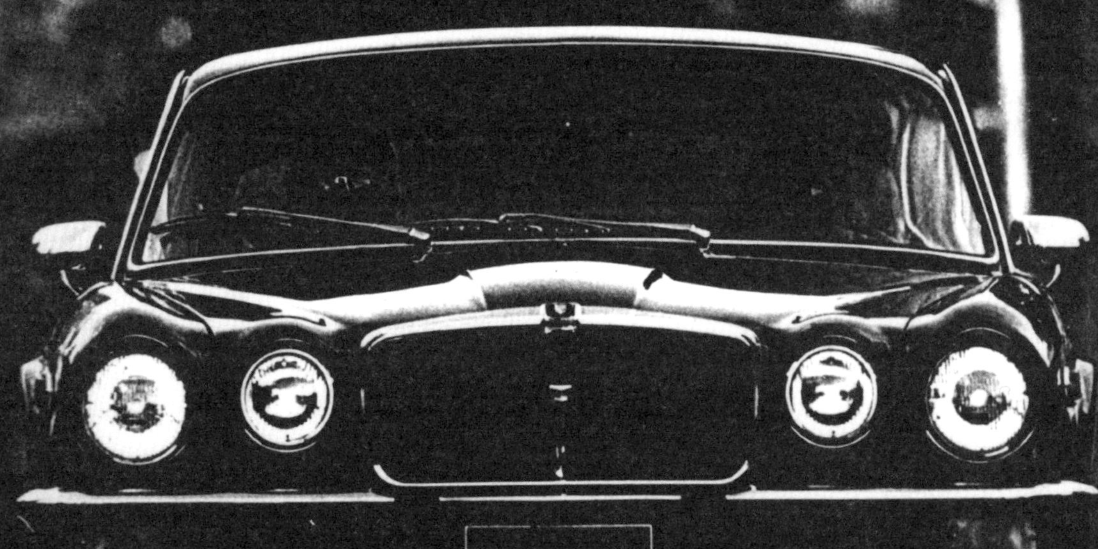

Jaguar, a breed apart. The new-generation Jaguar Executive has been born. And it has opened the door to a new world…a world that, because of its sophistication and sheer class, only a select few will enter.

It is a world that has been created for the leader, not the pack. For those who have made it and stand apart from the masses. For those whose success demands, and deserves, a quality of life that spells luxury, elegance, perfection.

Leyland South Africa

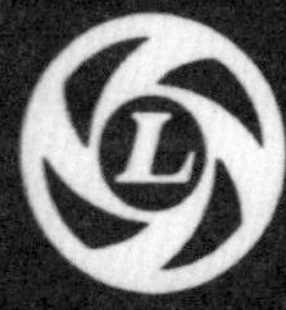

Mona Hatoum

KALEIDOSCOPE Live: lecture by Bridget Crone
2 June 2016

Mona Hatoum
5 April – 28 June 1998

MONA HATOUM

LIGHT SENTENCE / CORPS ETRANGER LAYOUT.

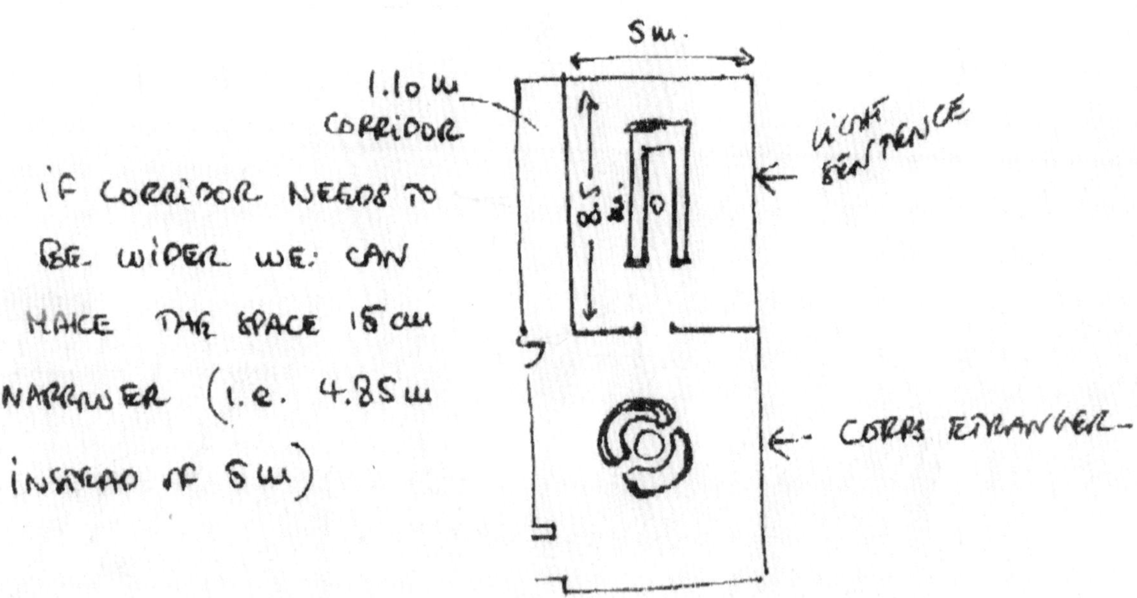

IF CORRIDOR NEEDS TO
BE WIDER WE CAN
MAKE THE SPACE 15 cm
NARROWER (i.e. 4.85 m
INSTEAD OF 5 m)

OTHER THINGS TO THINK ABOUT:

— ARE WE SHOWING THE VIDEOS ON PAL UMATIC
OR VHS?

— WILL IT BE ONE COMBINATION OF ALL 3
ON ONE MONITOR OR TWO MONITORS
AT EITHER ENDS OF THE ROOM.

— IN CHICAGO WE USED A PERSPEX SHEET
OVER HIGH RELIEF JUST SCREWED TO WALL (17.5 × 20")
DO WE WANT TO DO THE SAME HERE?

* Mona Hatoum *

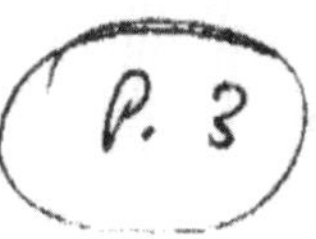

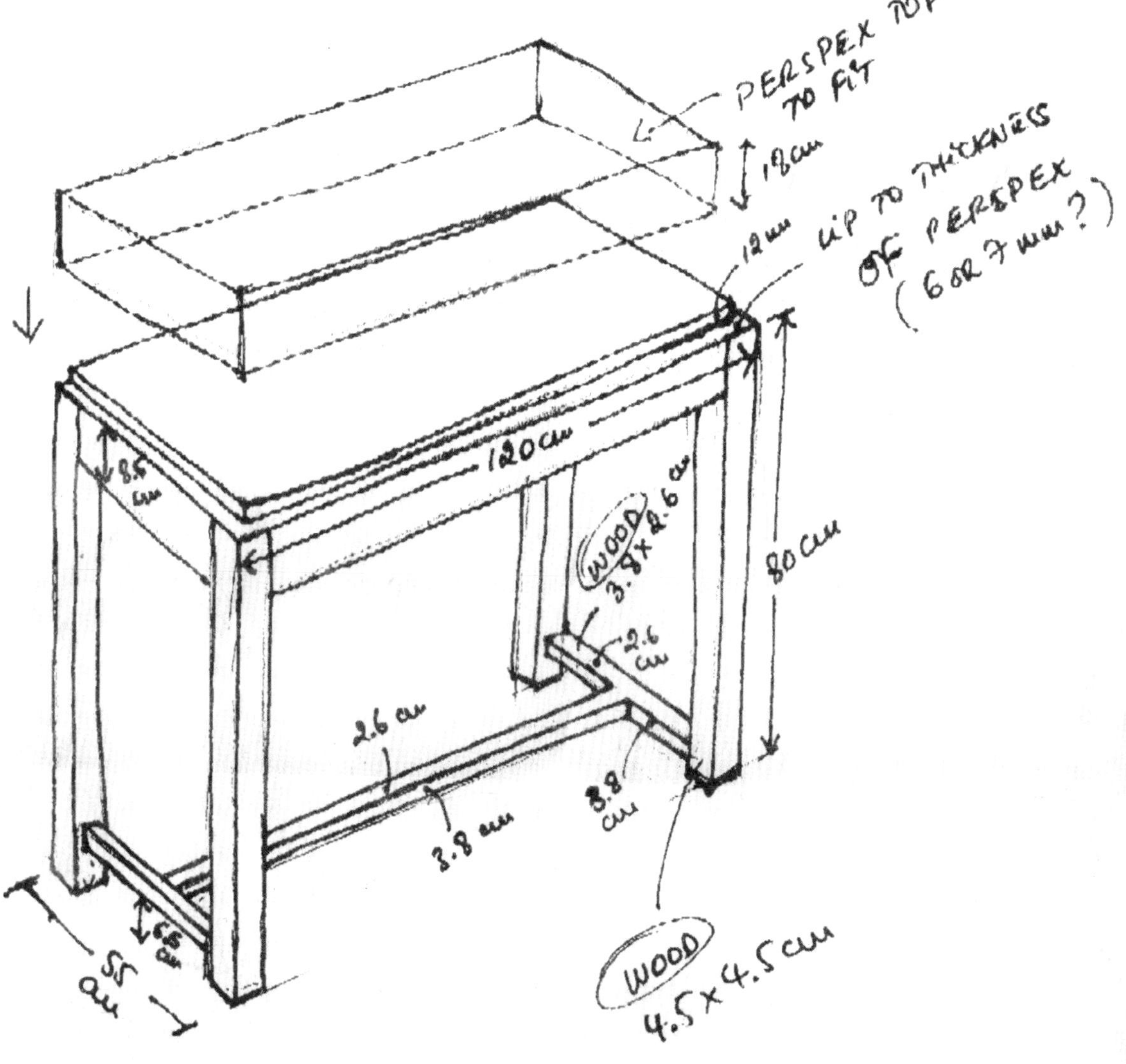

Faxed installation drawing, 1997

Mona Hatoum, Museum of Modern Art Oxford, 1998

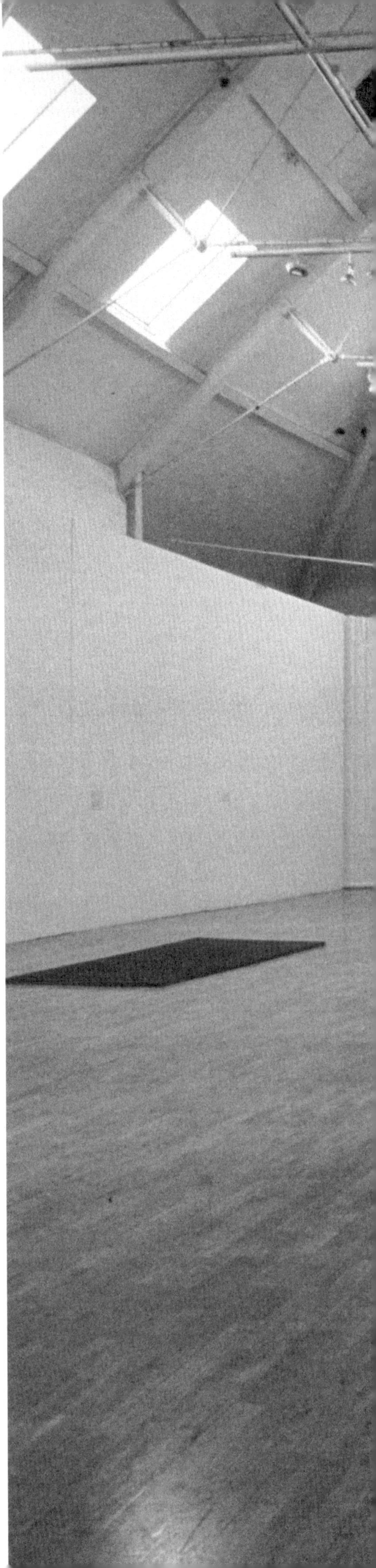

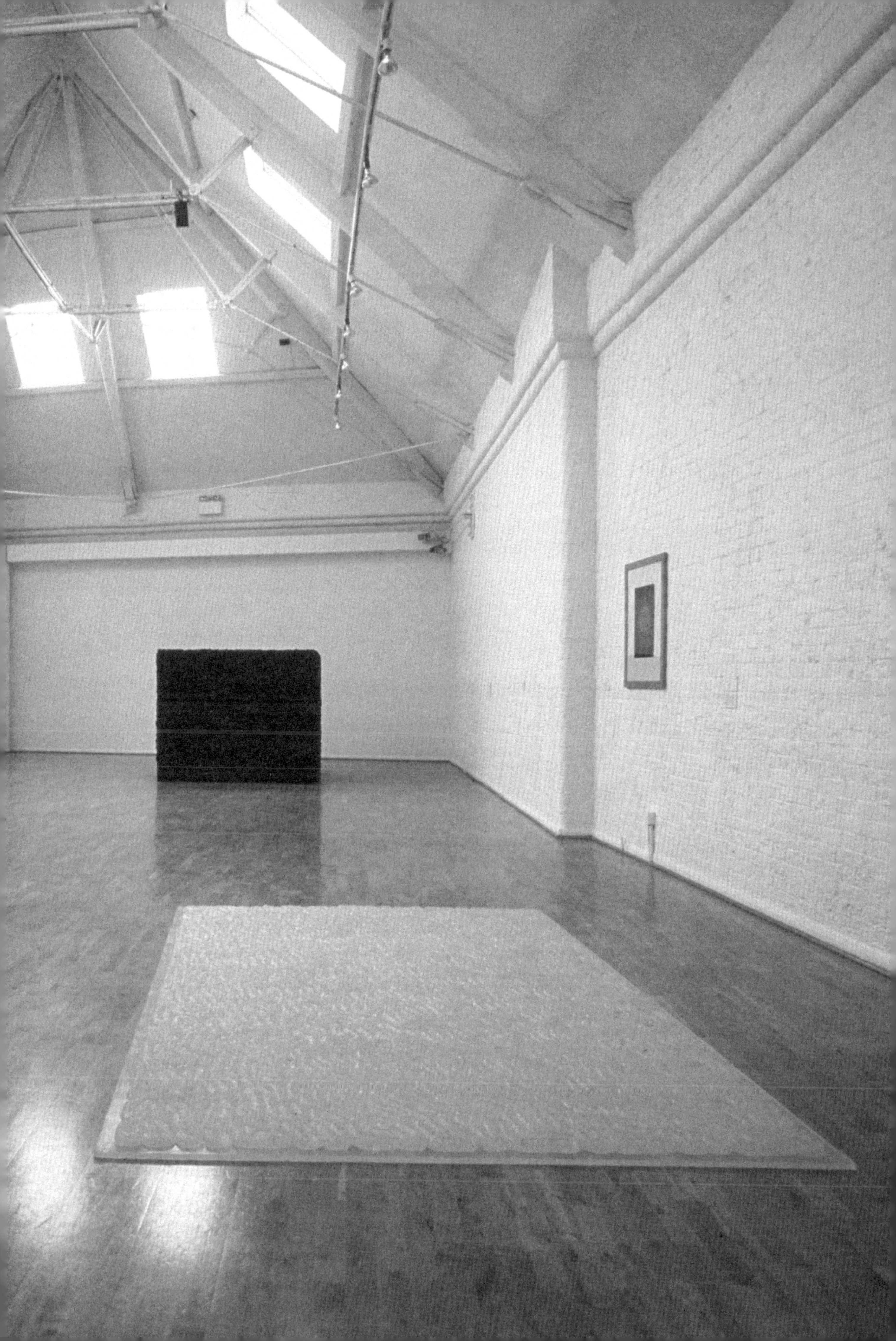

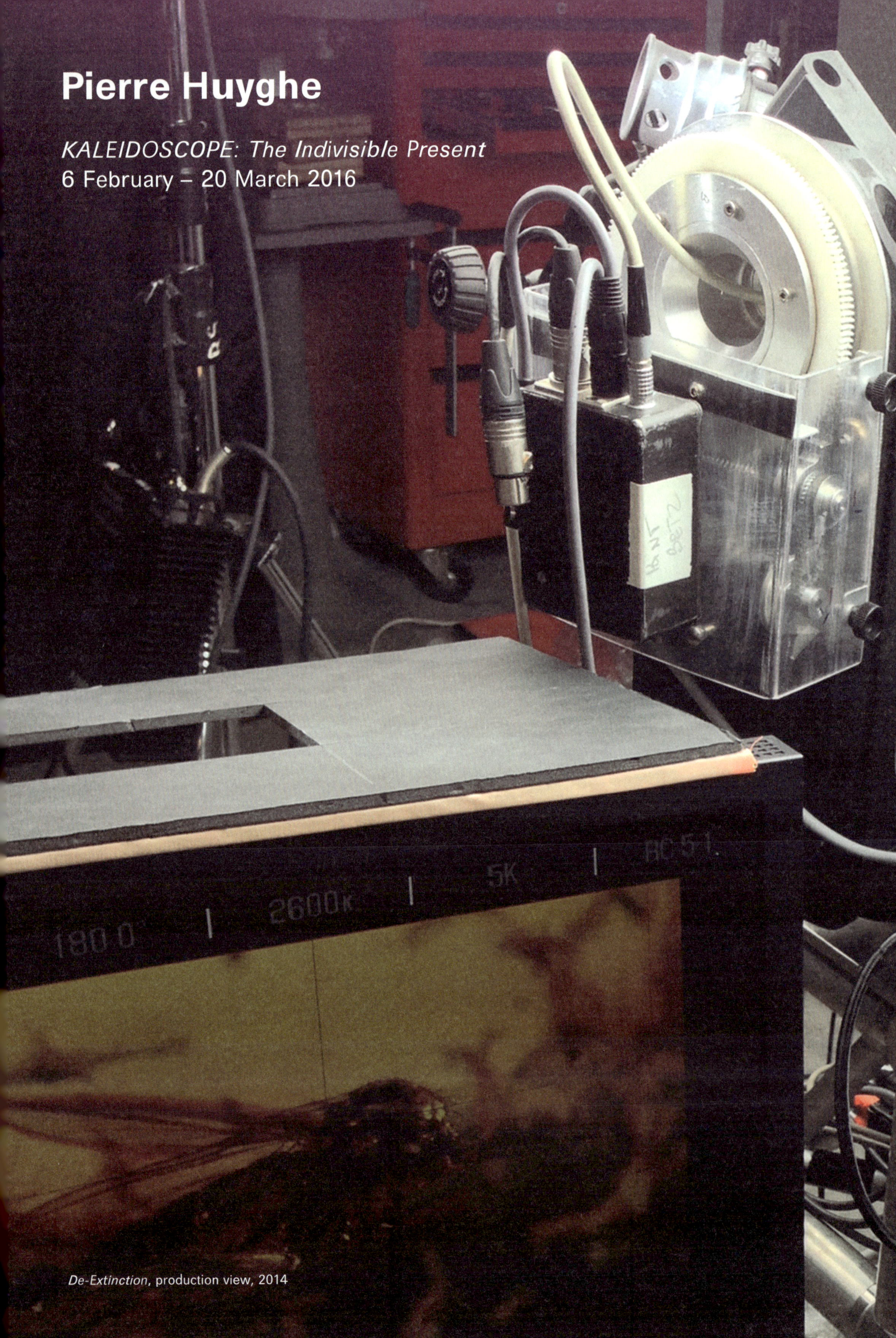

De-Extinction, production view, 2014

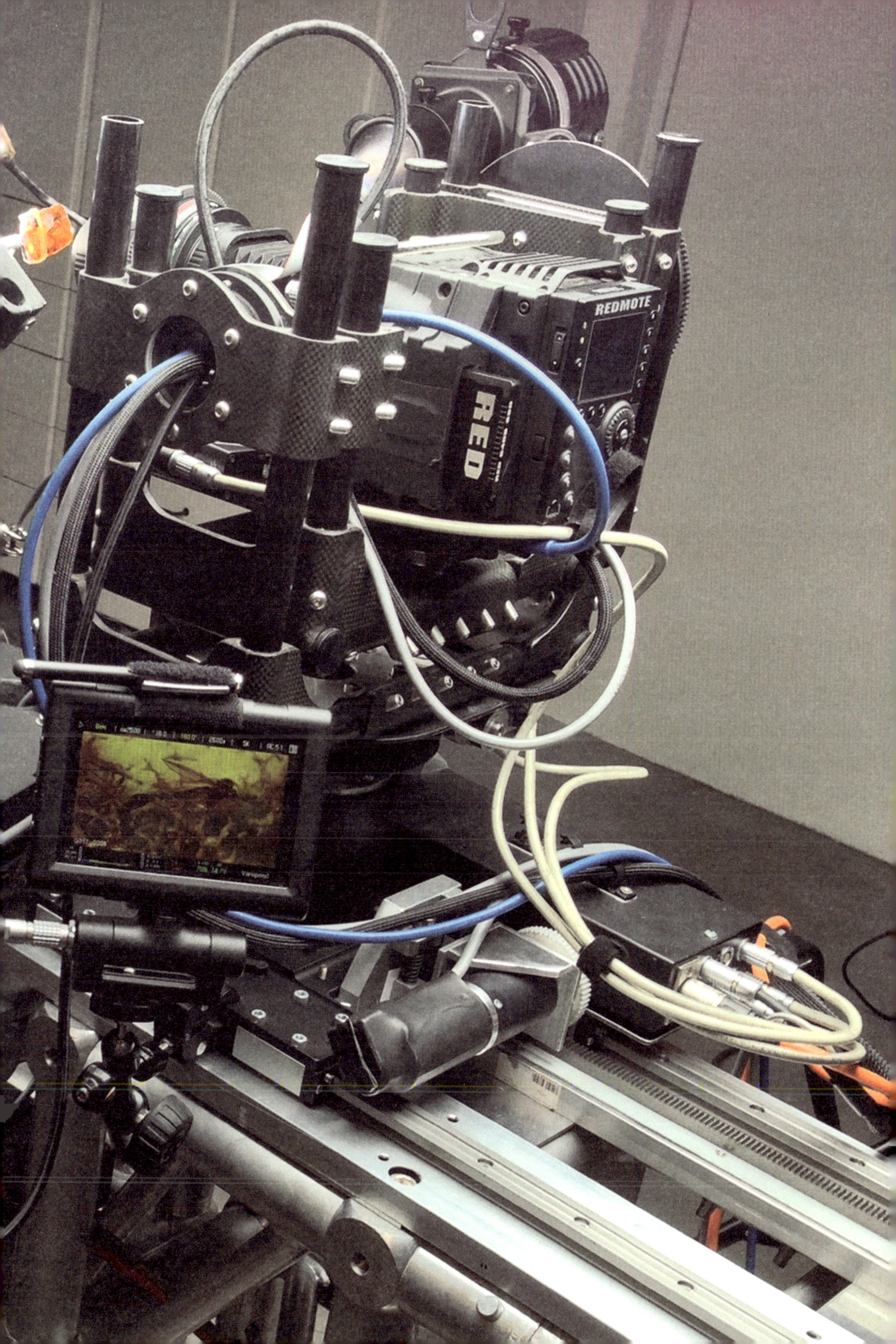

REDMOTE
RED

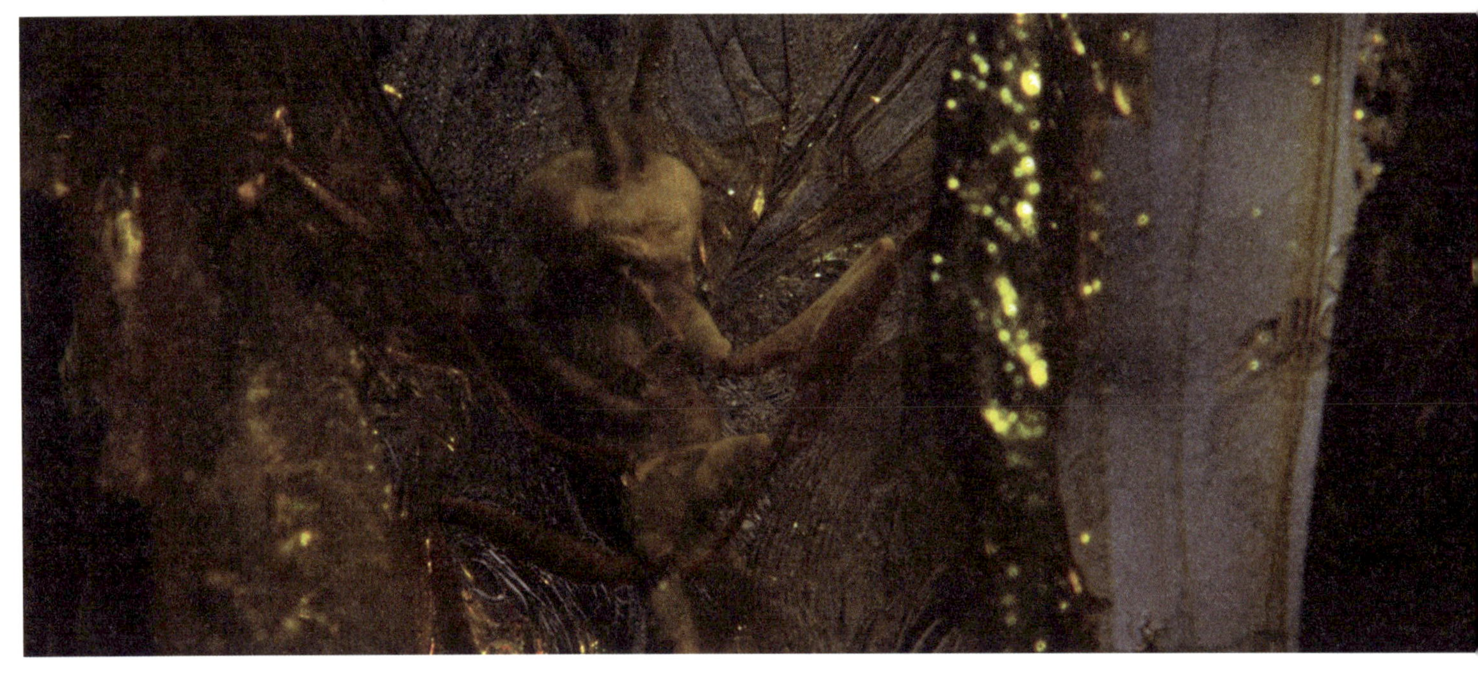

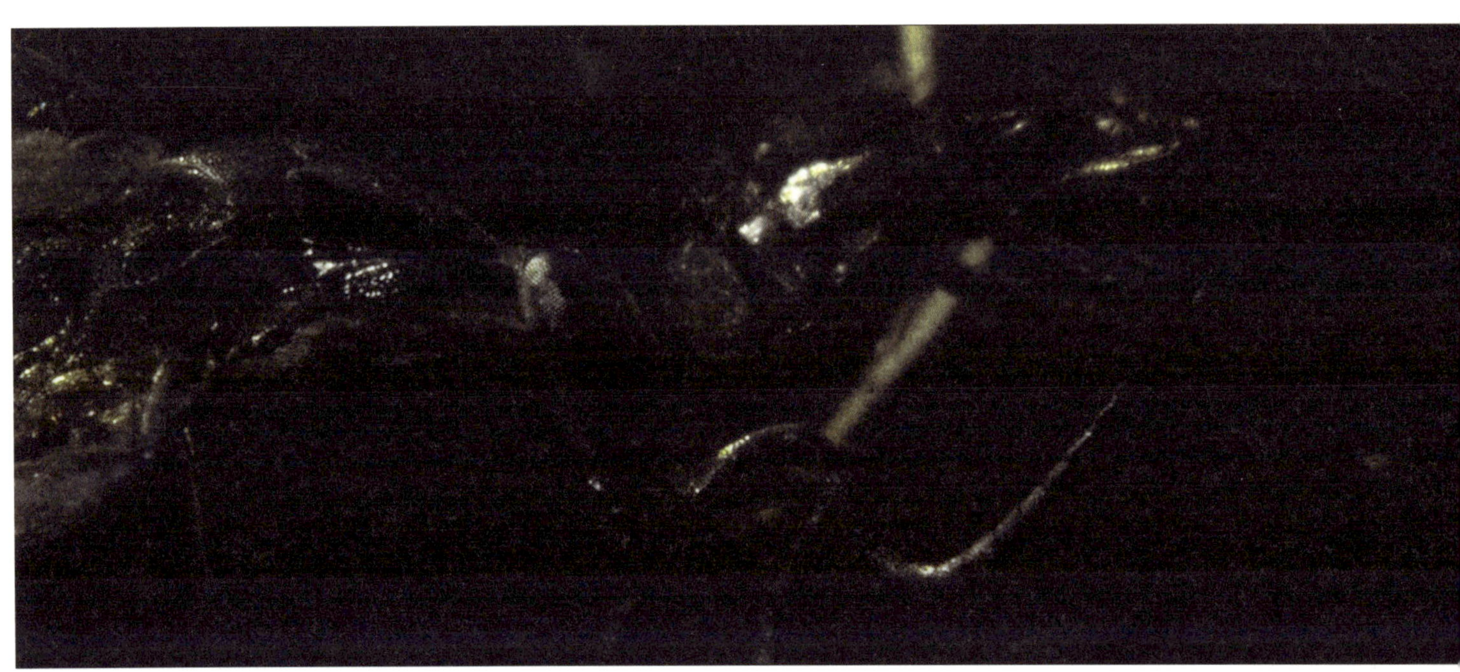

Pierre Huyghe, *De-Extinction,* film stills, 2014

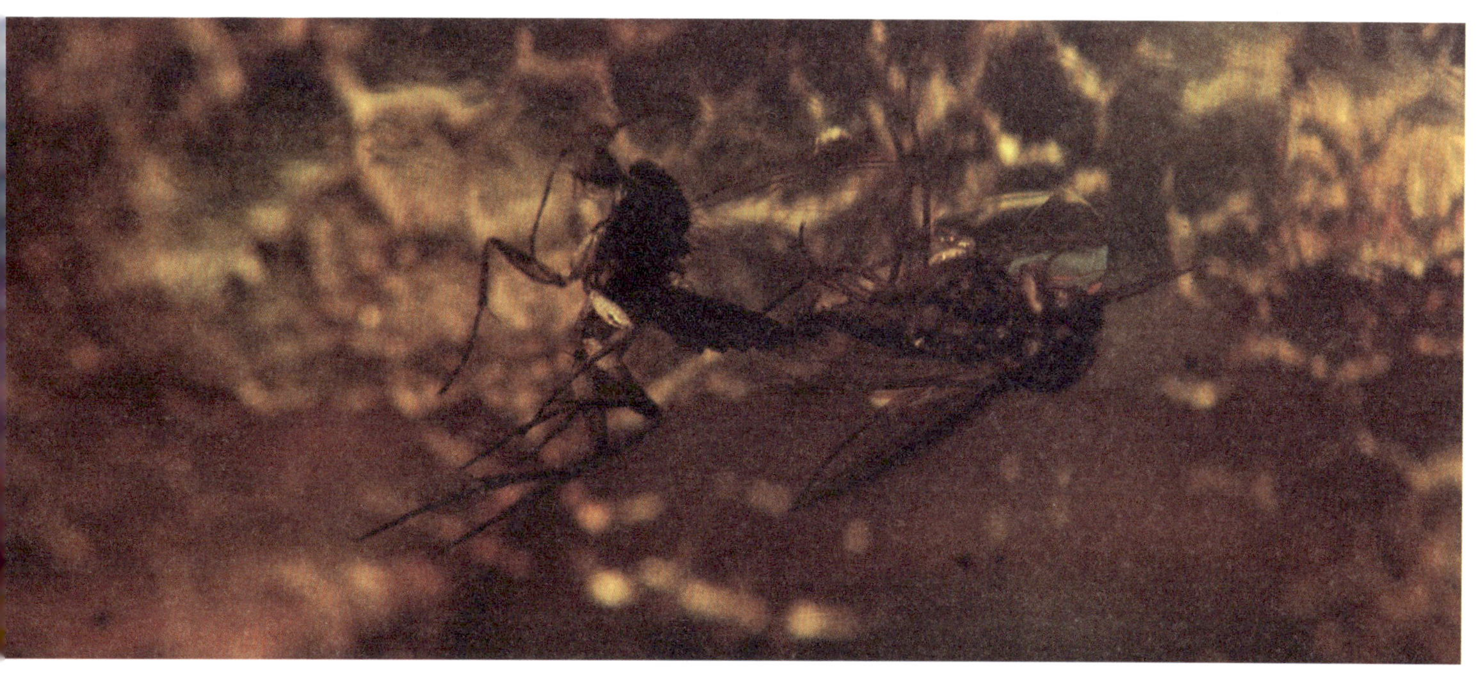

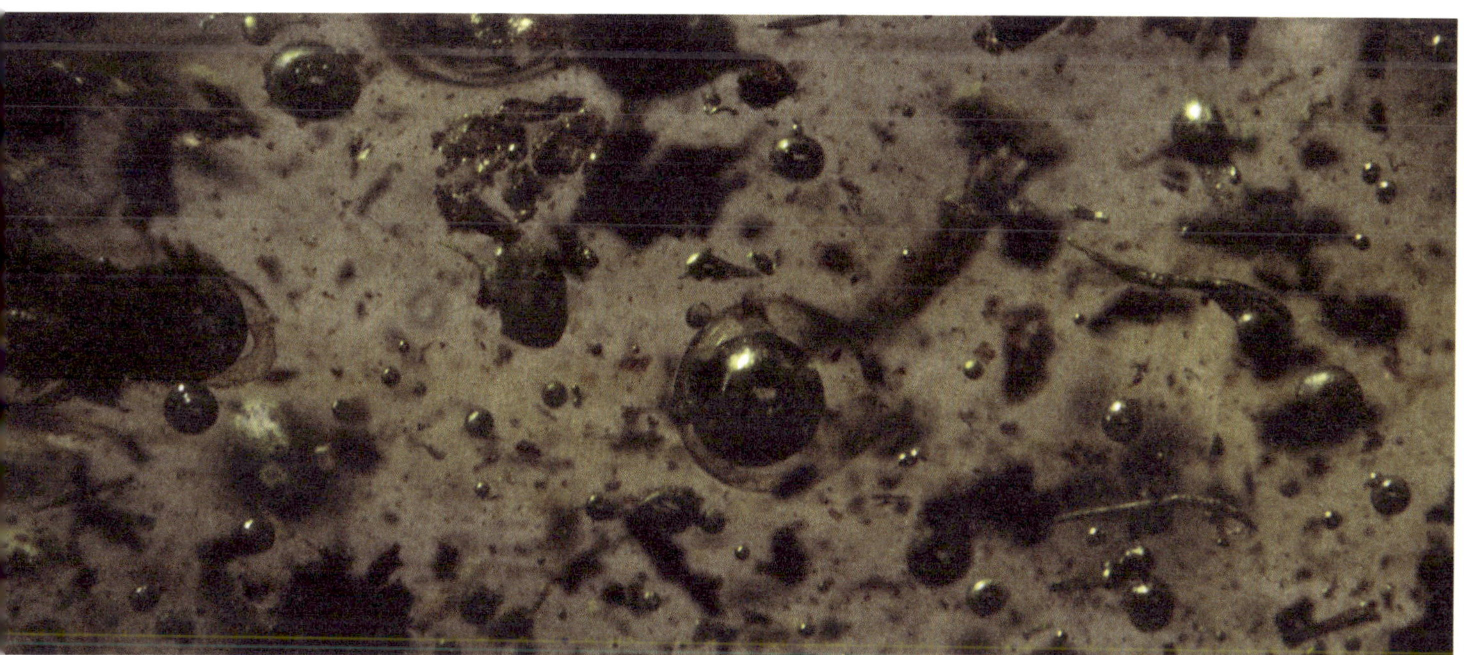

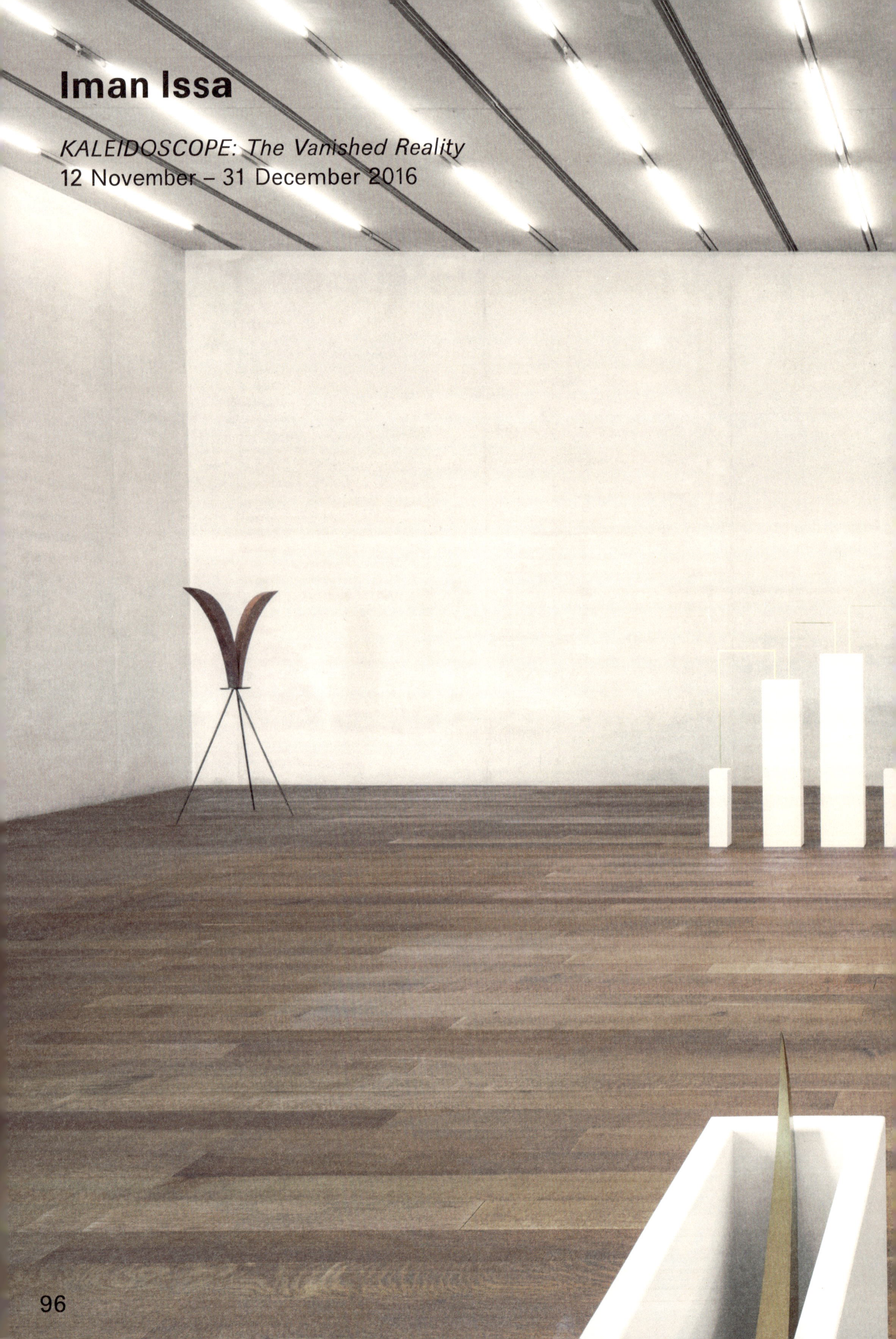

Iman Issa

KALEIDOSCOPE: The Vanished Reality
12 November – 31 December 2016

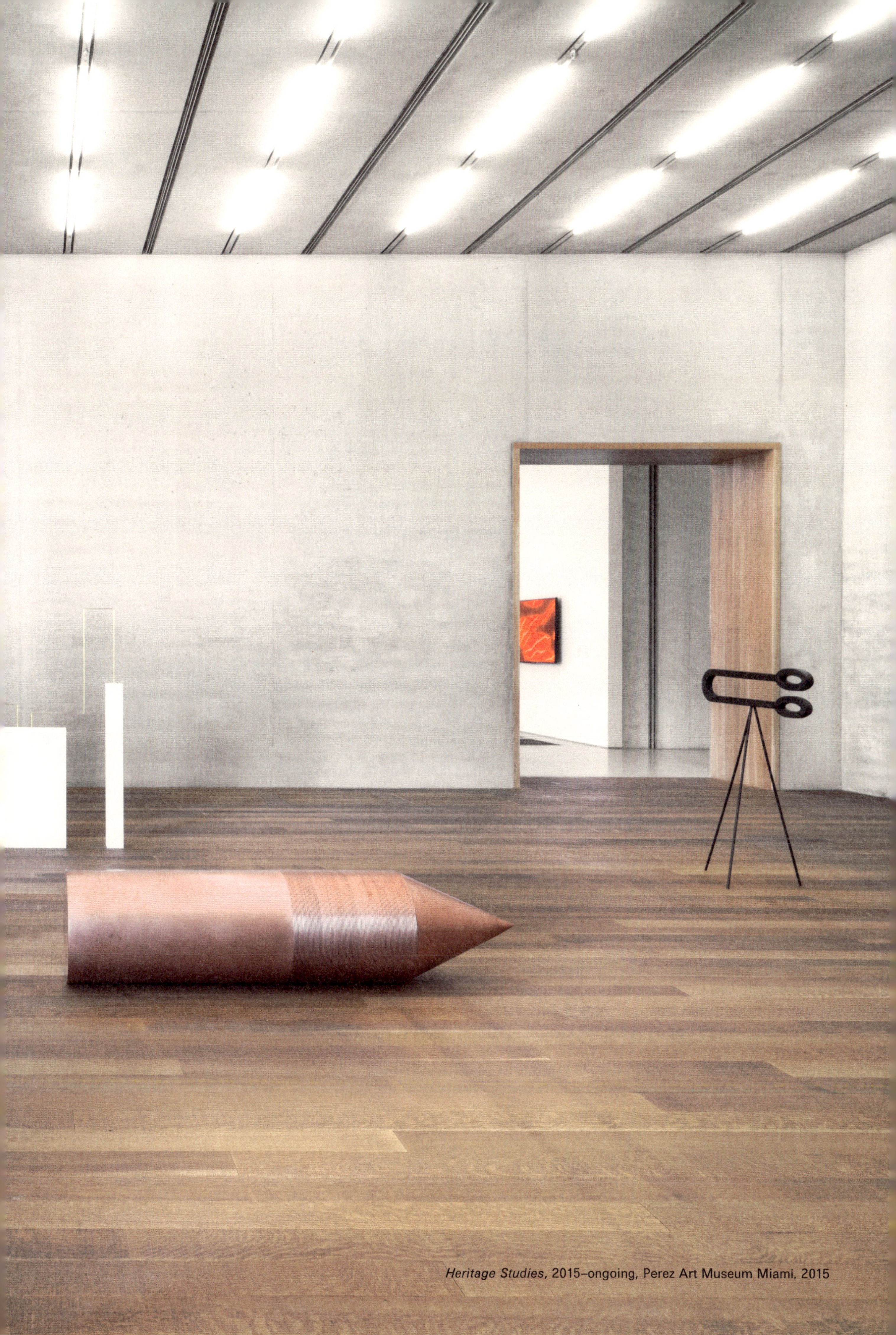

Heritage Studies, 2015–ongoing, Perez Art Museum Miami, 2015

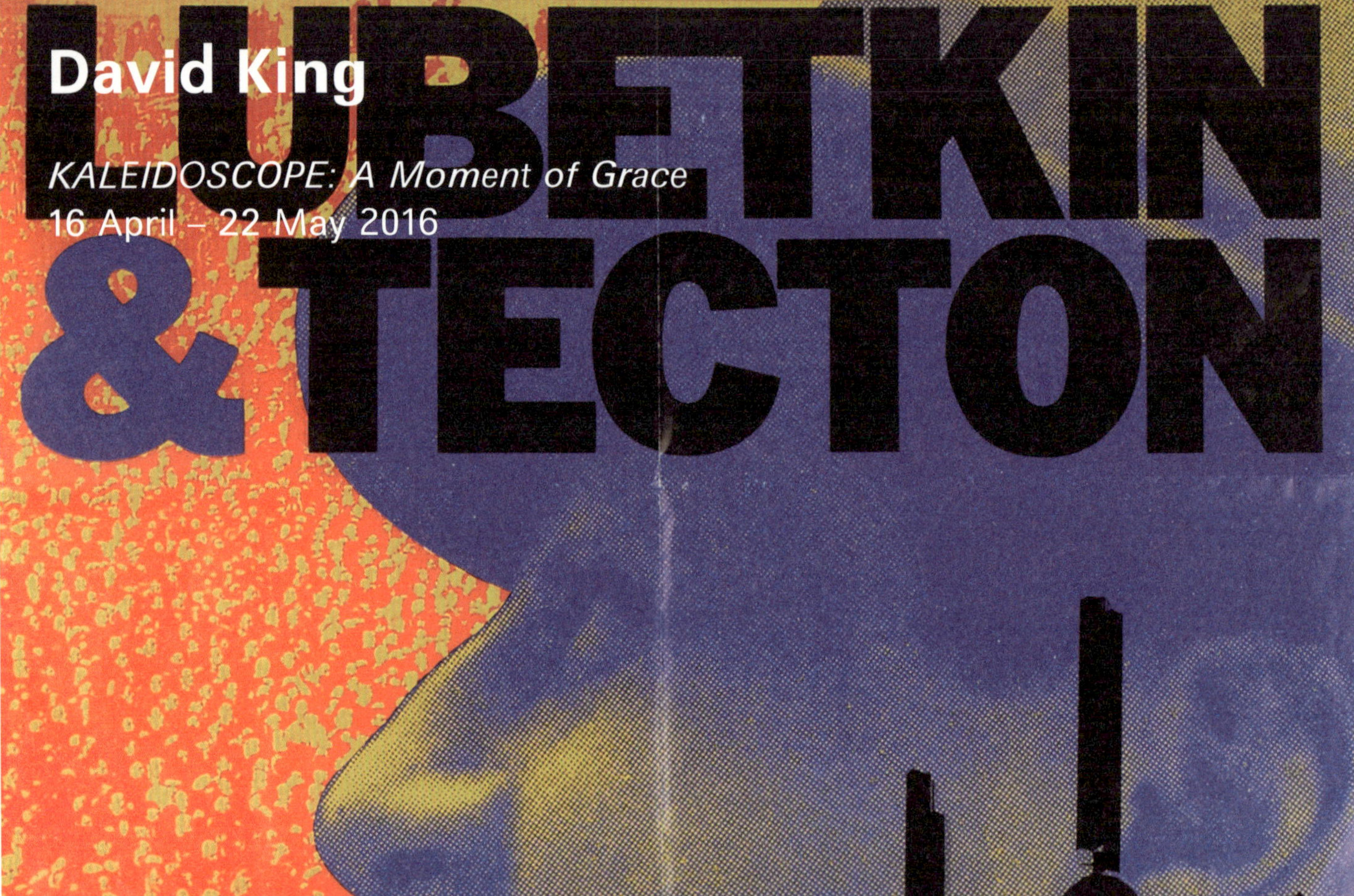

Lubetkin and Tecton: Architecture and Social Commitment poster, 1982

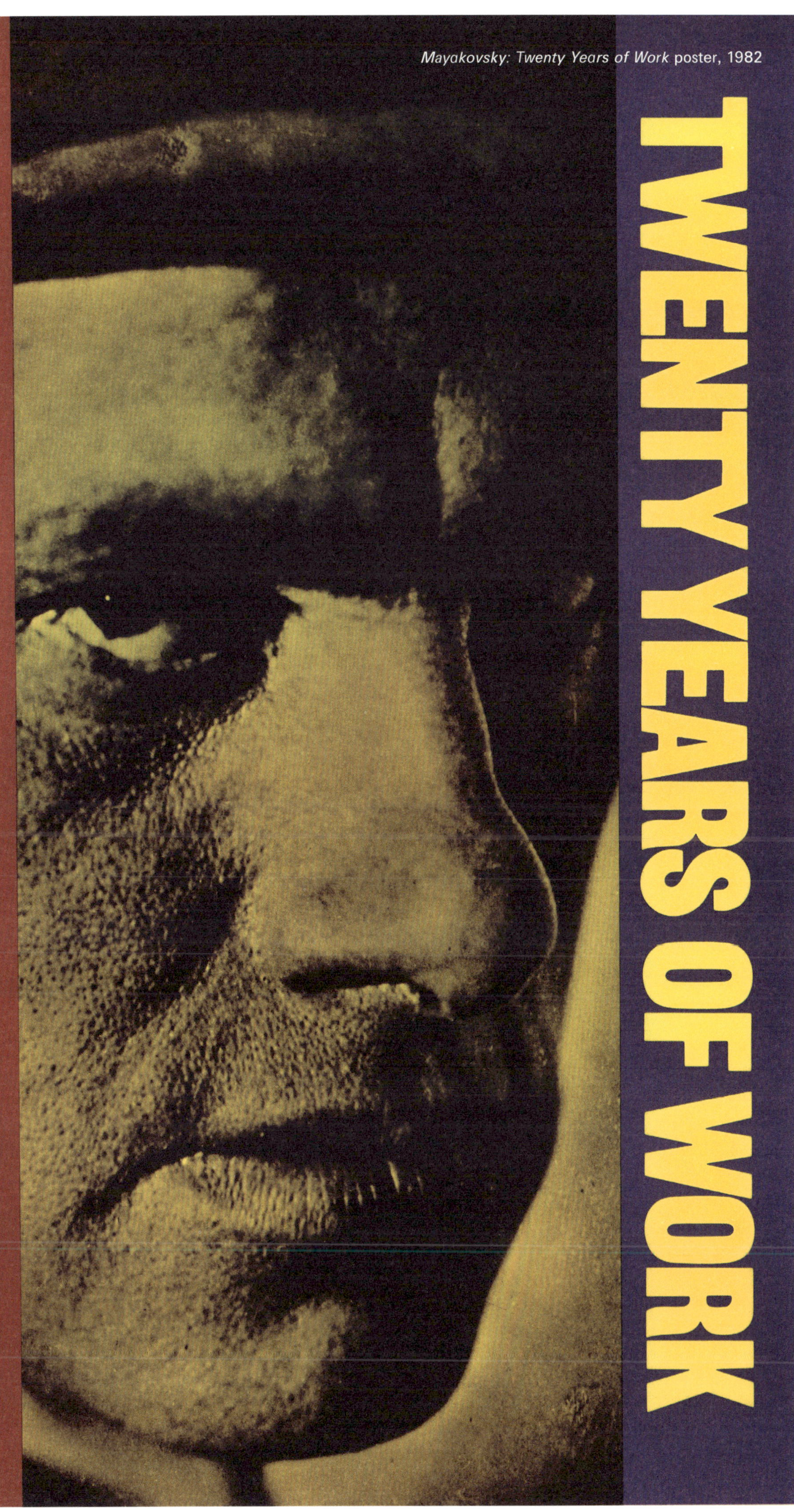

Mayakovsky: Twenty Years of Work poster, 1982

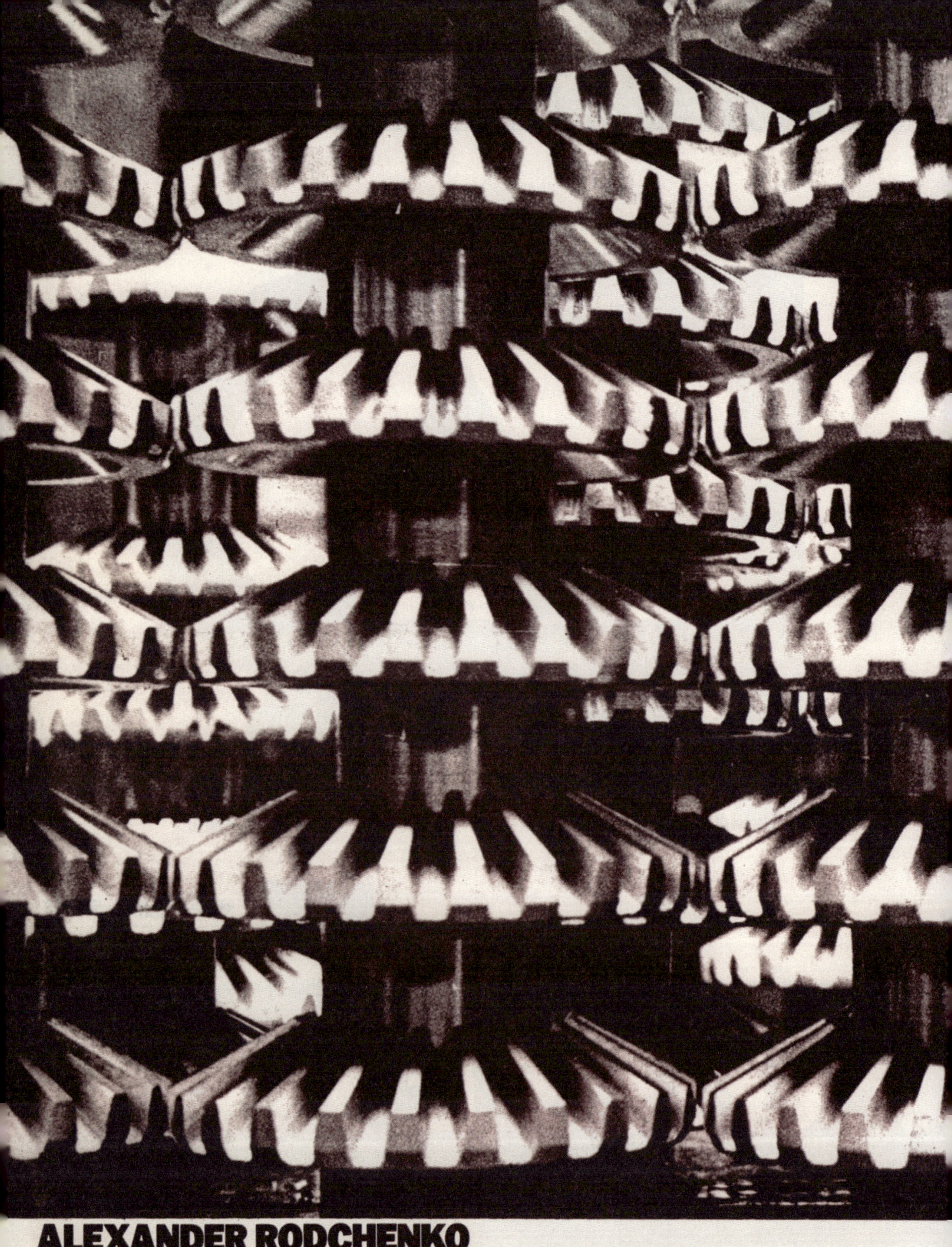

ALEXANDER RODCHENKO

EDITED BY DAVID ELLIOTT

David King, Alexander Rodchenko catalogue, 1979

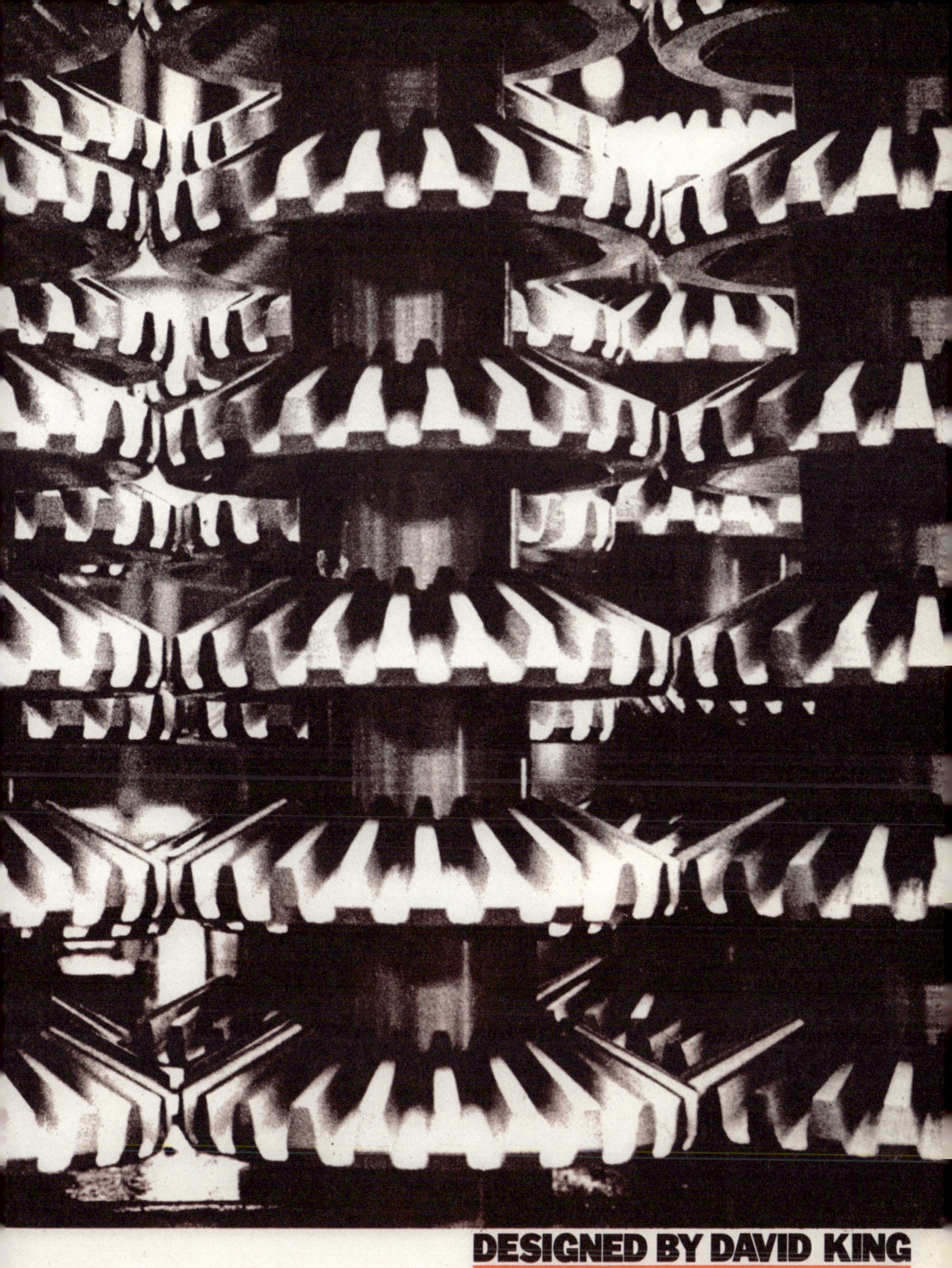
DESIGNED BY DAVID KING
MUSEUM OF MODERN ART OXFORD

Yayoi Kusama

KALEIDOSCOPE Live: lecture by Frances Morris
3 March 2016

Yayoi Kusama: *Soul Burning Flashes*
5 November 1989 – 7 January 1990

Handwritten list of works, 1989

YAYOI KUSAMA

MS CHRISSIE ILES

c/o The Museum of Modern Art of Oxford
30 Pembroke Street
Oxford OX1 1BP
England

Dear Ms Iles,

I am pleased to inform you that my private exhibition closed with a great success. Thank you most sincerely for the helpful support that you and your colleagues so kindly offered me in organizing my show.

I would be most appreciative if you would be so kind as to collect and send me tear sheets of the notices reporting on my exhibition that appeared in newspapers and magazines.

Thank you for your kind help.

Very sincerely,

yayoi Kusama

Letter from Yayoi Kusama to Chrissie Iles, undated

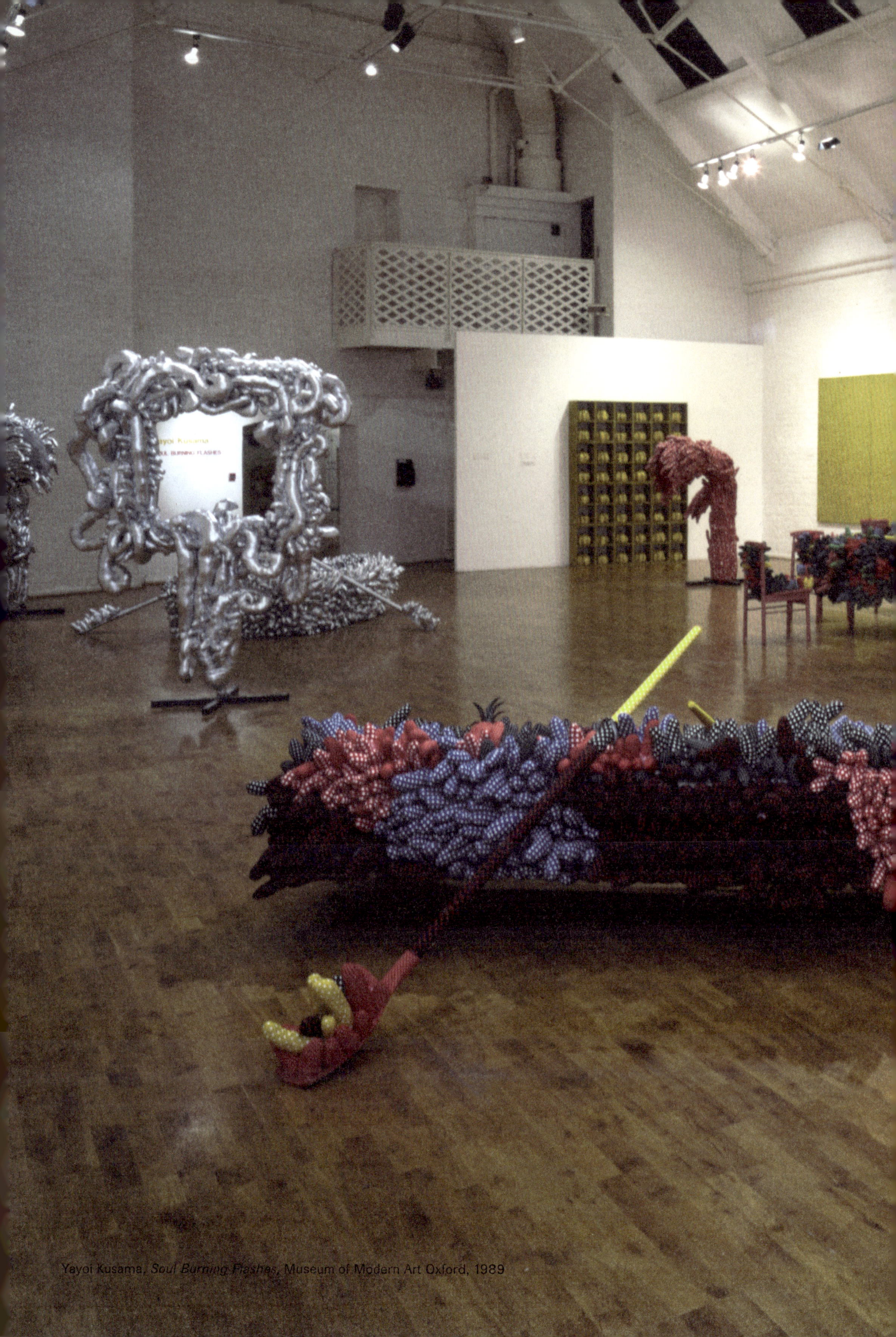

Yayoi Kusama, *Soul Burning Flashes*, Museum of Modern Art Oxford, 1989

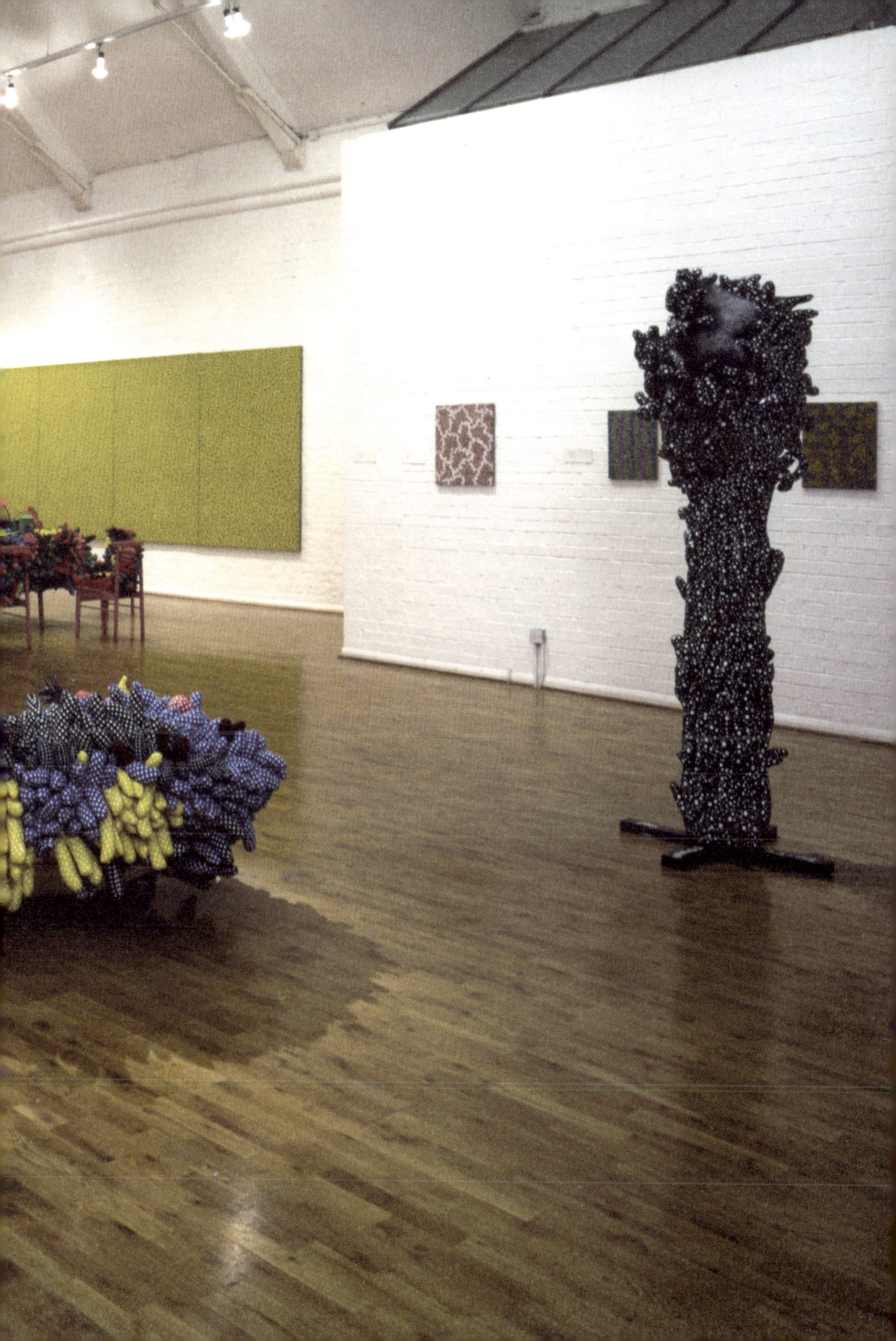

Darcy Lange

KALEIDOSCOPE: The Vanished Reality
12 November – 31 December 2016

Darcy Lange: *Work Studies in Schools*
22 March – 9 April 1977

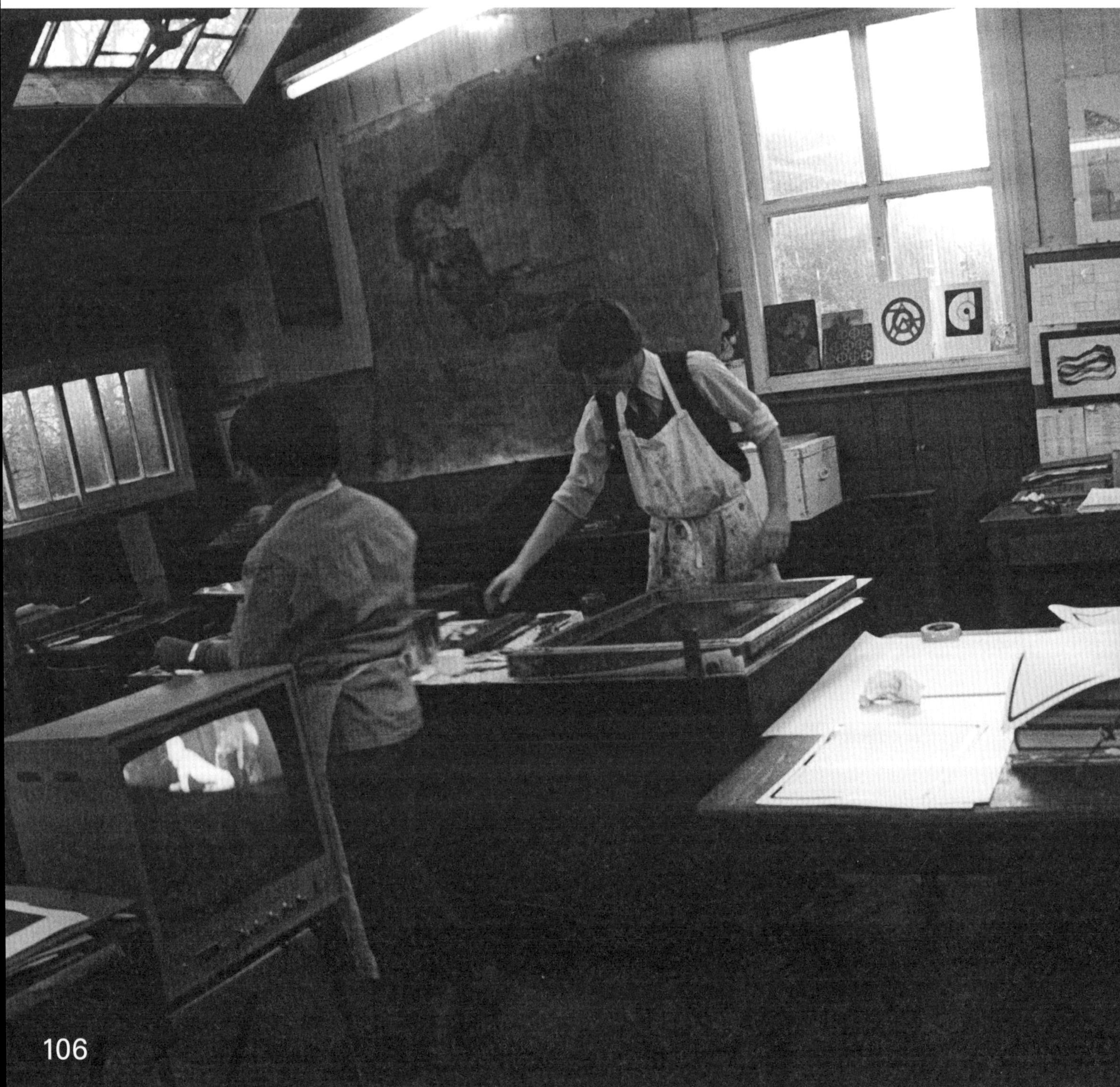

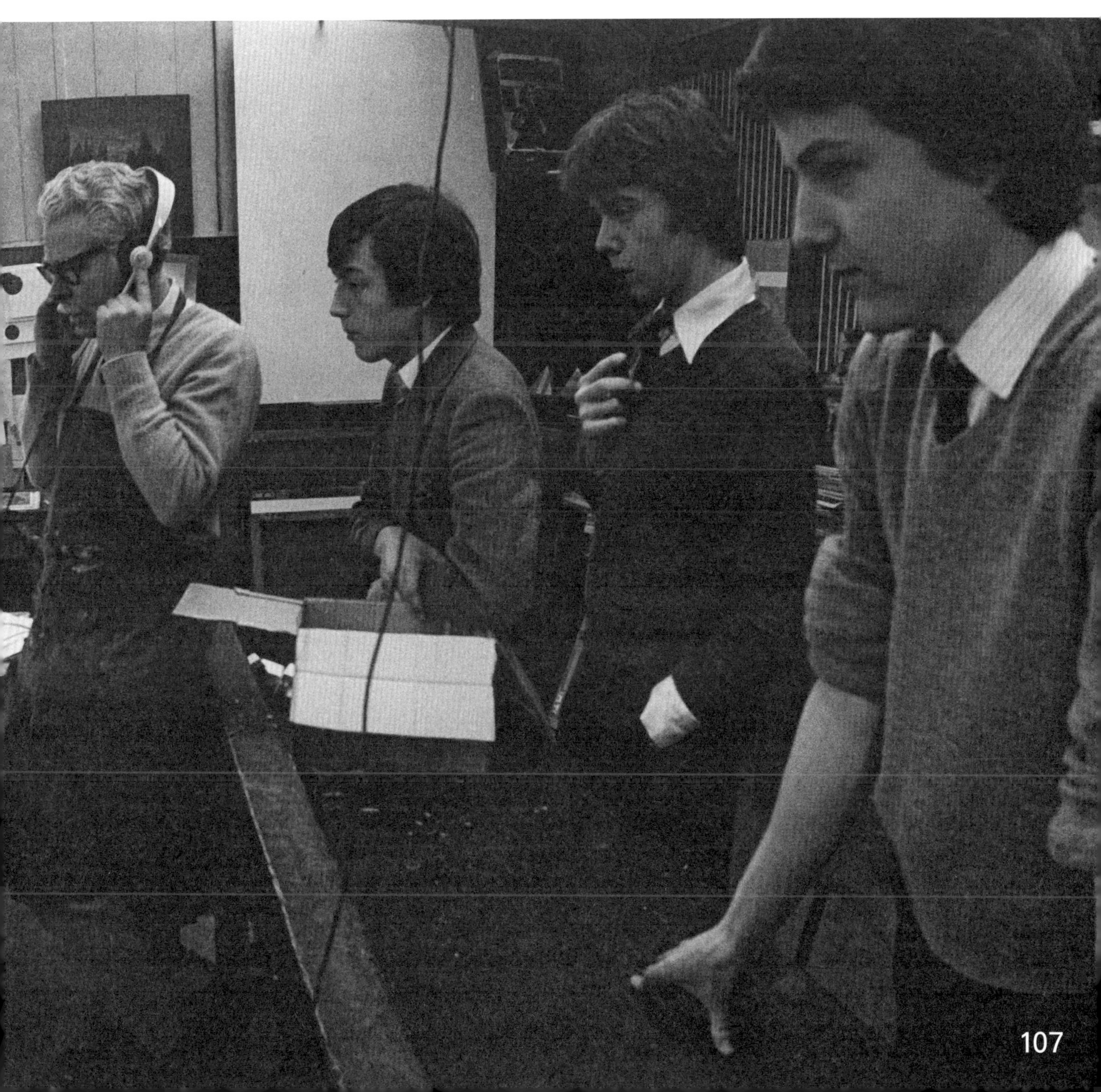

Studies of Teaching in Four Oxfordshire Schools, photographic still, 1977.
Charles Mussett and his students viewing the recording of the art class study

John Latham

KALEIDOSCOPE: The Indivisible Present
6 February – 20 March 2016

KALEIDOSCOPE: A Moment of Grace
16 April – 22 May 2016

John Latham: *Art After Physics*
13 October 1991 – 5 January 1992

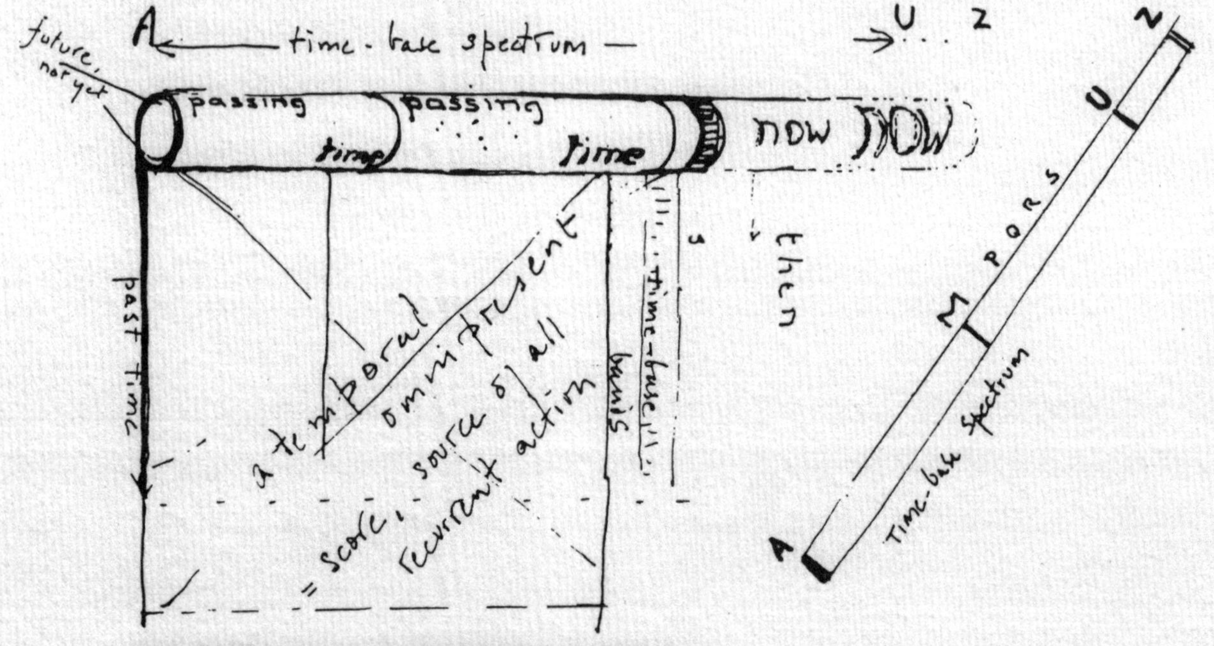

Government of the First and Thirteenth Chair performance invitation, 1991

to Chrissy Isles,
  MoMA, Oxford

29 Jan 91

Dear Chrissy

I have the feeling you need to get a notice out asap.
Can I suggest you quote this ...

... our future is in the hands of 3 institutions trying to propagate
an aspect of the world as the Big Truth. They originate at the same
point and follow the same early utterances. Each proclaims the Universe
to be a Person.   But they are each so barren of imagination that no
new idea has been added for 1400 years. In their terms of reference
and in those of the framework of science that they adopt, it has
become impossible to identify the dimensionality this Person inhabits.

     The rest of the world is disabled by other, equally insecure
institutions ...

Stuttgart ------------------------

   The press notice as translated seems to avoid reference to the
historic 20C point where everything coincides, and to this new
application. As far as I am in order suggesting what is to be made of
it, the work to date (to be represented in this exhibition) follows out
a logic from the point where modern art disappeared at a dimensionless
point along with literature and science. (Joyce 1941, Wittgenstein 1915
and 1951, Einstein 1915).

   What is to be found at this point?   The answer to that particular
one has beaten writers into their cocked hats.   I shift a basic
premise, from "object" to "event". When this is done the primitive
unit becomes an event, ie. an oscillation between Nothing and Not-
Nothing (see T-BDI 1975). When it is found that the mechanics of
objects in space is contra to event structure language based on that
dualised framework is placed in serious trouble; "person" is in a
category incompatible with "object".

   The idea of events as structured on a single principle seems obvious
enough. But it entails a different concept of order, having no literary
or scientific record. IT IS THIS THAT I AM POINTING OUT IN WRITTEN
PAPERS. Surely Oxford is able to cope with the proposition.?

   With the idea accepted, "marks and noises" precede writing and
words. A Least Mark precedes "drawing", and a Least Event precedes
mass/energy, space, subject-predicate grammar, anthropomorphism, common
sense perception. The result is a principle and dimensional framework
that describes person and that I have called Event Structure.
Perhaps the solution is too simple but let's have it out there.

? fotos any good?

best   *John*

john latham
210 bellenden road
london se15 4bw
tel: 01-639 3597

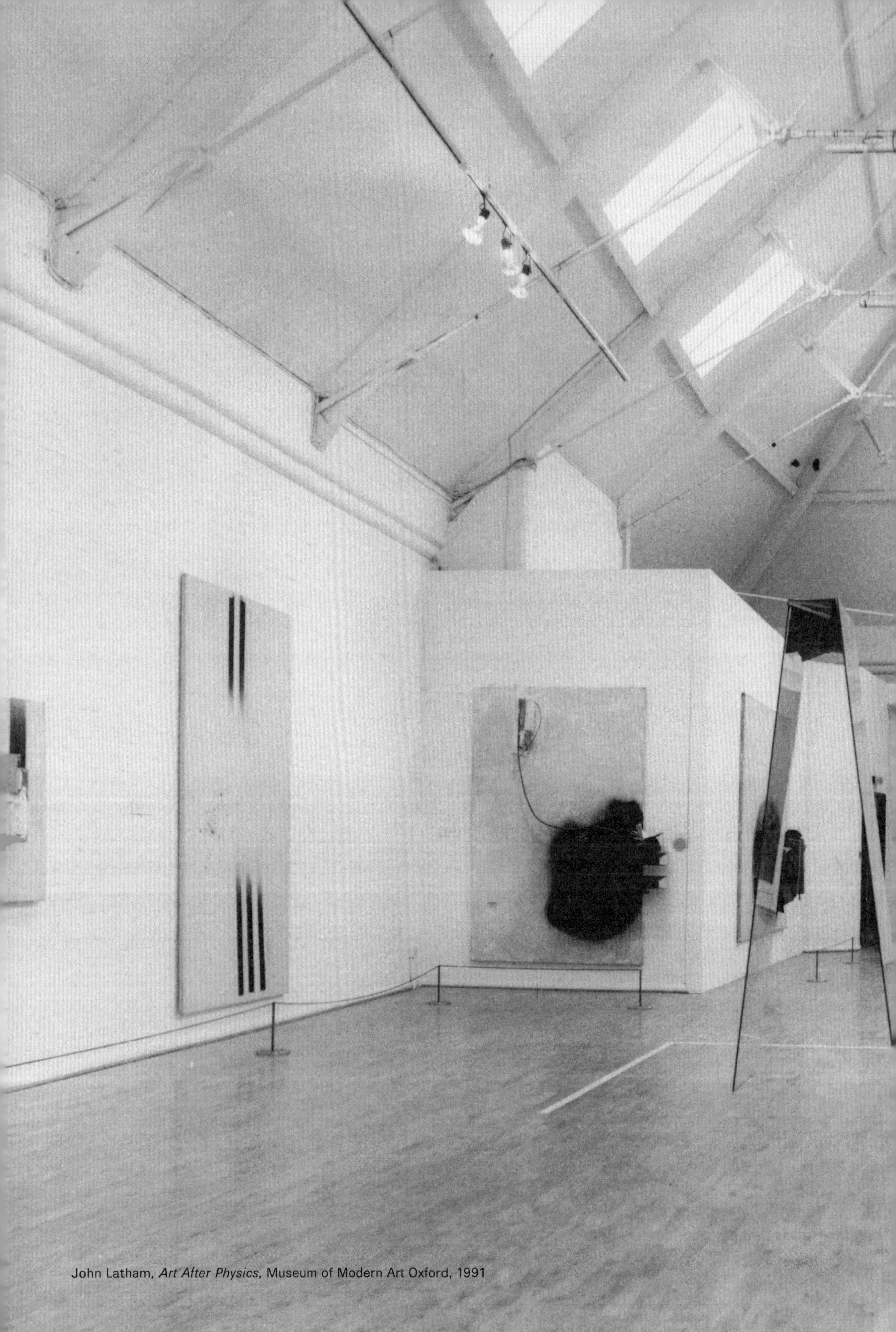

John Latham, *Art After Physics*, Museum of Modern Art Oxford, 1991

No Drones

Louise Lawler

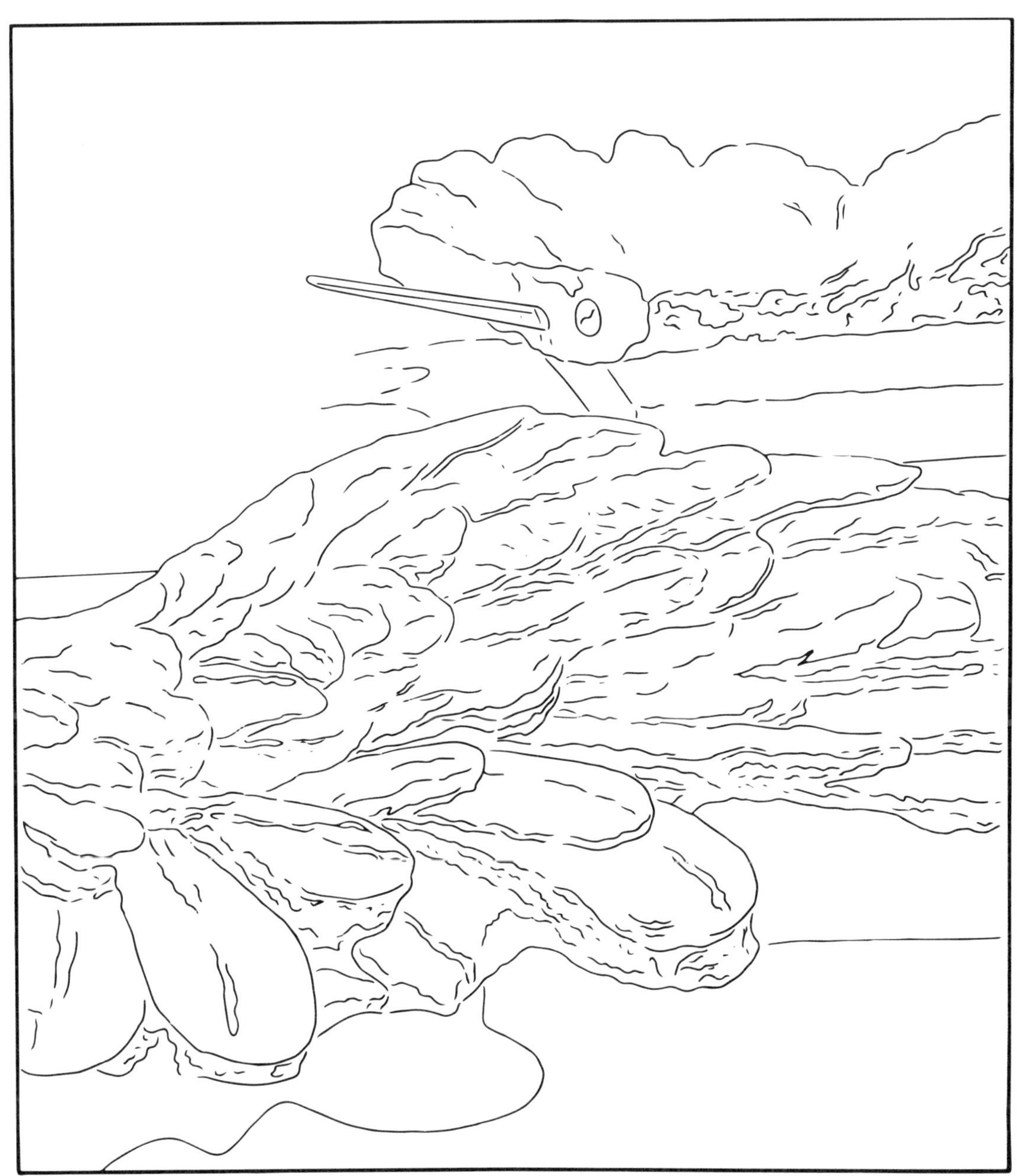

Grieving Mothers (Attachment) (traced)
2005/2016

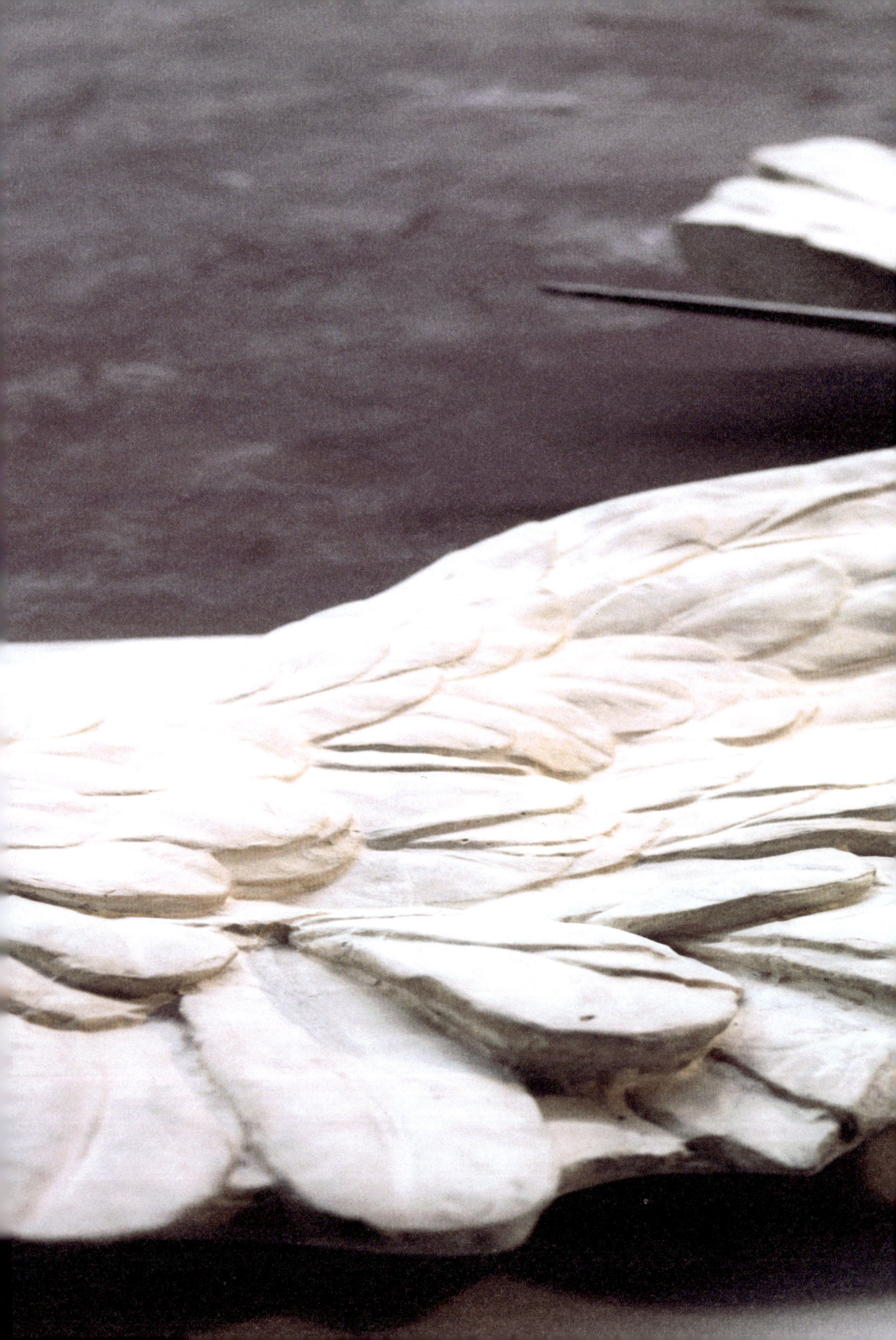

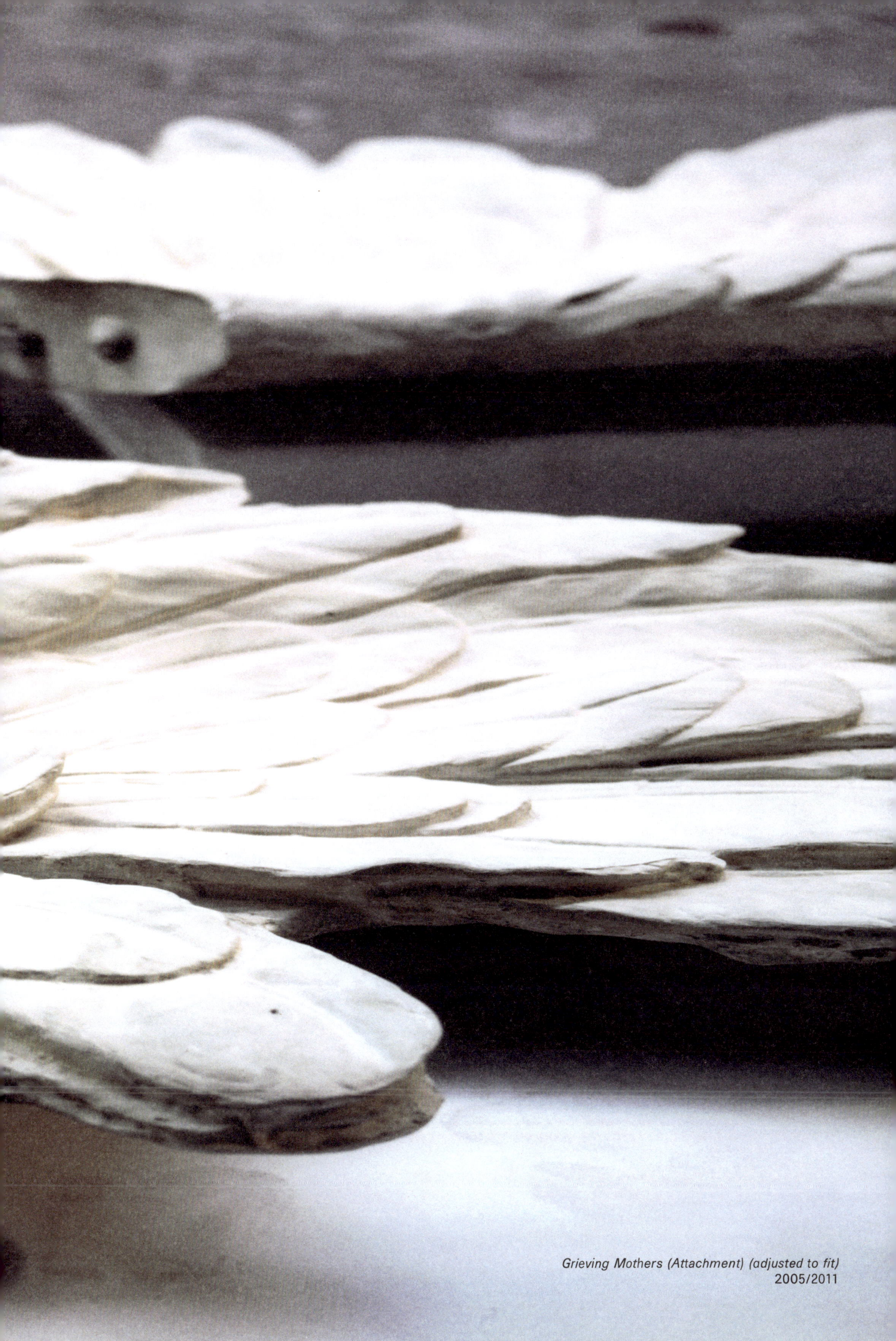

Grieving Mothers (Attachment) (adjusted to fit)
2005/2011

Jac Leirner

KALEIDOSCOPE: A Moment of Grace
16 April – 22 May 2016

Jac Leirner
14 July – 29 September 1991

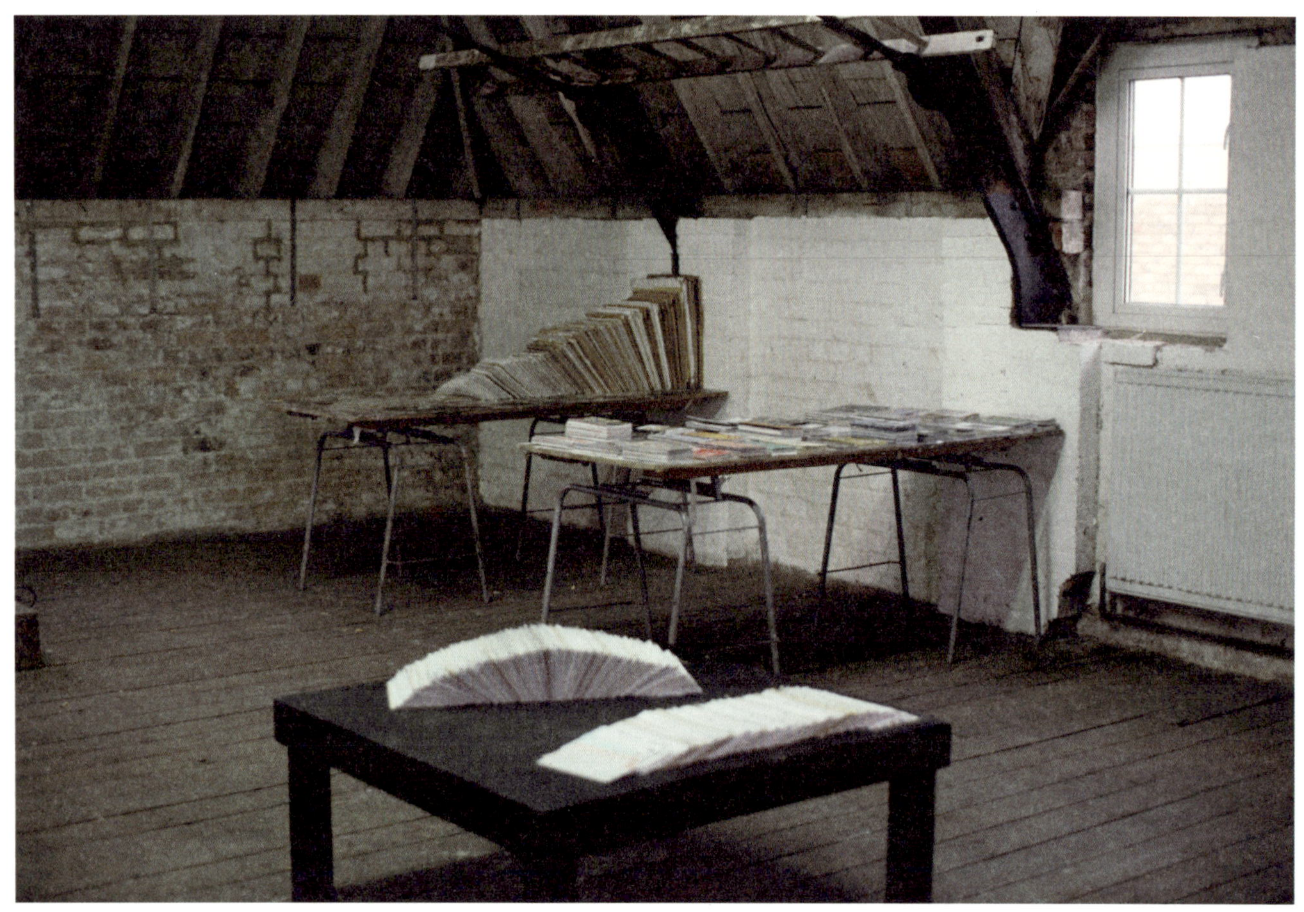

Residency at Museum of Modern Art Oxford, 1991

28 May 1991

John Leslie
The Museum of Modern Art
Oxford
FAX: 722573

Dear John, good afternoon!

Here is the text, it's ready.
The sequence <u>can't</u> be altered and there may be some mistakes
of writing to be corrected.
All the letters are small (<u>not A but a</u>) from beggining to end.
I hope you like it, John.
It shoul be read on its sequence.
Please, send me a copy of it when it's ready (photomounted)
I'd like to see it and other proves of the catalogue. What is
its size (of the catalogue)?

Last friday I sent by express post Chris Moore's picture for
the cover. It must be arriving tomorrow and may need some
retouching or a new copy.

Well, that's it for now, dear John...

Good Work!

We are in touch!

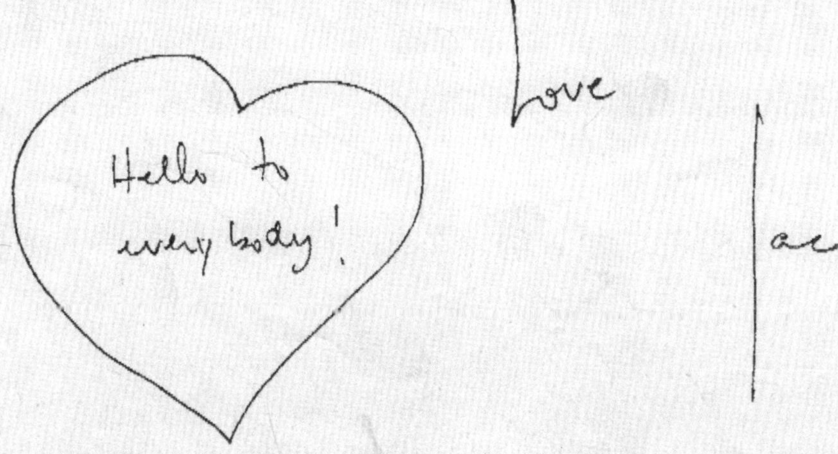

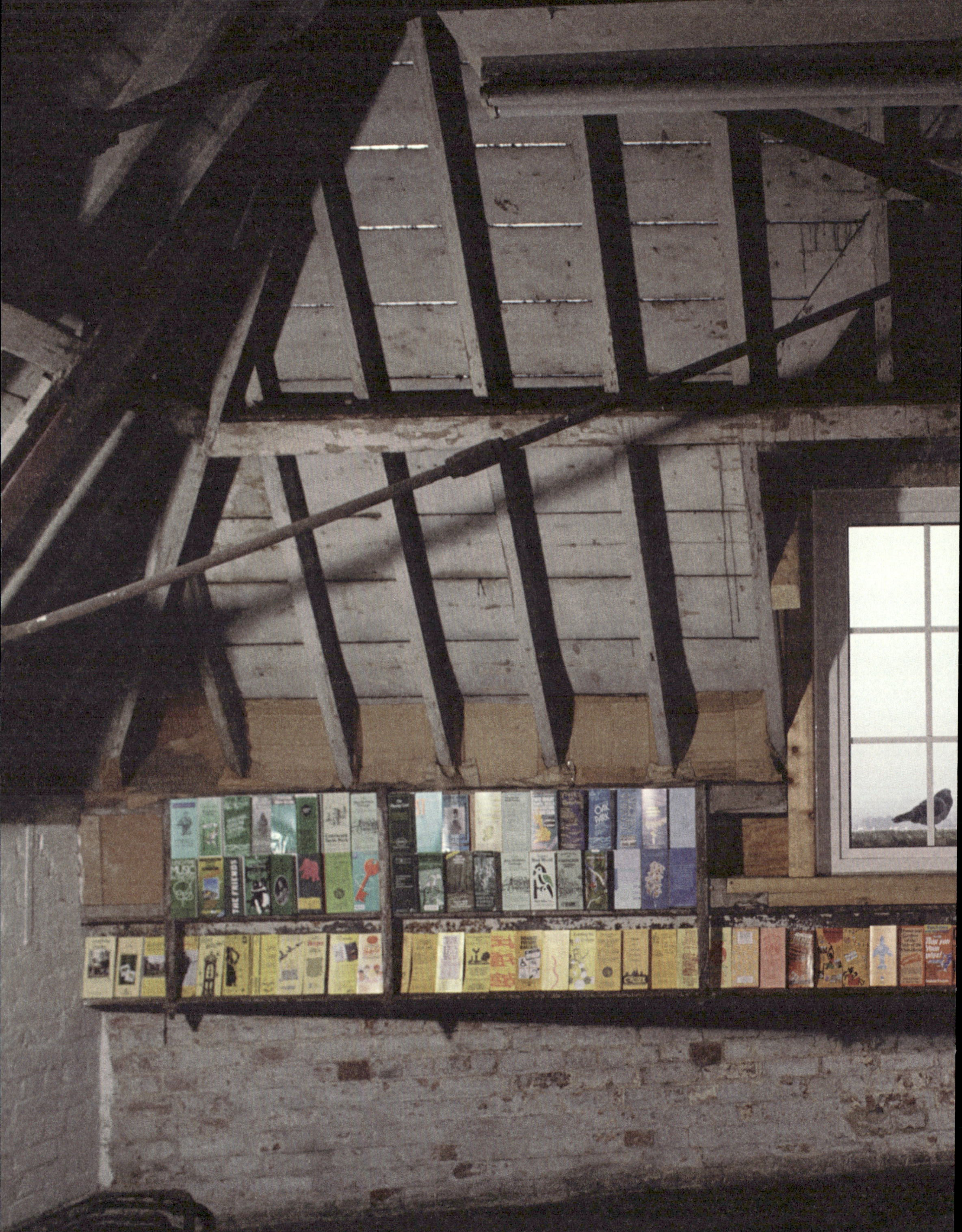

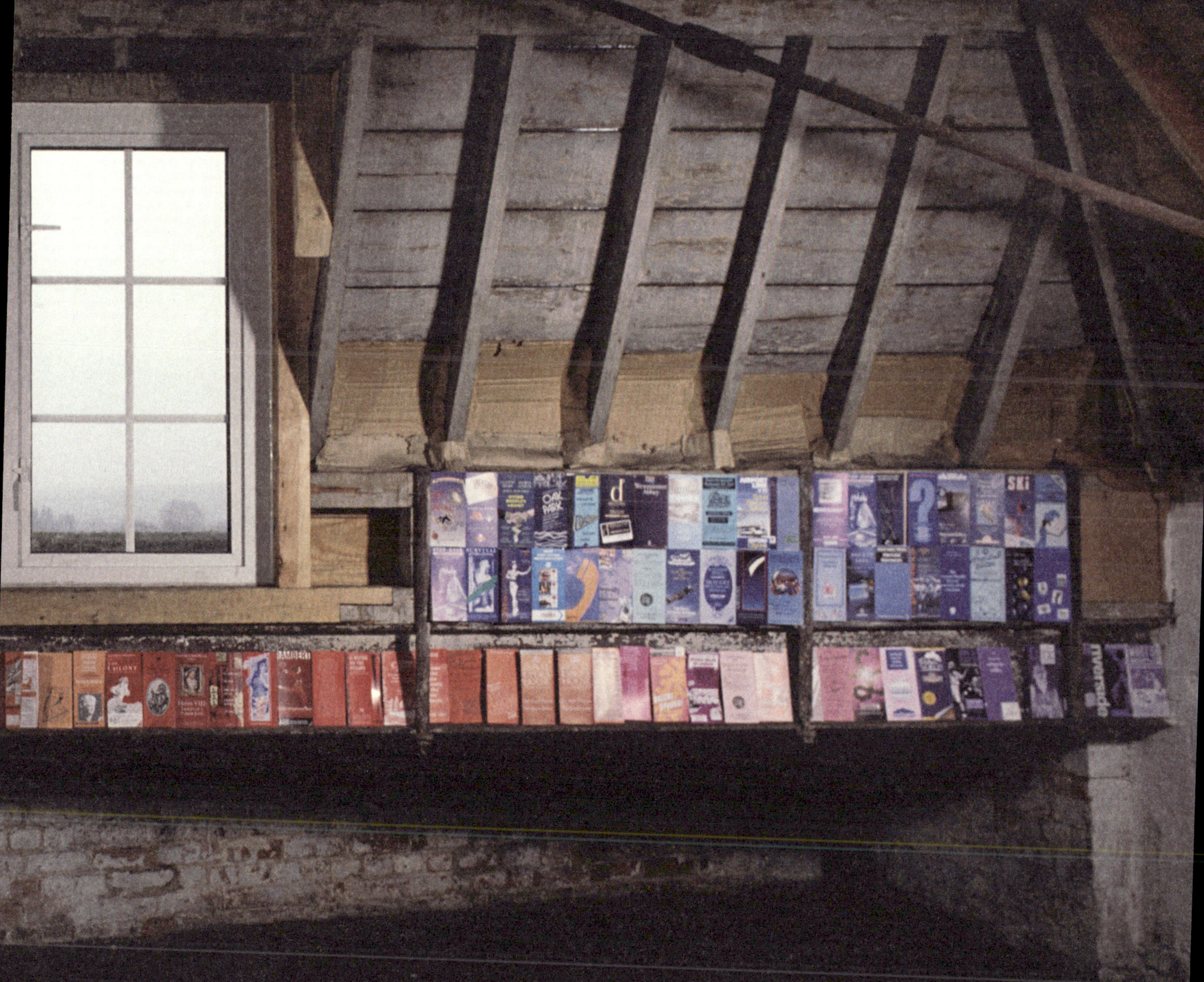

Sol LeWitt

KALEIDOSCOPE: Mystics and Rationalists
11 June – 31 July 2016

Sol LeWitt: *Structures 1962-1993*
24 January – 28 March 1993

Sol LeWitt: *Drawings 1958–1992*
24 January – 28 March 1993

Sol LeWitt: *Incomplete Open Cubes*
24 April – 29 May 1977

Sol LeWitt: *Wall Drawings*
28 April – 27 May 1973

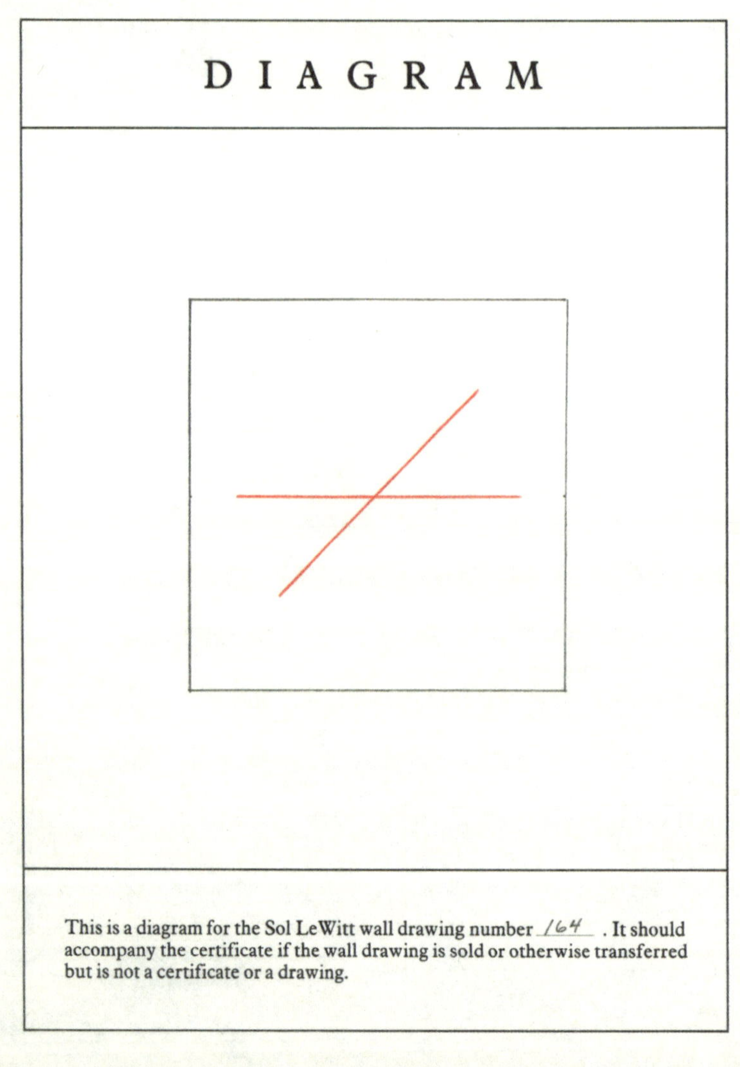

Diagram for *Wall Drawing #164*, 1973

Squares and Lines.

All squares are 8' and all lines are 6' long.

1. Horizontal line from mid-point of the left edge of the square.

2. Horizontal line, centered between the mid-points of the square.

3. Diagonal line from the upper left corner of the square.

4. Diagonal line centered between the upper left corner and the lower right corner of the square.

5. Diagonal line centered between the upper left corner and the lower right corner of the square crossing a diagonal line from the lower left corner of the square.

6. Diagonal lines from the lower left corner and lower right corner of the square.

7. Diagonal lines centered between the upper left and lower right and upper right and lower left corners of the square.

8. Horizontal line from the left edge and vertical line from the top of the square touching at the ends.

9. Horizontal line from the left edge and vertical line from the top of the square not touching.

10. Horizontal line from the mid-point of the left edge of the square touching the mid-point of a vertical line centered in the square.

11. Horizontal line centered between the mid-points axis of the square crossing a diagonal line centered between the upper right and lower left corners of the square.

Sol LeWitt.

(Plan for Wall-drawings, Oxford, April 28, 1973).

Sol LeWitt, *Wall Drawings*, Museum of Modern Art Oxford, 1973

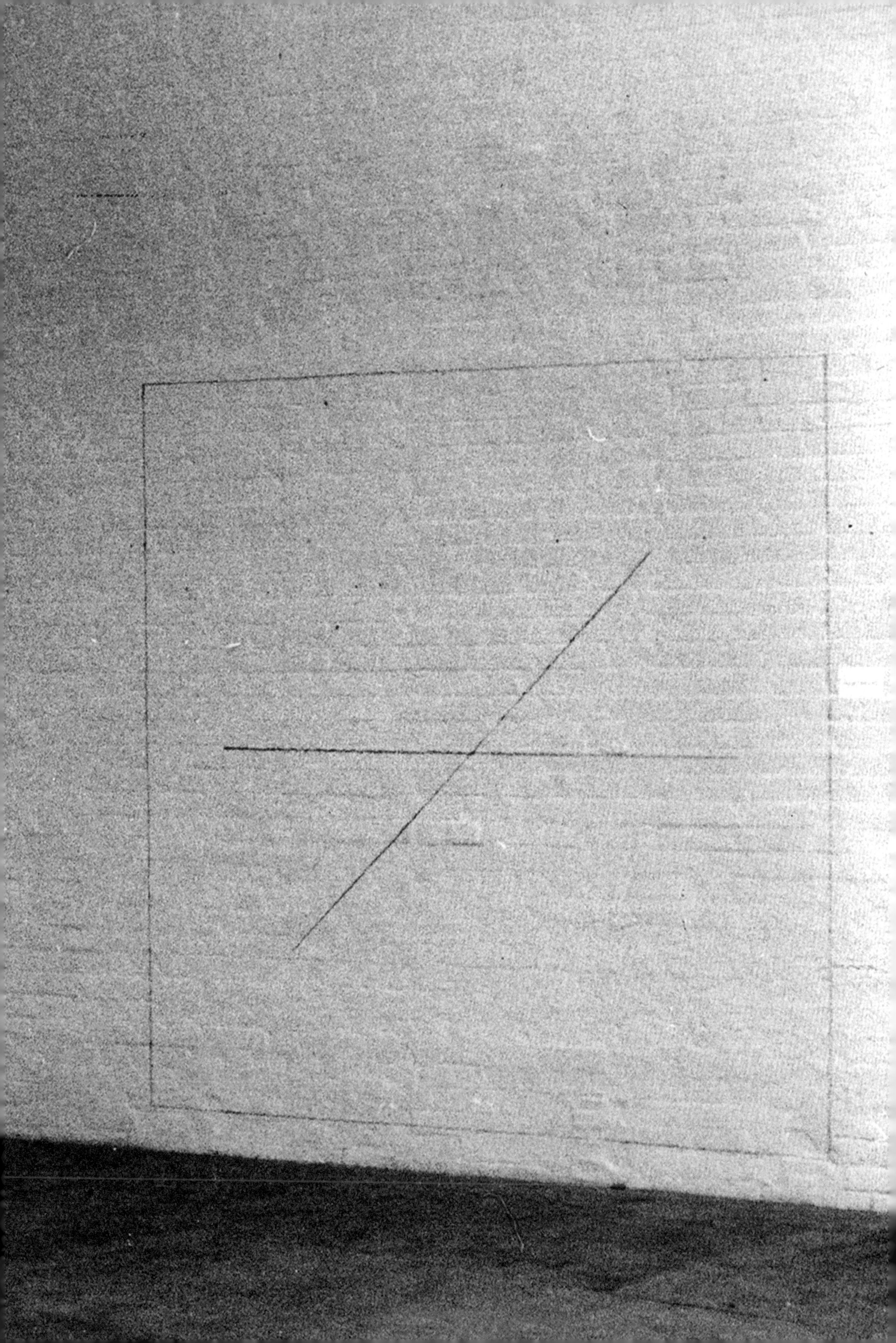

Maria Loboda

KALEIDOSCOPE: The Vanished Reality
12 November – 31 December 2016

124

TO , AS PROMISED

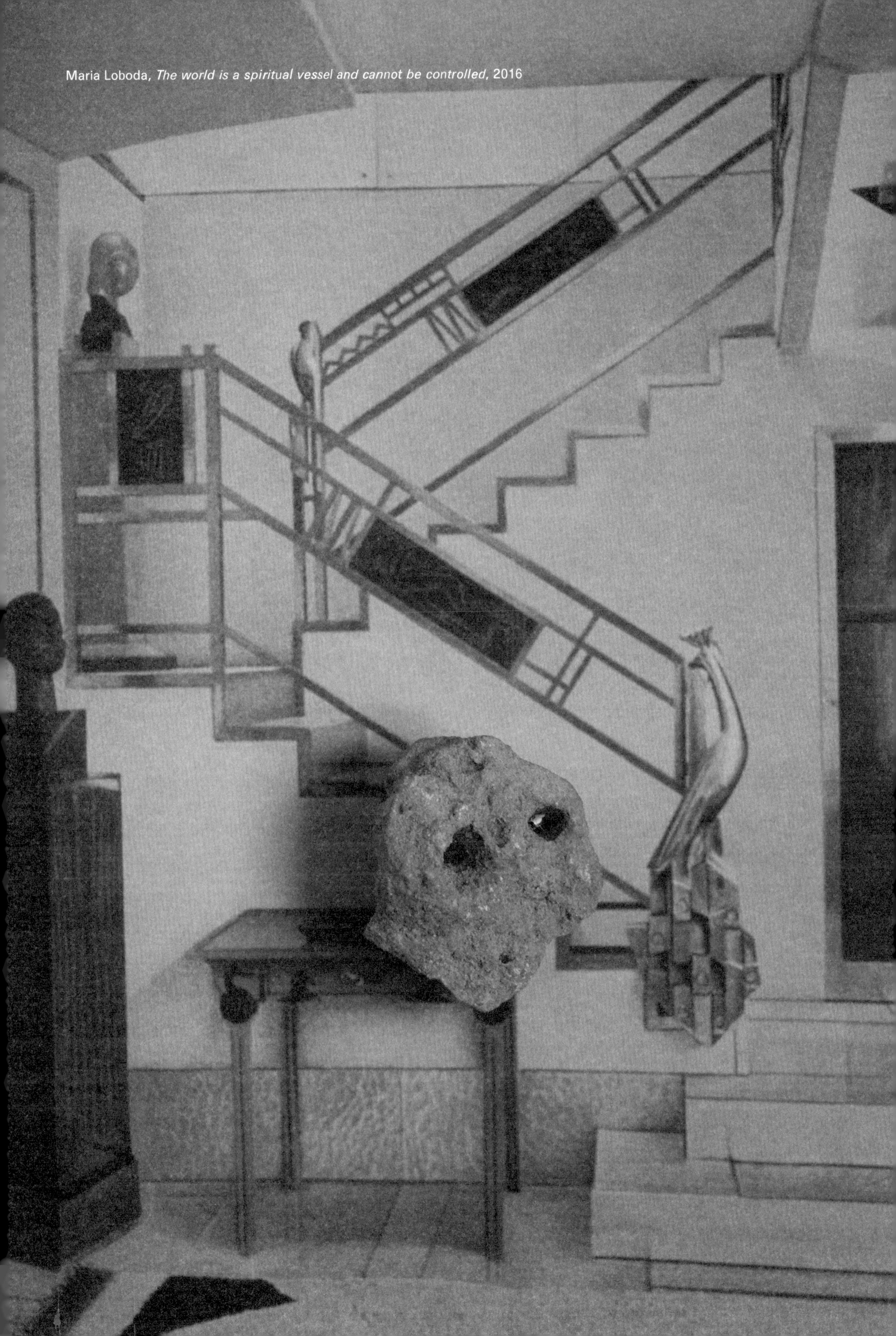

Maria Loboda, *The world is a spiritual vessel and cannot be controlled*, 2016

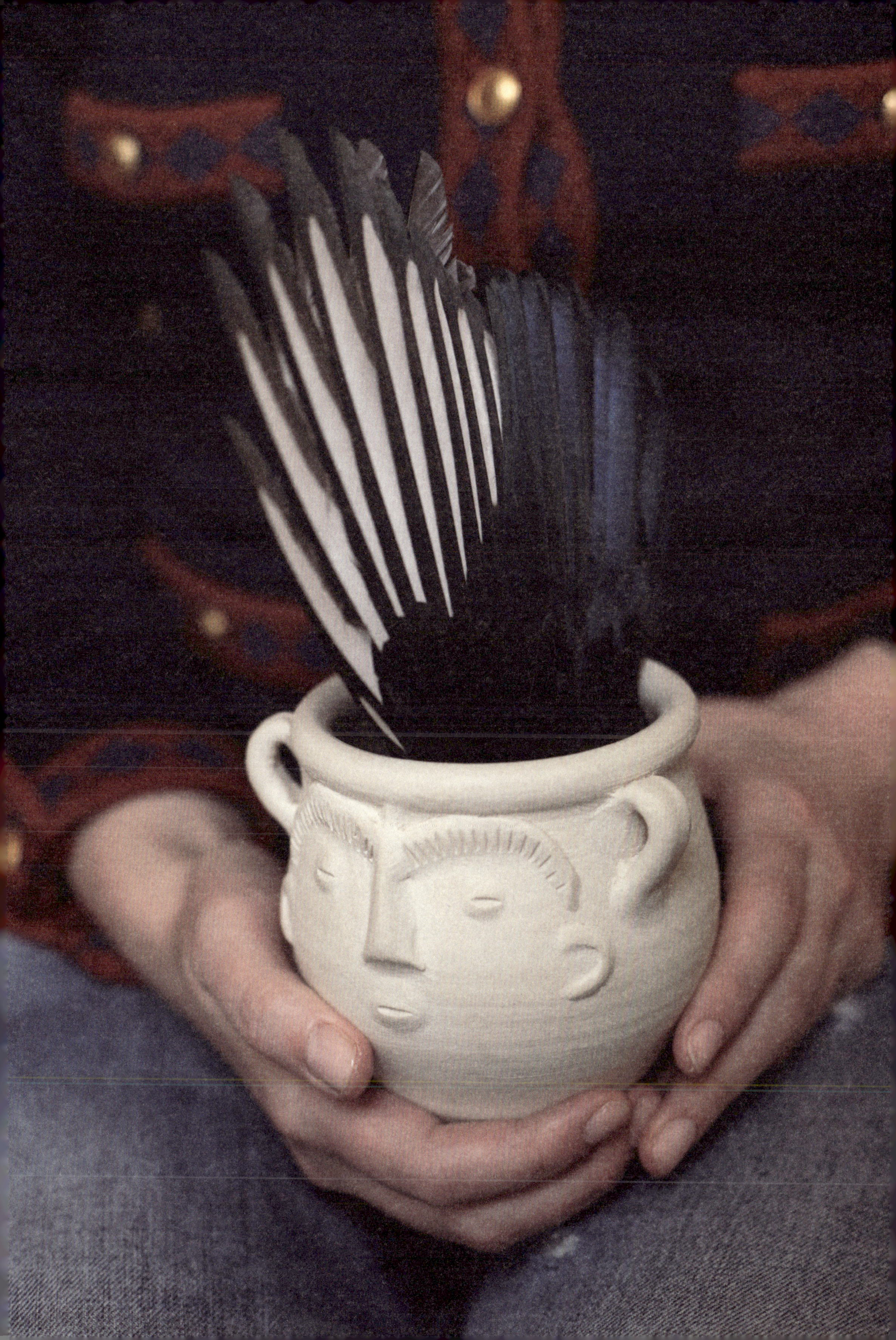

Richard Long

KALEIDOSCOPE: It's Me to the World
20 August – 16 October 2016

Richard Long
11 November – 23 December 1979

Richard Long
9 December – 23 December 1971

Letter from Richard Long to Peter Ibsen, undated, in answer to Ibsen's invitation
to exhibit at the museum. Ibsen's letter, dated 11 August 1971, opened with the
sentence, "Although I have been led to expect a negative answer from you, I would
very much like to ask if you would be interested in exhibiting here at the Museum."

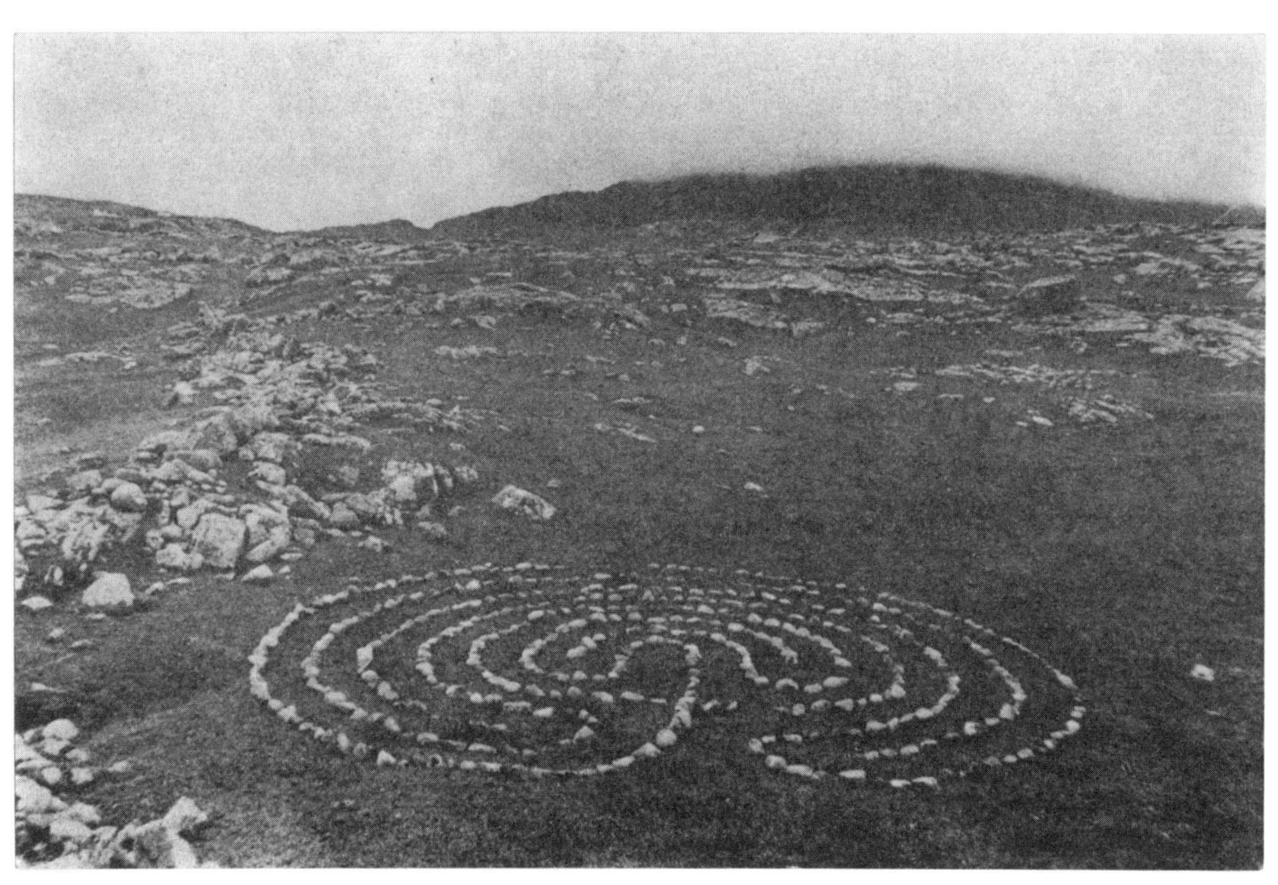

Exhibition invitation, 1971

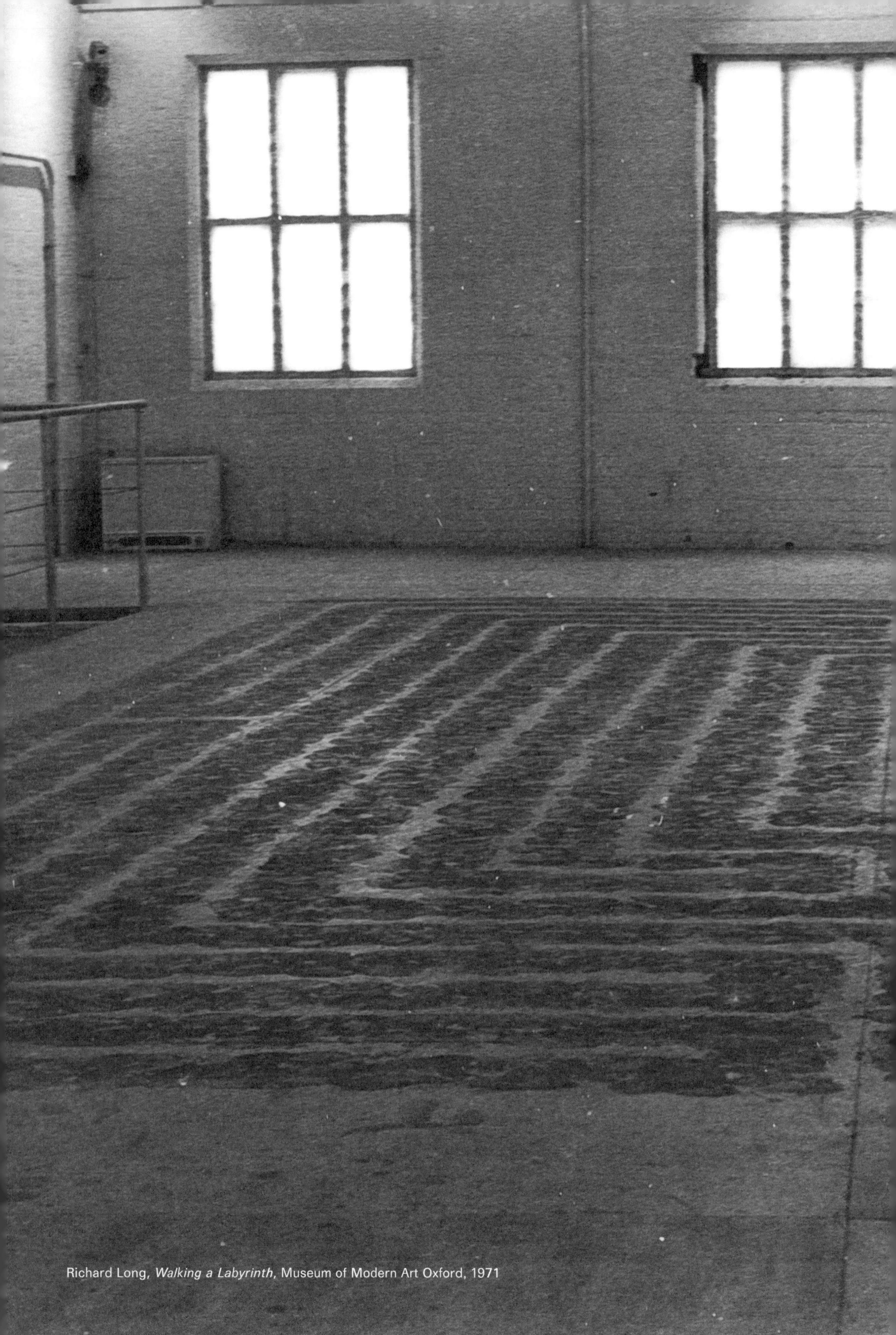

Richard Long, *Walking a Labyrinth*, Museum of Modern Art Oxford, 1971

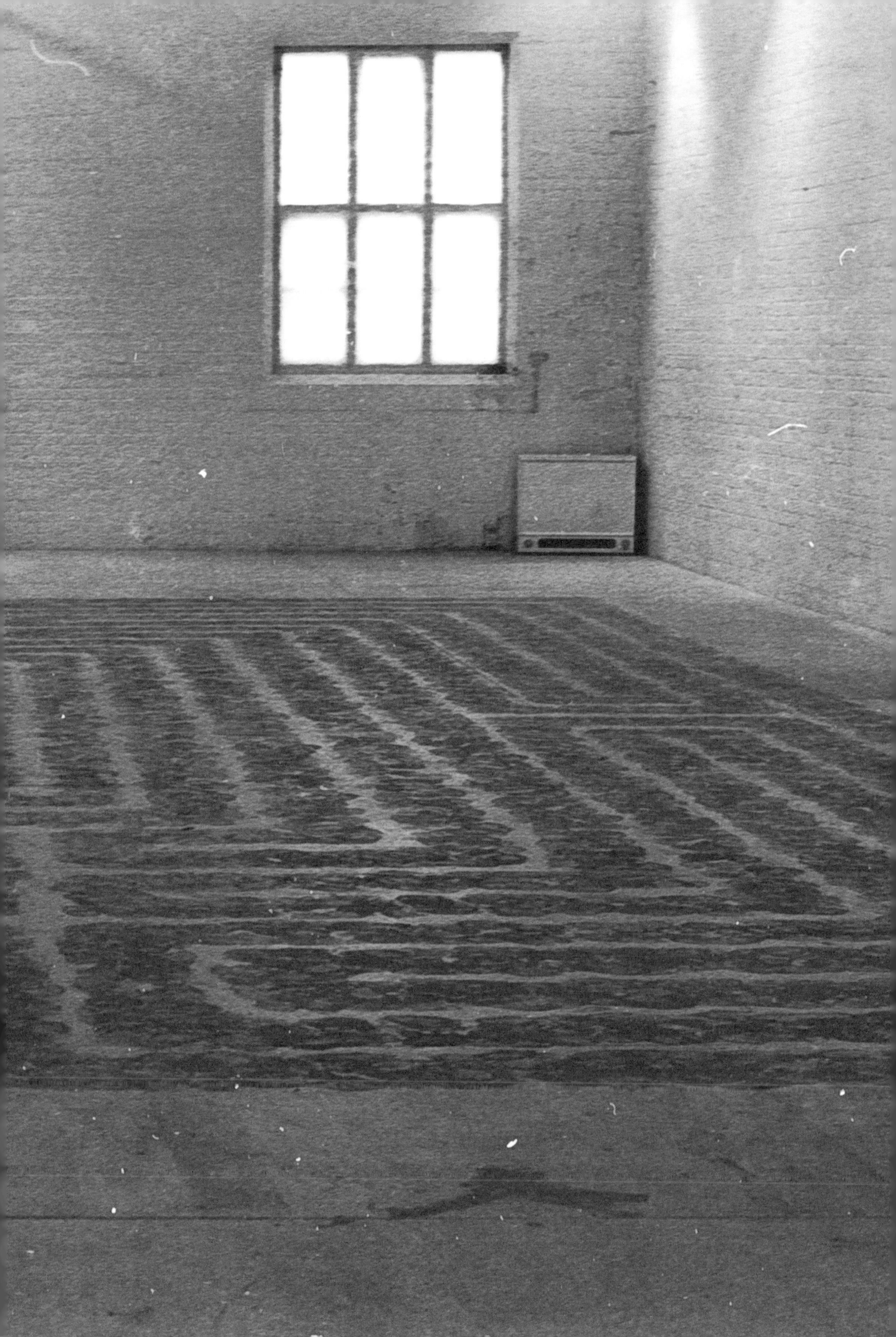

David Maljkovic

KALEIDOSCOPE: A Moment of Grace
16 April – 22 May 2016

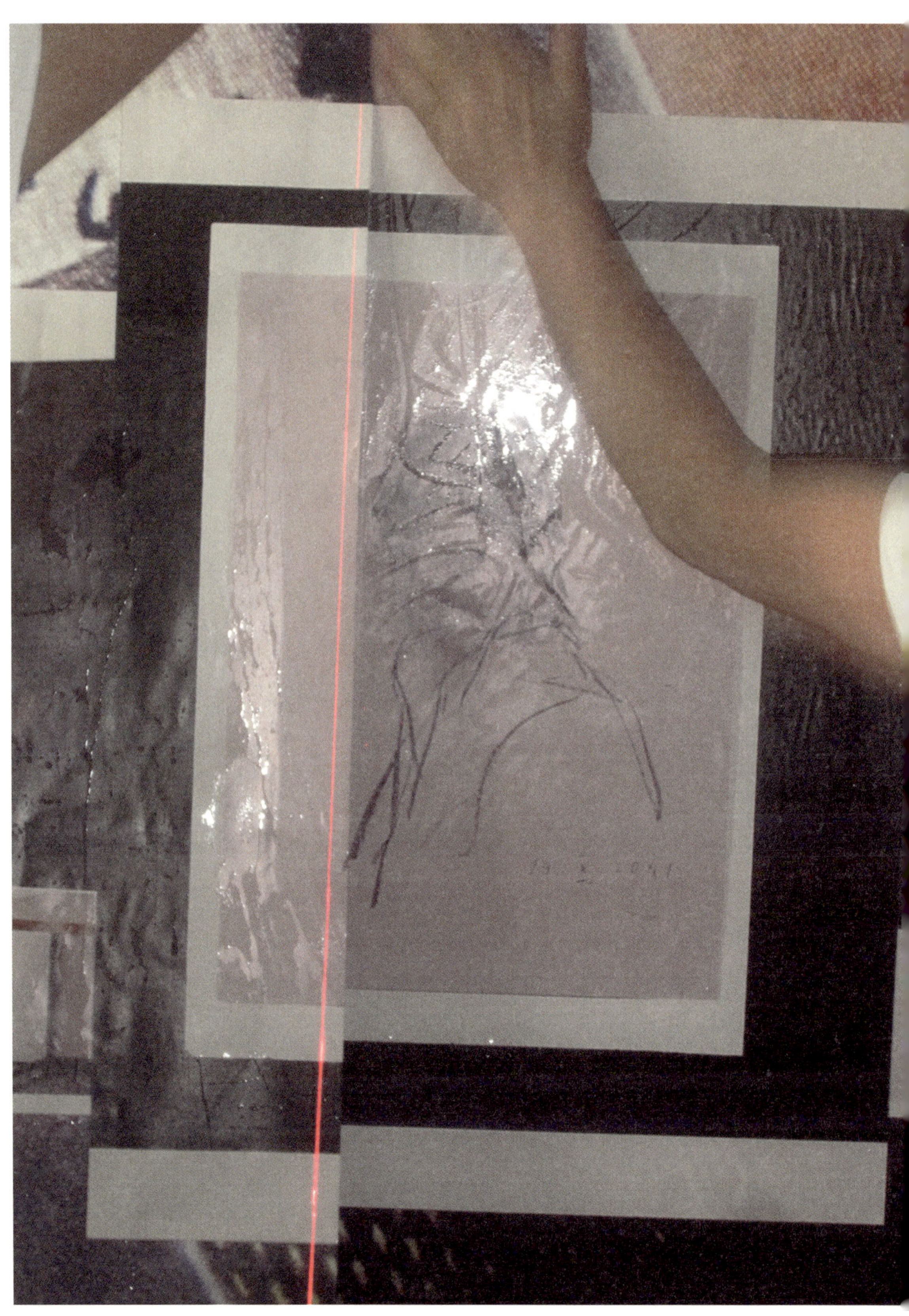

New Reproductions (process), 2013–15

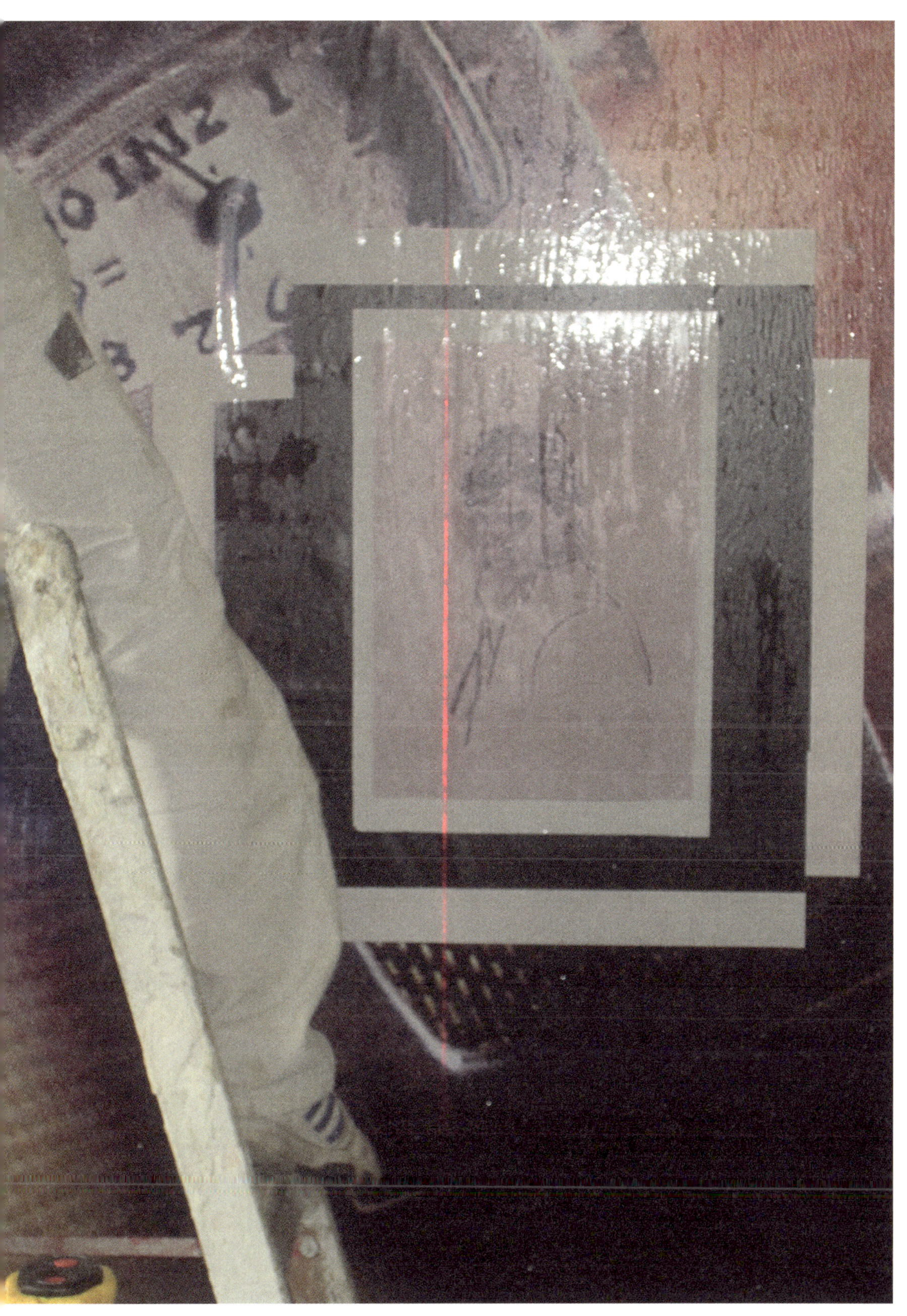

Kerry James Marshall

KALEIDOSCOPE: The Vanished Reality
12 November – 31 December 2016

Kerry James Marshall: *Along the Way*
25 July – 22 October 2006

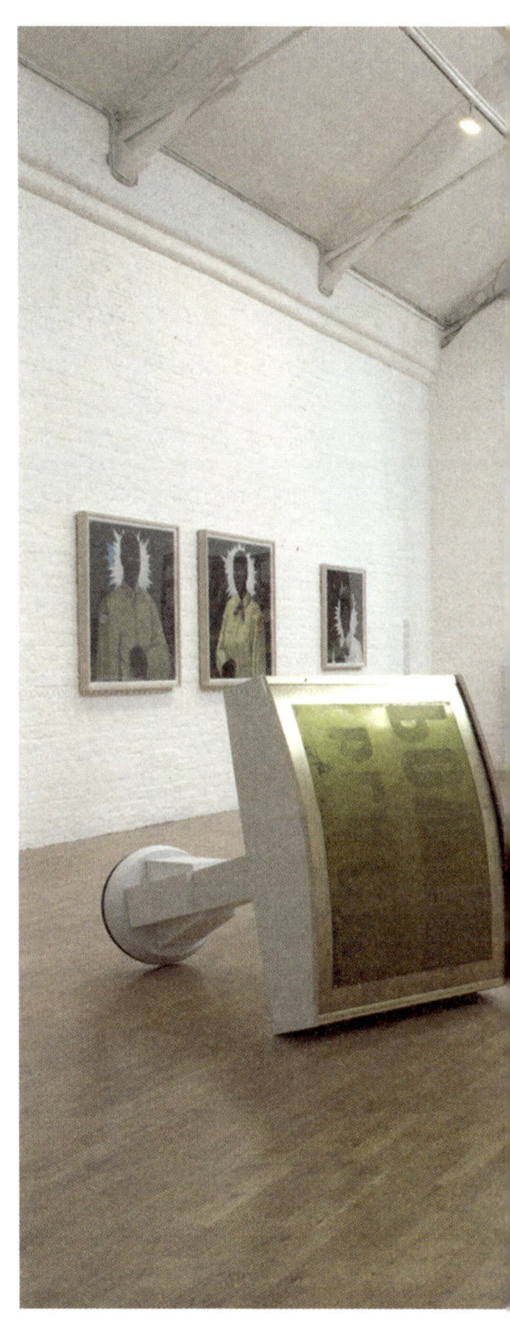

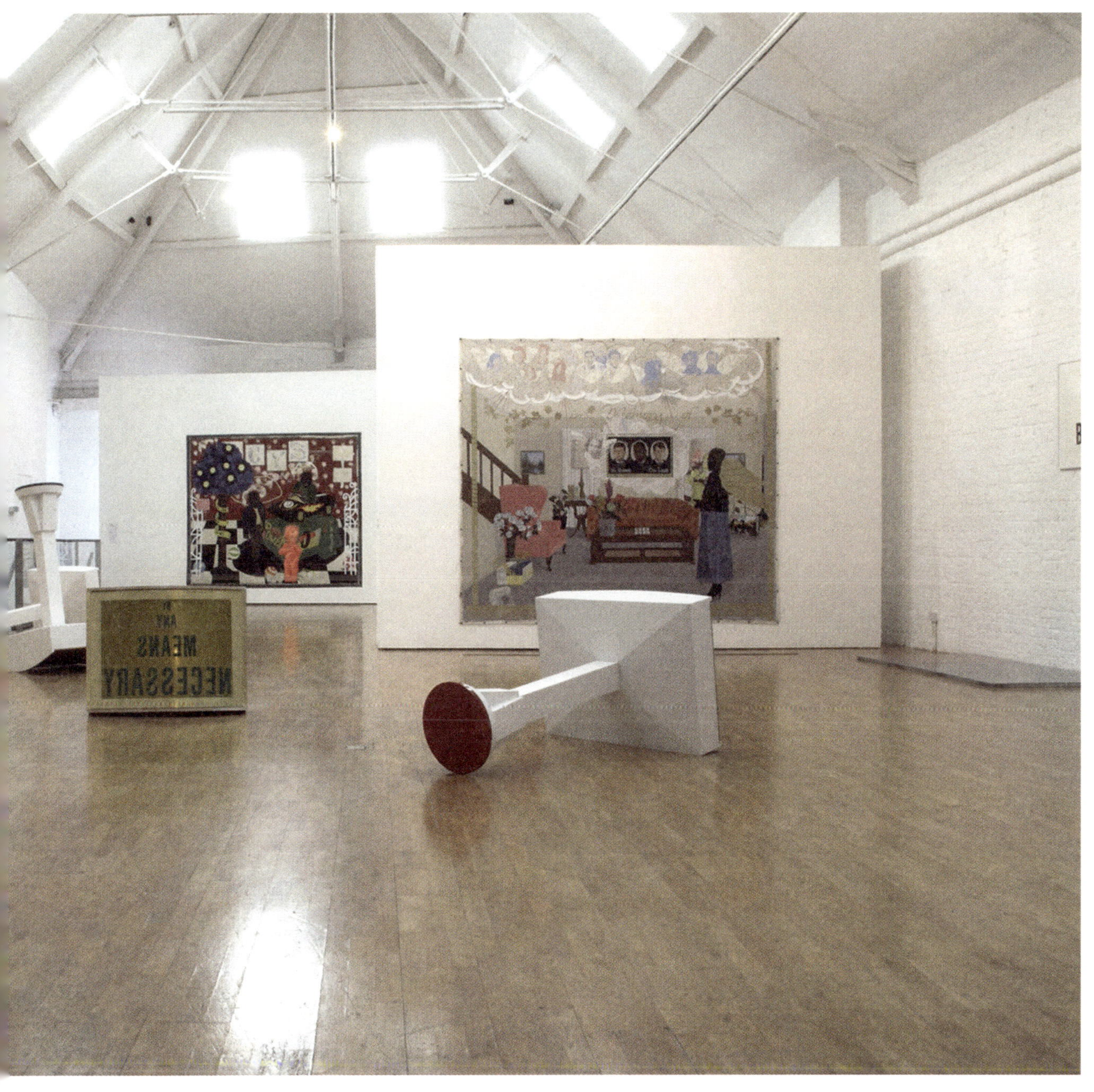

Along The Way, Modern Art Oxford, 2006

Agnes Martin

KALEIDOSCOPE: It's Me to the World
20 August – 16 October 2016

Agnes Martin: *On a Clear Day*
19 January – 23 February 1975

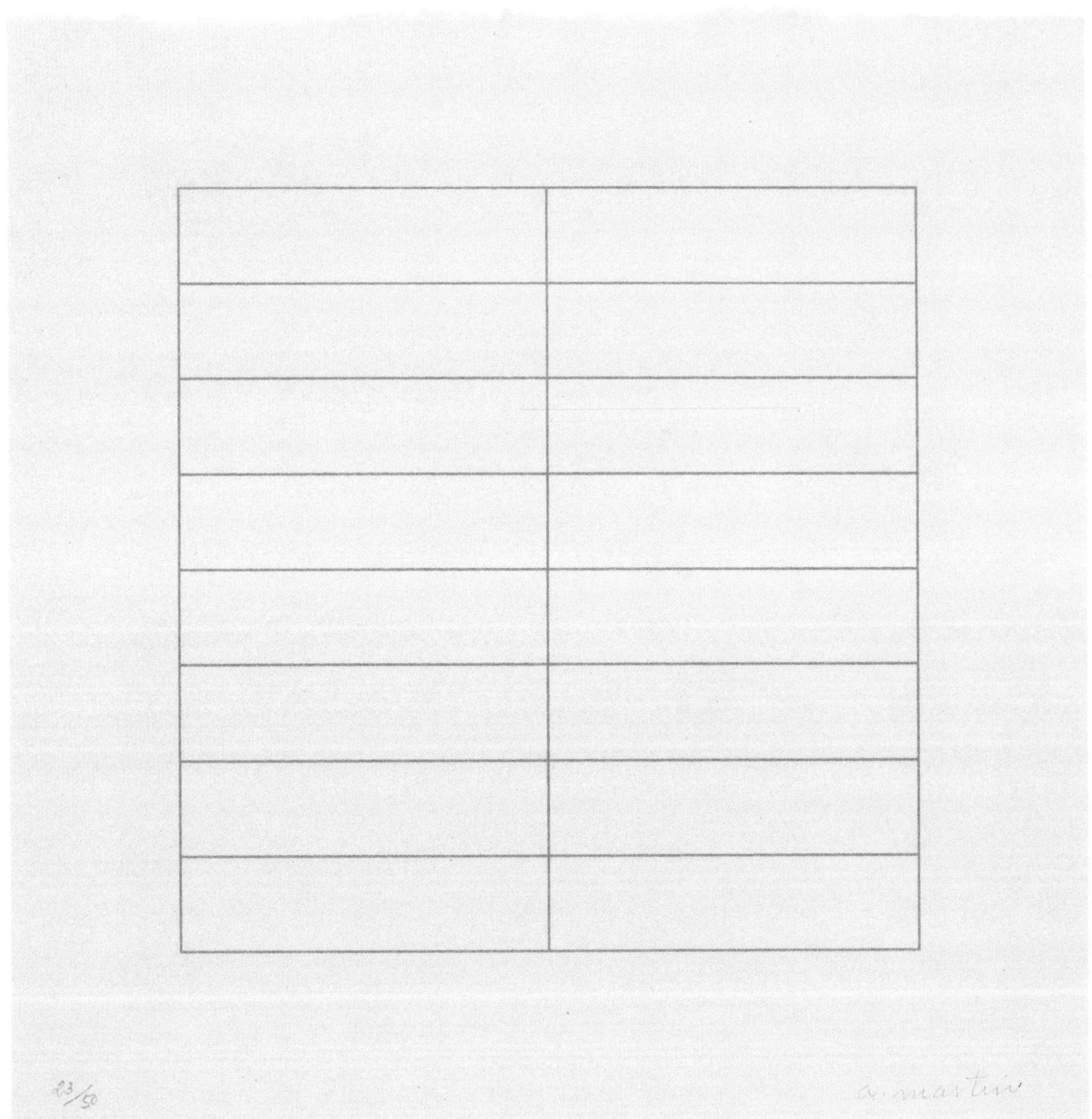

On a Clear Day, 1973

On a Clear Day, 1973

Gustav Metzger

KALEIDOSCOPE: A Moment of Grace
16 April – 22 May 2016

Gustav Metzger
25 October 1998 – 10 January 1999

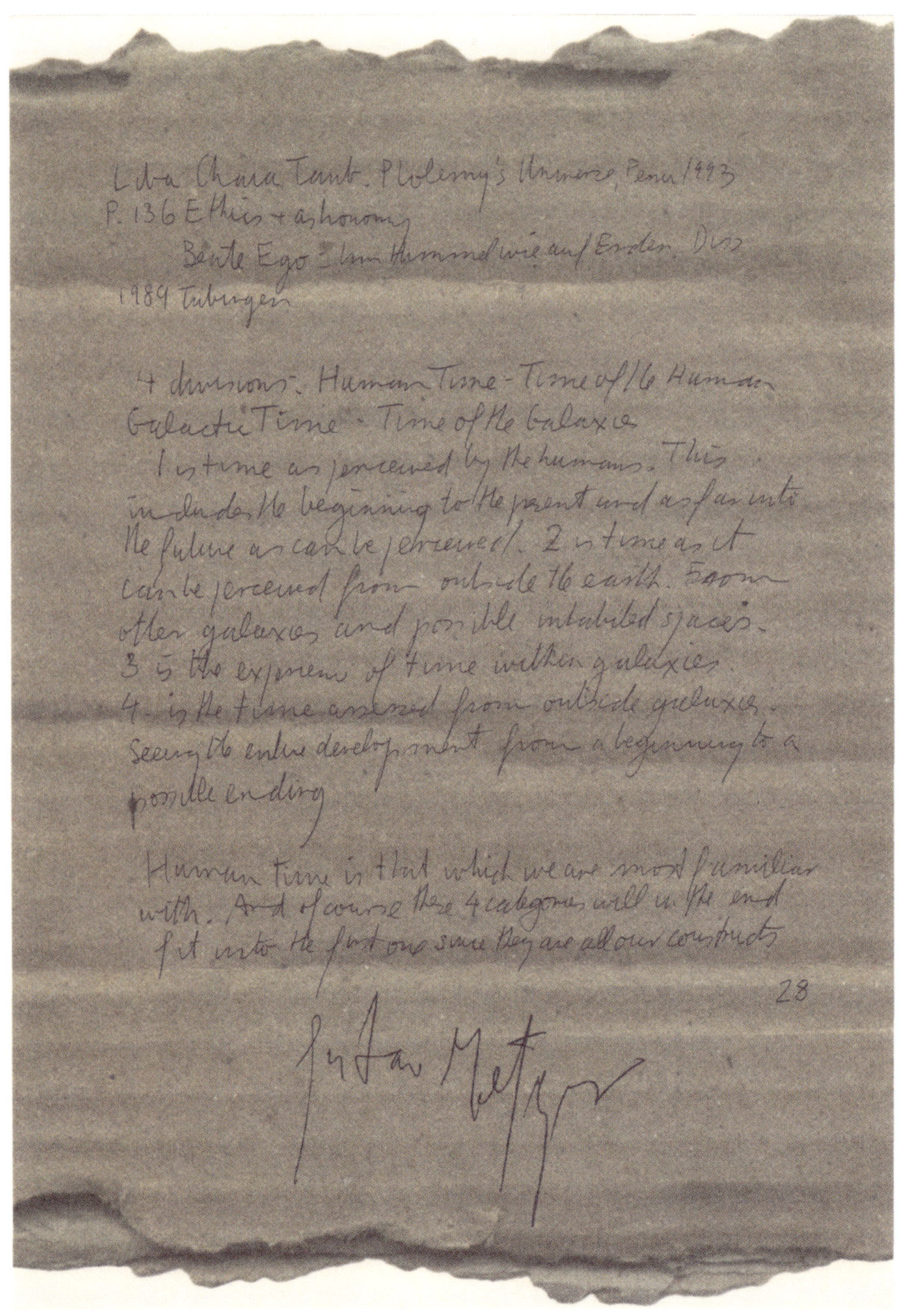

Exhibition invitation, 1998

Gustav Metzger
artist, activist

The exhibition *Gustav Metzger* presents a slice through Metzger's life as an artist and activist. The two large galleries - the Piper and Upper Galleries - represent with new work two poles of his art whilst the smallest - the New Gallery - holds examples of past projects. The first part of this guide presents extracts from some of Gustav Metzger's statements, manifestos and events from the late 1950s to the mid 1960s. The second part of the guide introduces the work on show with brief notes written by the artist.

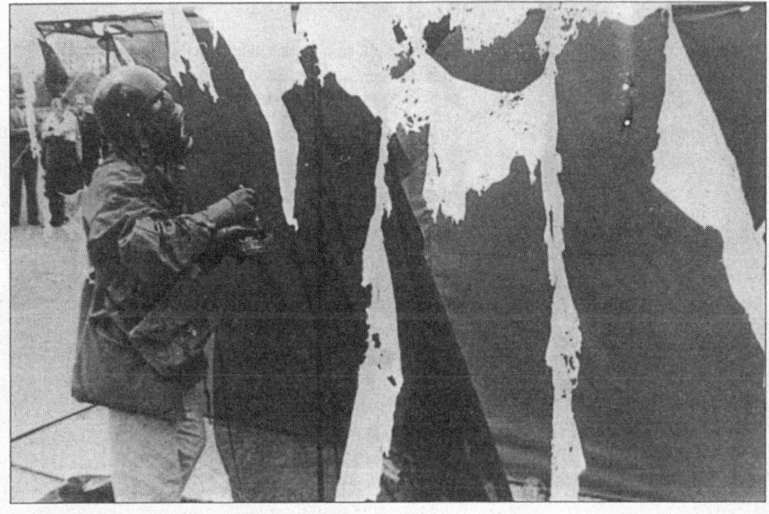

Gustav Metzger, *South Bank Demonstration, 3 July 1961.*

Courtesy of The Hulton Getty Picture Collection

Museum of Modern Art Oxford

Exhibition Guide

Exhibition guide, 1998

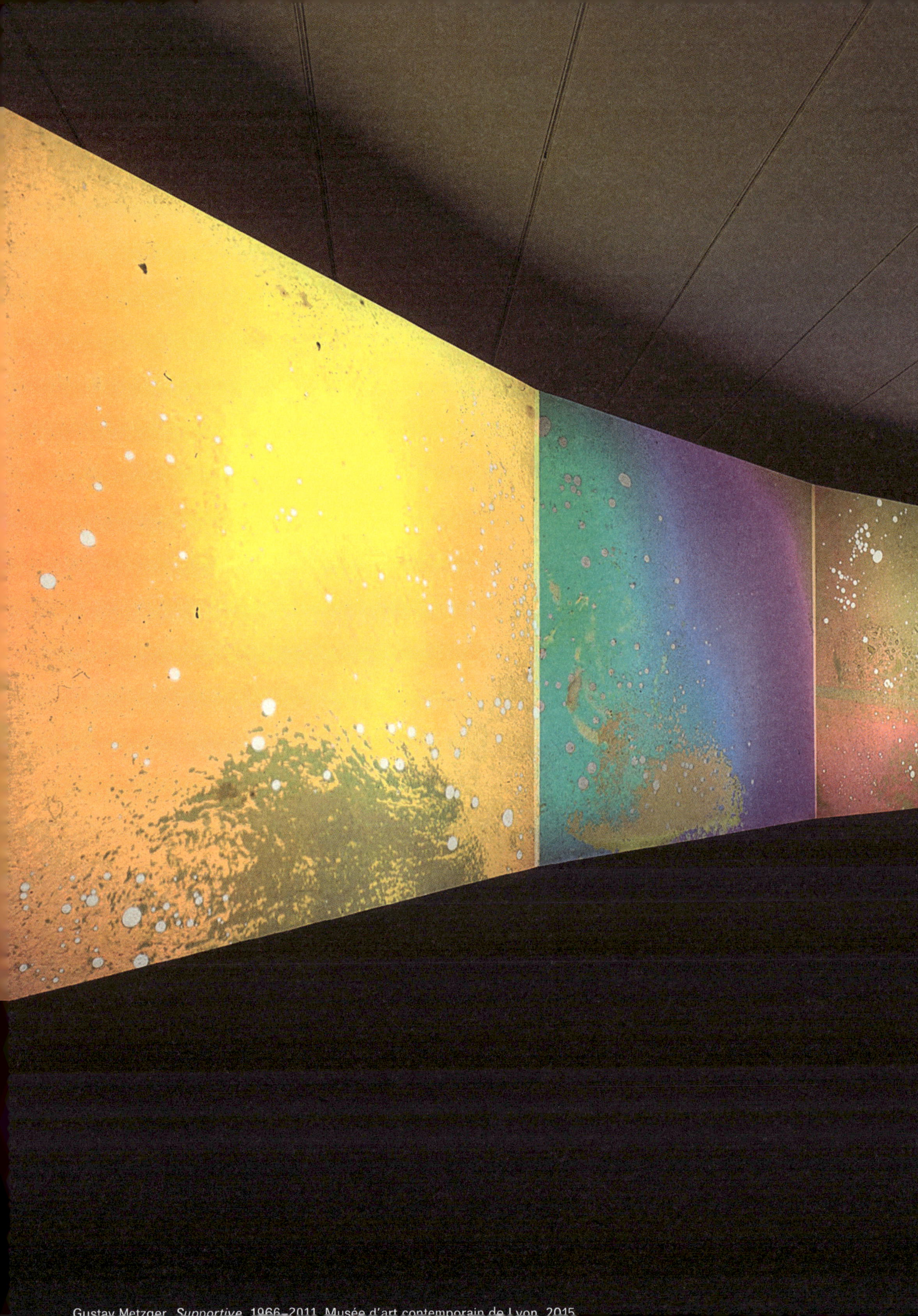

Gustav Metzger, *Supportive*, 1966–2011, Musée d'art contemporain de Lyon, 2015

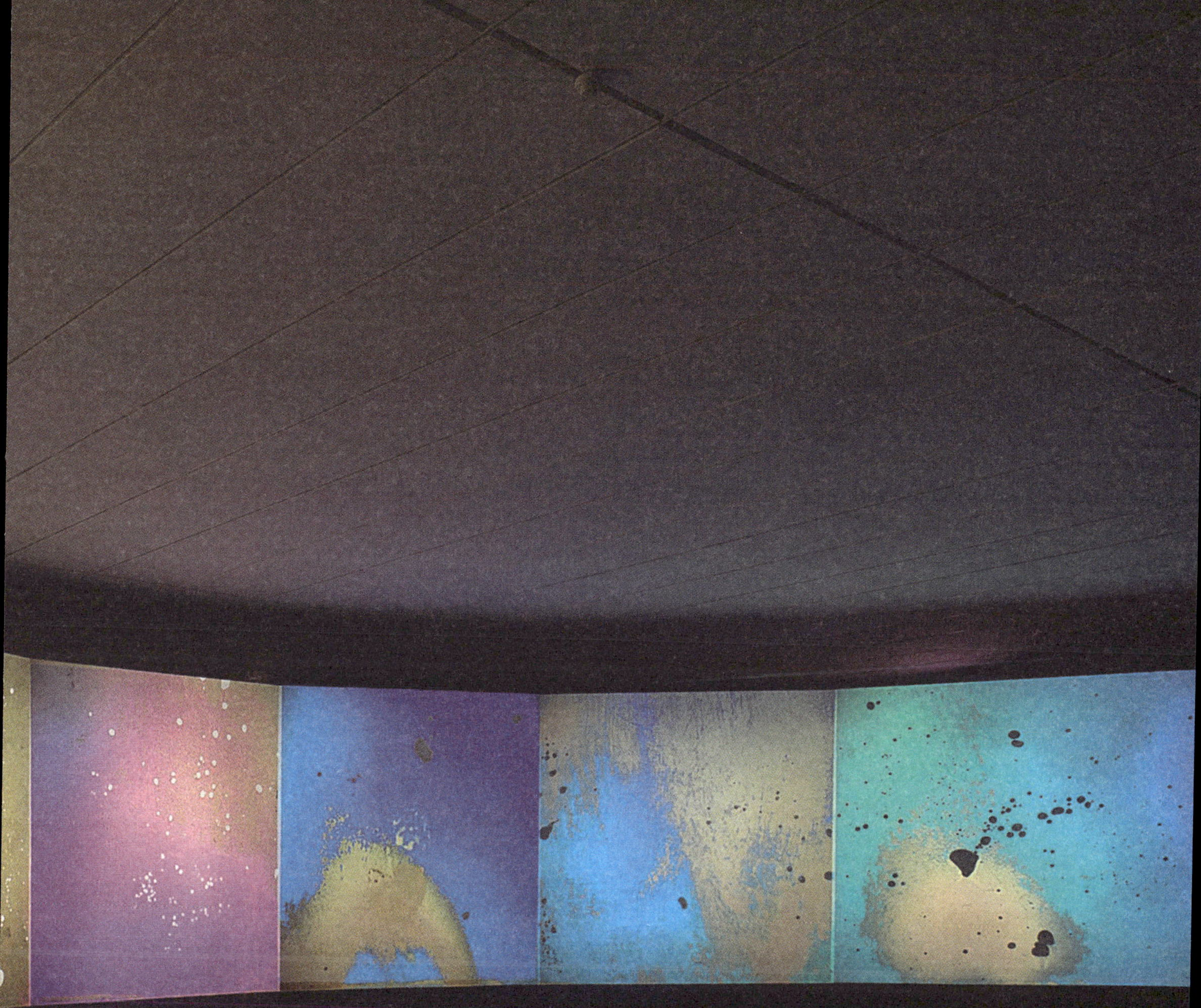

Mike Nelson

KALEIDOSCOPE Live: lecture by Jeremy Millar
22 September 2016

Mike Nelson: *Triple Bluff Canyon*
8 May – 4 July 2004

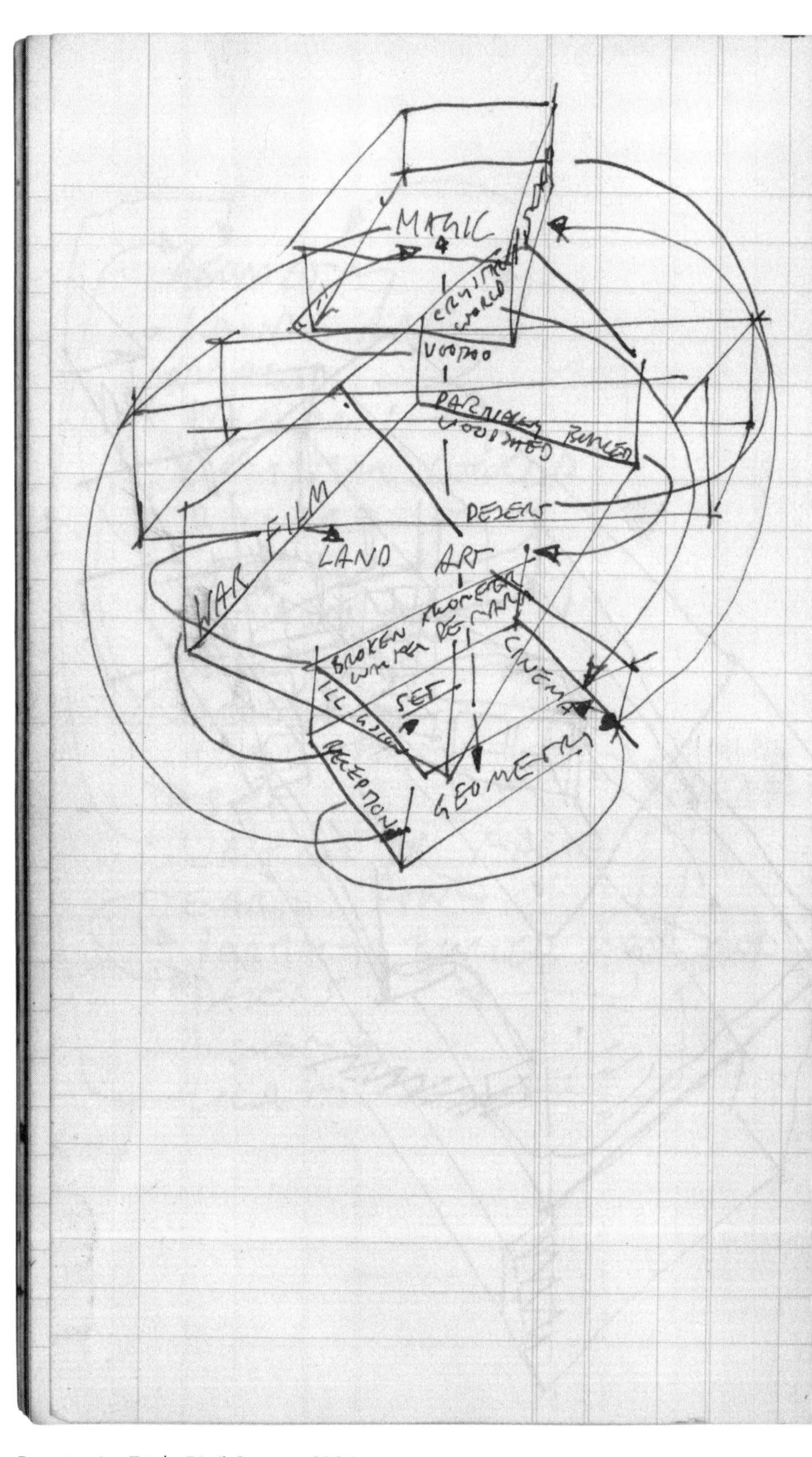

Drawing for *Triple Bluff Canyon*, 2004

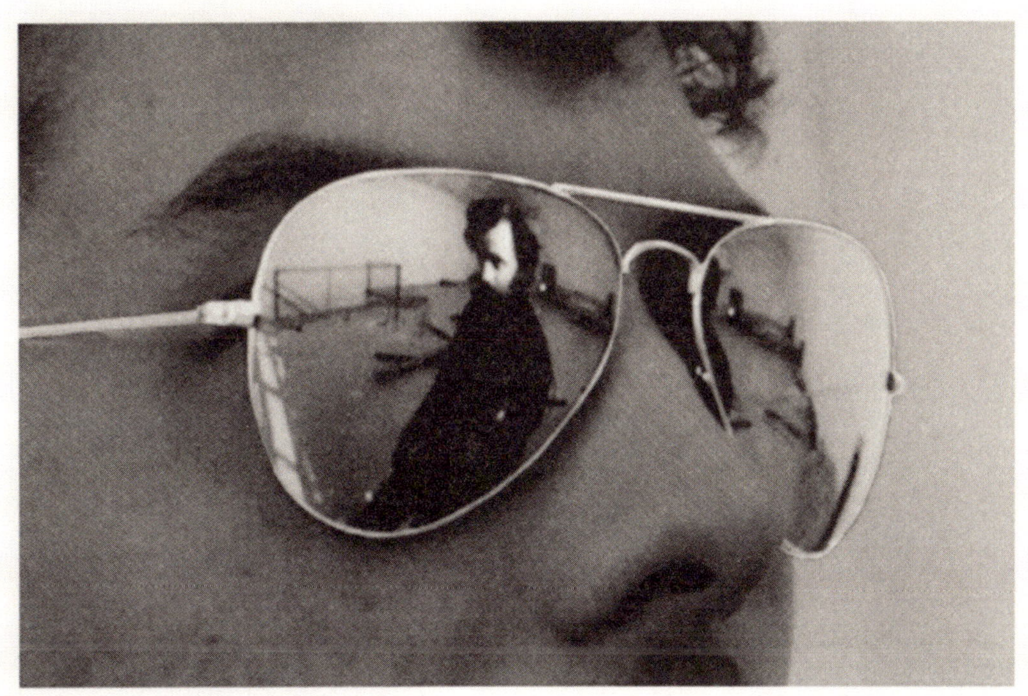

Exhibition invitation, 2004

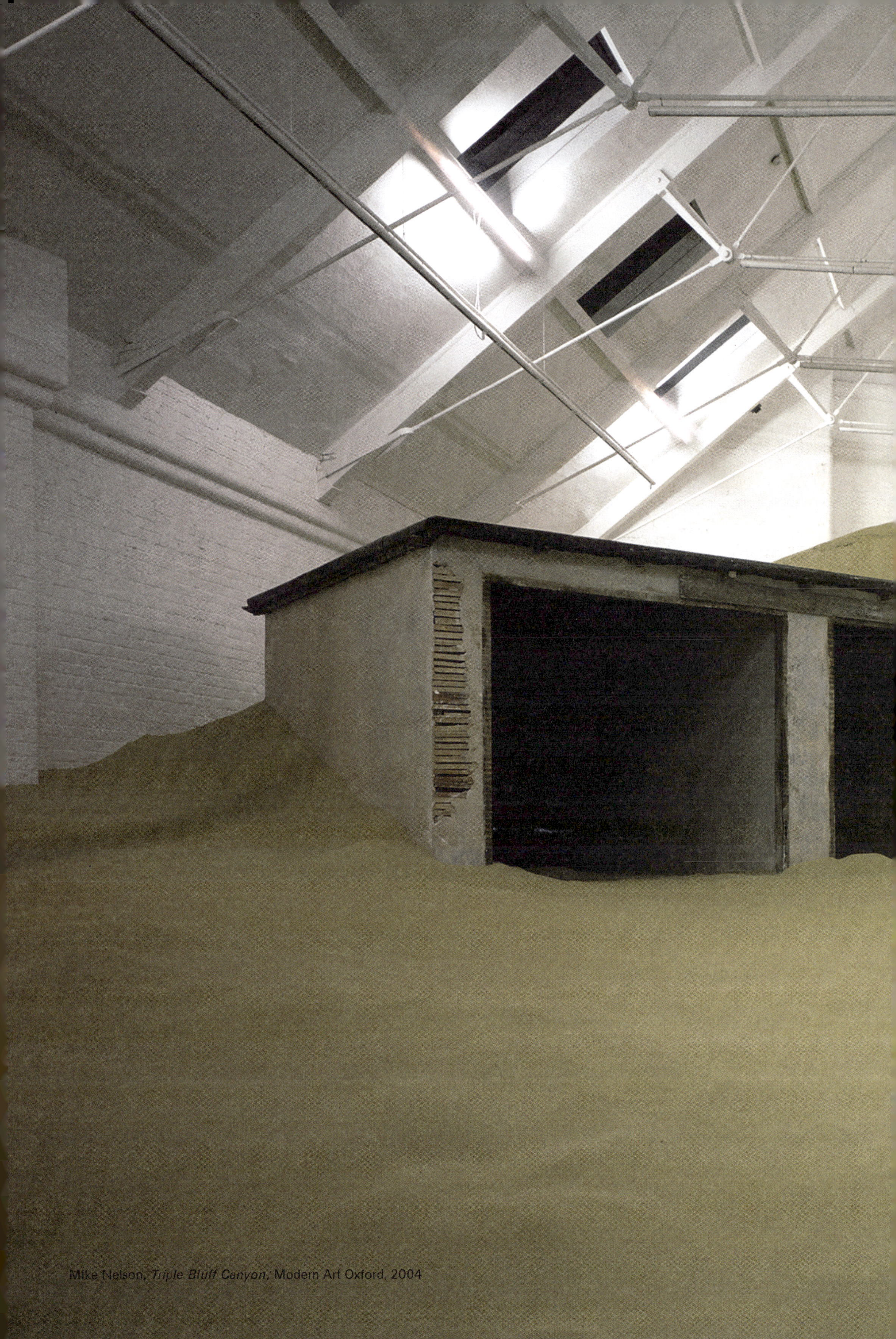

Mike Nelson, *Triple Bluff Canyon*, Modern Art Oxford, 2004

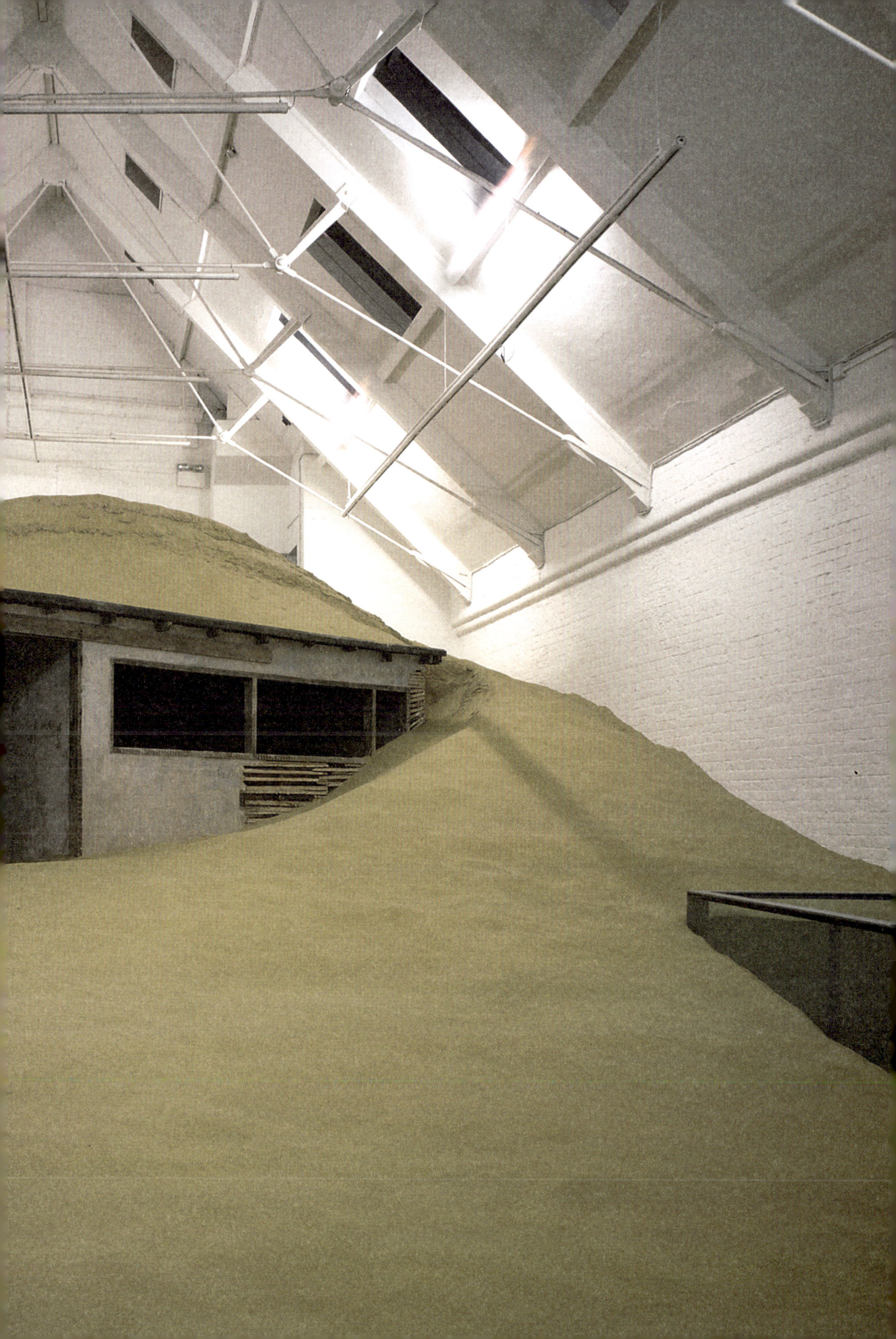

Otobong Nkanga

KALEIDOSCOPE: It's Me to the World
20 August – 16 October 2016

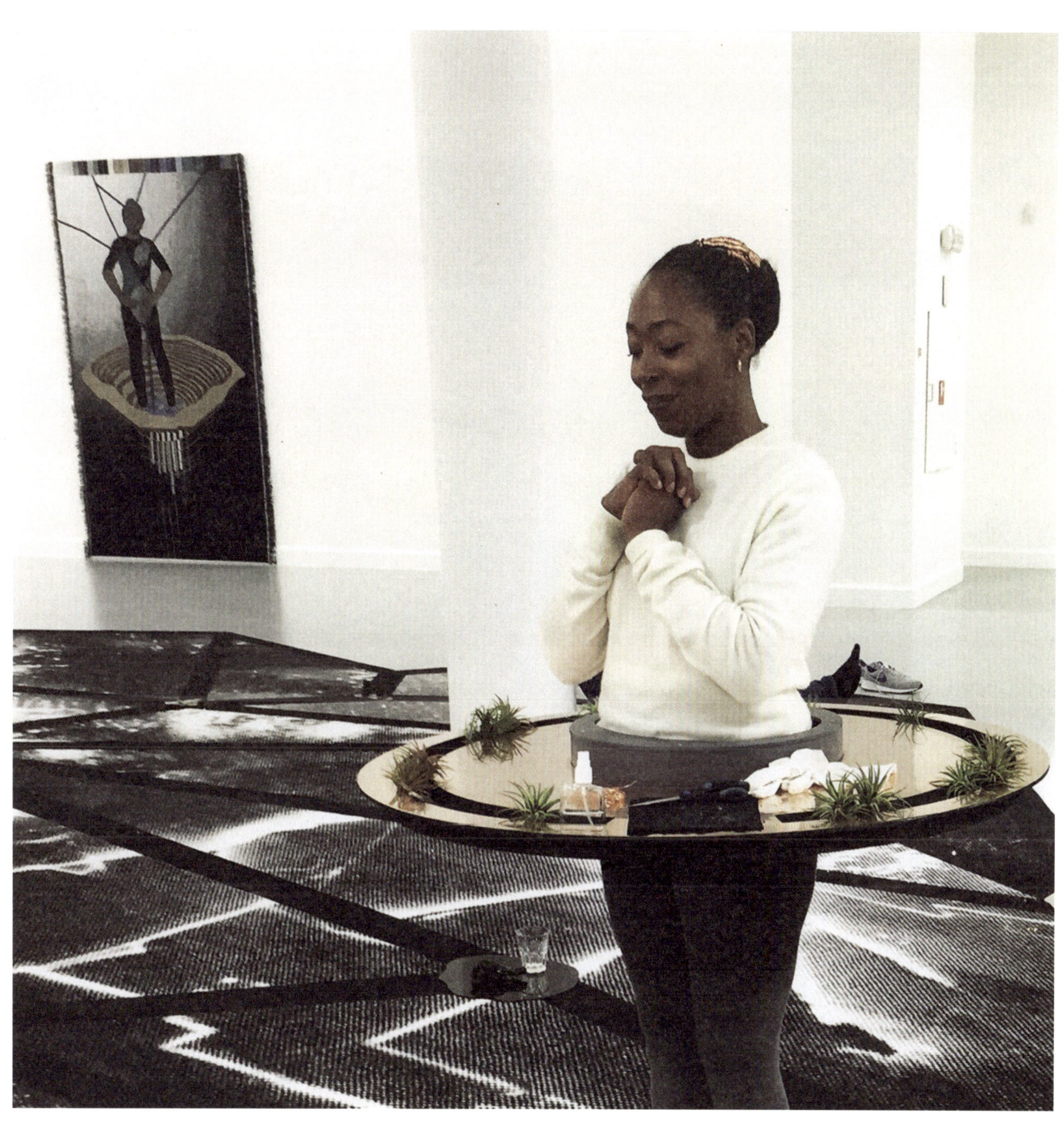

Performance still from *From Where I Stand – Glimmer Unfold*,
Museum of Contemporary Art, Antwerp (M HKA), 2015

Otobong Nkanga, *Tsumeb Fragments*, Kadist Art Foundation, 2015

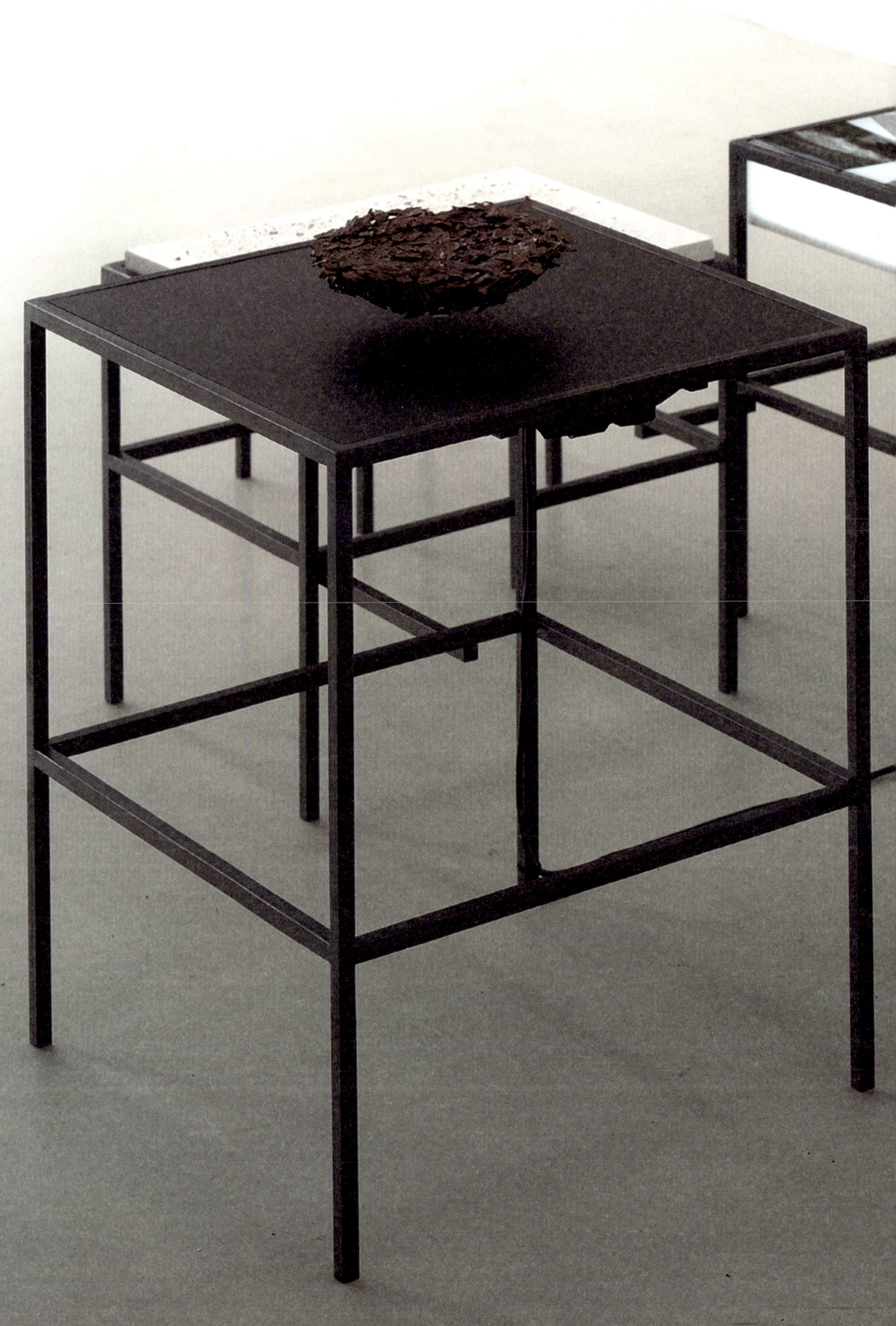

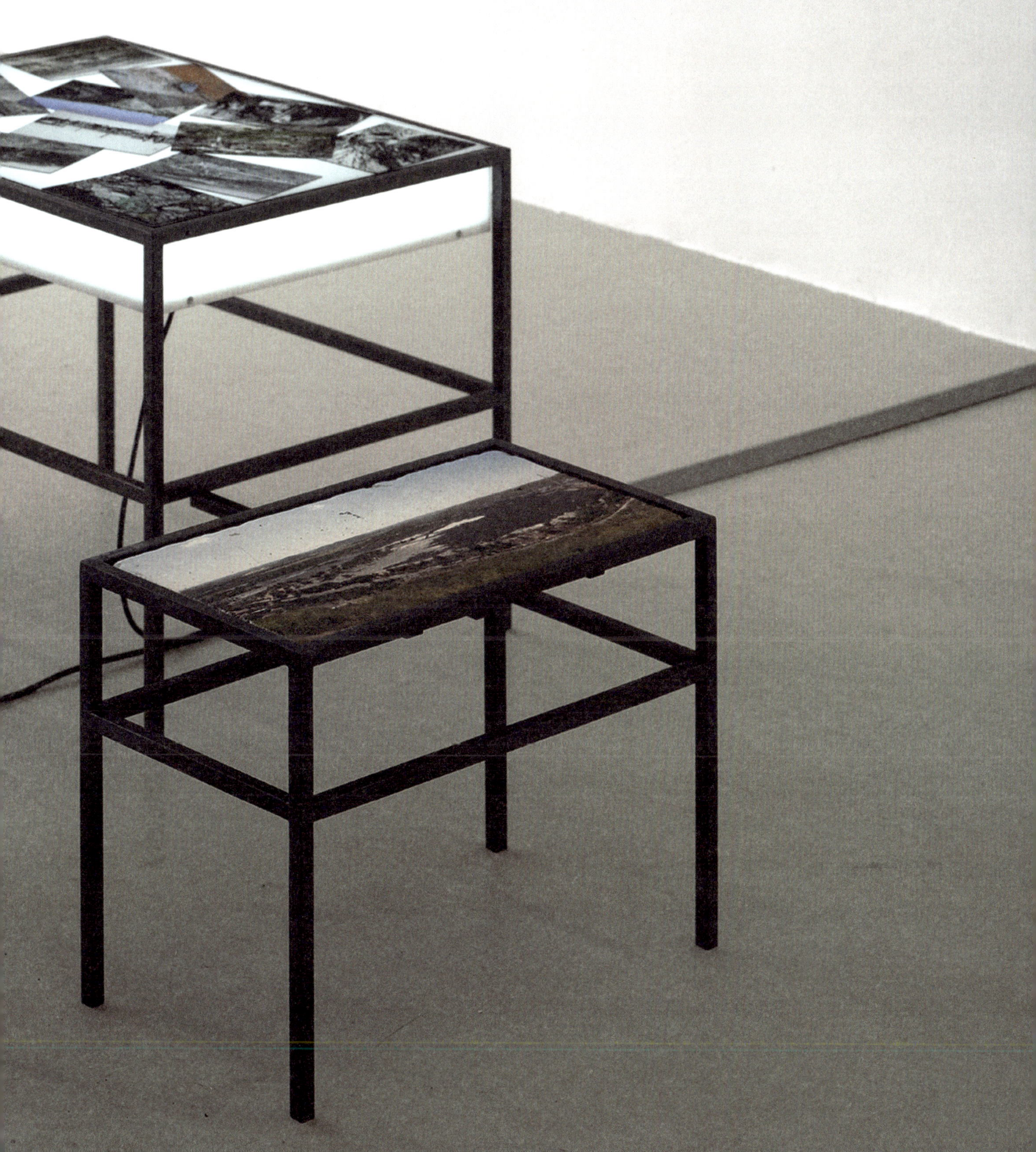

Katja Novitskova

KALEIDOSCOPE: The Vanished Reality
12 November – 31 December 2016

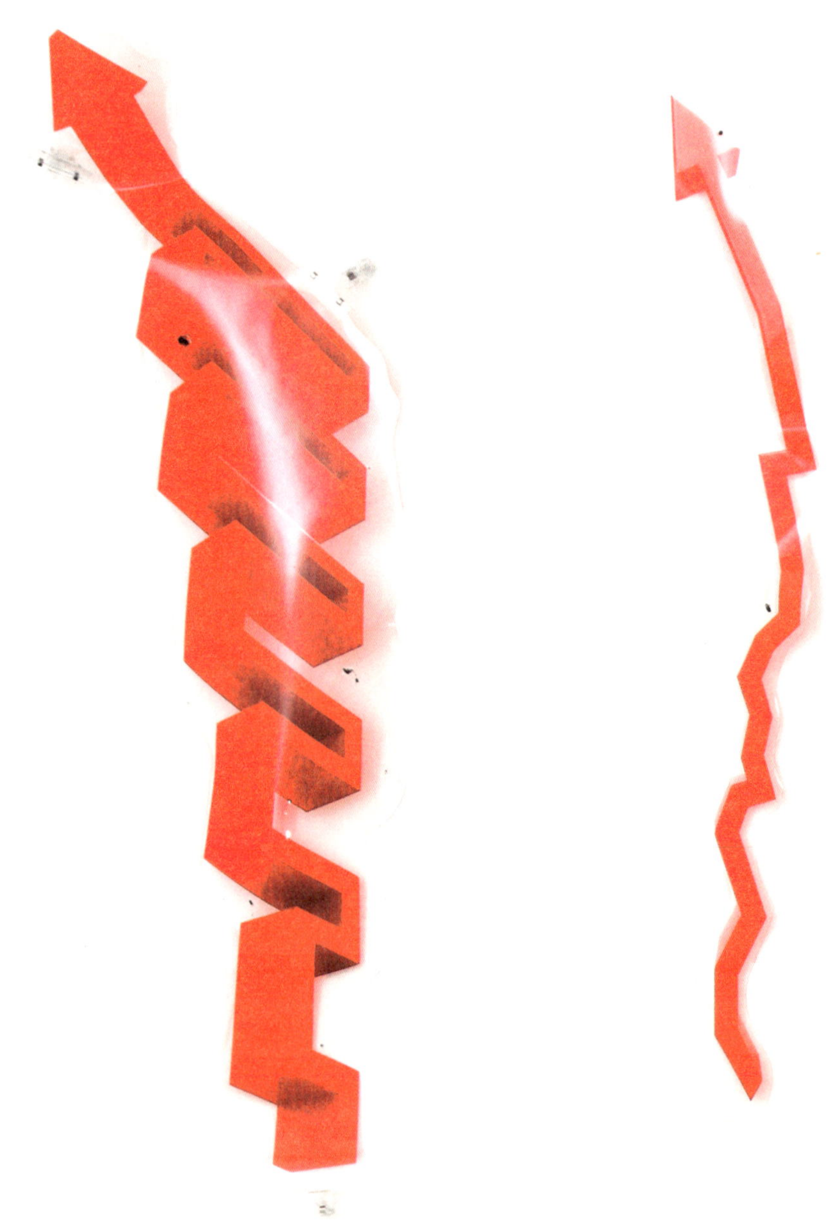

Growth Potentials (Mars), 2014

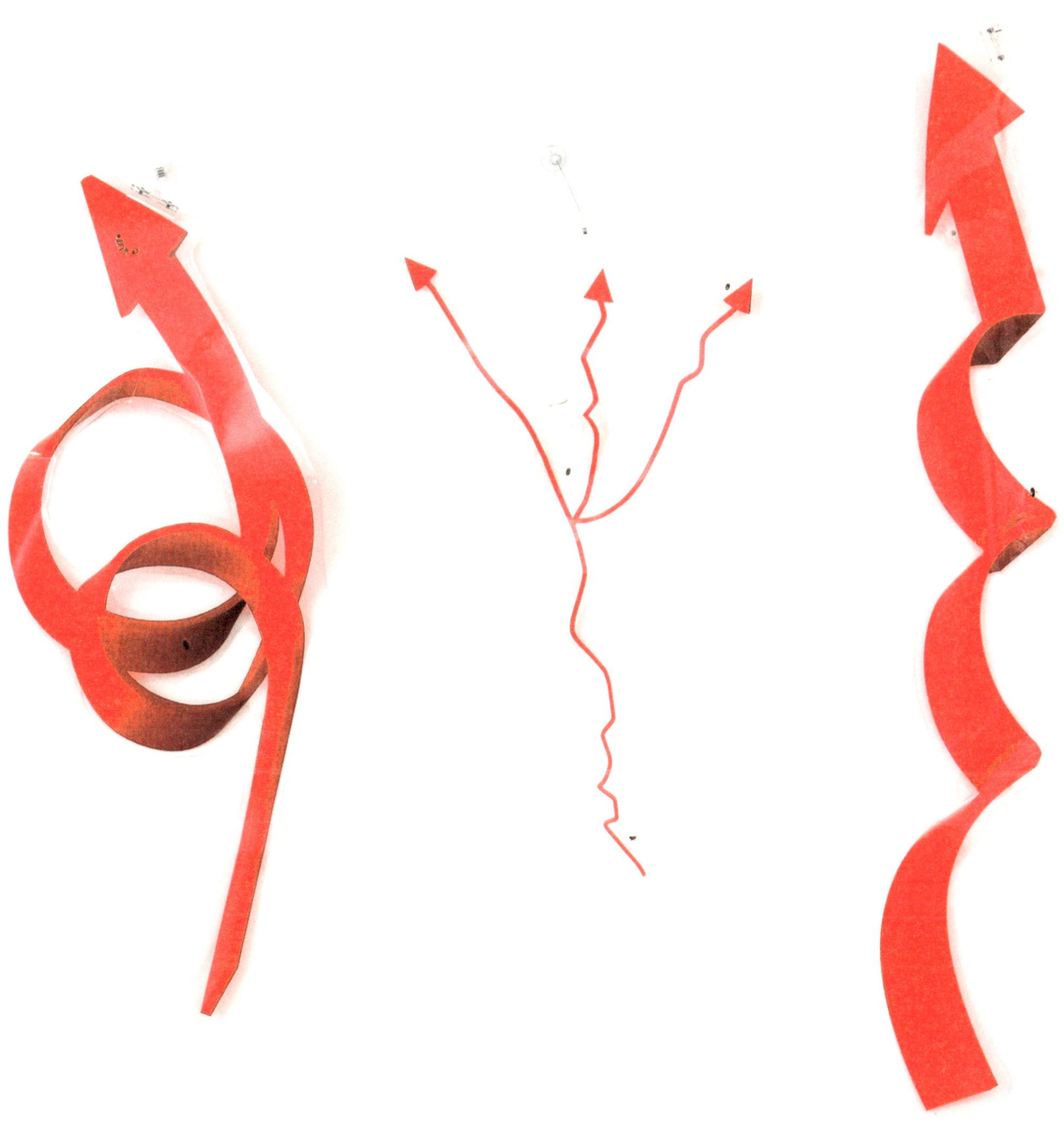

Gareth Nyandoro

KALEIDOSCOPE: A Moment of Grace
16 April – 22 May 2016

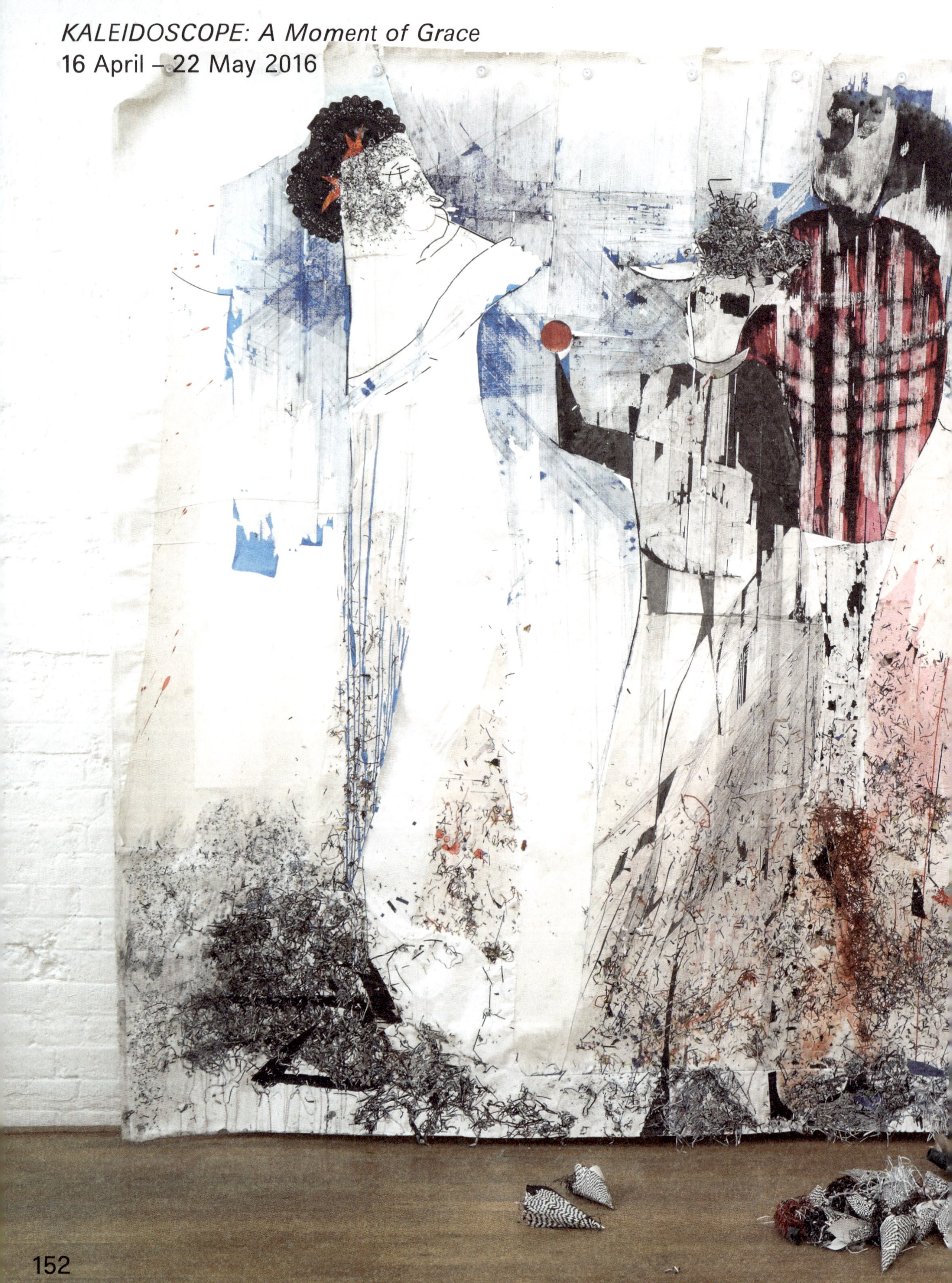

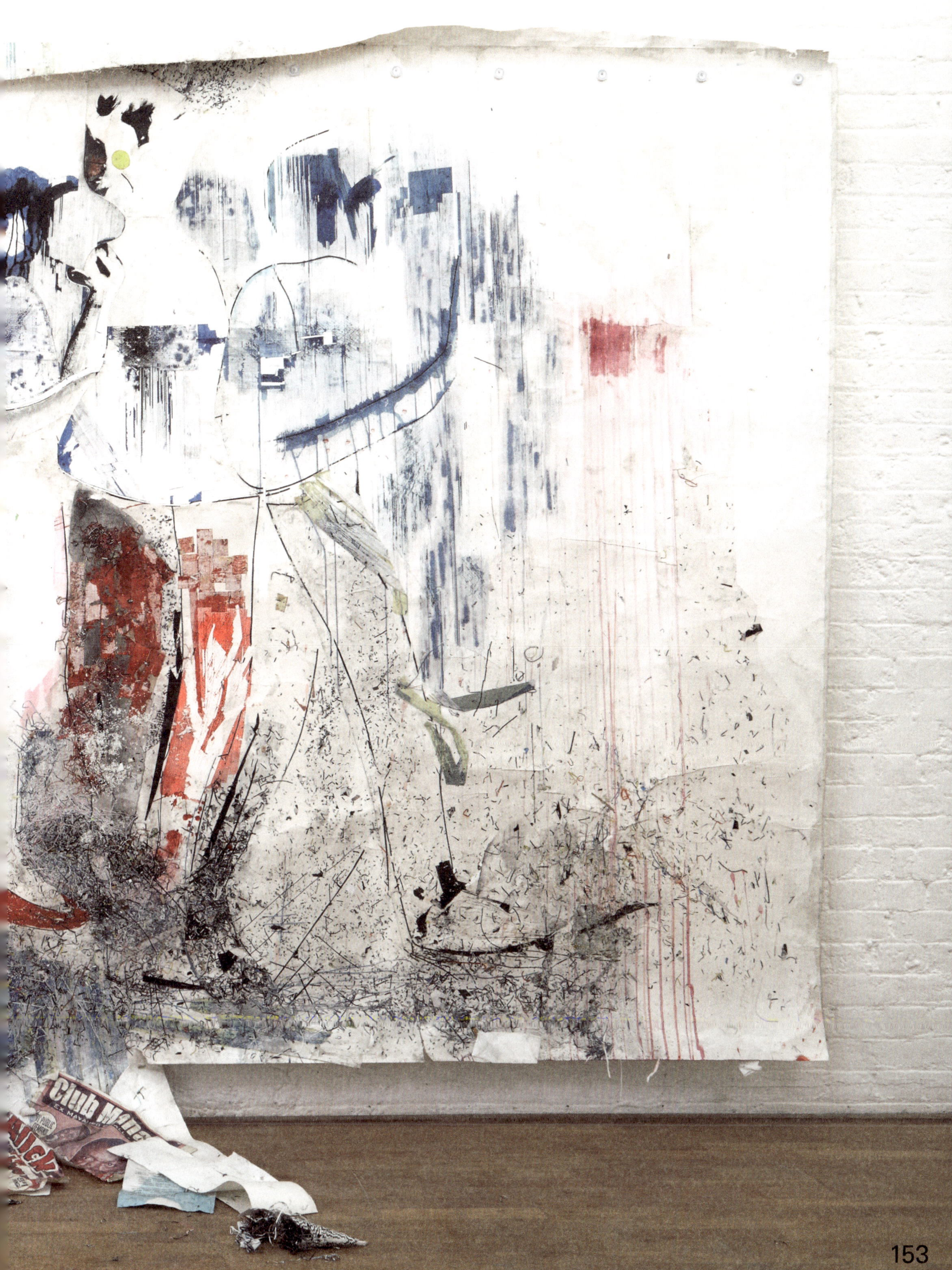

Kuguruguda Stambo (hypnotic lollipop eaters), Modern Art Oxford, 2016

153

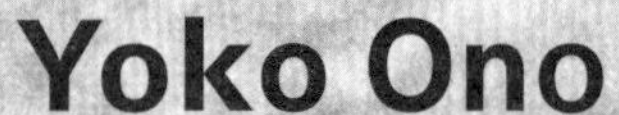

Yoko Ono

KALEIDOSCOPE
6 February – 31 December 2016

Yoko Ono: *Have you seen the horizon lately?*
23 November 1997 – 15 March 1998

Space Place: Constructed Space Participation
28 November – 24 December 1966

Yoko Ono

KALEIDOSCOPE
6 February – 31 December 2016

Yoko Ono writing on wall of Upper Gallery, Museum of Modern Art Oxford, 1997

YOKO ONO
23 November 1997 - 15 March 1998

Have you seen the horizon lately?

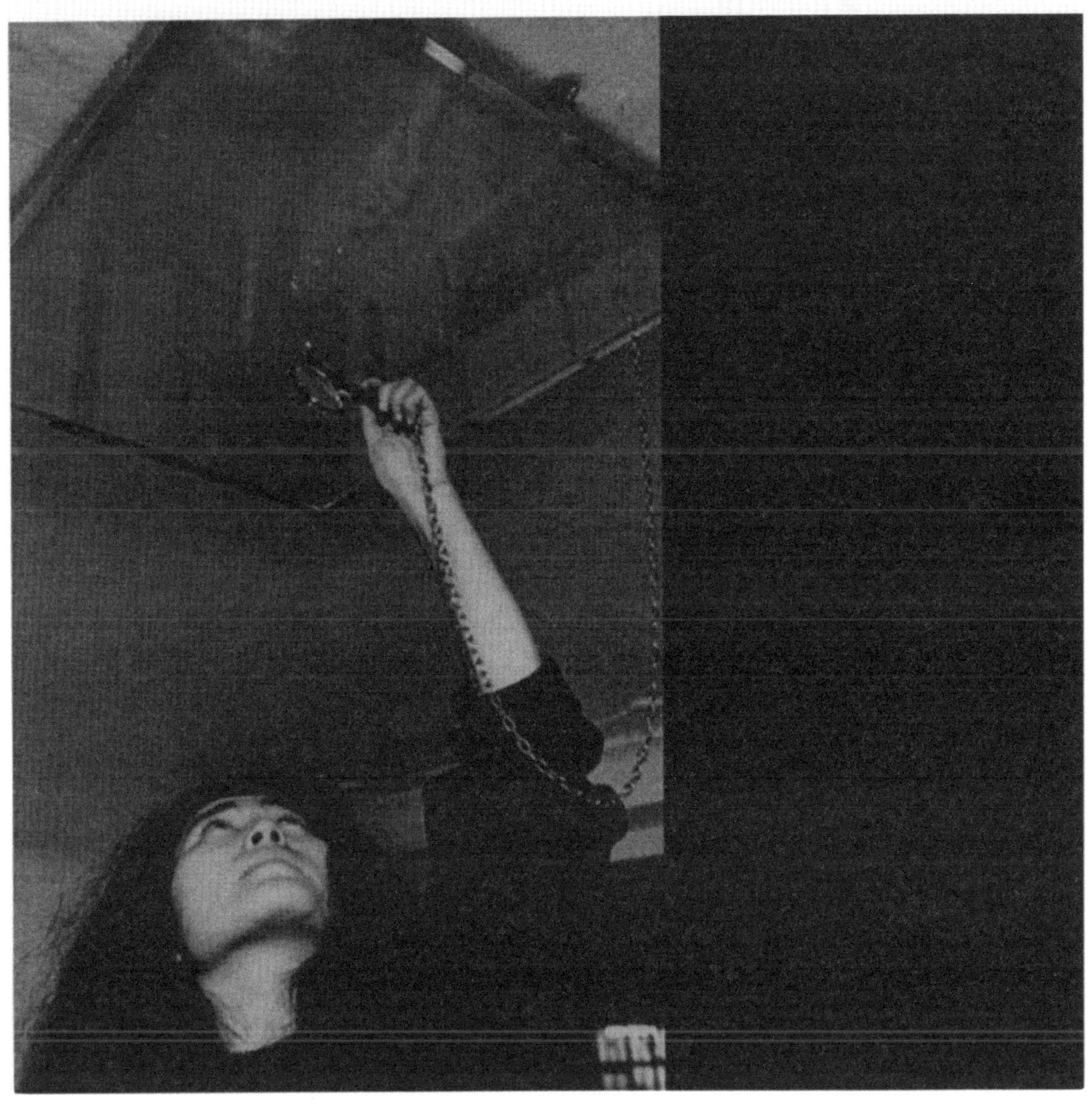

Exhibition invitation, 1997

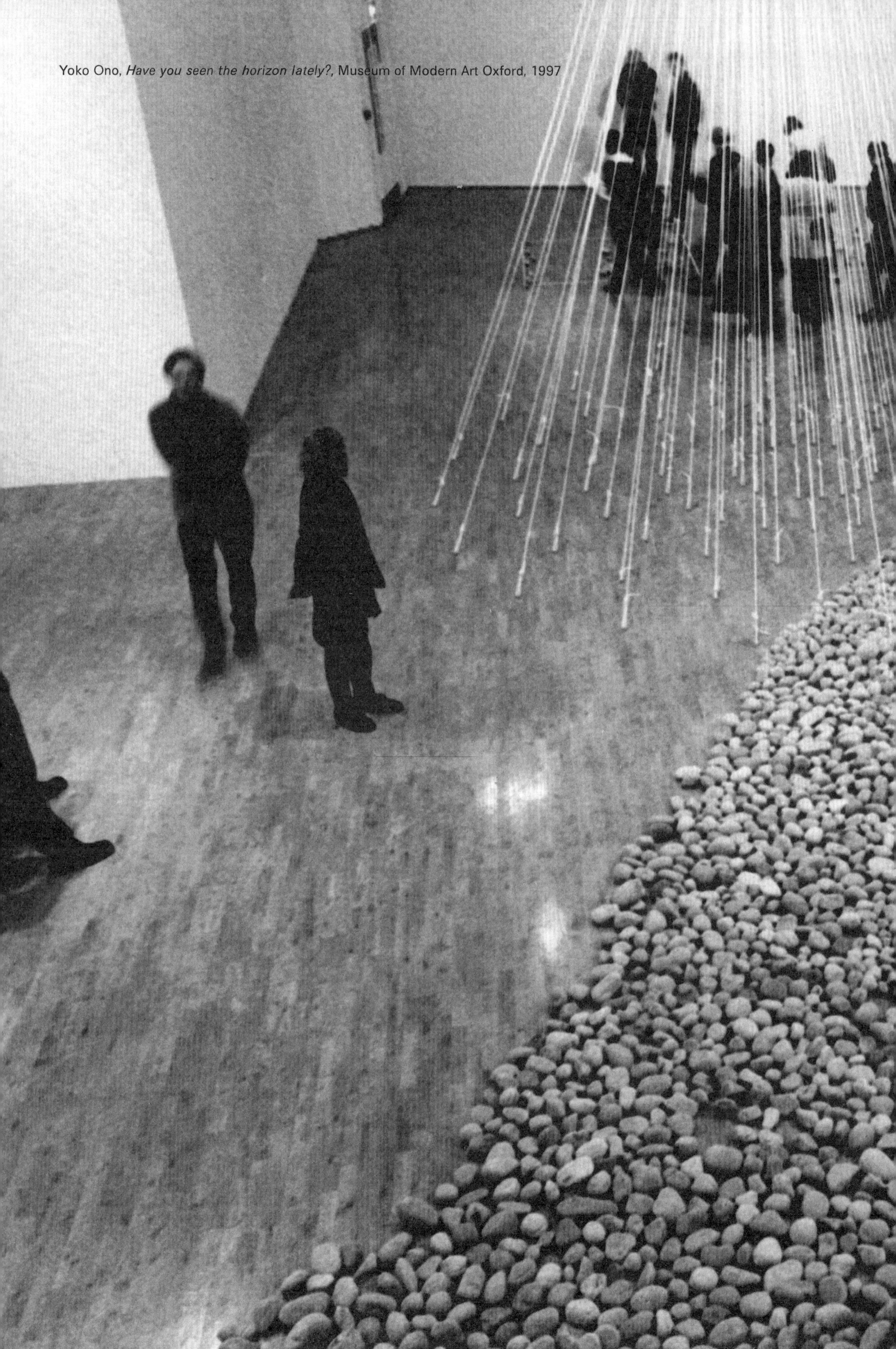

Yoko Ono, *Have you seen the horizon lately?*, Museum of Modern Art Oxford, 1997

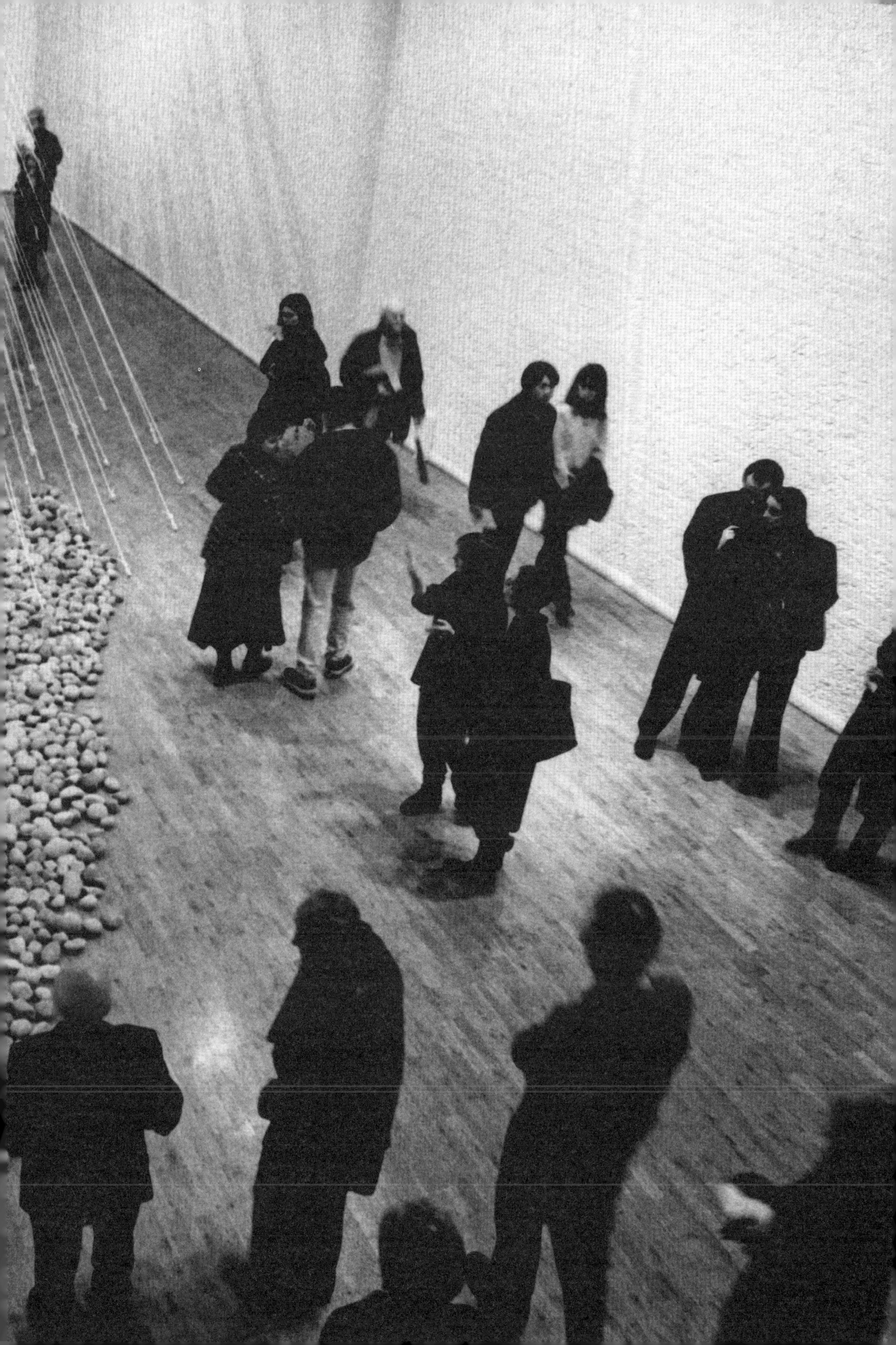

Open Music Archive

KALEIDOSCOPE: A Moment of Grace
16 April – 22 May 2016

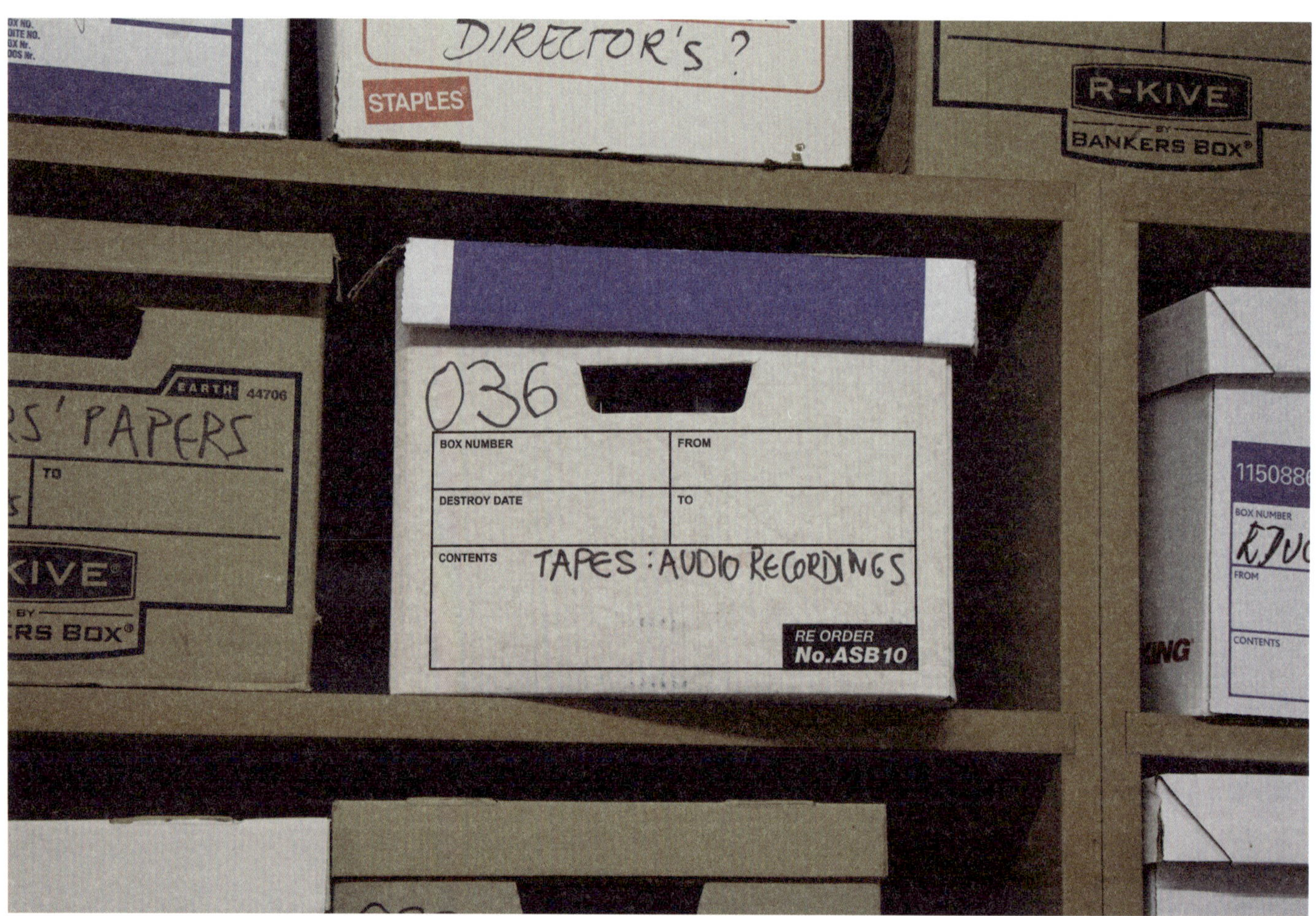

Research image, Archive, Modern Art Oxford, 2015

In the spirit of the 1960s project of the Museum of
Modern Art Oxford, to make contemporary art freely
accessible to the widest audience, artists Eileen Simpson
and Ben White produce an archive of recorded sounds
– auditory traces of activity in the gallery, available for
use by a future public, without restriction and beyond
the scope of the current copyright term.

Tape hiss, voices, musical fragments, audience shuffles
and applause, recorded at past public events, are
digitised from videotapes and audio cassettes held
in the Modern Art Oxford archive, to generate a new
sonic inventory. In addition, samples of chart hit records
from 1966, the museum's inaugural year, are ripped from
vinyl 45s. The artists process the archival sounds using
emerging information retrieval technologies, to create
a bank of source material and a new work for exhibition:
Premonition 2037. A series of live events with invited
collaborators, reanimate these sounds on a specially
assembled platform. The events are recorded and
stored in the archive for future release in 2037, the
year the material will legally fall into public ownership.
www.openmusicarchive.org/premonition2037

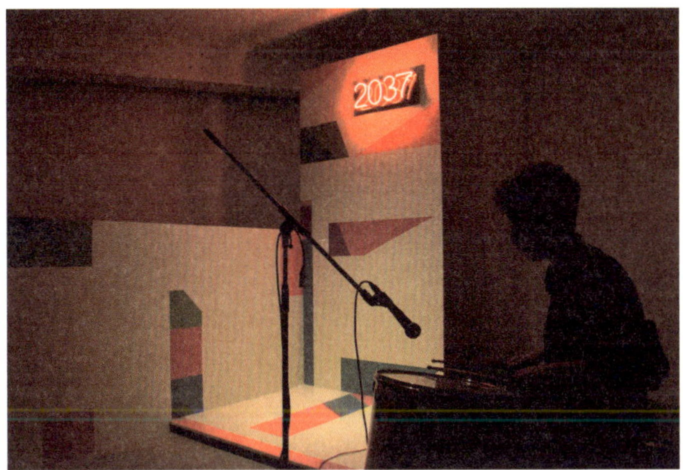

Premonition 2037, Modern Art Oxford, 2016

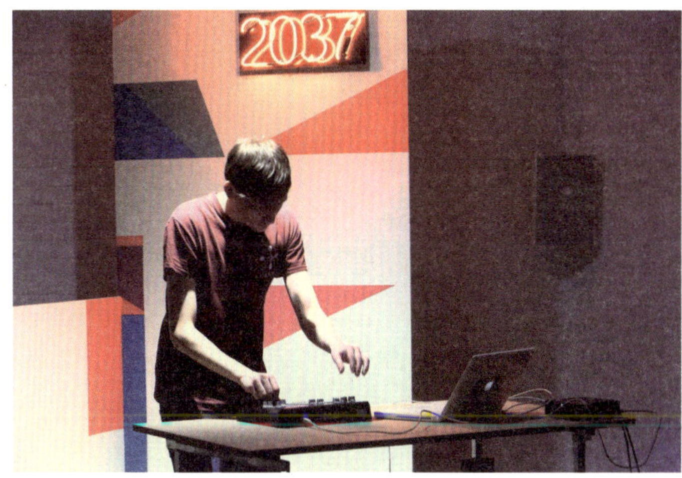

Premonition 2037, Modern Art Oxford, 2016

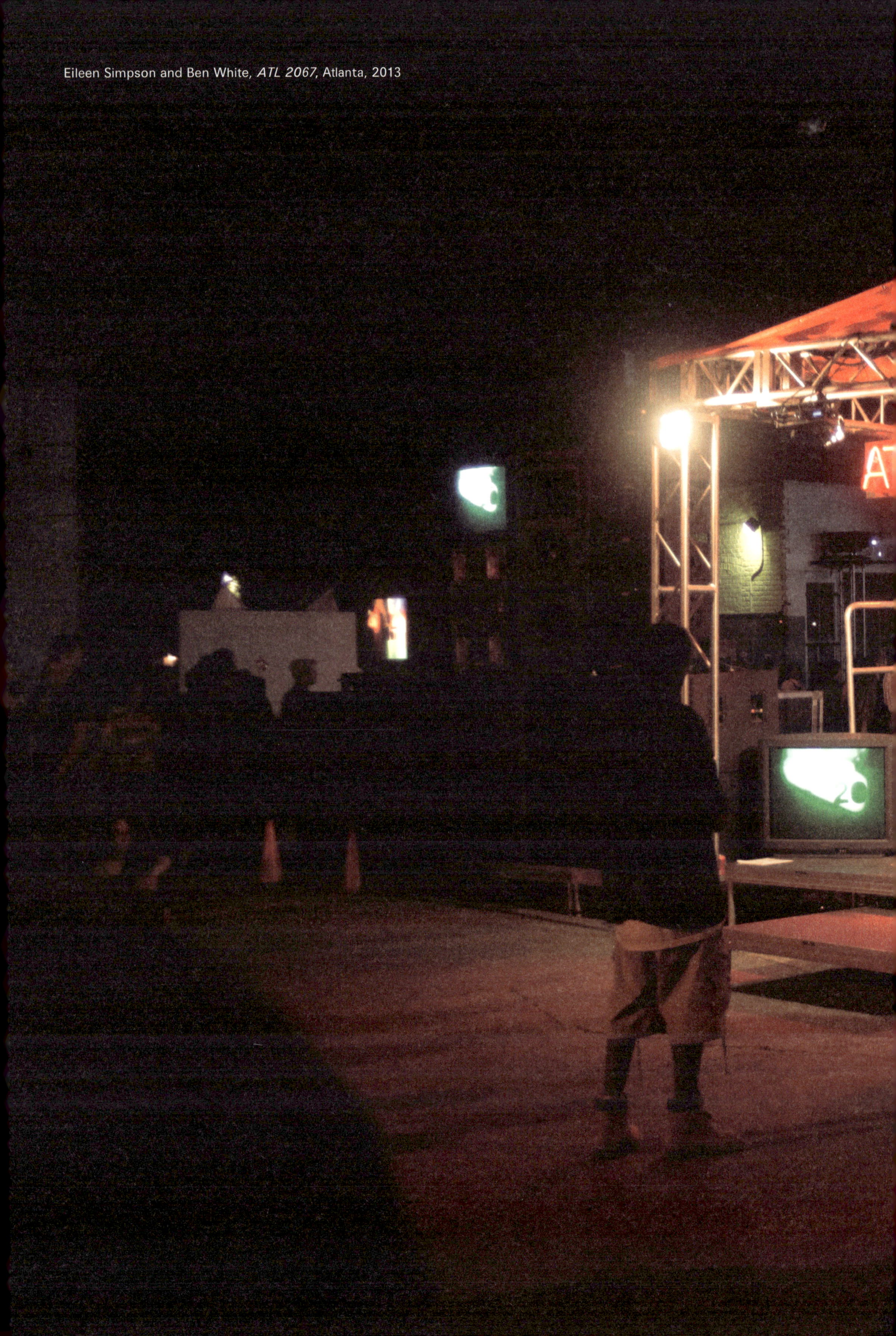

Eileen Simpson and Ben White, *ATL 2067*, Atlanta, 2013

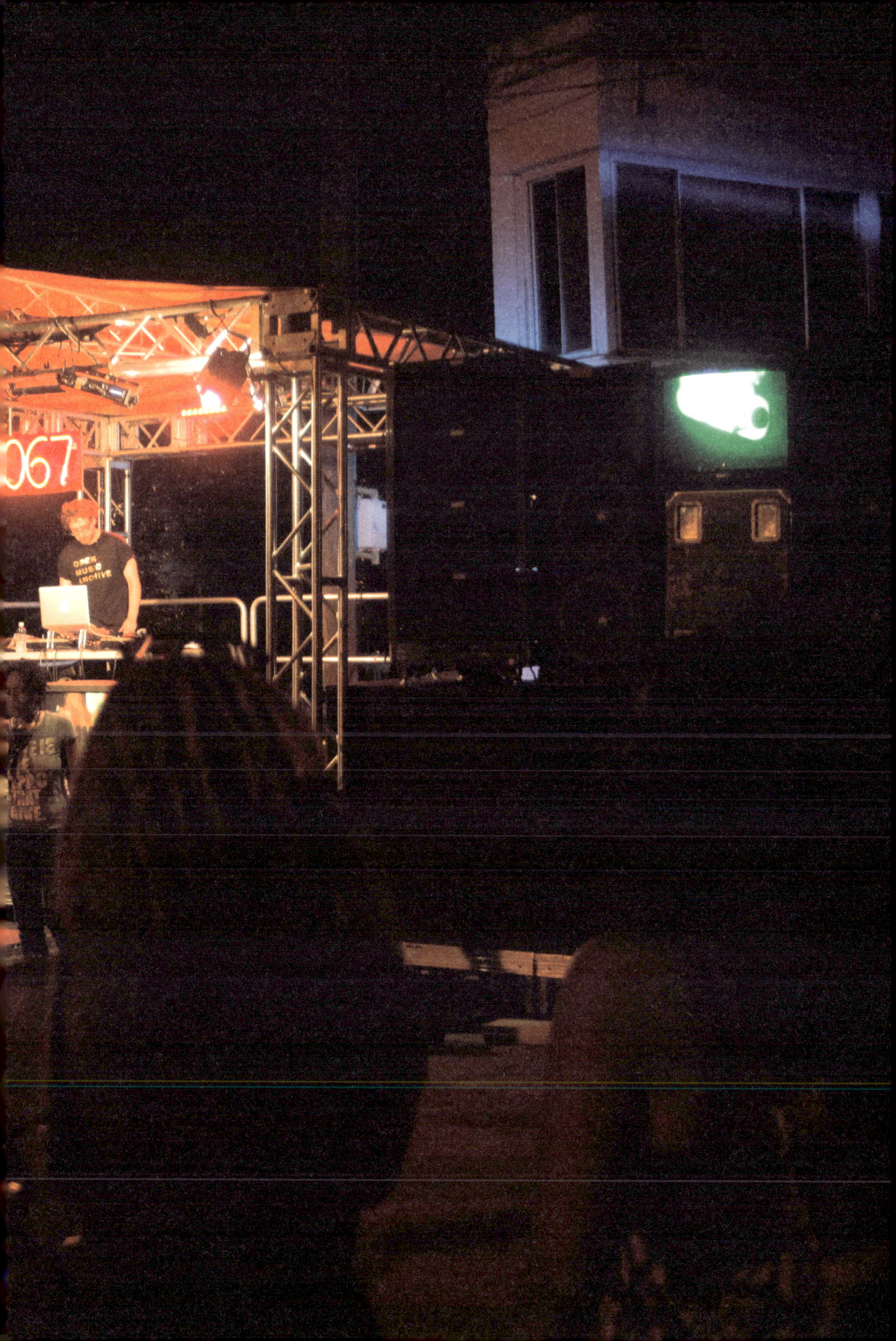

067
OPEN
MUSIC
ARCHIVE

Sally O'Reilly

KALEIDOSCOPE Writer in *Residence*
6 February – 31 December 2016

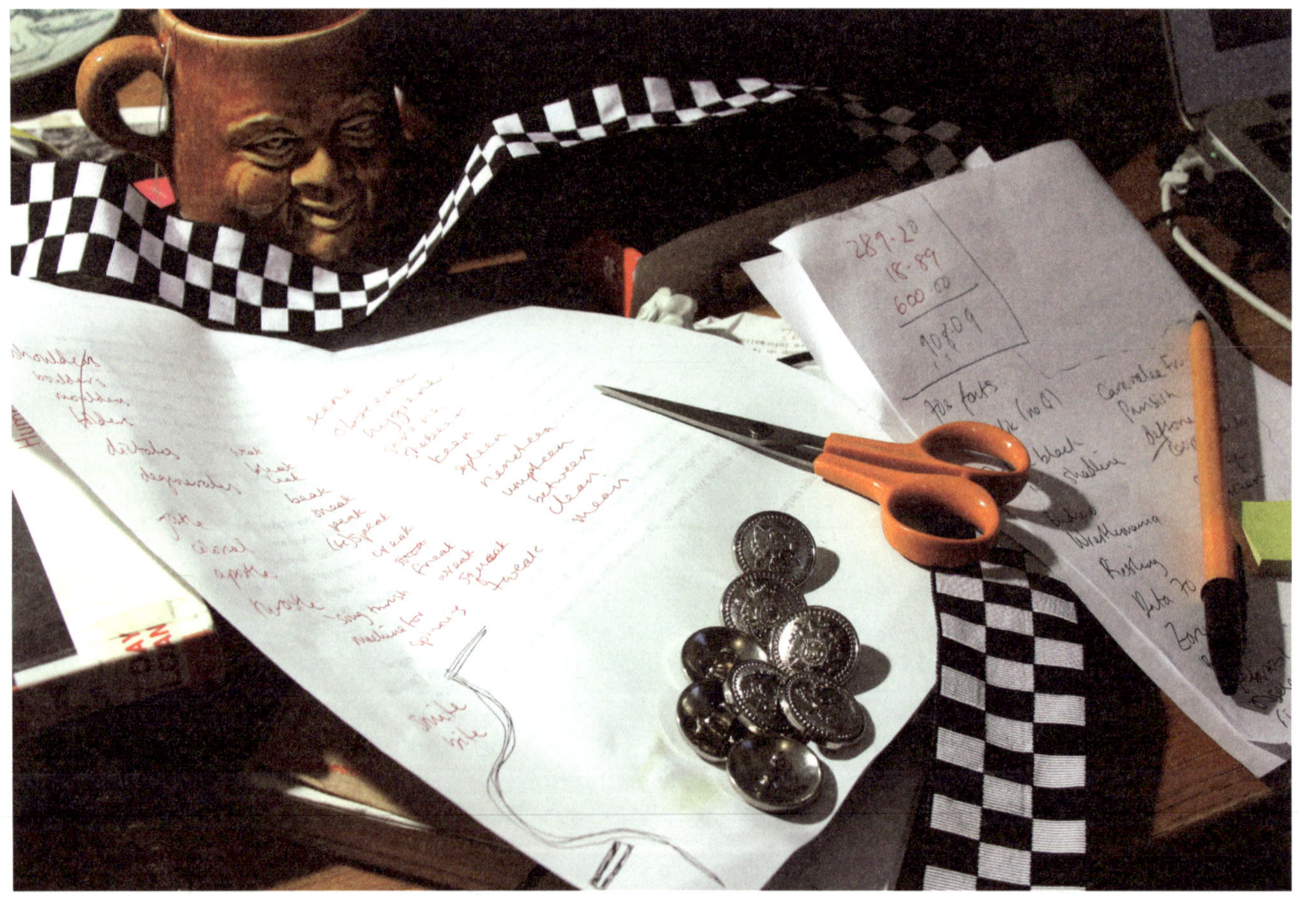

Work in progress image from the artist's studio, 2016

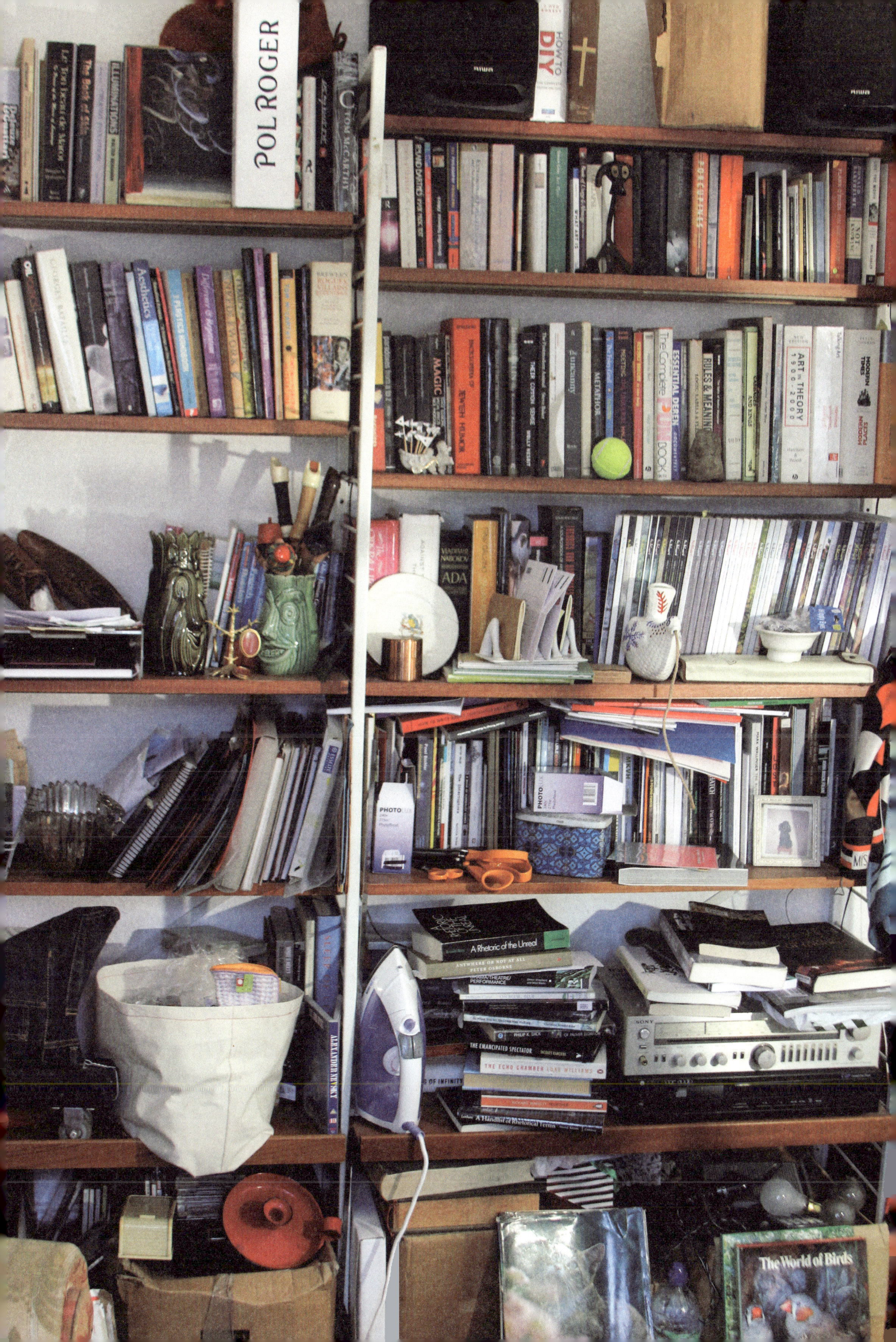

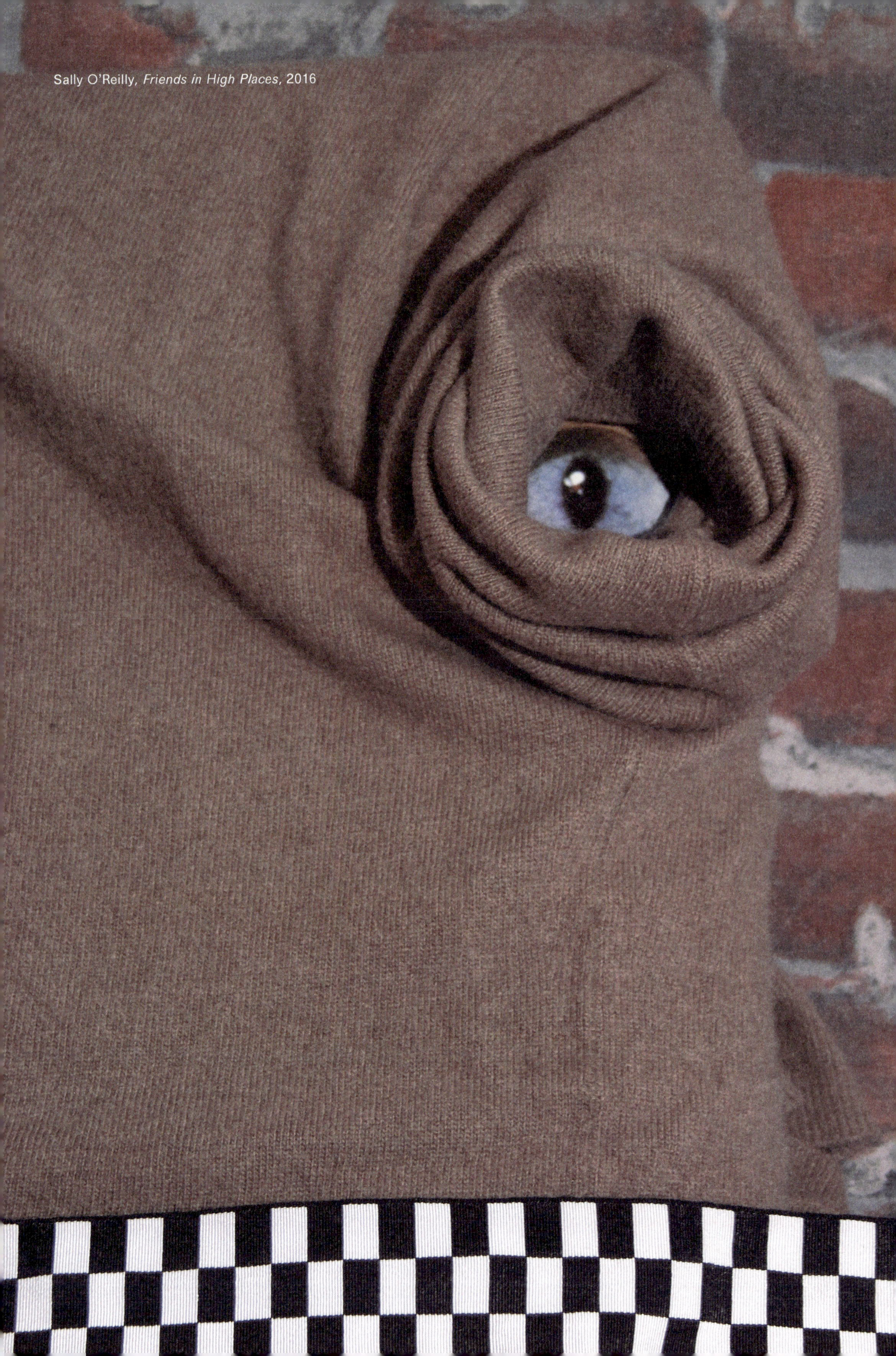
Sally O'Reilly, *Friends in High Places*, 2016

ACT 1, SCENE 3

Incidental music continued

GLITZY PRESENTER

I am delighted to announce that the weather is clement and also that for your pleasure
commentating the inspection for you this evening is Sir Dawnay Lemon, C.B.E., Q.P.M.
The Chief Constable of Kent.

SIR DAWNAY LEMON
(voiced by violin)

Good evening.

GLITZY PRESENTER

Good evening Sir Dawnay.
Gibbins, call Team A for inspection.

STEWARD

Calling Team A for inspec-shun!

SCENE 3

Fashion show music.
Spotlight moves across screen/catwalk for each promenade.
Pre-recorded footsteps pan left to right and back for each.
SOR appears to Foley footsteps.

SIR DAWNAY LEMON
(voiced by violin)

Our model here is Bobby for the Peelers, who feel that the traditional methods are taken
for granted, that people think it quite a matter of course that they sleep and wake in safety
in the midst of hordes of starving plunderers.
Bobby's motto is 'the police are servants of the community, armed with prestige, not power'.
That's a great sentiment, Bobby, and what a great look too.
This season is all about authority, and I love this jacket, which is channelling the pomp
of the military with those buttons.
And you get that lovely sharp four-pocket silhouette and those really defined shoulders,
all set off with a slight cinching at the knee.
And where would we be without a truncheon?
This is a great investment piece, a classic in city or countryside.

STEWARD

Team A dismissed!

Calling Team B for inspec-shun!

SIR DAWNAY LEMON

Next is Carl, from the Flying Squad.
Carl believes the police are enforcers of good laws against bad men,
strengtheners of moral fibre against the dirt of crime, vagrancy, dissipation and insubordination.
His motto is: 'Let them have it!'
As you can see, Carl has updated the classic look with some fabulous accessories.
This lovely asymmetrical vest is a really exciting way to add some volume and disguise
any lumps and bumps, giving you a little extra coverage, if you're feeling a bit exposed.
And I think that because blue-black has become such a central part of all our wardrobes,
the straps and pockets and guns give it that all-important extra bit of texture.

STEWARD

Team B dismissed!

Excerpt from *Live Illuminated Manuscript 1: Police Open Day 1971*, 2016

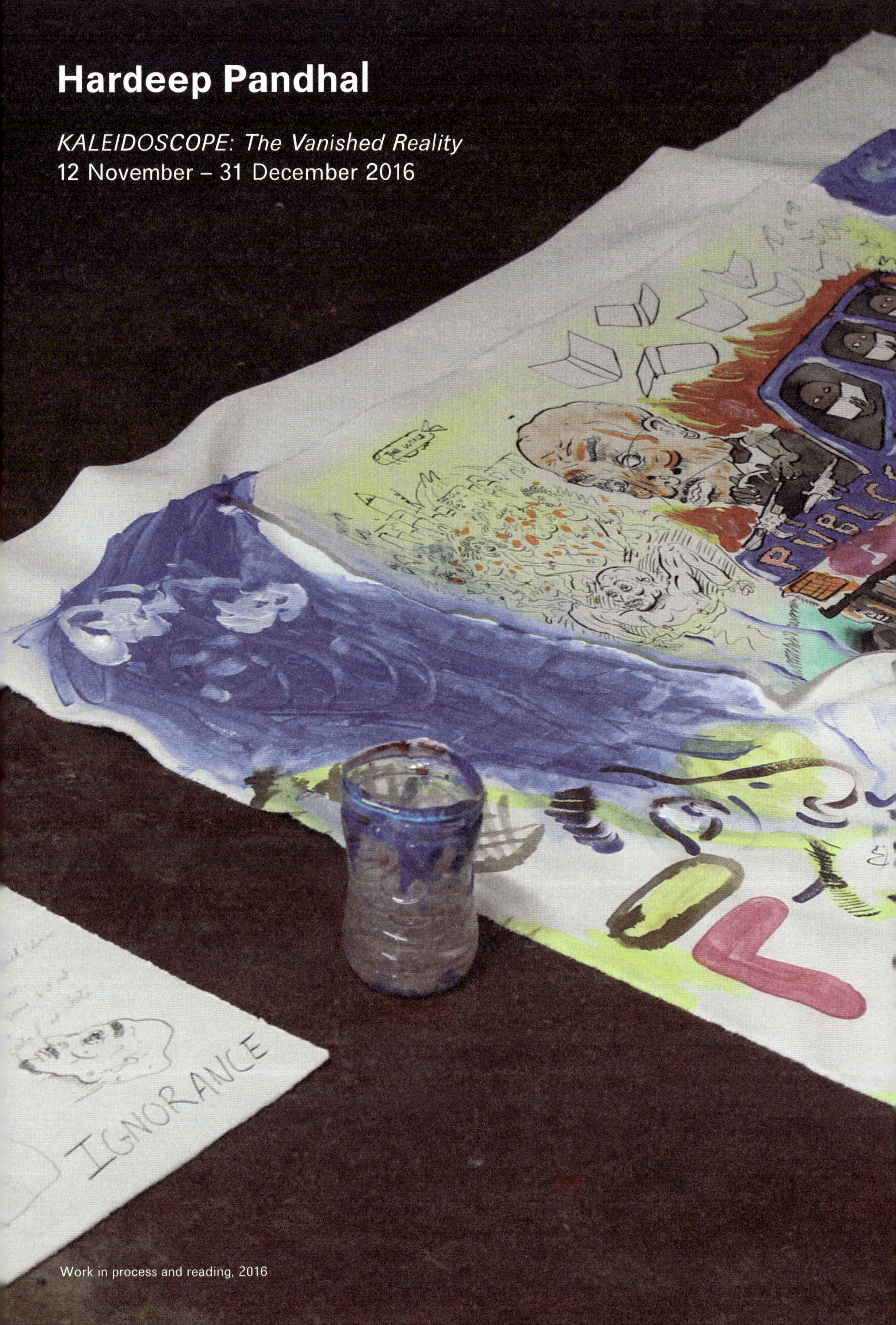

Hardeep Pandhal

KALEIDOSCOPE: The Vanished Reality
12 November – 31 December 2016

Work in process and reading, 2016

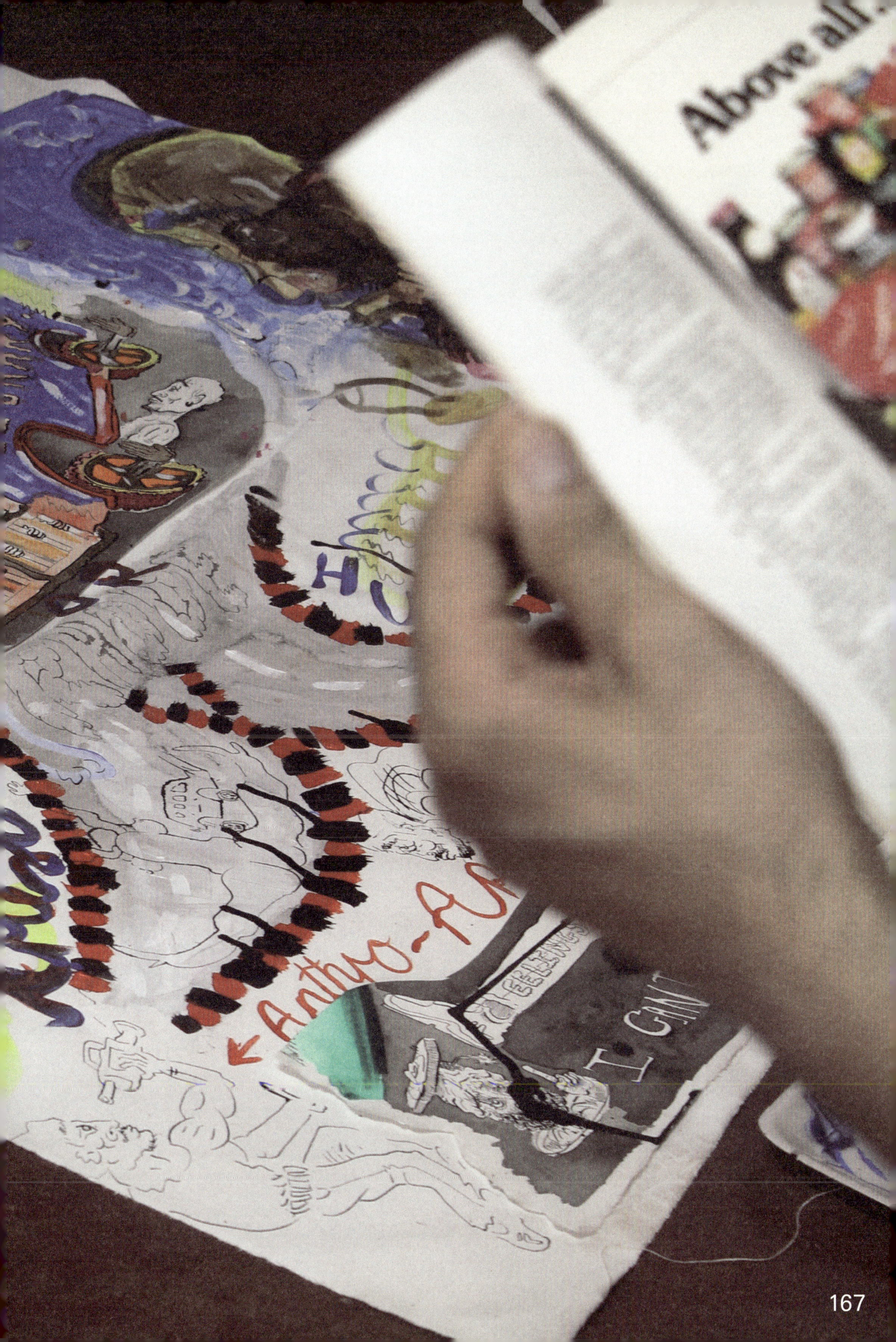

Above all:
Anthro-P
I CAN'T

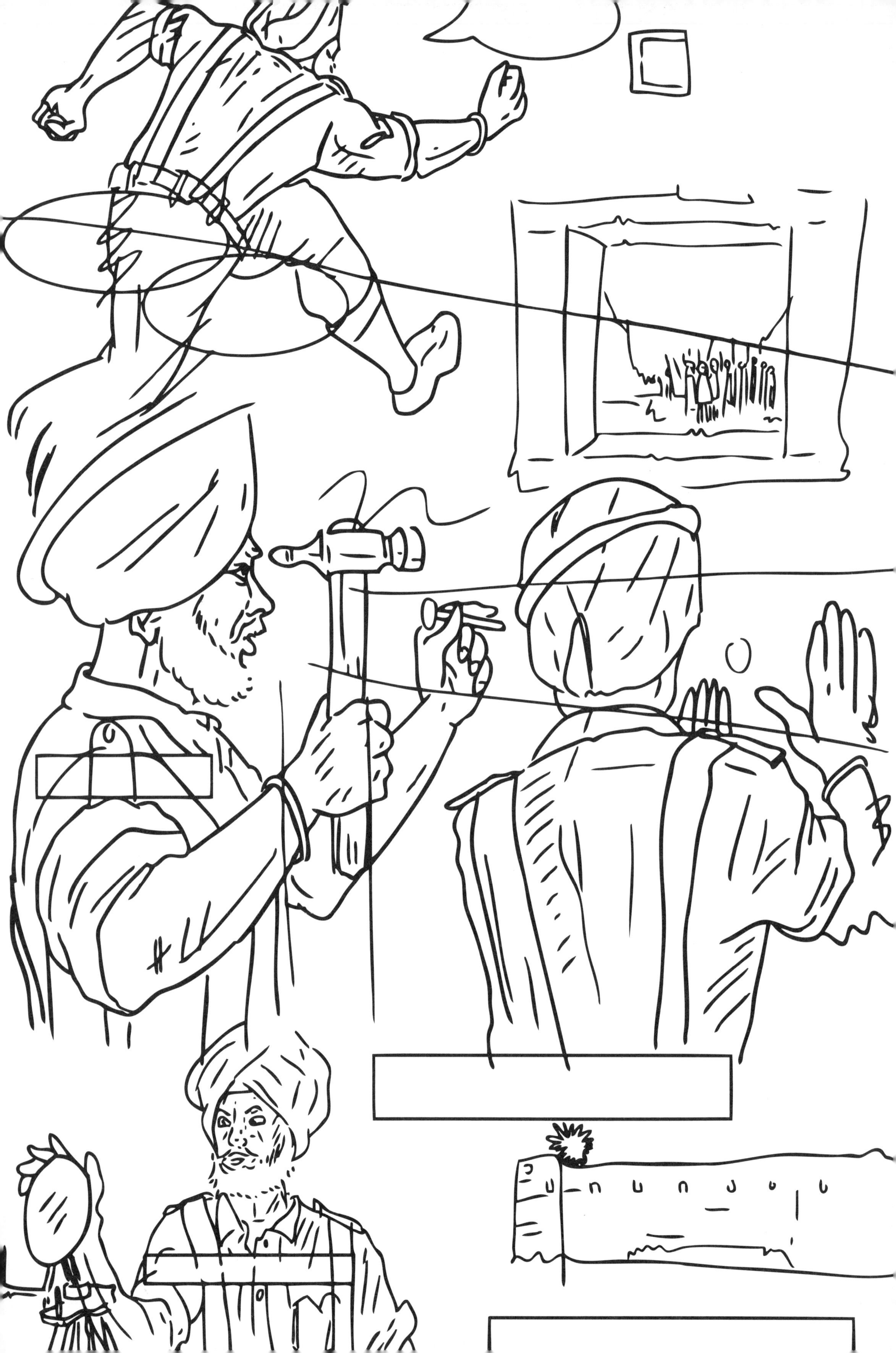

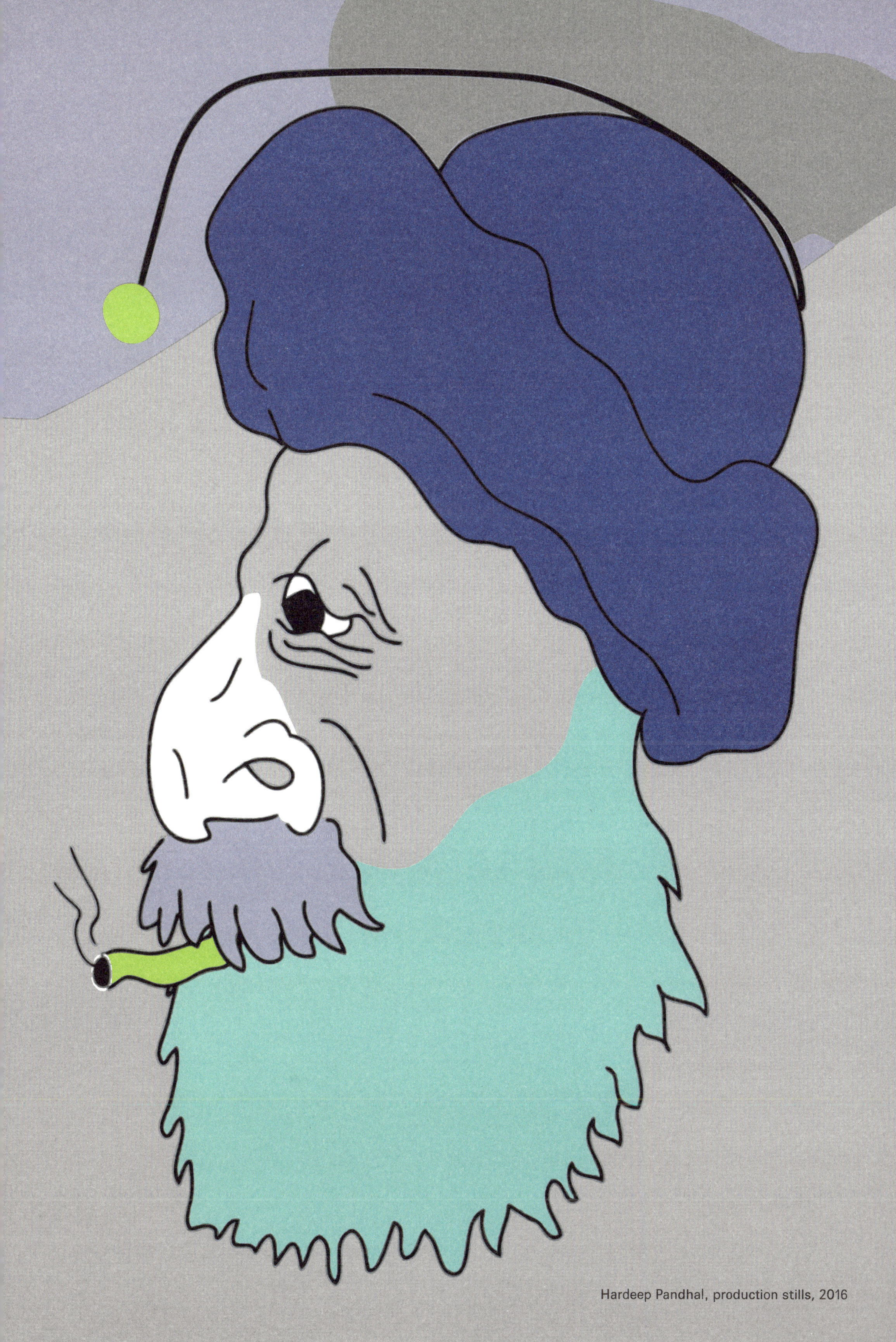

Hardeep Pandhal, production stills, 2016

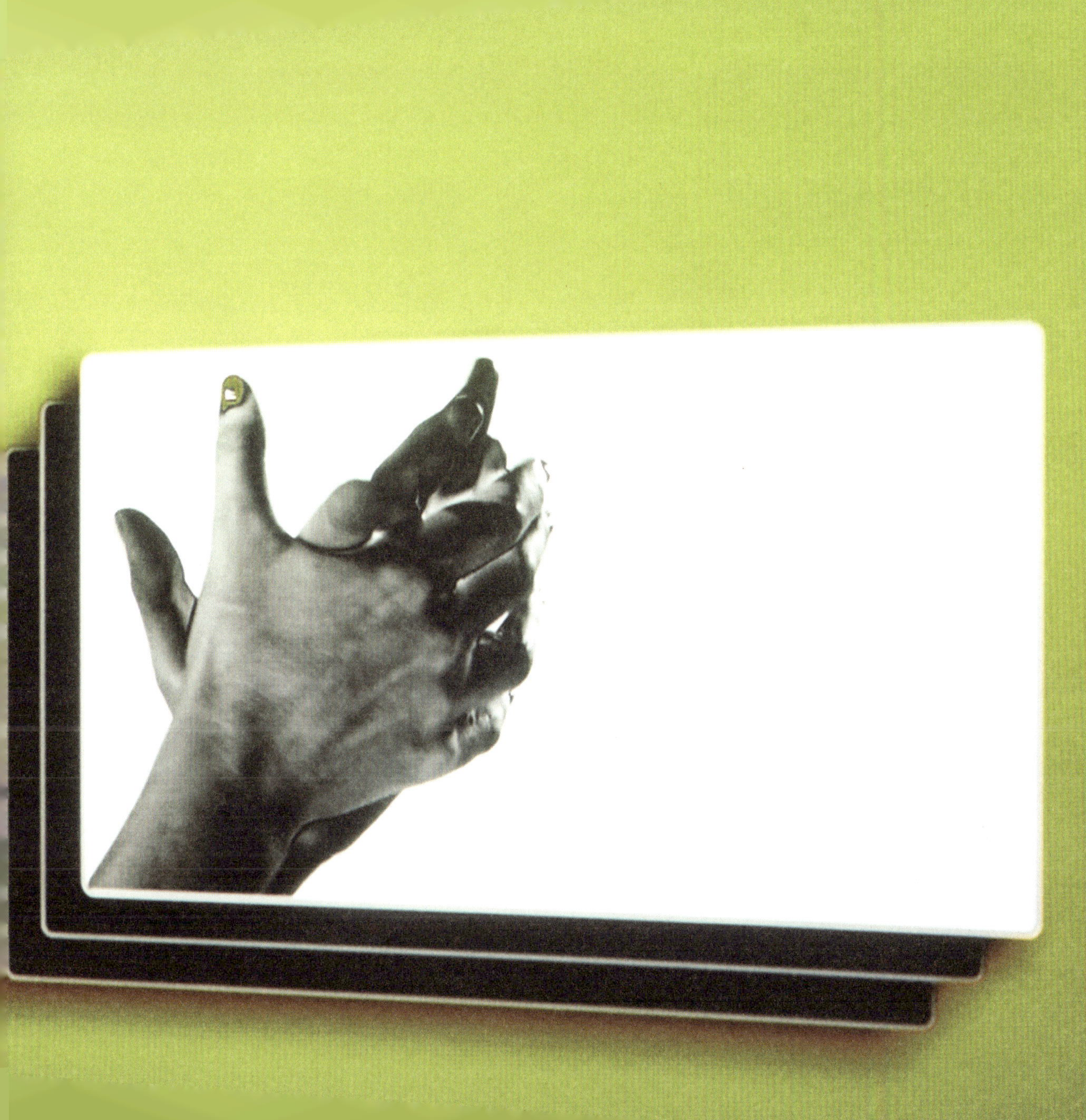

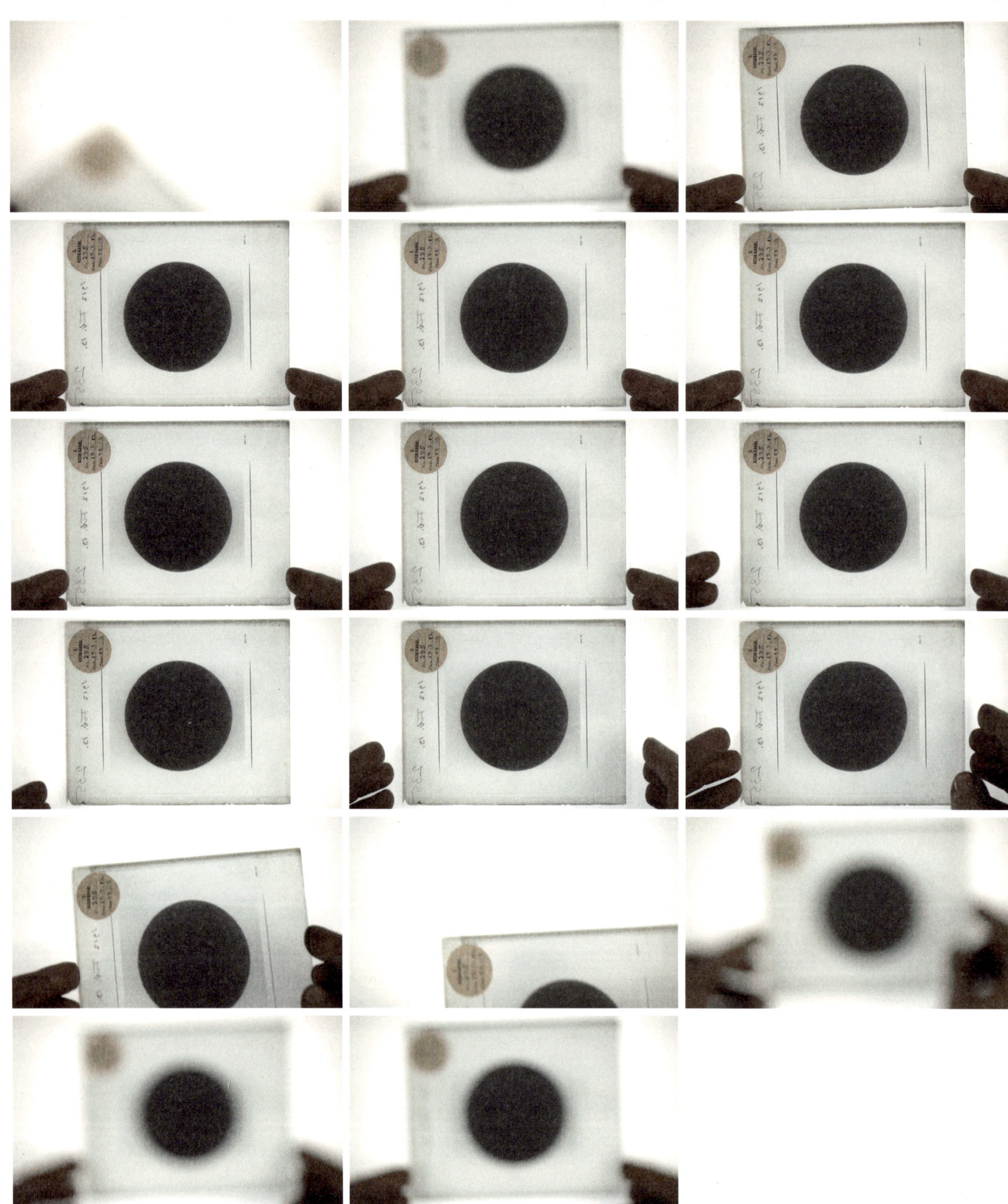

Elizabeth Price, *SLEEP*, source material, 2014

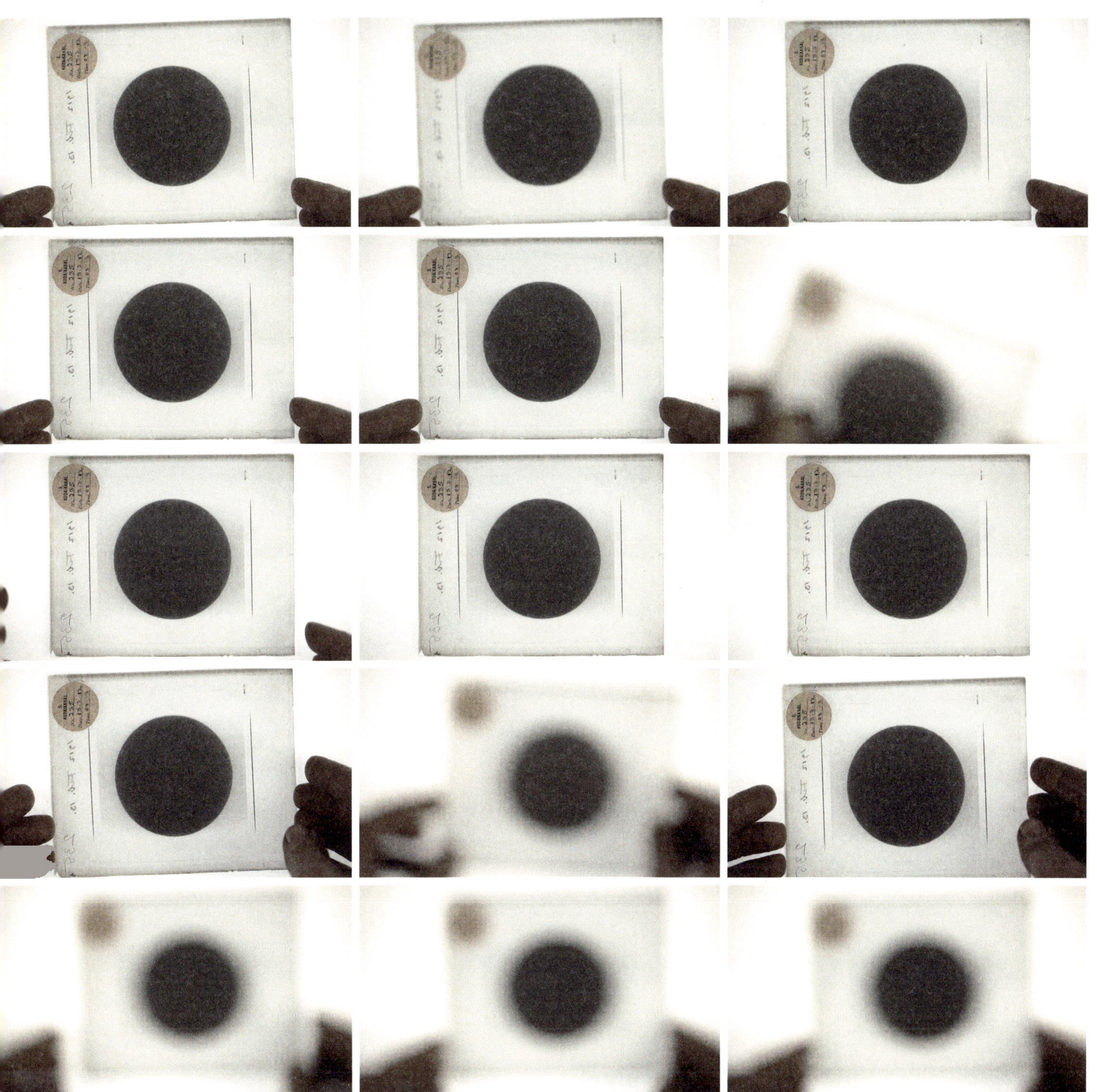

Hannah Rickards

KALEIDOSCOPE: It's Me to the World
20 August – 16 October 2016

Hannah Rickards: *To enable me to fix my attention on any
one of these symbols I was to imagine that I was looking at
the colours as I might see them on a moving picture screen*
15 February – 20 April 2014

A recording of a single clap of thunder was stretched
in length from eight seconds to seven minutes. The resulting
sound was transcribed into a musical score for six
instruments. The musical score was performed, recorded
and then reduced in length to eight seconds.

A flute, trumpet, trombone, cello, viola and violin now
replicate the original thunder.

Thunder, 2005

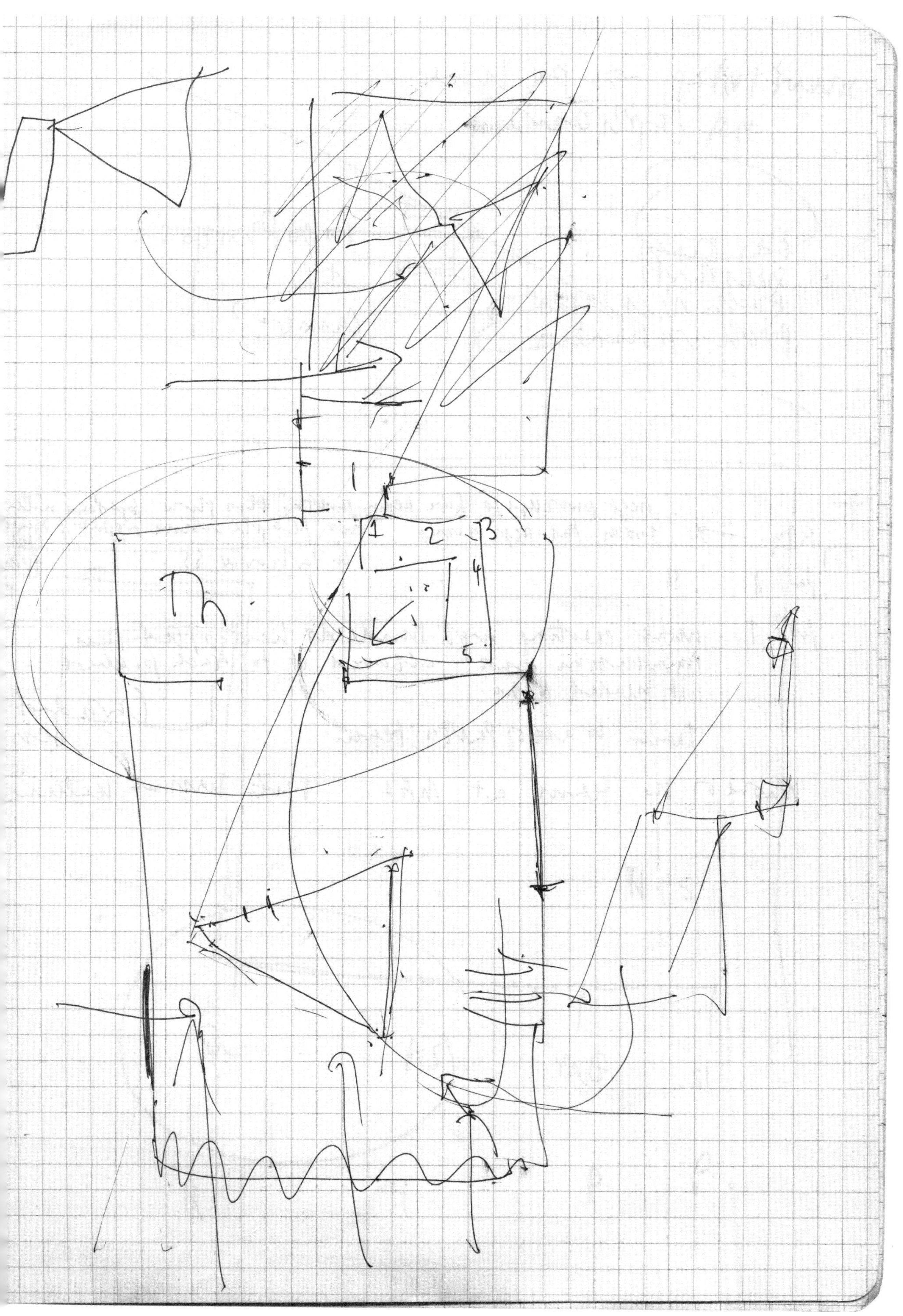

Exhibition plan, 2014

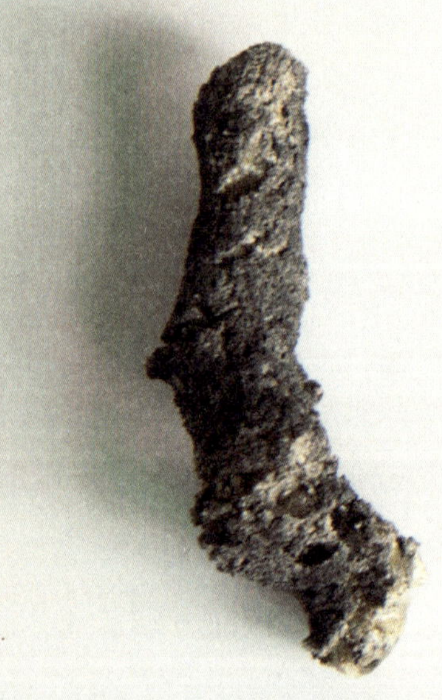

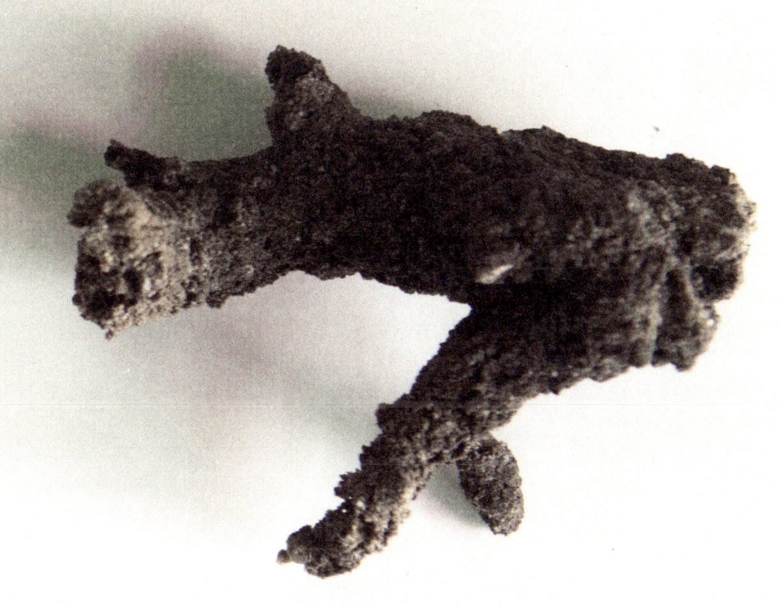

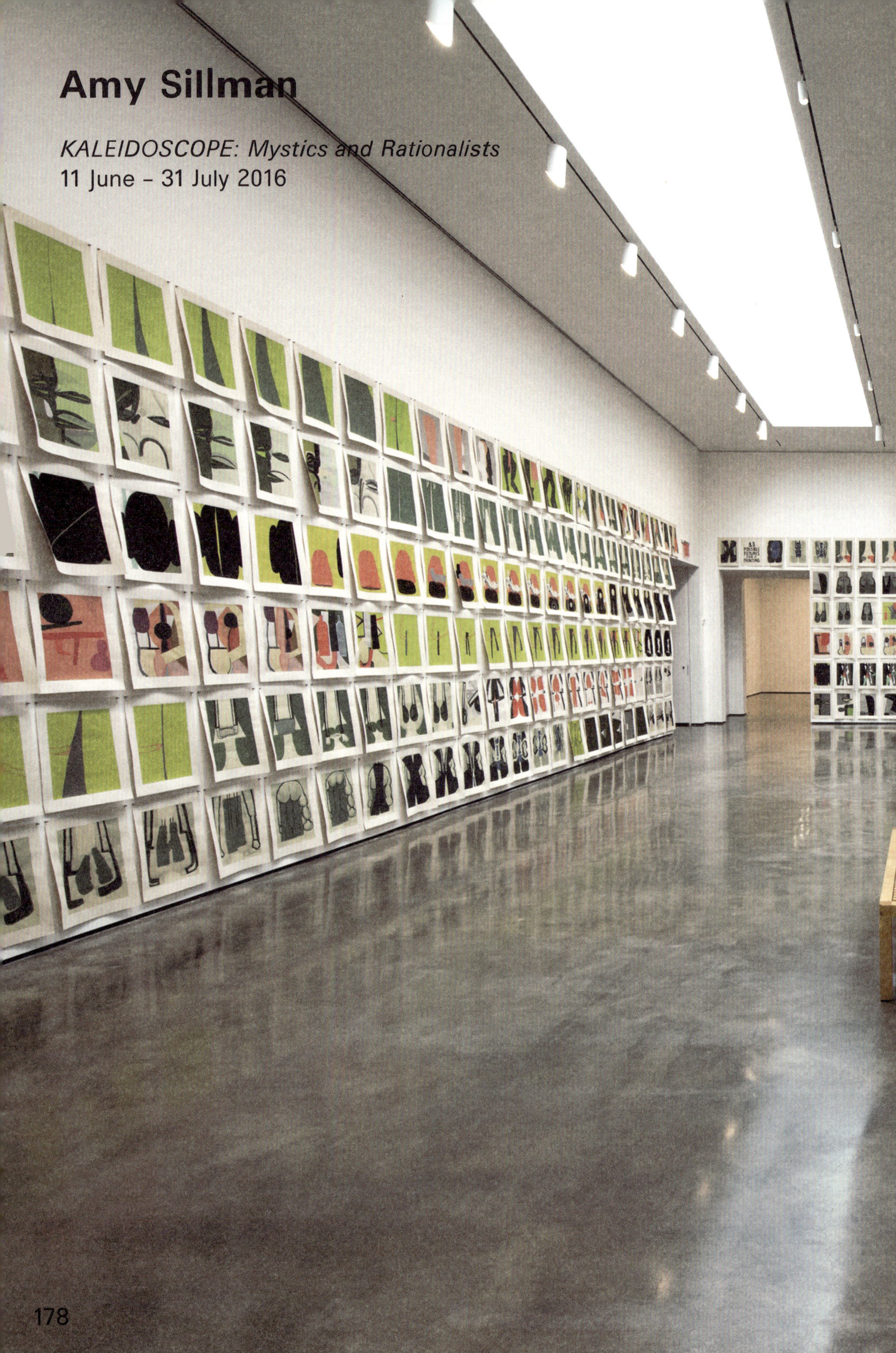
Amy Sillman
KALEIDOSCOPE: Mystics and Rationalists
11 June – 31 July 2016

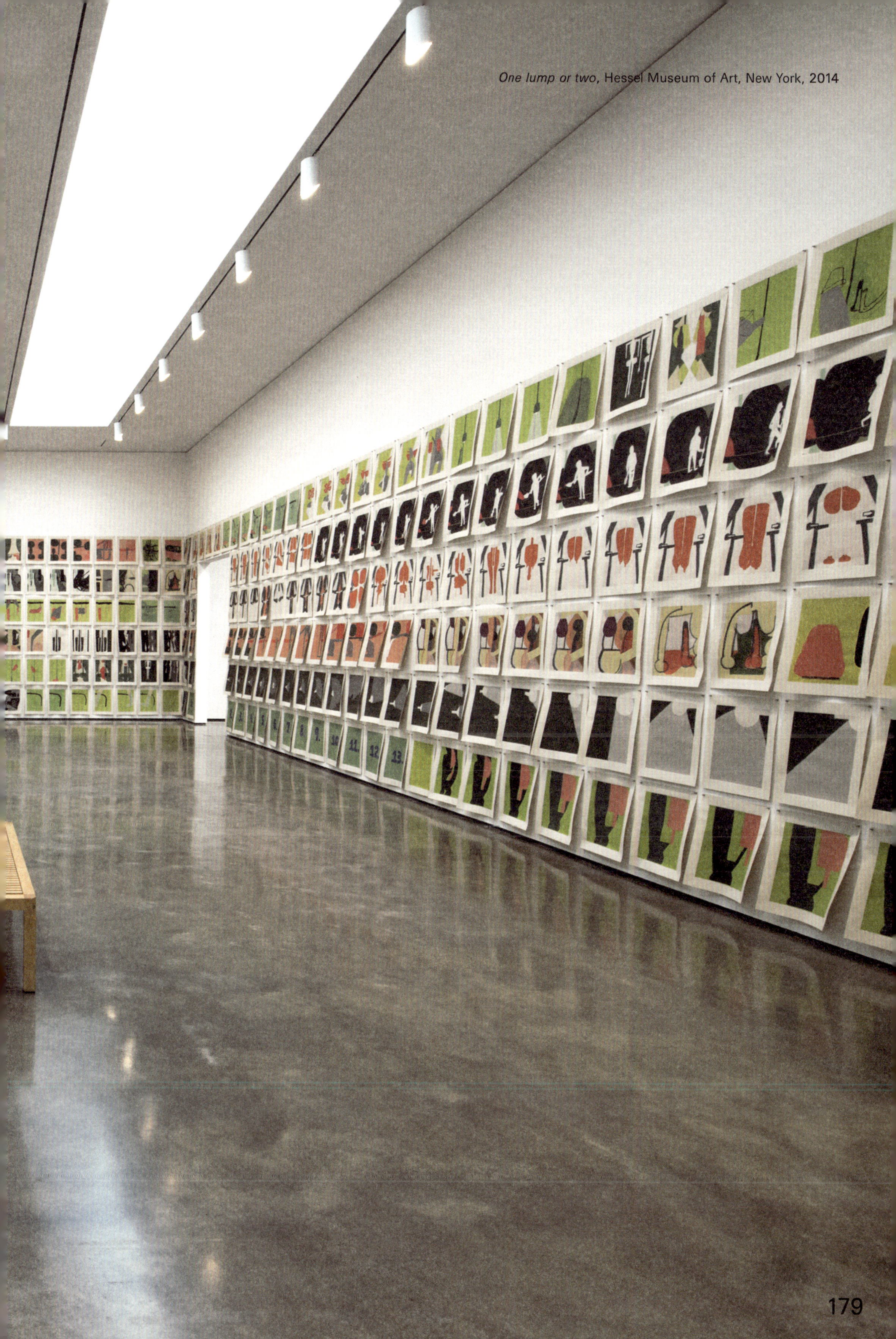

One lump or two, Hessel Museum of Art, New York, 2014

Corin Sworn

KALEIDOSCOPE: The Vanished Reality
12 November – 31 December 2016

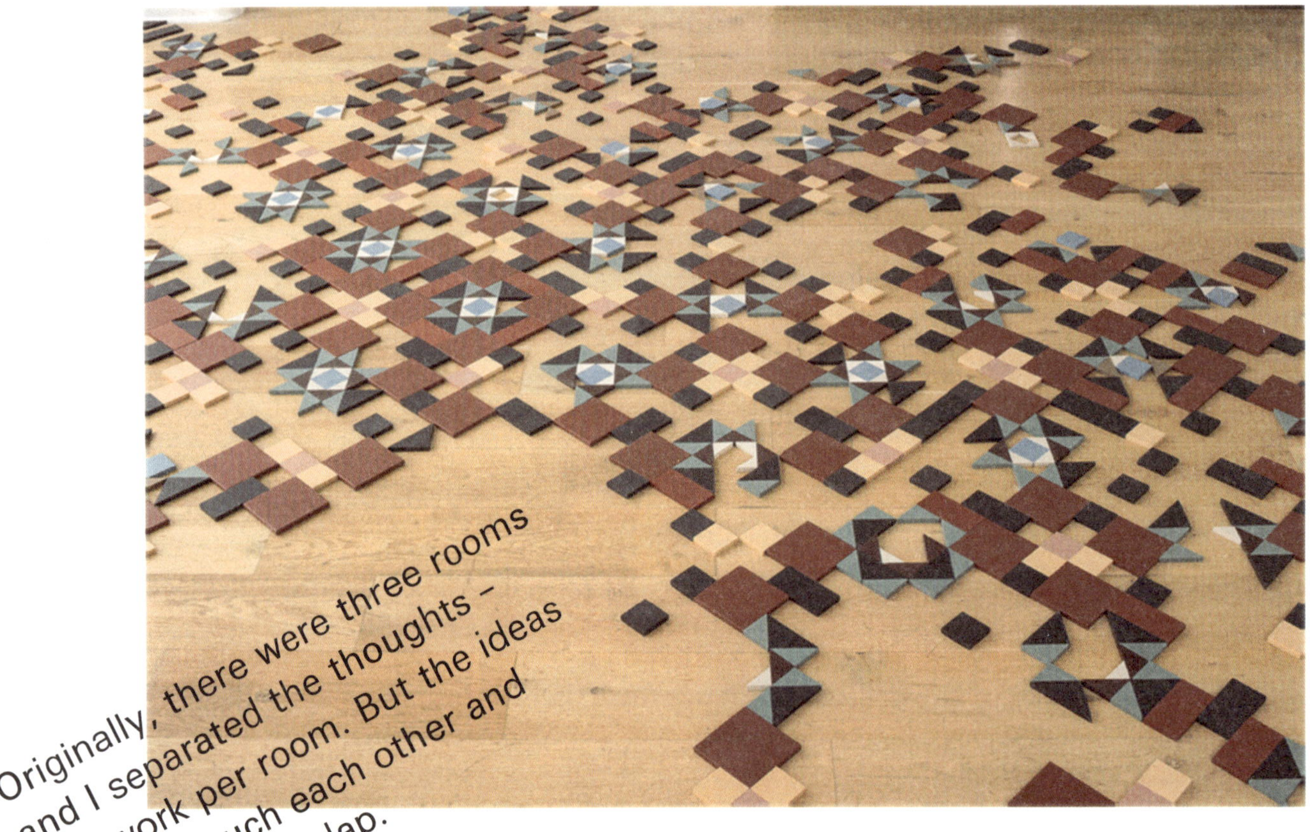

Originally, there were three rooms and I separated the thoughts – one work per room. But the ideas actually touch each other and sometimes overlap.

While making the video I placed one piece of footage next to another and sometimes I edited things out. I was trying to 'tell a story' but there were many.

The left-out materials have not disappeared.
They have drawn more information to them.
Restless and only partly formed they brood
about their utterance.

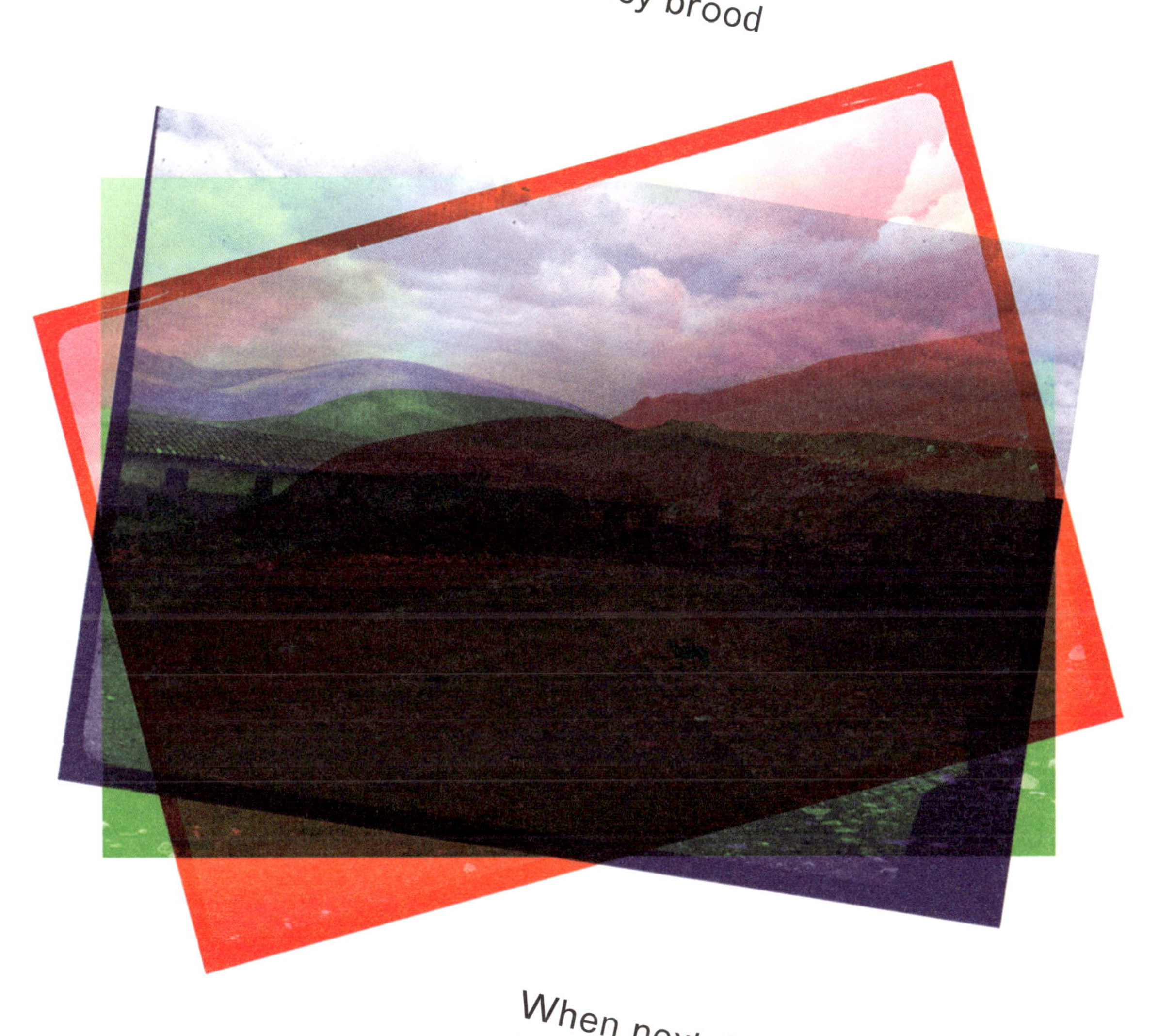

When next the exhibition is presented
it should be opened, all bits laid out
and these left untidy and chattering.

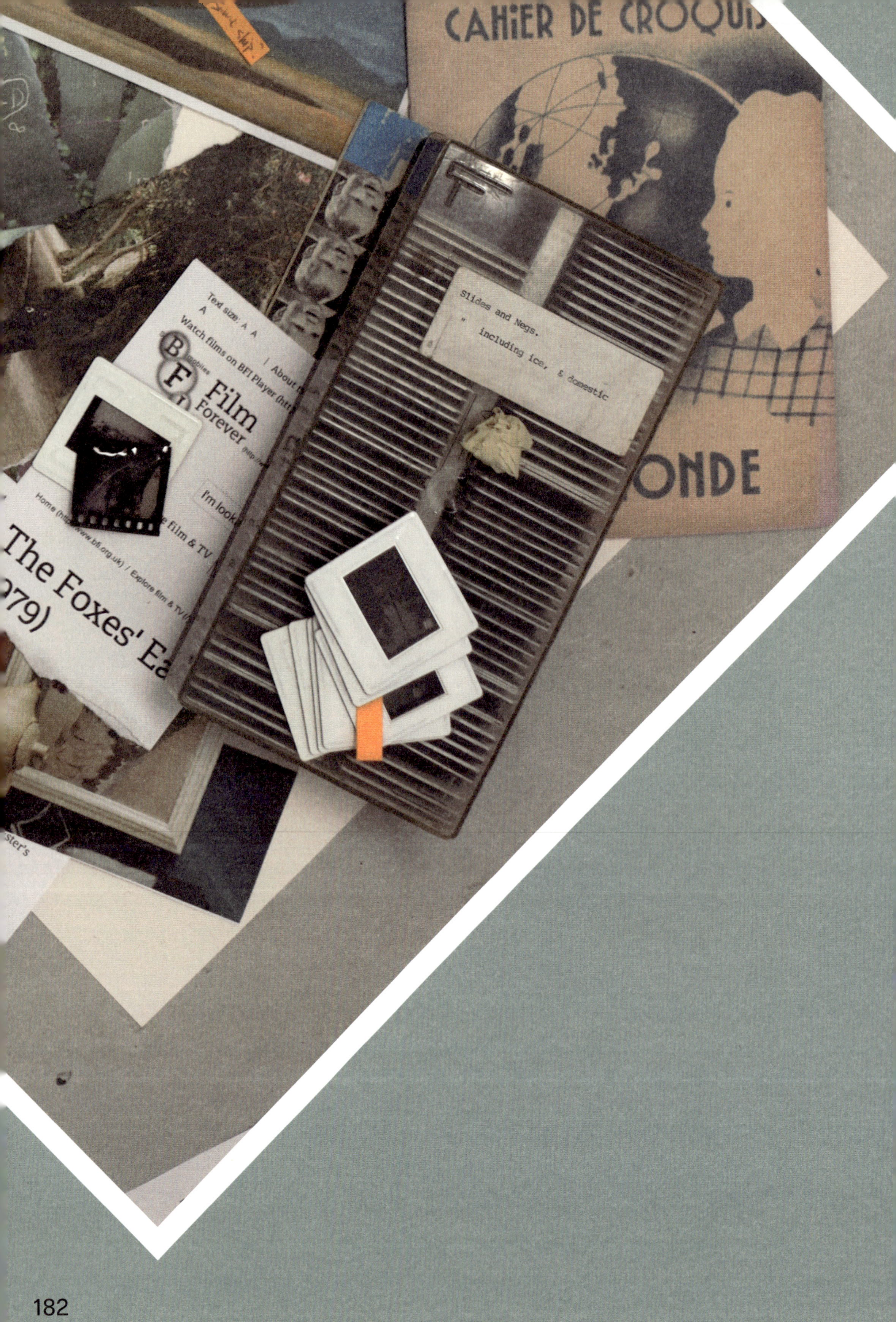
CAHiER DE CROQUIS
ONDE
Slides and Negs.
"   including ice, & domestic
Text size: A A
A
Watch films on BFI Player (htt
BFI Film
Forever
Home (http://www.bfi.org.uk) / Explore film & TV /
I'm look
The Foxes' Ea
79)

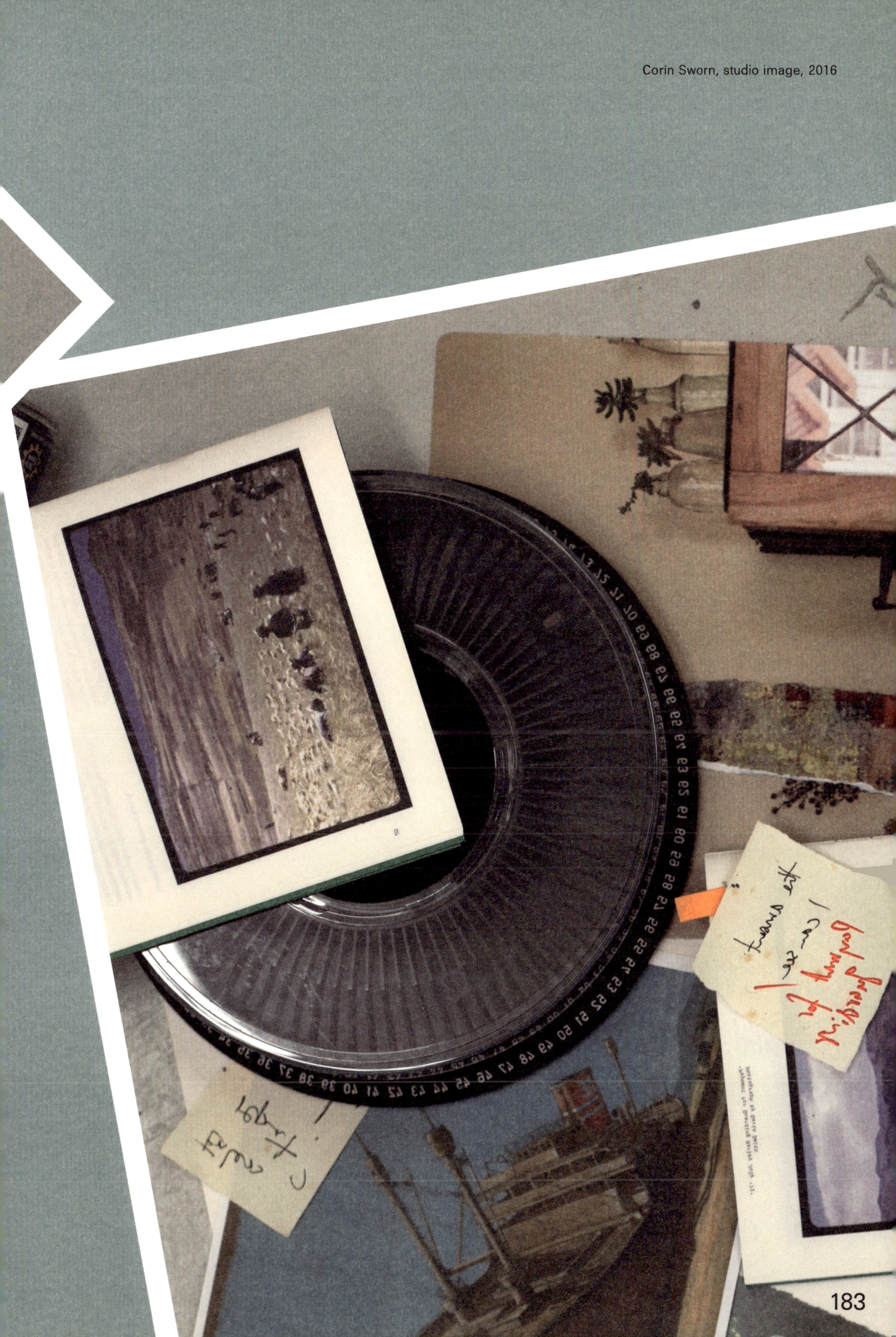

Viola Yeşiltaç

KALEIDOSCOPE: The Indivisible Present
6 February – 20 March 2016

I. Film   AO4   NEG.   ⑨
    F. 16   13 sec.
    C = 0   M 40   Y 35

II. Film   1915   NEG   ⑦ 12
     ₮16   11 sec
     CO M34 Y44   5   Y 43

     1917_44 | 3er paar [done!]
     1917_01   look up   39247_02
     (CO2_12 + CO2_08) paar
     AO6 _12
     1908_09   maybe stays single!
Couple (AO6 _11)   + ersten Abzug + 1914_47

Couple
     1915_12 im ersten +   done!
   + 1916_52

MONO CHROMES   1. Yellow, grün, blau
orange   Bei rosa schwarz   .Red   grau, orange
grau   blau   "   orange
gelb   gelb   "   - green
                               - blue

The Quality of a photograped Sculptu
· towards a Sculptre we look at

~~If a plastic is defined idea in our~~

~~in the tradition of sculpture~~

if we accept that plastic is
defined by Silouhette, line and
surface than maybe it is possible
to unfold a sculpture on a
twodimensional surface.

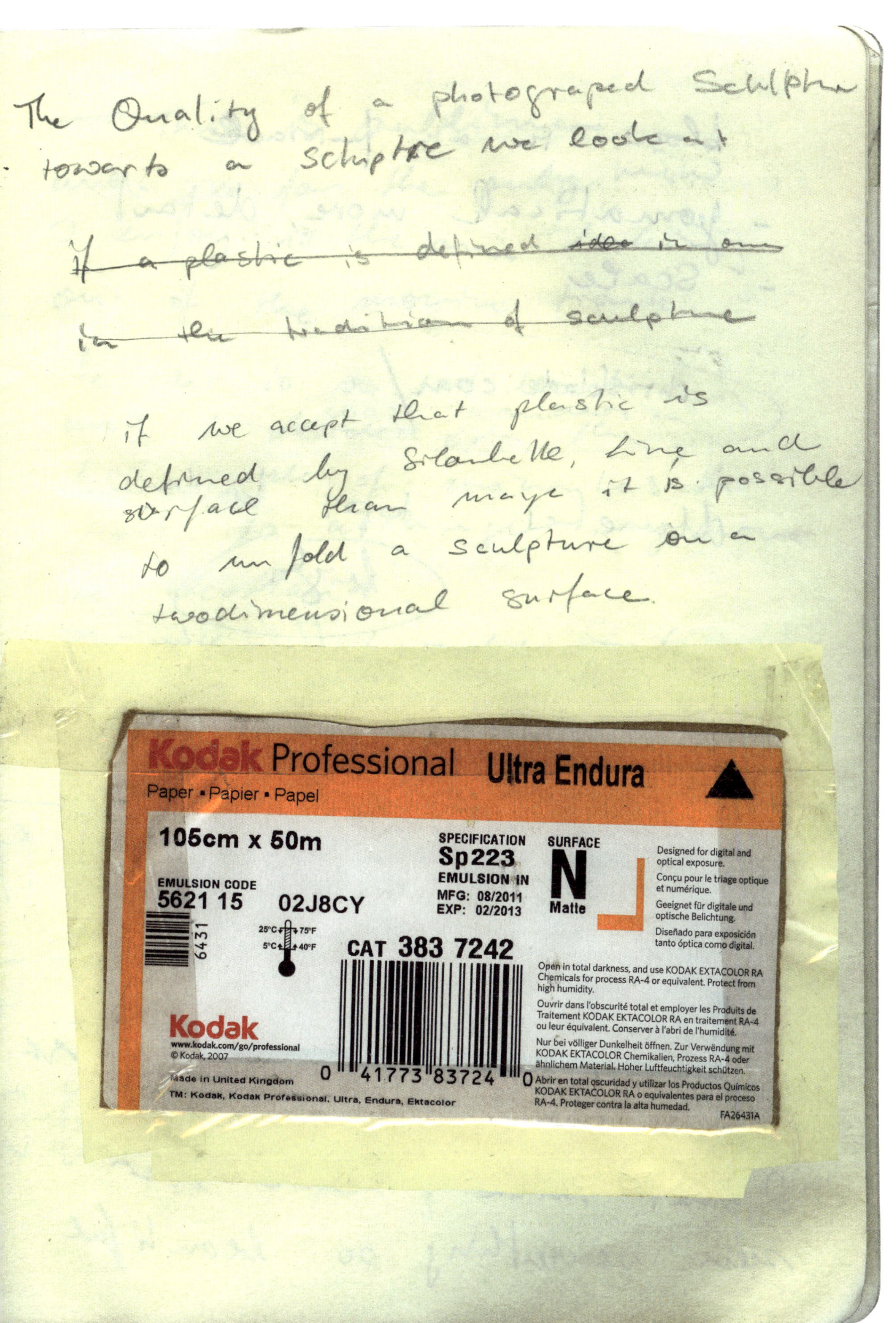

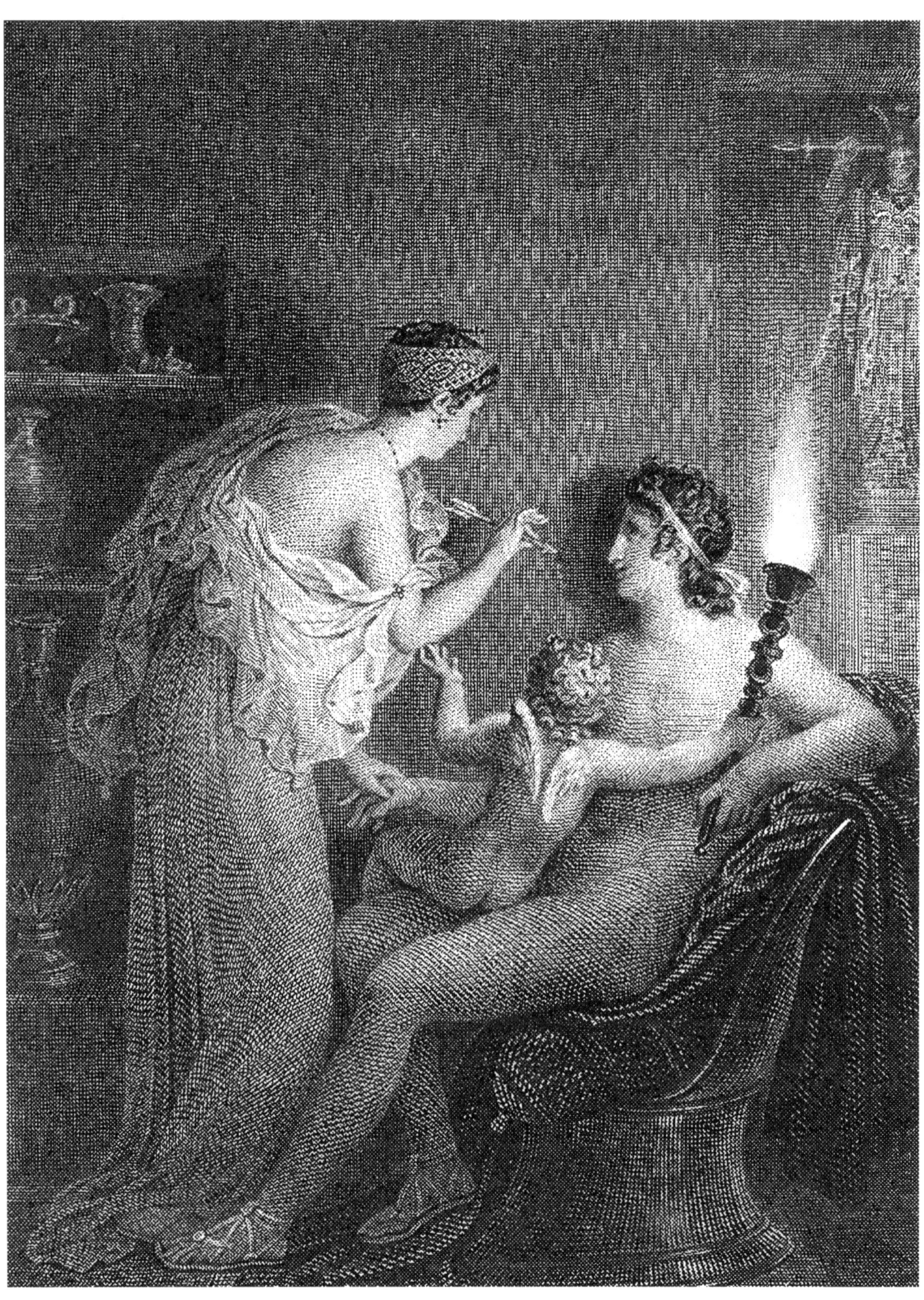

Anne-Louis Girodet de Roussy-Trioson, *The Origin of Drawing* (1829)

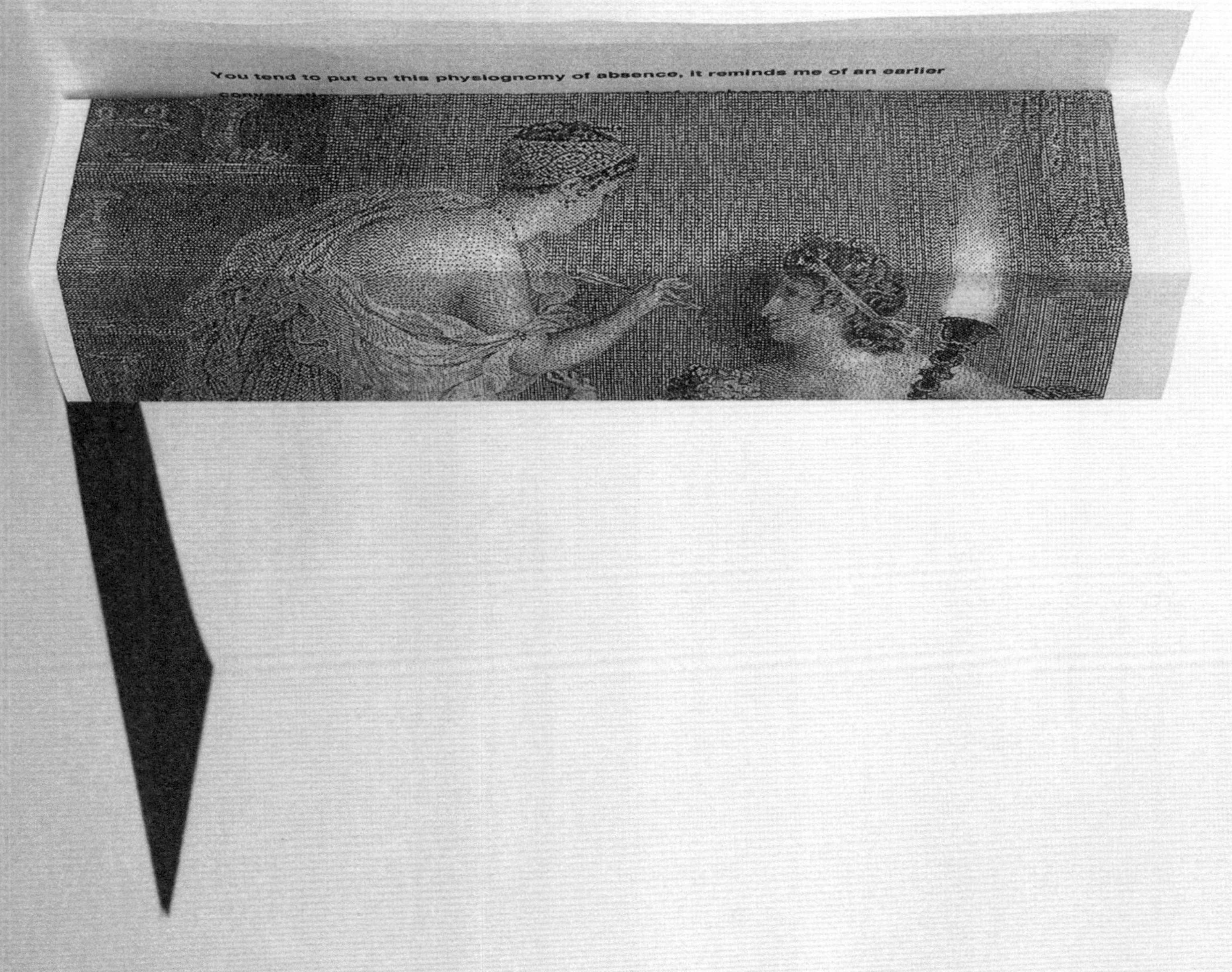
You tend to put on this physiognomy of absence, it reminds me of an earlier

Image Credits

All images © Modern Art Oxford unless otherwise stated.

p.2 Founder Trevor Green onsite at the future Museum of Modern Art Oxford, 1966, courtesy of *Oxford Mail and Times*, Newsquest Oxfordshire

p.6 Bear Lane Gallery, precursor to the Museum of Modern Art Oxford, c.1960

p.6 *Platform '70*, installation view, Museum of Modern Art Oxford, 1970

p.7 *PoPA at MoMA: Pioneers of Part-Art*, Museum of Modern Art Oxford, 1971

p.7 Museum of Modern Art Oxford façade, 1971

p.7 *Fluxshoe*, Performance documentation, Museum of Modern Art Oxford, 1973, courtesy of *Oxford Mail and Times*, Newsquest Oxfordshire

p.7 Photo-souvenir: Daniel Buren, *Sanction of the Museum*, installation view, Museum of Modern Art Oxford, 1973 © DB-ADAGP Paris

p.8 Bruce McLean, *Early Works 1967–71* exhibition invitation, 1975

p.8 *Andre Flavin Judd LeWitt: Sculptures, Prints and Drawings*, installation view, Museum of Modern Art Oxford, 1976

p.8 Jan Dibbets, installation view, Museum of Modern Art Oxford, 1977

p.9 Richard Long, installation view, Museum of Modern Art Oxford, 1979

p.9 Leon Kossoff, *Paintings From a Decade 1970–80*, installation view, Museum of Modern Art Oxford, 1981

p.9 *Lubetkin and Tecton: Architecture and Social Commitment*, installation view, Museum of Modern Art Oxford, 1982

p.10 Tolly Cobbold, *Eastern Arts Fourth National Exhibition*, installation view, Museum of Modern Art Oxford, 1983

p.10 Leonard McComb, installation view, Museum of Modern Art Oxford, 1983

p.10 *Reconstructions: Avant-Garde Art in Japan 1945–65*, installation view, Museum of Modern Art Oxford, 1985

p.10 Entrance to the Museum of Modern Art Oxford, 1986

p.11 K.G. Subramanyan at work in temporary studio, Museum of Modern Art Oxford, 1988

p.11 Young people use movement and shadow to transpose Indian dance into paint, Museum of Modern Art Oxford, 1989

p.11 Jac Leirner, installation view, Museum of Modern Art Oxford, 1991

p.12 Museum of Modern Art Oxford façade during *New Art from China*, 1993. Photo: Chris Moore

p.12 Marina Abramović, *Objects Performance Video Sound*, private view, Museum of Modern Art Oxford, 1995

p.12 Yoko Ono, *Have you seen the horizon lately?* exhibition invitation, 1997

p.13 Jake and Dinos Chapman, *The Rape of Creativity*, installation view, Modern Art Oxford, 2003

p.13 Jannis Kounellis, installation view, Modern Art Oxford, 2004. Photo: Manolis Baboussis

p.13 Angela Bulloch, installation view, Modern Art Oxford, 2005. Photo: Carsten Eisfeld

p.13 *Out of Beirut*, installation view, Modern Art Oxford, 2006. Photo: Steve White

p.13 Mircea Cantor, *The Need for Uncertainty*, installation view, Modern Art Oxford, 2008. Photo: Andy Keate

p.13 Miroslaw Balka, *Topography*, installation view, Modern Art Oxford, 2009. Photo: Marcus J. Leith

p.14 Haegue Yang, *Teacher of Dance*, installation view, Modern Art Oxford, 2011. Photo: Stuart Whipps

p.14 Jenny Saville, installation view, Modern Art Oxford, 2012. Photo: Mike Bruce

p.14 Tim Head, *Displacement*, installation view, Modern Art Oxford, 2013. Photo: Stuart Whipps

p.14 *Love is Enough*, installation view, Modern Art Oxford 2014. Photo: Andy Stagg

p.14 Kiki Kogelnik, *Fly Me to the Moon*, installation view, Modern Art Oxford 2015. Photo: Ben Westoby

p.15 *KALEIDOSCOPE: The Indivisible Present*, installation view, Modern Art Oxford, 2016. Photo: Ben Westoby

pp.16–17 *KALEIDOSCOPE: A Moment of Grace*, installation view, Modern Art Oxford, 2016. Photo: Ben Westoby

pp.18–19 *KALEIDOSCOPE: Mystics and Rationalists*, installation view, Modern Art Oxford, 2016. Photo: Ben Westoby

p.26 Marina Abramović, *Objects Performance Video Sound* exhibition preview, Museum of Modern Art Oxford, 1995

p.27 Marina Abramović, *Objects Performance Video Sound* exhibition poster, 1995

pp.28–29 Marina Abramović, *Objects Performance Video Sound*, installation view, Museum of Modern Art Oxford, 1995

p.30 Mohammed Qasim Ashfaq, *SHIFT*, copperplate etching on velin arches noir with Kiki the Cat, 2016, courtesy of the artist and Lesley Sharpe

p.31 Mohammed Qasim Ashfaq, *BLACK HOLE IV*, 2014, pencil on paper, 155 × 150 cm, diameter 120 cm, courtesy of the artist

pp.32–33 Mohammed Qasim Ashfaq, charcoal test for site-specific wall drawing, 2015

p.35 Kevin Beasley, shoes found outside the artist's studio, 2015, courtesy of the artist

pp.36–37 Kevin Beasley, artist's studio during the production of *...for this moment, this moment is yours...*, 2013, courtesy of the artist

p.38 Postcard from Joseph Beuys, undated, courtesy of the artist and Modern Art Oxford

p.39 Artist's lecture, Museum of Modern Art Oxford, 1974

pp.40–41 Joseph Beuys, *The Secret Block for a Secret Person in Ireland, Drawings 1948–72*, installation view, Museum of Modern Art Oxford, 1974 © DACS 2016

pp.42–43 Karla Black, exhibition invitation, 2009

pp.44–45 Karla Black, installation view, Modern Art Oxford, 2009. Photo: Andy Keate

p.46 Marcel Broodthaers, *Le Privilege de l'Art*, exhibition invitation, 1975 © Estate Marcel Broodthaers

p.47 Portrait of Marcel Broodthaers at Museum of Modern Art Oxford, 1975. Photo: Yves Gevaert © Estate Marcel Broodthaers

pp.48–49 Marcel Broodthaers, *Le Privilège de l'Art*, installation view, Museum of Modern Art Oxford, 1975 © Estate Marcel Broodthaers

p.50 Daniel Buren, *Sanction of the Museum*, private view invitation, 1973

p.51 Photo-souvenir: Daniel Buren, sketch for *Sanction of the Museum*, Museum of Modern Art Oxford, 1973. © DB-ADAGP Paris

pp.52–53 Photo-souvenir: Daniel Buren, *From Three Windows – 5 Colours for 252 Places*, work *in situ*, *Intervention II*, Modern Art Oxford, (detail), 2006 © DB-ADAGP Paris

pp.54–55 Letter from Helen Chadwick to Chrissie Iles and David Elliott, 1989

pp.56–57 Helen Chadwick, *Viral Landscapes*, installation view, Museum of Modern Art Oxford, 1989

p.58 Njideka Akunyili Crosby, *Cassava Garden* (in progress), 2015, acrylic, transfers, coloured pencils, charcoal and commemorative fabric on paper, 6 × 5 ft. Photo: Njideka Akunyili Crosby, courtesy of the artist and Victoria Miro, London

p.59 Njideka Akunyili Crosby, *Something Split and New*, 2013, acrylic, charcoal, pastel, colour pencils, marble dust, collage and transfers on paper, 7 × 9.30 ft. Photo: Joshua White Photography, courtesy of the artist and Victoria Miro, London

p.60 Njideka Akunyili Crosby, *"The Beautyful Ones" Series #2*, 2013, acrylic, colour pencils, pastel and transfers on paper, 5 × 3.5 ft. Photo: Njideka Akunyili Crosby, courtesy of the artist and Victoria Miro, London

p.61 Njideka Akunyili Crosby, *"The Beautyful Ones" Series #1c*, 2014, acrylic, colour pencils, and transfers on paper, 5 × 3.5 ft. Photo: Joshua White Photography, courtesy the artist and Victoria Miro, London

p.62 Dorothy Cross, *Studio with Cuvier's whale bones*, 2016, courtesy of the artist

p.63 Dorothy Cross, *Studio with Basking Shark Currach*, 2016, courtesy of the artist

pp.64–65 Dorothy Cross, *Eye of Shark, KALEIDOSCOPE: Mystics and Rationalists*, installation view, Modern Art Oxford, 2016. Photo: Ben Westoby

pp.66–67 Dog Kennel Hill Project, participation session for *Shelley on a Loop*, 2015. Photo: Tony Wadham, courtesy of the artists

pp.68–69 Dog Kennel Hill Project, *Argument Finished*, 2016, courtesy of the artists

pp.70–71 Ibrahim El-Salahi, Drawings from the artist's sketchbook, 2016, courtesy of the artist

p.72 Ibrahim El-Salahi, *Untitled XII*, watercolour on paper, 25.4 × 25.4 cm, 2001. Photo: Justin Piperger, courtesy of Vigo gallery and the artist

p.73 Ibrahim El-Salahi, *The Tree*, coloured ink on watercolour paper, 29.5 × 29.5 cm, 2001. Photo: Justin Piperger, courtesy of Vigo gallery and the artist

pp.74–75 Douglas Gordon, *24 Hour Psycho*, installation sketch, Museum of Modern Art Oxford, 1999

pp.76–77 Douglas Gordon, *24 Hour Psycho*, 1993, *KALEDIOSCOPE: The Indivisible Present*, installation view, dimensions variable, video installation, Modern Art Oxford, 2016. Photo: Ben Westoby © Studio lost but found / VG Bild-Kunst, Bonn 2016, from *Psycho*, 1960, USA. Directed and produced by Alfred Hitchcock. Distributed by Paramount Pictures © Universal City Studios

p.78 Postcard from Dan Graham to David Elliott, 1979, courtesy of the artist and Modern Art Oxford

p.79 Dan Graham, transcript from *Past Future Split Attention*, 1972

p.80 Dan Graham, *Inflatable Beachside Floats*, Highway Store, New Jersey, 2006, courtesy of the artist

p.81 Dan Graham, *Mafia Mansion*, Deal, New Jersey, 2006, courtesy of the artist

p.82 Guan Xiao, *Slight Dizzy*, coloured bronze, camera tripods, umbrella, 154 × 28 × 150 cm in edition of 3 (+ 1AP), 2014. Photo: Hans-Georg Gaul, courtesy of the artist and Kraupa-Tuskany Zeidler

p.83 Guan Xiao, *Rolling Beating*, coloured bronze, car tyre, 127 × 48 × 22 cm in edition of 3 (+ 1AP), 2014. Photo: Hans-Georg Gaul, courtesy of the artist and Kraupa-Tuskany Zeidler

p.84 Hans Haacke, *A Breed Apart* exhibition drawings, 1978, courtesy of the artist and Modern Art Oxford

p.86 Hans Haacke, *A Breed Apart* newspaper advertisement, 1978

pp.86–87 Hans Haacke, *A Breed Apart*, 2 of 7 panels, 1978, courtesy of the artist

pp.88–89 Mona Hatoum, faxed installation drawing, 1997, courtesy of the artist and Modern Art Oxford

pp.90–91 Mona Hatoum, installation view, Museum of Modern Art Oxford, 1998

pp.92–93 Pierre Huyghe, *De-Extinction*, 2014, production view, courtesy the artist and Hauser & Wirth, London

pp.94–95 Pierre Huyghe, *De-Extinction*, 2014, film stills, courtesy the artist and Hauser & Wirth, London

pp.96–97 Iman Issa *Heritage Studies*, 2015-ongoing, installation view, 2015, courtesy of the artist and Perez Art Museum, Miami

p.98 David King, *Lubetkin and Tecton: Architecture and Social Commitment* poster, 1982, courtesy of the artist and Modern Art Oxford

p.99 David King, *Mayakovsky: Twenty Years of Work* poster, 1982, courtesy of the artist and Modern Art Oxford

pp.100–101 David King, *Alexander Rodchenko* catalogue cover, 1979, courtesy of the artist and Modern Art Oxford

p.102 Yayoi Kusama, handwritten list of works for the exhibition, 1989, courtesy of the artist and Modern Art Oxford

p.103 Letter from Yayoi Kusama to Chrissie Iles, undated, courtesy of the artist and Modern Art Oxford

pp.104–105 Yayoi Kusama, *Soul Burning Flashes*, installation view, Museum of Modern Art Oxford, 1989

pp.106–107 Darcy Lange, *Studies of Teaching in Four Oxfordshire Schools*, 1977. Charles Mussett and his students viewing the recording of the art class study. Photographic still, courtesy of the Darcy Lange Estate

p.108 John Latham, *Government of the First and Thirteenth Chair* performance invitation, 1991, courtesy of Modern Art Oxford

p.109 Letter from John Latham to Chrissie Iles, 29 January 1991, courtesy of Modern Art Oxford

pp.110–111 John Latham, *Art After Physics*, installation view, Museum of Modern Art Oxford, 1991

pp.112–113 Louise Lawler, *Grieving Mothers (Attachment) (traced)*, 2005/2016, courtesy of the artist

pp.114–115 Louise Lawler, *Grieving Mothers (Attachment) (adjusted to fit)*, 2005/2011, courtesy of the artist

p.116 Jac Leirner, residency at Museum of Modern Art Oxford, 1991 © the artist and White Cube. Photo: Chris Moore

p.117 Letter from Jac Leirner to John Leslie, 29 May 1991, courtesy of the artist and Modern Art Oxford

pp.118–119 Jac Leirner, *Cromático precário*, 1991 © the artist and White Cube. Photo: Chris Moore

p.120 Sol LeWitt, diagram for *Wall Drawing #164*, first installation: Museum of Modern Art Oxford, 1973 © Estate of Sol LeWitt, 2016

p.121 Sol LeWitt, *Wall Drawings*, exhibition instructions, 1973, courtesy of the artist and Modern Art Oxford

pp.122–123 Sol LeWitt, *Wall Drawings*, installation view, Museum of Modern Art Oxford, 1973 © Estate of Sol LeWitt, 2016

pp.124–125 Page design by Maria Loboda, courtesy of the artist

pp.126–127 Maria Loboda, *The world is a spiritual vessel and cannot be controlled*, 2016. Photo: Friederike Seifert, courtesy the artist

p.128 Letter from Richard Long, undated, courtesy of the artist and Modern Art Oxford

p.129 Richard Long, exhibition invitation, 1971

pp.130–131 Richard Long, installation view, Museum of Modern Art Oxford, 1971

pp.132–133 David Maljkovic, *New Reproductions (process)*, 2013-2015, courtesy of the artist, Sprüth Magers Berlin London Los Angeles and Metro Pictures, New York

pp.134–135 Kerry James Marshall, *Along the Way*, installation view, Modern Art Oxford, 2006. Photo: Steve White

pp.136–137 Agnes Martin, *On a Clear Day*, 1973, screenprint, 30.8 × 30.5 cm © Agnes Martin / DACS 2016

p.138 Gustav Metzger, *Retrospectives* exhibition invitation, 1998

p.139 Gustav Metzger, *Retrospectives* exhibition guide, 1998 pp.140–141 Gustav Metzger, *Supportive*, 1966–2011, Musée d'art contemporain de Lyon, 2015, courtesy of the artist

p.142 Mike Nelson, notebook drawing for *Triple Bluff Canyon*, 2004, courtesy of the artist and Modern Art Oxford

p.143 Mike Nelson, *Triple Bluff Canyon* exhibition invitation, 2004

pp.144–145 Mike Nelson, *Triple Bluff Canyon*, installation view, Modern Art Oxford, 2004. Photo: Mike Nelson, courtesy the artist and 303 Gallery, New York; Galleria Franco Noero, Turin; Matt's Gallery, London; and neugerriemschneider, Berlin

p.147 Otobong Nkanga, *From Where I Stand – Glimmer Unfold*, performance still, Museum of Contemporary Art, Antwerp (M HKA), Saturday 28 November 2015. Photo: Ciara Moloney, courtesy of the artist

pp.148–149 Otobong Nkanga, *Tsumeb Fragments*, sculpture, 5 modular metallic structures, cement, copper, 12 images inkjet printed on plexiglas, images inkjet printed on Galala, limestone, lightbox, Tsumeb minerals, 2015. Photo: Aurelien Mole, courtesy the artist and Kadist Art Foundation

pp.150–151 Katja Novitskova, *Growth Potentials (Mars)*, economical growth stock images, digital print on film, polyurethane rubber, insects, 2014, courtesy of Katja Novitskova and Kraupa-Tuskany Zeidler

pp.152–153 Gareth Nyandoro, *Kuguruguda Stambo (hypnotic lollipop eaters)*, *KALEIDOSCOPE: A Moment of Grace*, installation view, Modern Art Oxford, 2016. Photo: Ben Westoby

p.154 Yoko Ono writing on wall of Upper Gallery, Museum of Modern Art Oxford, 1997

p.155 Yoko Ono, *Have you seen the horizon lately?*, exhibition invitation, 1997

pp.156–157 Yoko Ono, *Have you seen the horizon lately?*, installation view, Museum of Modern Art Oxford, 1997

p.158 Eileen Simpson and Ben White, Research image, Archive, Modern Art Oxford, 2015, courtesy of the artists and Modern Art Oxford

p.159 Eileen Simpson and Ben White, *Premonition 2037*, Modern Art Oxford, 2016, courtesy of the artists

pp.160–161 Eileen Simpson and Ben White, *ATL 2067*, street level sound system for live event with open mic, Atlanta, 2013 (cc) by-sa 3.0, courtesy of the artists

p.162 Sally O'Reilly, work in progress image from the artist's studio, 2016, courtesy of the artist

p.163 Sally O'Reilly, image of the artist's studio (detail), 2016, courtesy of the artist

p.164 Sally O'Reilly, *Friends in High Places*, 2016, courtesy of the artist.

pp.166 Hardeep Pandhal, work in process and reading, 2016, courtesy of the artist

pp.168–169 Hardeep Pandhal, production stills, 2016, courtesy of the artist

pp.170–171 Elizabeth Price, *SLEEP, KALEIDOSCOPE: The Indivisible Present*, installation view, Modern Art Oxford, 2016. Photo: Ben Westoby

p.172–173 Elizabeth Price, *SLEEP*, source material, 2014, photographs of glass-plate slides recording the Sun, 1875–1945. From the archives of the Rutherford Appleton Laboratory, Oxfordshire

p.174 Hannah Rickards, *Thunder*, 2005, courtesy of the artist

p.175 Hannah Rickards, *To enable me to fix my attention on any one of these symbols I was to imagine that I was looking at the colours as I might see them on a moving picture screen* exhibition plan, 2014, courtesy of the artist

pp.176–177 Hannah Rickards, *Fulgurite from a lightning strike which occurred in Oswego, New York, at 43.464 N Lat. by 76.501 W Long. on August 2nd, 2008. Collected by Michael Walter on August 25th, 2008*, courtesy of the artist

pp.178–179 Amy Sillman, *One lump or two*, installation view, Hessel Museum of Art, Center for Curatorial Studies, Bard College, Annandale-on-Hudson, NY, 2014. Photo: Chris Kendall

pp.180–181 Page design by Corin Sworn, courtesy of the artist

pp.182–183 Corin Sworn, studio image, courtesy of the artist

pp.184–185 Viola Yeşiltaç, pages from the artist's notebook, 2016, courtesy of the artist

p.186 Anne-Louis Girodet de Roussy-Trioson, *The Origin of Drawing* (1829). Photograph courtesy of the University of Chicago Library

p.187 Viola Yeşiltaç, *Untitled*, 2011, silver gelatin print, 71.1 × 61 cm, courtesy of the artist

Endpapers (in order of appearance):

Bear Lane Gallery, precursor to the Museum of Modern Art Oxford, c. 1960

Museum of Modern Art Oxford, 1977

Elevation of the Museum of Modern Art Oxford, 1966

Entrance to the Museum of Modern Art Oxford, 1968

Published by Modern Art Oxford
on the occasion of the
50th anniversary programme:

KALEIDOSCOPE
6th February – 31st December 2016

Modern Art Oxford
30 Pembroke Street
Oxford OX1 1BP
United Kingdom
+ 44 (0) 1865 722733
modernartoxford.org.uk

Programme team:

Scot Blyth, Hilary Floe, Ciara Moloney,
Andy Owen, Curt Riegelnegg,
Emma Ridgway, Ben Roberts,
Sally Shaw, Jonathan Weston

Publication edited by Ciara Moloney
Editorial assistance by Jonathan Weston
Historical research by Hilary Floe
Archival assistance by Sarka Fenclova
and Hannah Keating
Design by Fraser Muggeridge studio
Proofreading by Eileen Daly

Printed in edition of 1,000

© Modern Art Oxford
and the authors, 2016

ISBN: 978-1-901352-65-8

A catalogue record for this book is
available from the British Library

Museum of Modern Art Limited
Registered charity no. 313035

With special thanks to our lenders:

Trustees of the British Museum,
London; Marcel Broodthaers Estate;
Galerie Gisela Capitain, Cologne;
Thomas Dane Gallery, London;
Sindika Dokolo Collection;
The George Economou Collection;
Electronic Arts Intermix; Ibrahim
El-Salahi; Frith Street Gallery, London;
Douglas Gordon; Hauser & Wirth,
London; Kadist Art Foundation;
Kerlin Gallery, Dublin; Kraupa-Tuskany
Zeidler, Berlin; Darcy Lange Estate;
John Latham Estate; Sol LeWitt
Estate; Lisson Gallery, London;
Nicholas Logsdail; Anne Madden;
Metro Pictures, New York; Migros
Museum für Gegenwartskunst;

MOT International, London; Museo
de Arte de Lima; Valeria & Gregorio
Napoleone Collection, London;
Yoko Ono; Rodeo, London; Richard
Saltoun Gallery; Jack Shainman Gallery;
Sprüth Magers, London and Berlin;
Stedelijk Museum; Tate & the
National Galleries of Scotland; Tiwani
Contemporary, London; Victoria Miro,
London; Walker Art Gallery; White Cube
Gallery, London; Andreas Wittmann;
Zabludowicz Collection

The contributors to the publication:

Stu Allsopp, James Attlee,
Mohamed Bishara, brook & black,
Kerry Brougher, Andrew Charlwood,
Suzanne Cotter, Jeremy Deller,
David Elliott, Tracey Emin,
Sarka Fenclova, Dr. Hilary Floe,
Dan Fox, Mark Francis, Helen Ganly,
Will Gompertz, Barbara Grodecka
Lewis, Hanneke Grootenboer,
Mark Haddon, Gill Hart,
Darren Henley, John Hoole,
Antoinette Ibsen, David Isaac,
Vera Jefferson, Leah Jones,
Armin Kekil, Barbara Kruger,
Marco Livingstone, Jon Lockhart,
Ciara Moloney, Sarah Mossop,
Andrew Nairne, Sandy Nairne,
Valeria Napoleone, Bob Price,
Emma Ridgway, Sally Shaw,
Eric Shiner, Ronnie Sonneborn,
Zahra Tehrani, David Thorp,
Richard Wentworth and Anthony White

And our supporters:

Modern Art Oxford is supported
by Oxford City Council and
Arts Council England.

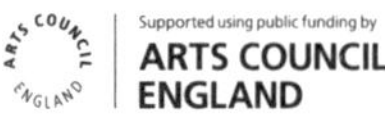

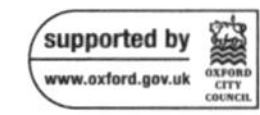

The 50th Anniversary Artist Patrons
are Marina Abramović, Jake &
Dinos Chapman, Jeremy Deller,
Tracey Emin, Lynn Hershman Leeson,
Howard Hodgkin, Barbara Kruger,
Yoko Ono, Michelangelo Pistoletto
and Richard Wentworth.

Modern Art Oxford receives
support from corporate partners;
Lavazza Coffee, Warburg Pincus,
Bonhams, HMG Law, Laurent-Perrier,
Oxford Bus Company, Penny & Sinclair
and Wenn Townsend, plus a number
of generous trusts and foundations
including the Heritage Lottery Fund,
John S. Cohen Foundation,
the Henry Moore Foundation,
the Staples Trust, the Rothschild
Foundation

With thanks to Modern Art Oxford's
Director's Circle, Patrons, Friends
and Council of Management;
David Isaac (Chair), Heidi Baravalle,
Hussein Barma, Patrick Holmes,
Diana Parker, Amanda Poole,
Robert Rickman, Tania Rotherwick,
Andy Verschoyle and Anna Yang.

This publication was made possible
through the support of the Art Fund.

Art Fund_

We are grateful to the following
companies for their generous support
of the 50th anniversary celebrations:

LAVAZZA

Penny & Sinclair, HMG Law,
Laurent-Perrier, Castello di Ama.

Modern Art Oxford staff:

Ruba Asfahani, Communications Manager
John Berridge, Visitor Assistant
Scot Blyth, Production Manager
Mohamed Bishara, Visitor Assistant
Juliette Carlton Thoquenne,
Visitor Assistant
Lusiana Castiglione, Visitor Assistant
Laura Catsellis, Visitor Assistant
Andrew Charlwood, Visitor Assistant
Helen Corley, Development and
Communications Assistant
Hilary Floe, Curatorial researcher
Lauren Greenaway, Visitor Assistant
Simone Hesselberg, Visitor Assistant
Paul Hobson, Director
Jumana Hokan, Information and Bookings
Assistant and Duty Manager
Paulette Mae, Visitor Assistant
Deb Martindale, Visitor Assistant
Ciara Moloney, Curator of Exhibitions
and Projects
Ellie Nixon, Information
and Bookings Assistant
Michelle O'Donohue, Visitor Assistant
Andy Owen, Assistant Production Manager
Fennah Podschies, Head of Resources
and Enterprise
Hayley Raines, Executive Assistant
and Project Manager
Emma Ridgway, Head of Programme
Shona Ritchie, Shop Assistant
Odette Rivas, Retail and
External Events Manager
Ben Roberts, Curator of Education
and Public Programmes
Annie Le Santo, Visitor Assistant
Curt Riegelnegg, Project Manager
Kay Sentance, Assistant Operations
Manager
Sally Shaw, Head of Programme
Helen Shilton, Head of Operations
and Visitor Services
Jamie Simmons, Visitor Assistant
Verity Slater, Director of Development
and Communications
Liz Smith, Development Manager
Lorraine Stone, Finance Manager
Kiran Tasneem, Visitor Assistant
George Townsend, Visitor Assistant
Jenny Vafeidon, Visitor Assistant
Jon Weston, Programme Coordinator
Joe Wilson, Assistant Operations Manager

Technical team:

Harrison Blyth, Aaron Head, Chris Jackson,
Kamila Janska, Tom Milnes, Marcus Orlandi,
Diane Prayle, Sean Reynard, Seb Thomas

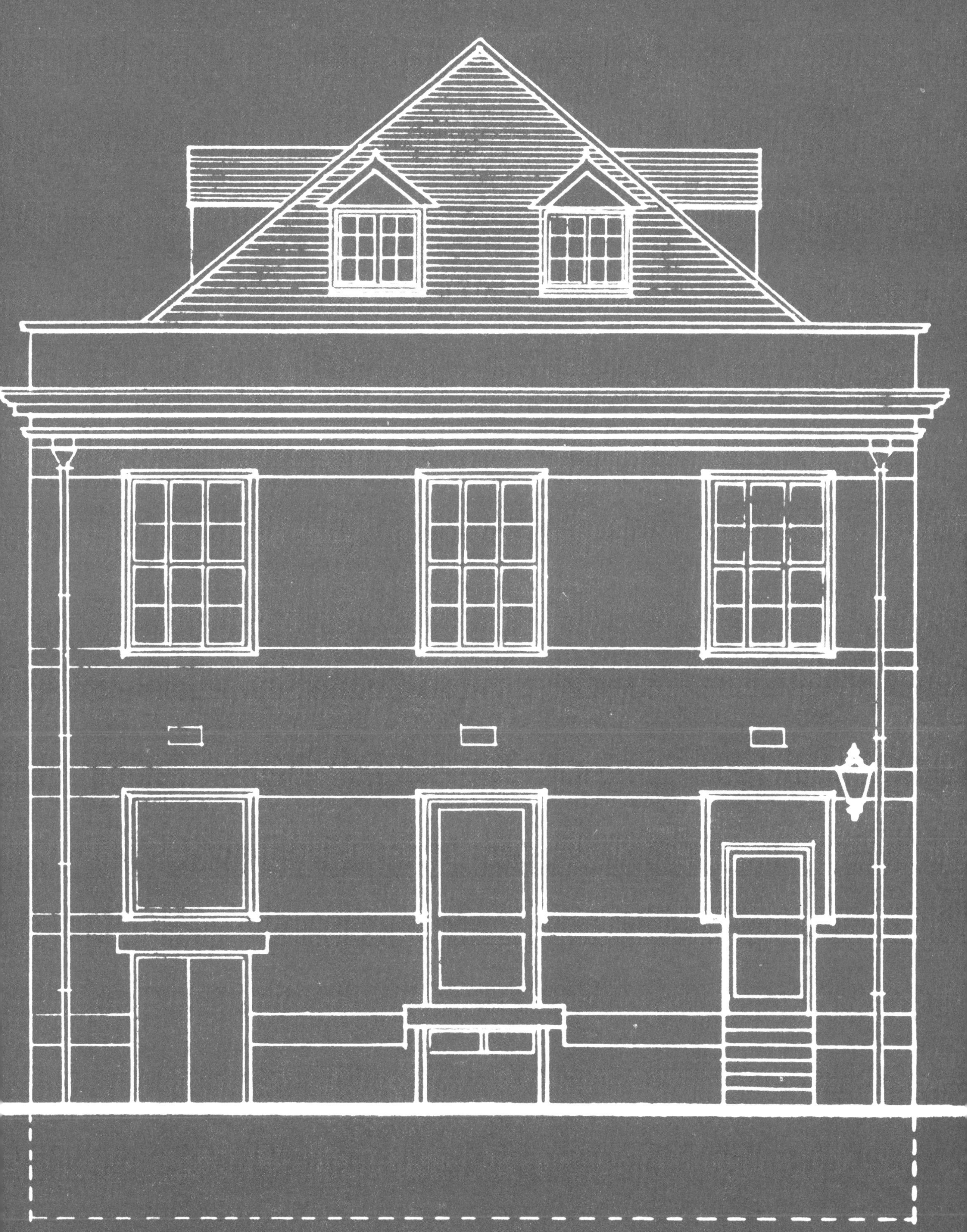

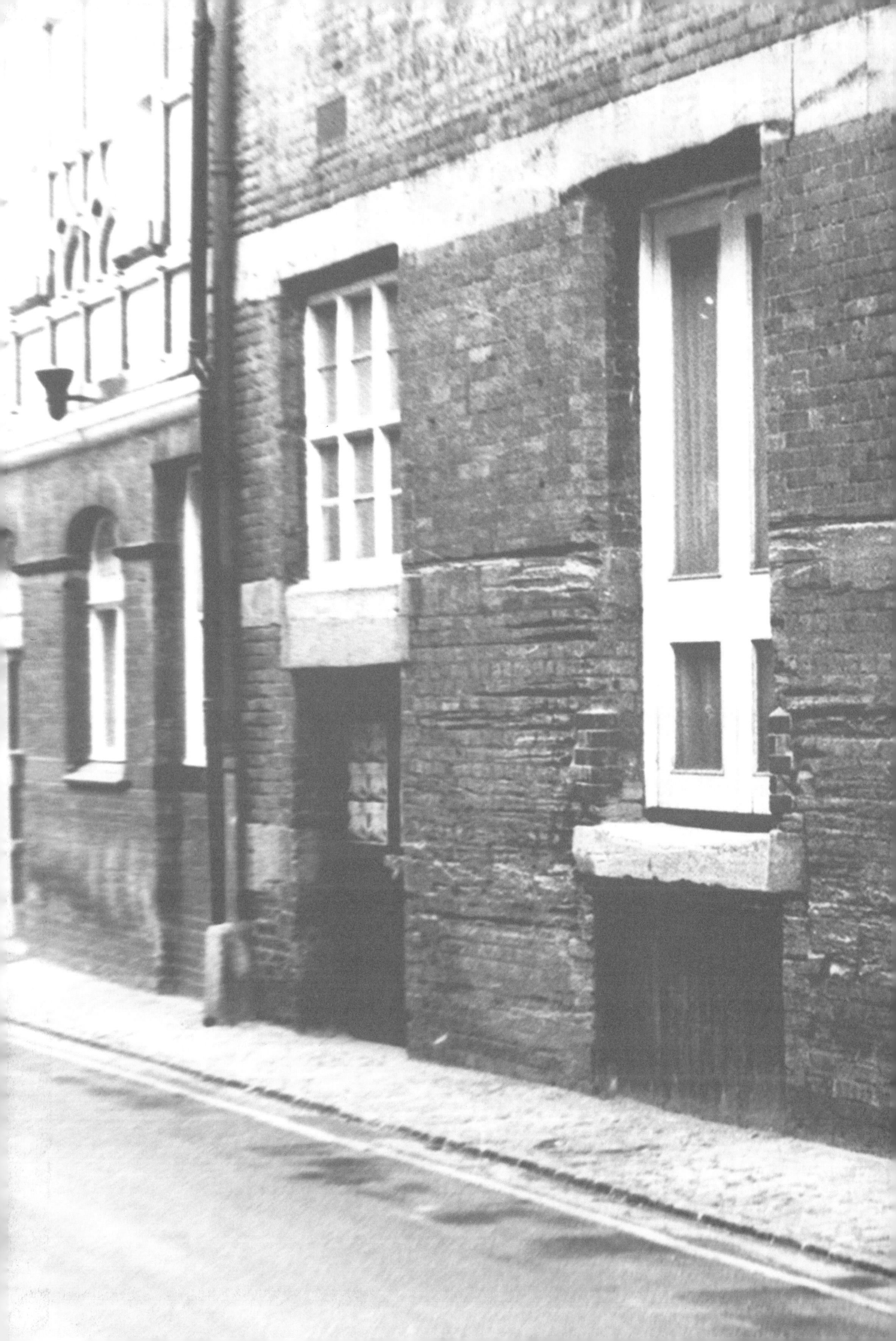